# A Midsummer Night's Dream

## Texts and Contexts

Giovanni
Madison
Junior II
emma :)

WILLIAM SHAKESPEARE

# A Midsummer Night's Dream

## Texts and Contexts

━━━━━━━━━━━━━━━ ✍ ━━━━━━━━━━━━━━━

Edited by

## GAIL KERN PASTER

George Washington University

## SKILES HOWARD

Rutgers University at New Brunswick

*Bedford/St. Martin's*        BOSTON ◆ NEW YORK

*For Bedford/St. Martin's*
*Executive Editor:* Karen S. Henry
*Associate Editor:* Michelle Clark
*Production Supervisor:* Joe Ford
*Production Management:* Publisher's Studio, a division of Stratford Publishing Services, Inc.
*Marketing Manager:* Charles Cavaliere
*Text Design:* Claire Seng-Niemoeller
*Cover Design:* Donna Lee Dennison
*Cover Art:* Sheldon tapestry, *Spring.* Hatfield House.
*Composition:* Stratford Publishing Services, Inc.
*Printing and Binding:* Haddon Craftsmen, an R. R. Donnelley & Sons Company

*President:* Charles H. Christensen
*Editorial Director:* Joan E. Feinberg
*Director of Editing, Design, and Production:* Marcia Cohen
*Manager, Publishing Services:* Emily Berleth

Library of Congress Catalog Card Number: 98-86158

Manufactured in the United States of America.

5  4  3  2  1  0
o  n  m  l  k  j

*For information, write:* Bedford/St. Martin's, 75 Arlington Street, Boston, MA 02116 (617–399–4000)

ISBN-10: 0–312–16621–4 (paperback)
         0–312–21822–2 (hardcover)
ISBN-13: 978-0–312–16621–2

Published and distributed outside North America by

MACMILLAN PRESS LTD
Houndmills, Basingstoke, Hampshire RG21 6XS and London
Companies and representatives throughout the world.

ISBN: 0–333–76396–3

*For Emily and Timothy Paster*
*and for Howard T. Howard,*

*"Ever true in loving be"*

# *About the Series*

————————————————>‹‹————————————————

Shakespeare wrote his plays in a culture unlike, though related to, the culture of the emerging twenty-first century. The Bedford Shakespeare Series resituates Shakespeare within the sometimes alien context of the sixteenth and seventeenth centuries while inviting students to explore ways in which Shakespeare, as text and as cultural icon, continues to be part of contemporary life. Each volume frames a Shakespearean play with a wide range of written and visual material from the early modern period, such as homilies, polemical literature, emblem books, facsimiles of early modern documents, maps, woodcut prints, court records, other plays, medical tracts, ballads, chronicle histories, and travel narratives. Selected to reveal the many ways in which Shakespeare's plays were connected to the events, discourses, and social structures of his time, these documents and illustrations also show the contradictions and the social divisions in Shakespeare's culture and in the plays he wrote. Engaging critical introductions and headnotes to the primary materials help students identify some of the issues they can explore by reading these texts with and against one another, setting up a two-way traffic between the Shakespearean text and the social world these documents help to construct.

Jean E. Howard
Columbia University
Series Editor

# About This Volume

—➤✦—

It is an axiom of contemporary criticism that the meaning of a literary work is context-bound but that contexts themselves are boundless (Culler 27). For a play such as *A Midsummer Night's Dream*, with its own rich, centuries-old history of theatrical production and critical interpretation, this critical belief has particular force. There are many possible, overlapping contexts for reading a play as beloved as this romantic comedy. And, as the possible contexts change to support different critical points of view, the play will change — will come to be different from itself — from one reading to another.

The contexts for this edition of *A Midsummer Night's Dream* are mainly historical and literary ones, which means that documents and illustrations of several different kinds have been organized into four chapters in order to suggest how Shakespeare's play is marked by, and responds to, its moment in time over four centuries ago. Each chapter contains its own introduction, as do the individual documents. The chapter introductions are intended to set each chapter's documents in relation to one another and to Shakespeare's play, and to do so in a way that opens up questions for debate and inquiry. Thus we invite readers of this edition to imagine the twenty illustrations and thirty-eight documents contained herein as engaged in a dialogue, separately and in combination, with Shakespeare's comedy. As with the best dialogues, this one should be understood as dynamic, interactive, egalitarian, and ongoing. By reading the documents on their own and in conjunction with the play, students can question simple distinctions between "literature" and "primary documents," between literature and history. This kind of approach replaces the traditional relationship between the "text" in the foreground and the "contexts" in the background with a more fluid and dynamic textual interaction. Texts and contexts change places. The play no longer holds a secure and central place in our regard, but takes its place among other texts. It no longer speaks on its own, but speaks in concert and even in competition with other voices from the past. Out of this more complex sense of textual categories and intertextual possibilities, we hope that students will develop the intellectual basis for historical interpretation. The result, we believe, is an enriched experience and enhanced understanding of the play.

Like *A Midsummer Night's Dream* itself, then, all the textual artifacts from early modern England included here require and reward critical analysis. We present them in order to offer students the opportunity to assess documentary evidence as historians and literary scholars do. And we invite students to respond to the language in these documents with the same appetite for complex meaning, ambiguity, irony, and wordplay that they bring to Shakespeare's works. We have edited the texts, modernizing their spelling and glossing their possible obscurities, so as to facilitate such an engaged response. For, as many teachers know from their own attempts at photocopying primary materials for classroom use, direct encounter with sixteenth- and seventeenth-century texts presents formidable difficulties for most students. Manuscript materials, written in unfamiliar hands, seem illegible to all but those expert readers trained in early modern paleography. To illustrate this — and to suggest what historians and literary scholars actually do while spending time in archives and research libraries poring over pages from rare books and manuscripts — we have reprinted a manuscript page from the diary of Simon Forman, a physician who lived in Elizabethan London (decipher it if you can!). Early printed sources, while certainly more available and theoretically more accessible, present students with unfamiliar orthography and typography, obscure allusions and references, and hard-to-read typefaces, such as the black-letter type of ballad broadsheets. (We have illustrated this, too, with examples of pages from early books.) Such features are, of course, part of the historical and material character of these artifacts, and their erasure does involve a certain loss. But, by removing students' difficulties with basic comprehension through modernization and glossing, we hope to make the experience of reading primary materials as rewarding as possible and to give students the means for arriving at their own interpretations of the cultural conditions prevailing when *A Midsummer Night's Dream* was first performed.

No single narrative about these cultural conditions can or should be inferred from any selection of historical documents, however stimulating those documents may be. One of the most important historical lessons to be drawn from this edition might be the recognition that any document set, no matter how large, would by definition be partial. All document sets require interpretation, offering only glimpses of a past that is, like our present moment, finally unknowable in richness and complexity — even to itself. A good example of this unknowability might come from comparing the two versions of Queen Elizabeth's address to her troops, the received version often quoted by scholars and a lesser-known version recently brought to scholars' attention. In this sense, the many differences between the two texts are less important than the problems of interpretation and accuracy that such differences pose for historians. *A Midsummer Night's Dream* cannot be fully subsumed into its cultural moment, should never become indistinguishable from its "background" or regarded merely as a vehicle for understanding that background. But this edition does seek to decenter the play by insisting that its relationship to Elizabethan culture is dynamic and reciprocal: the play does not mirror its moment in time as a passive, reflective object would do. Rather it transforms its moment through the act of representation and it does so intentionally. This means that, just as our interpretations of the play can be changed and enriched by a greater understanding of Shakespeare's culture, so too is our reading of that culture changed and enriched by our experience of the play.

We offer these thirty-eight documents in full recognition of the fact that another pair of editors might have made a different set of choices of contexts for *A Midsummer Night's Dream*. This is to suggest not that our choices are arbitrary or unrelated to the play, but that for a play as rich in implication as this one, contexts are, to repeat, practically limitless. What occupies the most time and attention in the action of the play itself, the love-chase of the crossed couples in the forest, is not foregrounded by our documents. What we have tried to do, instead, is to situate the lovers' experience in the social context of Elizabethan society. We seek to highlight the play's status as an entertainment and to recognize its explicit, self-conscious representation of the conditions of theatrical performance — who performs what to whom, on what basis, and for what purposes. Thus we have included a selection of documents about other forms of entertainment in Elizabethan England, including holiday pastimes, amateur theatricals, as well as the one-time-only entertainments created for the queen while on summer holiday. The point here is not only to indicate something of the range and cultural history of performance in Elizabethan England, but also to suggest how every kind of entertainment, including *A Midsummer Night's Dream*, grows from a specific set of local conditions. And those local conditions are often marked by controversy and complaint, as Robert Laneham's *Letter* suggests.

The centrality of heterosexual romance to the play's action and to the culture of Western Europe is part of what has made the play seem timeless in its appeal. But our contexts offer up a slightly different picture of the play's men and women than merely as lovers or would-be lovers. Rather we invite readers to see the play's male characters in terms of Elizabethan social theory and self-description. The play does not dwell on what makes a leader or a gentleman; it assumes its audience comprehends that often-disputed subject matter. Was gentility a matter of birthright and blood only or could it be acquired? If it could be acquired, how could it be acquired and by whom? The question was not unimportant, for on its answer the claims to the many rights and privileges of gentlemanly rank depended. Thus it seemed important to us to include primary materials about leadership and gentility, including in that category Plutarch's influential biographies of classical heroes like Theseus. The play suggests, implicitly, that a young gentleman free to meditate on the qualities of his own beloved or chase the beloved of another young man is so different from a workingman living in the same city that they might never have occasion to meet. Thus it seemed important to acknowledge the Elizabethan workingman, the occupations he might have had, his wages and his conditions of work, as Elizabethan parliaments sought repeatedly to regulate them. And while the play does not dwell on Theseus's defeat of the Amazons as a precondition of his marrying Hippolyta, we wish to. The figure of the warrior woman and other kinds of women resistant to marriage preoccupied the Elizabethans at least in part because their transition as a nation from Roman Catholic to Protestant belief required changes in all forms of social practice, including the practices of courtship and marriage. The grounds of women's resistance have been forgotten in optimistic histories of love and marriage, but such resistance is evident in the many different source materials we print here (and in those we might have printed). We thought it important to include the writing of women themselves contemplating the history of warrior women forebears and imagining the conditions of exclusively female community. Because this play begins by asserting the prerogatives of fathers over daughters and ends by apparently setting them aside, it also seemed important to offer some examples of Elizabethan conduct manuals about the expected behaviors of daughters and wives. Even as we do so, however, we wish to insist on the difference between prescription and description: the printed texts that prescribe how people in the past should live do not describe how they did live.

Finally, we want to contextualize the play's emphasis on supernatural agency, an emphasis not unique to this play either among Shakespeare's plays or among plays in the period, but one that begs to be interpreted historically. The play's central stage picture of the metamorphosed Bottom embraced by a doting Titania is, as we shall suggest, a meeting place of traditions — literary and popular, classical and contemporary, political and religious, allegorical and erotic. We hope students reading our selection from Ovid's *Metamorphoses* will experience something of the great imaginative power that Shakespeare found in reading that poem as well as the possibilities for theatrical parody. And we hope they will be surprised and provoked by Reginald Scot's vehement denunciation of any belief in metamorphosis as well as his habit of literal interpretation. Even more important, by including ballads about Robin Goodfellow, first-person reminiscences about Elizabethan fairy beliefs, and Richard Corbett's partisan endorsement of fairy beliefs, we want students to learn something about how even creatures as apparently fanciful as Shakespeare's fairy characters represent the comedy's response to real social conflicts about the spirit world and supernatural agency.

## EDITORIAL POLICY

In choosing texts of the historical documents included in this volume, we have consulted these works directly by looking at the early books themselves or more indirectly in the form of facsimile editions, microfilm reproduction, or modern editions. We have generally reproduced the first or only editions of early books. Exceptions include those works, such as John Stow's *Annals of England* or *Survey of London*, that were revised and expanded over time. In cases of multiple editions, we used that edition closest in time to *A Midsummer Night's Dream* itself, which scholars have dated 1594–1595. When a modern, old-spelling edition of a work was available, we have usually used it as copy-text, although we have compared the modern edition against the original text whenever we could. The edition is always indicated in the source note. In reproducing manuscript or other archival sources, as for example *The Autobiography of Simon Forman*, the proclamation regarding Chester wages, or court records from the *Calendar of Assize Records*, we have had to rely on modern sources alone. Such material, while distant from its original source in public records offices or manuscript archives, is derived from reliable modern sources, the sources all historians of the period must rely on for textual evidence unless they visit the archives where such data are stored. For works in translation, such as the selections from Ovid's *Metamorphoses* or Plutarch's "Life of Theseus," we have preferred translations close in time to the play over modern translations, even though, when judged by modern standards of translation, the earlier versions are often faulty on textual, semantic, or stylistic grounds. (As we note in the headnote to Sir Thomas North's translation of Plutarch, for example, North himself translated *The Lives of the Noble Grecians and Romans* into English from a French translation of the original Greek.) Our rationale in dealing with translations was always to put before our readers the words and phrasings that an Elizabethan reader would have seen when reading Ovid or Plutarch in English. We have consulted the texts in the original languages, whenever it seemed essential to do so, and compared early translations against modern ones in order to clarify our own understanding of the originals and to help us gloss the texts.

Our goal has been to make texts as accessible as possible by modernizing spelling, including place-name spellings, expanding contractions, and using modern standards for capitalization, punctuation, abbreviations, and other features of early print format. Otherwise, we have not changed or altered early modern grammar or locutions, relying on paraphrases in the glosses in order to clarify the sometimes obscure structure of sixteenth- and seventeenth-century sentences. The only exception to this practice is Spenser's *Shepheardes Calendar* where, though we have omitted E. K.'s glosses, we have retained Spenser's deliberately archaic spelling. We have used *The Oxford English Dictionary* (*OED*) in glossing words, the *Dictionary of National Biography* (*DNB*) for biographical information about English authors, and a host of reference works too numerous and various to record here for help with fairies, classical mythology, classical and English place-names, and the other material, historical and literary, that readers will find in our notes and glosses.

Because we have reproduced or referred to the original pagination of sixteenth- and seventeenth-century texts, a word of explanation about early modern printing practices may be in order. In early printed books, signature markings sometimes appear instead of or in addition to page numbers. Signature numbers indicate how sheets of paper were folded for printing (into two for folios, four for quartos, or eight for octavos). After folding, the gathered pages were stitched together to form the book. The signature markings in early printed books differ, but usually appear like this: in a quarto volume, A or the first signature has eight pages, the front sides of which are marked A, A2, A3, A4. Because the back sides of the page are not marked, modern bibliographers distinguish between them, calling the front *r* for recto and the back *v* for verso. So a modern bibliographer would designate the back side of the last page of signature A as A4v and this page would be followed by the first page of the next gathering, designated B1r. In some texts (represented in this volume by *The Autobiography of Simon Forman* and *The Bishops' Bible*), pages are called folios, but their recto and verso sides are also specified.

## ACKNOWLEDGMENTS

A collaboration such as this one may accumulate more than the usual number of debts to friends, fellow scholars, and supporting institutions, which we are delighted to record here. Both of us, but especially Gail Paster, are grateful to the Folger Shakespeare Library for its archival and human resources. That most of the illustrations reproduced in this volume come from the Folger's collection only begins to suggest the extent of our indebtedness. Skiles Howard wishes to extend special thanks to Mark Wittop and Ryan Tebbitt of the British Library, Nicola Pollock and David Weston of the Department of Special Collections at the Glasgow University Library, and Anne Steinberg of the Ashmolean Museum, Oxford.

For their bracing readings of our manuscript along the way from prospectus to final product, we are indebted to Michael Bristol, Fran Dolan, Barbara Freedman, Margo Hendricks, Jean Howard, Coppélia Kahn, Leah Marcus, Bruce Smith, and David Young. In addition, Skiles Howard wants to thank Michelle Cella, who generously shared her knowledge of classical studies. On a host of particular matters, Gail Paster has benefited from the counsel, encouragement, and sorely needed expertise of Peter Blayney, Cynthia Herrup, Gil Harris, Robert Miola, Russ McDonald, Barbara Mowat, Susan Snyder, Leslie Thomson, and Georgianna Ziegler, whom she is pleased to thank. With entirely characteristic generosity, Barbara Traister supplied her own transcripts of Simon Forman's dreams, as well as photocopies of the originals, and added to them information about Forman's life from her important biographical research. It is a pleasure to remember such wonderful collegiality here. Working with Karen Henry and her colleagues Michelle Clark and Emily Berleth at Bedford/St. Martin's throughout this project has been, by turns, exciting, challenging, and inspiring. We have been buoyed by their enthusiasm and are grateful for their care.

# Contents

><

# *Illustrations*

———————— ✣ ————————

# Introduction

>‹‹

*A Midsummer Night's Dream* is enchanting, lyrical, and very funny. So say generations of readers and audiences captivated by the play's eclectic mingling of lovers, fairies, and artisan actors in an action filled with mythological allusions and moved by the combined power of love, magic, and self-conscious theatricality. Thematically, the play stands forth as a comedy about romantic desire and the trials of imagination. Its two central actions — the love chase of Hermia, Helena, Lysander, and Demetrius and the encounter between a metamorphosed Bottom and the fairy queen Titania — symbolize the arbitrary power of lovers' imaginations to transform the beloved from just another human being into an incomparable individual. In its framing and subsidiary actions — the nuptial festivities of Theseus and Hippolyta and the artisans' hilarious rehearsal and performance of their version of "Pyramus and Thisbe" — the play extends its social reach to bring figures from classical legend together with humble (but aspiring) workingmen. In the melding of these comic materials, Shakespeare suggests that courtship, marriage, and putting on a play have much in common. All three are unpredictable, creative enterprises requiring daring, hope, and a willingness to look foolish in the eyes of others.

In the Athens of Theseus, the protocols of love are full of comic potential. Bottom opines wisely to Titania that "reason and love keep little company together nowadays" (3.1.119–20). In this summary judgment and commonplace wisdom, only the qualifying adverb "nowadays" is suspect. Nothing in the play's texture of allusion and mythology suggests that love was *ever* rational or comprehensible to the spectator from the outside or the desiring subject from within. In action, the onset of love produces events that are painful and/or hilarious to witness. From the opening of the play, Shakespeare hints at what troubles lovers in the passage from courtship to marriage. Theseus has had to conquer a woman's desire for autonomy — symbolized here by the Amazon Hippolyta. The four young lovers have to conquer various obstacles, both internal and external, ranging from the volatility of male desire to the opposition of Hermia's father and the mutual suspicions harbored by all four of them. These young lovers, while seeming overwhelmed by passion, have reason to be suspicious of love. When the men change from loving Hermia to loving Helena, their change of heart is violently expressed as hatred for the disavowed one: "Hang off, thou cat, thou burr," Lysander shouts to the bewildered Hermia, "Or I will shake thee from me like a serpent!" (3.2.260–61). Lysander and Demetrius seem to know no intermediate form of address to the women, oscillating between extremes of adoration and degradation. Oberon has transformed their vision, has altered the object of their desire, but he is not responsible for everything that Lysander and Demetrius say. And, given Oberon's (mis)management of his powers to create and destroy desire through magical love juice, the three couples at the end of the play will need fairy blessings and more to stay faithful to one another, to bear and raise happy children, and to keep their houses from harm.

For their part, the fairy spouses quarrel so bitterly over custody of Titania's foster child that Oberon is moved to punish and humiliate his queen by causing her to dote absurdly on Bottom. When Puck reports how it came to pass that "Titania waked and straightway loved an ass," Oberon replies with delight: "This falls out better than I could devise" (3.2.34–35). But its depiction of love as irrational, sudden, and even self-destructive does not prevent *A Midsummer Night's Dream* from finally endorsing romantic love as the basis of marriage, even if such endorsement requires myth, magic, and amnesia for its consummation. "These things seem small and undistinguishable," Demetrius says with puzzlement when the four lovers awake after their strife-filled night in the woods, "Like far-off mountains turnèd into clouds" (4.1.182–83). The job of comedy — so the play's joyous conclusion implies — is to imagine the attainment of long life, true love, and good children not as an arbitrary accident of fortune but as a reward for suffering, albeit the limited and predictable kind of suffering that goes here under the fanciful rubric of romantic misadventure in the woods. Perhaps it is this complex combination of recognition and endorsement that has recommended the play to generation after generation of playgoers.

Its enduring popularity and its undeniable charm are proof of *A Midsummer Night's Dream*'s greatness as comedy. But questions other than the play's greatness have also preoccupied scholars for a long time; we intend to address them, at least in part, through the documents included in this volume. In the last two decades, much literary scholarship has been engaged in showing that Shakespeare's plays, including the romantic comedies, are deeply entwined in the sociocultural circumstances of early modern England. In the case of *A Midsummer Night's Dream*, understanding of the play has been complicated and deepened by critical attention to the political tensions and social conflicts embedded in its contextual history. Scholars have investigated, for example, the play's reproduction of the social structures of rank and gender. They have noted that the play treats Peter Quince and his fellow laboring men as less than fully adult. The mechanicals even seem to acquiesce in such infantilizing treatment, referring repeatedly to themselves as "every mother's son." Some scholars have wondered whether this affectionate but somewhat condescending portrayal is linked, defensively, to Elizabethan social tensions in the wake of widespread unrest and local uprisings in the mid-1590s (Leinwand, "'I believe'"); others have seen the mechanicals as a complexly ironic self-representation by Shakespeare the professional man of the theater, as a playful strategy for distancing his company of the Lord Chamberlain's Men from amateur players (Montrose, *Purpose* 205).

As with the mechanicals, so with other elements of the play: tracing out the play's complex interconnections with its culture has led scholarship in many directions. Thus some scholars have wished to follow the leads offered by the text's geographical allusions to "the farthest step of India" (2.1.69), where Titania's beloved foster child was born and whence Oberon has come to witness the wedding of Hippolyta to Theseus. In these geographical references, post-colonialist critics argue, we may glimpse the early traces of England's imperial future and its emerging preoccupation with the structures of racial and geographical difference (Hendricks). For feminist historians in particular, the play's opening allusion to the conquered Amazons and Theseus's strange pronouncement to Hippolyta that he has "won thy love doing thee injuries" (1.1.17) have prompted historical and theoretical critique. Feminists have noted the gender tensions, the note of complaint directed at all women, implied in the impatient bridegroom Theseus's comparison of the moon to "a stepdame or a dowager / Long withering out a young man's revenue" (1.1.5–6). Rather than dismissing the opening dispute between Hermia and her father as merely the generic furniture of comedy, the romantic conflict required to move the action, scholars have paid serious historical attention to the generational, gender, and religious tensions suggested by so prominent a disagreement over whose desire counts most in the matter of marital choice. To them, Theseus's dictum to Hermia that "to you your father should be as a god" (1.1.47) sounds less like a patriarch's serene orthodoxy and more like his embattled hope. And, of course, cultural historians of all stripes have sought to understand the full force and political implications of the play's several allusions to Queen Elizabeth. It is she, and not Titania, whom literate Elizabethans would have identified as "the fairy queen," whether or not they had read Edmund Spenser's great romantic poem. More specifically, in *A Midsummer Night's Dream*, it is Elizabeth to whom Oberon refers as "a fair vestal thronèd by the west," the "imperial vot'ress" (2.1.158, 163). In the play's mythmaking, she alone is said to be immune to the lovebolts of Cupid, in her "maiden meditation, fancy-free" (164).

Flattering acknowledgment of offstage royal beings is characteristic — indeed virtually required — of court entertainments. It is one reason why arguments continue to flourish about whether or not *A Midsummer Night's Dream* was originally commissioned to celebrate an aristocratic wedding (Chambers 1: 358). Evidence to support such claims remains inconclusive (if tantalizing), and it seems safer to assume with Louis Montrose that Shakespeare, the public playwright, would have wanted to write plays with broad appeal, plays suitable for private performance at court or an aristocratic household (*Purpose* 160–61). Even so, flattery of royal personages is much less characteristic of plays written for the public theaters where kings and queens never came. Furthermore, it is important to recognize that the play's treatment of *its* fairy queen is far more complex and ambivalent than mere flattery would warrant. Hence scholars have seen real if ambiguous tensions in the play's relations to the monarch, perhaps fueled by what Montrose has called "processes of disenchantment," which are "increasingly evident in Elizabethan cultural productions of the 1580s and 1590s" (*Purpose* 165). It has been important for recent scholarship to explicate the play's varied strategies of allusion and disenchantment, to note the tensions of class, gender, and generation often embedded in the play's metaphorical language or, as with the Amazons and the Indian boy, given importance through reference rather than representation. In such metaphors and allusions we may trace the cultural dialogue in which the play is rooted.

In the commentary and documents of this volume, we have sought to include what seem to us the most important of the many perspectives introduced by such recent historical scholarship, though to do them all justice would require many more pages and many more documents than we have space for. Suffice it to say that we, like others before us, see the play's text saturated by the massive, overarching social and cultural changes occurring in post-Reformation England over the course of the sixteenth century. While it may always be difficult to detail the effect of such changes on the production of specific literary texts, it is almost impossible to overstate their overall transformation of cultural practices. As historian Charles Phythian-Adams has suggested,

> for urban communities in particular, the middle and later years of the six-teenth century represented a more abrupt break with the past than any period since the era of the Black Death or before the age of industrialization. Not only were specific customs and institutions brusquely changed or abol-ished, but a whole, vigorous, and variegated popular culture, the matrix of everyday life, was eroded and began to perish. (57)

In England, the kind of changes that we highlight in this volume were wrought, directly and indirectly, by the Protestant Reformation — what happened during the 1530s when the English abandoned their allegiance to Roman Catholicism and created the national church, today's Church of England. We understand that Reformation not merely as a change in reli-gious practice and doctrine, but rather as a large-scale social, cultural, and intellectual transformation. The revolutionary changes of most interest to us here include (but obviously are not limited to) the following: a transforma-tion of holiday customs, festive practices, and the official calendar; the dis-appearance of monastic ways of life, especially for women; the centralization of state power around a charismatic ruler and the regularization of the patri-archal nuclear family; and a massive redefinition of supernatural agency and the proper objects of belief.

A history of the English Reformation is of course well beyond our inten-tions or authority. But our selection of documents is intended to illustrate our firm conviction — and that of other historical scholars of the play — that the Protestant Reformation spreads across the cultural map of early modern England like the letters on a road map, which get harder to see as they increase in size and sprawl across the page. The Reformation's influ-ence on the play is so pervasive and widespread as to be almost invisible. This influence extends, for example, well beyond the obvious effect on the play's representation of marriage and the family (which we document espe-cially in Chapter 3) into such apparently unlikely areas as the play's repre-sentation of holiday customs (Chapter 1), its allusive treatment of the Amazons (Chapter 3), and its characterization of the fairies (Chapter 4).

The Reformation's several effects on early modern English culture are of course interrelated. In the later Middle Ages, some 9,300 English men and women (or about 0.26 percent of the population) lived in monasteries or convents, with convents numbering approximately 138 (Crawford, *Women and Religion* 219, n.10). After the dissolution of monastic ways of life, many adults of both sexes, but women especially, found their life choices significantly constrained. Convent life had offered women an honored vocation, a large degree of self-government under the authority of abbesses and prioresses, and independence from the demands of family (Crawford, *Women and Religion* 22). The modern model of an affectionate marriage within a small, nuclear household became the newly normative — and even perhaps the only truly acceptable — basis of mature social identity. This relatively new cultural insistence upon marriage for women suggests why the defeat of the Amazons, that community of self-governing women, should serve as historical precursor for the opening events of the play. The state's dissolution of the conventual way of life may also account for Theseus's disparagement of female celibacy when he informs a defiant Hermia of the harsh Athenian law concerning women's marriages. It is your choice, Theseus informs her without a trace of irony, whether to die by state-sponsored execution (its exact means unspecified), to "live a barren sister all your life" (1.1.72), or to marry the man whom father Egeus wants as son-in-law. Students may gauge the extent of this social transformation by remembering Chaucer's Wife of Bath, who begins her own self-portrait as a much-married woman by defending marriage as a worthy way of life for men and women against the superior perfection of virginity. "Virginitee is greet perfeccion, / And continence eek with devocioun," she admits, but defiantly declares "I wol bistowe the flour of al my age, / In the actes and the fruyt of mariage" (*Wife of Bath's Prologue* 105–06, 113–14). In England two centuries later, she need not have bothered to defend herself or the goodness and necessity of marriage.

Of other major changes brought about in the wake of the Reformation most relevant to *A Midsummer Night's Dream*, we have selected documents that highlight the change in belief practices implied in the play's treatment of the supernatural. As we will spell out in chapter 4, change in the official religion changed the consensus about the nature of supernatural agency. Belief in fairies, like belief in witches, became a matter of real debate instead of a matter of indifference or neutral disagreement. Medieval Catholicism had considered belief in fairies as paganism. Ironically, now that Catholicism was itself the superseded religion in England, Protestant reformers identified it with superstitious beliefs and practices. Placating fairies with gifts of food, as country people were said to do, now smacked of ignorant superstition or worse. But such disagreement about the supernatural is linked — as we shall see — to redefinitions of the natural and a reexamination of the possible. Are marvels the direct work and judgment of God, people increasingly began to wonder, or events susceptible to scientific explanation?

It is this complex of interlinked and overlapping historical issues on which we focus in the following chapters. Chapter 1 has the most general application to English culture, since it concerns holiday celebrations at a moment in the nation's social history when festive practices — May Day observances, civic theatricals, royal entertainments — had begun to divide and differentiate, had begun to signify "popular" or "elite." Chapter 2 takes up the play's representation of male hierarchy and narratives of male development, both the normative development of an upper-class English male and the exceptional but still broadly symbolic development of a legendary hero such as Theseus. The social tensions surrounding the proper formation of the male subject surface in the fairies' custody dispute over the Indian boy. (They would have not quarreled at all, we must remember, had the child been a girl: Oberon's court is a household of male intimates.) Chapter 3 turns to women, first to representations of those who, both alone and in communities, sought to elude or resist marriage, then to representative selections from the literature that prescribed the duties of daughters and wives and narrated the exemplary lives and deaths of dutiful wives. Chapter 4 is occupied by many elements of the play's dazzling supernaturalism. We understand the play's magic as motivated, at least in part, by a rich post-Reformation debate about the causes of things (especially extraordinary or monstrous things). By highlighting this debate, we seek to offer an alternative to the folkloric interpretations that have sentimentalized the fairies — and often the rest of the play as a result. We define the play's make-believe as an intervention in competing post-Reformation beliefs and practices with the fairies as unknowing players in the religious controversies of late Elizabethan culture. In this context, the following parts of the play come together: Titania's allusions to the wet summers and successive bad harvests of the mid-1590s, the comic treatment of current theological debates about the scope and nature of supernatural agency, Ovidian mythological narratives about wonderful metamorphoses, Bottom's transformation and erotic encounter with Titania, the sin of bestiality, and contemporary theories of monstrous birth.

Romantic comedy's representation of love and marriage cannot escape the determinations of its historical moment, even when the romantic comedy in question is, like *A Midsummer Night's Dream*, explicitly distanced in time and place from the society where it was first performed. Thus when

Titania and Oberon meet onstage for the first time and, for their benefit and our own, rehearse the grounds of their profound marital quarrel, we learn that their separation has had disastrous consequences in the natural order:

> No night is now with hymn or carol blessed.
> Therefore the moon, the governess of floods,
> Pale in her anger, washes all the air,
> That rheumatic diseases do abound.
> And thorough this distemperature we see
> The seasons alter. . . .   (2.1.102-07)

These references to wet weather, bad air, and poor harvests must have reminded Shakespeare's audiences of the succession of stormy springs and cold, wet summers that had caused several years of harvest failure not just in England but also in many parts of northern Europe. These events in nature had affected them all. Perhaps the lines evoked, more generally, the sense of crisis that hung over the last decade of the sixteenth century. For Europeans living in those years, and for the historians who have studied them, the 1590s seem to have been a terrible time. Political disorder, religious warfare, widespread inflation in the price of basic goods, collapse of the agricultural economy in many countries, subsistence and mortality crises, recurrent epidemics of plague — all these factors in combination created a general sense of crisis, even of catastrophe. Predictions of the end of the world were not uncommon (Clark, "Introduction" 4). England did not suffer the depopulation that afflicted other parts of Europe, including northern Ireland; indeed London was then undergoing a population explosion thanks to an influx of newcomers from elsewhere in England and abroad. To many, the urban landscape was violent and crime-infested, inundated with foreigners, threatened by rioting apprentices and other sources of unrest (some included in this category the theaters themselves). England was also spared the internal religious warfare that devastated France, though it too suffered ferocious ideological conflicts between Protestantism and Catholicism of the sort that had spawned warfare on the continent. But overseas warfare — naval expeditions against Spain, military involvement in the Netherlands and France, and recurrent forays against the Irish — took a high toll on English society in the 1590s. It hindered trade, raised taxes, and took a steady stream of able-bodied men out of the labor force only to return some of them, much less able-bodied, as veterans.

*A Midsummer Night's Dream*, written during difficult years, cannot help being influenced by them, especially since the perception of crisis was a contemporary one. More to the point, Titania's obvious allusions to the recent bad weather seem to invite an audience's critical attention, to offer up the play's action and characters as magical encodings of their own time and space. This impression is reinforced by the play's unusually specific allusions to Queen Elizabeth, mentioned above. But the allusion seems to function here almost as a disclaimer, preventing the scandalous liaison between Titania and Bottom from being understood as a satiric attack on Queen Elizabeth and her manner of bestowing favors and attention upon favorites. The disclaimer cannot work, except tactically, of course. In Elizabethan England, no representation of a fairy queen could ever claim *not* to concern the real queen at some level. The question, as always, is to figure out just what social meanings are encoded in fictive transformations of the real.

# PART ONE

## WILLIAM SHAKESPEARE

## *A Midsummer Night's Dream*

*Edited by David Bevington*

# A Midſommer nights dreame.

As it hath beene ſundry times pub-
*lickely acted*, *by the Right honoura-*
ble, the Lord Chamberlaine his
*ſeruants.*

*Written by William Shakeſpeare.*

¶ Imprinted at London, for *Thomas Fiſher*, and are to
be ſoulde at his ſhoppe, at the Signe of the White Hart,
in *Fleeteſtreete.* 1600.

FIGURE I    *Title page of the Quarto* A Midsummer Night's Dream.

# A Midsummer Night's Dream

---

[DRAMATIS PERSONAE

THESEUS, *Duke of Athens*
HIPPOLYTA, *Queen of the Amazons, betrothed to Theseus*
PHILOSTRATE, *Master of the Revels*
EGEUS, *father of Hermia*

HERMIA, *daughter of Egeus, in love with Lysander*
LYSANDER, *in love with Hermia*
DEMETRIUS, *in love with Hermia and favored by Egeus*
HELENA, *in love with Demetrius*

OBERON, *King of the Fairies*
TITANIA, *Queen of the Fairies*
PUCK, *or* ROBIN GOODFELLOW
PEASEBLOSSOM,
COBWEB,
MOTE,                    *Fairies attending Titania*
MUSTARDSEED,
*Other* FAIRIES *attending*

PETER QUINCE, *a carpenter,*       ⎫           PROLOGUE
NICK BOTTOM, *a weaver,*         ⎪           PYRAMUS
FRANCIS FLUTE, *a bellows mender,* ⎬ *representing*   THISBE
TOM SNOUT, *a tinker,*            ⎪           WALL
SNUG, *a joiner,*                ⎪           LION
ROBIN STARVELING, *a tailor,*     ⎭           MOONSHINE

*Lords and Attendants on Theseus and Hippolyta*

SCENE: *Athens, and a wood near it*]

## ACT I, SCENE I°

*Enter Theseus, Hippolyta, [and Philostrate,] with others.*

THESEUS:
   Now, fair Hippolyta, our nuptial hour
   Draws on apace. Four happy days bring in
   Another moon; but, O, methinks, how slow
   This old moon wanes! She lingers° my desires,
   Like to a stepdame° or a dowager°                  5
   Long withering out° a young man's revenue.
HIPPOLYTA:
   Four days will quickly steep themselves° in night;
   Four nights will quickly dream away the time;
   And then the moon, like to a silver bow
   New bent in heaven, shall behold the night        10
   Of our solemnities.°
  THESEUS:           Go, Philostrate,
   Stir up the Athenian youth to merriments.
   Awake the pert and nimble spirit of mirth.
   Turn melancholy forth to funerals;
   The pale companion° is not for our pomp.°     *[Exit Philostrate.]*  15
   Hippolyta, I wooed thee with my sword°
   And won thy love doing thee injuries;
   But I will wed thee in another key,
   With pomp, with triumph,° and with reveling.

---

ACT I, SCENE I. **Location:** Athens. Theseus's court.   **4. lingers:** postpones, delays the fulfill-
ment of.   **5. stepdame:** stepmother.  **a dowager:** i.e., a widow (whose right of inheritance
from her dead husband is eating into her son's estate).   **6. withering out:** causing to dwindle.
**7. steep themselves:** saturate themselves, to be absorbed in.   **11. solemnities:** festive ceremonies of marriage.   **15. companion:** fellow.  **pomp:** ceremonial magnificence.   **16. with
my sword:** in a military engagement against the Amazons, when Hippolyta was taken captive.
**19. triumph:** public festivity.

*Enter Egeus and his daughter Hermia, and Lysander, and Demetrius.*

EGEUS:

Happy be Theseus, our renownèd duke!                                       20

THESEUS:

Thanks, good Egeus. What's the news with thee?

EGEUS:

Full of vexation come I, with complaint
Against my child, my daughter Hermia. —
Stand forth, Demetrius. — My noble lord,
This man hath my consent to marry her. —                                   25
Stand forth, Lysander. — And, my gracious Duke,
This man hath bewitched the bosom of my child.
Thou, thou Lysander, thou hast given her rhymes
And interchanged love tokens with my child.
Thou hast by moonlight at her window sung                                  30
With feigning° voice verses of feigning love,
And stol'n the impression of her fantasy°
With bracelets of thy hair, rings, gauds,° conceits,°
Knacks,° trifles, nosegays, sweetmeats — messengers
Of strong prevailment in° unhardened youth.                                35
With cunning hast thou filched my daughter's heart,
Turned her obedience, which is due to me,
To stubborn harshness. And, my gracious Duke,
Be it so° she will not here before Your Grace
Consent to marry with Demetrius,                                           40
I beg the ancient privilege of Athens:
As she is mine, I may dispose of her,
Which shall be either to this gentleman
Or to her death, according to our law
Immediately° provided in that case.                                        45

THESEUS:

What say you, Hermia? Be advised, fair maid.
To you your father should be as a god —
One that composed your beauties, yea, and one
To whom you are but as a form in wax
By him imprinted, and within his power                                     50

---

**31. feigning:** (1) counterfeiting (2) faining, desirous.   **32. And . . . fantasy:** and made her fall in love with you (imprinting your image on her imagination) by stealthy and dishonest means.   **33. gauds:** playthings.   **conceits:** fanciful trifles.   **34. Knacks:** knickknacks.   **35. prevailment in:** influence on.   **39. Be it so:** if.   **45. Immediately:** directly, with nothing intervening.

To leave° the figure or disfigure° it.
Demetrius is a worthy gentleman.

HERMIA:
So is Lysander.

THESEUS:            In himself he is;
But in this kind,° wanting° your father's voice,°
The other must be held the worthier.                                        55

HERMIA:
I would my father looked but with my eyes.

THESEUS:
Rather your eyes must with his judgment look.

HERMIA:
I do entreat Your Grace to pardon me.
I know not by what power I am made bold,
Nor how it may concern° my modesty                                          60
In such a presence here to plead my thoughts;
But I beseech Your Grace that I may know
The worst that may befall me in this case
If I refuse to wed Demetrius.

THESEUS:
Either to die the death° or to abjure                                       65
Forever the society of men.
Therefore, fair Hermia, question your desires,
Know of your youth, examine well your blood,°
Whether, if you yield not to your father's choice,
You can endure the livery° of a nun,                                        70
For aye° to be in shady cloister mewed,°
To live a barren sister all your life,
Chanting faint hymns to the cold fruitless moon.
Thrice blessèd they that master so their blood
To undergo such maiden pilgrimage;                                          75
But earthlier happy° is the rose distilled°
Than that which, withering on the virgin thorn,
Grows, lives, and dies in single blessedness.

HERMIA:
So will I grow, so live, so die, my lord,
Ere I will yield my virgin patent° up                                       80

51. **leave:** i.e., leave unaltered. **disfigure:** obliterate. 54. **kind:** respect. **wanting:** lacking. **voice:** approval. 60. **concern:** befit. 65. **die the death:** be executed by legal process. 68. **blood:** passions. 70. **livery:** habit, costume. 71. **aye:** ever. **mewed:** shut in. (Said of a hawk, poultry, etc.) 76. **earthlier happy:** happier as respects this world. **distilled:** i.e., to make perfume. 80. **patent:** privilege.

Unto his lordship, whose unwishèd yoke
My soul consents not to give sovereignty.

THESEUS:

Take time to pause, and by the next new moon —
The sealing day betwixt my love and me
For everlasting bond of fellowship —                    85
Upon that day either prepare to die
For disobedience to your father's will,
Or° else to wed Demetrius, as he would,
Or on Diana's altar to protest°
For aye austerity and single life.                       90

DEMETRIUS:

Relent, sweet Hermia, and, Lysander, yield
Thy crazèd° title to my certain right.

LYSANDER:

You have her father's love, Demetrius;
Let me have Hermia's. Do you marry him.

EGEUS:

Scornful Lysander! True, he hath my love,               95
And what is mine my love shall render him.
And she is mine, and all my right of her
I do estate unto° Demetrius.

LYSANDER:

I am, my lord, as well derived° as he,
As well possessed;° my love is more than his;           100
My fortunes every way as fairly° ranked,
If not with vantage,° as Demetrius';
And, which is more than all these boasts can be,
I am beloved of beauteous Hermia.
Why should not I then prosecute my right?               105
Demetrius, I'll avouch it to his head,°
Made love to Nedar's daughter, Helena,
And won her soul; and she, sweet lady, dotes,
Devoutly dotes, dotes in idolatry
Upon this spotted° and inconstant man.                  110

THESEUS:

I must confess that I have heard so much,
And with Demetrius thought to have spoke thereof;

---

88. **Or:** either.   89. **protest:** vow.   92. **crazèd:** cracked, unsound.   98. **estate unto:** settle or
bestow upon.   99. **as well derived:** as well born and descended.   100. **possessed:** endowed
with wealth.   101. **fairly:** handsomely.   102. **vantage:** superiority.   106. **head:** i.e., face.
110. **spotted:** i.e., morally stained.

But, being overfull of self-affairs,°
My mind did lose it. But, Demetrius, come,
And come, Egeus, you shall go with me;                            115
I have some private schooling° for you both.
For you, fair Hermia, look you arm° yourself
To fit your fancies° to your father's will,
Or else the law of Athens yields you up —
Which by no means we may extenuate° —                             120
To death or to a vow of single life.
Come, my Hippolyta. What cheer, my love?
Demetrius and Egeus, go° along.
I must employ you in some business
Against° our nuptial, and confer with you                         125
Of something nearly that° concerns yourselves.

EGEUS:
    With duty and desire we follow you.    *Exeunt [all but Lysander and Hermia].*

LYSANDER:
    How now, my love, why is your cheek so pale?
    How chance the roses there do fade so fast?

HERMIA:
    Belike° for want of rain, which I could well                  130
    Beteem° them from the tempest of my eyes.

LYSANDER:
    Ay me! For aught that I could ever read,
    Could ever hear by tale or history,
    The course of true love never did run smooth;
    But either it was different in blood° —                       135

HERMIA:
    O cross!° Too high to be enthralled to low.

LYSANDER:
    Or else misgrafted° in respect of years —

HERMIA:
    O spite! Too old to be engaged to young.

LYSANDER:
    Or else it stood upon the choice of friends° —

---

113. **self-affairs:** my own concerns.   116. **schooling:** admonition.   117. **look you arm:** take
care you prepare.   118. **fancies:** likings, thoughts of love.   120. **extenuate:** mitigate, relax.
123. **go:** i.e., come.   125. **Against:** in preparation for.   126. **nearly that:** that closely.
130. **Belike:** very likely.   131. **Beteem:** grant, afford.   135. **blood:** hereditary station.
136. **cross:** vexation.   137. **misgrafted:** ill grafted, badly matched.   139. **friends:** relatives.

HERMIA:

O hell, to choose love by another's eyes!                          140

LYSANDER:

Or if there were a sympathy° in choice,
War, death, or sickness did lay siege to it,
Making it momentany° as a sound,
Swift as a shadow, short as any dream,
Brief as the lightning in the collied° night                       145
That in a spleen° unfolds° both heaven and earth,
And ere a man hath power to say "Behold!"
The jaws of darkness do devour it up.
So quick° bright things come to confusion.°

HERMIA:

If then true lovers have been ever crossed,°                       150
It stands as an edict in destiny.
Then let us teach our trial patience,°
Because it is a customary cross,
As due to love as thoughts, and dreams, and sighs,
Wishes, and tears, poor fancy's° followers.                        155

LYSANDER:

A good persuasion.° Therefore, hear me, Hermia:
I have a widow aunt, a dowager
Of great revenue, and she hath no child.
From Athens is her house remote seven leagues;
And she respects° me as her only son.                              160
There, gentle Hermia, may I marry thee,
And to that place the sharp Athenian law
Cannot pursue us. If thou lovest me, then,
Steal forth thy father's house tomorrow night;
And in the wood, a league without° the town,                       165
Where I did meet thee once with Helena
To do observance to a morn of May,°
There will I stay for thee.

HERMIA:                          My good Lysander!
I swear to thee, by Cupid's strongest bow,

---

141. **sympathy:** agreement.   143. **momentany:** lasting but a moment.   145. **collied:** black-ened (as with coal dust), darkened.   146. **in a spleen:** in a swift impulse, in a violent flash.
**unfolds:** reveals.   149. **quick:** quickly; also, living, alive. **confusion:** ruin.   150. **ever crossed:** always thwarted.   152. **teach . . . patience:** i.e., teach ourselves patience in this trial.   155. **fancy's:** amorous passion's.   156. **persuasion:** doctrine.   160. **respects:** regards.
165. **without:** outside.   167. **do . . . May:** perform the ceremonies of May Day.

By his best arrow° with the golden head,                              170
By the simplicity° of Venus' doves,°
By that which knitteth souls and prospers loves,
And by that fire which burned the Carthage queen°
When the false Trojan° under sail was seen,
By all the vows that ever men have broke,                             175
In number more than ever women spoke,
In that same place thou hast appointed me
Tomorrow truly will I meet with thee.

LYSANDER:
Keep promise, love. Look, here comes Helena.

*Enter Helena.*

HERMIA:
God speed, fair° Helena! Whither away?                                180

HELENA:
Call you me fair? That "fair" again unsay.
Demetrius loves your fair.° O happy fair!°
Your eyes are lodestars,° and your tongue's sweet air°
More tunable° than lark to shepherd's ear
When wheat is green, when hawthorn buds appear.                       185
Sickness is catching. O, were favor° so,
Yours would I catch, fair Hermia, ere I go;
My ear should catch your voice, my eye your eye,
My tongue should catch your tongue's sweet melody.
Were the world mine, Demetrius being bated,°                          190
The rest I'd give to be to you translated.°
O, teach me how you look and with what art
You sway the motion° of Demetrius' heart.

HERMIA:
I frown upon him, yet he loves me still.

HELENA:
O, that your frowns would teach my smiles such skill!                 195

---

170. **best arrow:** (Cupid's best gold-pointed arrows were supposed to induce love; his blunt leaden arrows, aversion.)   171. **simplicity:** innocence.   **Venus' doves:** i.e., those that drew Venus's chariot.   173, 174. **Carthage queen, false Trojan:** (Dido, Queen of Carthage, immolated herself on a funeral pyre after having been deserted by the Trojan hero Aeneas.)   180. **fair:** fair-complexioned (generally regarded by the Elizabethans as more beautiful than a dark complexion).   182. **your fair:** your beauty (even though Hermia is dark complexioned).   **happy fair:** lucky fair one.   183. **lodestars:** guiding stars.   **air:** music.   184. **tunable:** tuneful, melodious.   186. **favor:** appearance, looks.   190. **bated:** excepted.   191. **translated:** transformed.   193. **sway the motion:** control the impulse.

HERMIA:
I give him curses, yet he gives me love.

HELENA:
O, that my prayers could such affection° move!°

HERMIA:
The more I hate, the more he follows me.

HELENA:
The more I love, the more he hateth me.

HERMIA:
His folly, Helena, is no fault of mine. 200

HELENA:
None, but your beauty. Would that fault were mine!

HERMIA:
Take comfort. He no more shall see my face.
Lysander and myself will fly this place.
Before the time I did Lysander see
Seemed Athens as a paradise to me.° 205
O, then, what graces in my love do dwell,
That he hath turned a heaven unto a hell?

LYSANDER:
Helen, to you our minds we will unfold.
Tomorrow night, when Phoebe° doth behold
Her silver visage in the watery glass,° 210
Decking with liquid pearl the bladed grass,
A time that lovers' flights doth still° conceal,
Through Athens' gates have we devised to steal.

HERMIA:
And in the wood, where often you and I
Upon faint° primrose beds were wont to lie, 215
Emptying our bosoms of their counsel° sweet,
There my Lysander and myself shall meet,
And thence from Athens turn away our eyes
To seek new friends and stranger companies.°
Farewell, sweet playfellow. Pray thou for us, 220
And good luck grant thee thy Demetrius!
Keep word, Lysander. We must starve our sight
From lovers' food till morrow deep midnight.

197. **affection:** passion. **move:** arouse. **204–05. Before . . . to me:** (Hermia seemingly means that love has led to complications and jealousies, making Athens hell for her.) **209. Phoebe:** Diana, the moon. **210. glass:** mirror. **212. still:** always. **215. faint:** pale. **216. counsel:** secret thought. **219. stranger companies:** the company of strangers.

LYSANDER:
I will, my Hermia. (*Exit Hermia.*) Helena, adieu.
As you on him, Demetrius dote on you!                    *Exit Lysander.* 225
HELENA:
How happy some o'er other some can be!°
Through Athens I am thought as fair as she.
But what of that? Demetrius thinks not so;
He will not know what all but he do know.
And as he errs, doting on Hermia's eyes,                                    230
So I, admiring of° his qualities.
Things base and vile, holding no quantity,°
Love can transpose to form and dignity.
Love looks not with the eyes, but with the mind,
And therefore is winged Cupid painted blind.                               235
Nor hath Love's mind of any judgment taste;°
Wings and no eyes figure° unheedy haste.
And therefore is Love said to be a child,
Because in choice° he is so oft beguiled.°
As waggish° boys in game° themselves forswear,                             240
So the boy Love is perjured everywhere.
For ere Demetrius looked on Hermia's eyne,°
He hailed down oaths that he was only mine;
And when this hail some heat from Hermia felt,
So he dissolved, and showers of oaths did melt.                            245
I will go tell him of fair Hermia's flight.
Then to the wood will he tomorrow night
Pursue her; and for this intelligence°
If I have thanks, it is a dear expense.°
But herein mean I to enrich my pain,                                       250
To have his sight thither and back again.                          *Exit.*

---

226. o'er . . . can be: can be in comparison to some others.    231. admiring of: wondering at.
232. holding no quantity: i.e., unsubstantial, unshapely.    236. Nor . . . taste: i.e., nor has
Love, which dwells in the fancy or imagination, any *taste* or least bit of judgment or reason.    237. figure: are a symbol of.    239. in choice: in choosing.    beguiled: self-deluded,
making unaccountable choices.    240. waggish: playful, mischievous.    game: sport, jest.
242. eyne: eyes (old form of plural).    248. intelligence: information.    249. dear: costly.
a dear expense: i.e., a trouble worth taking on my part, or a begrudging effort on his part.

## ACT I, SCENE 2°

*Enter Quince the carpenter, and Snug the joiner, and Bottom the weaver, and Flute the
bellows mender, and Snout the tinker, and Starveling the tailor.*

QUINCE:   Is all our company here?

BOTTOM:   You were best to call them generally,° man by man, according to
the scrip.°

QUINCE:   Here is the scroll of every man's name which is thought fit,
through all Athens, to play in our interlude° before the Duke and the     5
Duchess on his wedding day at night.

BOTTOM:   First, good Peter Quince, say what the play treats on, then read
the names of the actors, and so grow to° a point.

QUINCE:   Marry,° our play is "The most lamentable comedy and most cruel
death of Pyramus and Thisbe."     10

BOTTOM:   A very good piece of work, I assure you, and a merry. Now, good
Peter Quince, call forth your actors by the scroll. Masters, spread yourselves.

QUINCE:   Answer as I call you. Nick Bottom,° the weaver.

BOTTOM:   Ready. Name what part I am for, and proceed.     15

QUINCE:   You, Nick Bottom, are set down for Pyramus.

BOTTOM:   What is Pyramus? A lover or a tyrant?

QUINCE:   A lover, that kills himself most gallant for love.

BOTTOM:   That will ask some tears in the true performing of it. If I do it,
let the audience look to their eyes. I will move storms; I will condole° in     20
some measure. To the rest — yet my chief humor° is for a tyrant. I could
play Ercles° rarely, or a part to tear a cat° in, to make all split.°

   "The raging rocks
   And shivering shocks
   Shall break the locks     25
      Of prison gates;
   And Phibbus' car°
   Shall shine from far
   And make and mar
      The foolish Fates."     30

This was lofty! Now name the rest of the players. This is Ercles' vein, a
tyrant's vein. A lover is more condoling.

---

ACT I, SCENE 2. **Location:** Athens.   **2. generally:** (Bottom's blunder for "individually.")
**3. scrip:** scrap. (Bottom's error for "script.")   **5. interlude:** play.   **8. grow to:** come to.
**9. Marry:** (A mild oath; originally the name of the Virgin Mary.)   **14. Bottom:** (As a
weaver's term, a *bottom* was an object around which thread was wound.)   **20. condole:** lament,
arouse pity.   **21. humor:** inclination, whim.   **22 Ercles:** Hercules. (The tradition of ranting
came from Seneca's *Hercules Furens.*)   **tear a cat:** i.e., rant.   **make all split:** i.e., cause a stir,
bring the house down.   **27. Phibbus' car:** Phoebus', the sun god's, chariot.

QUINCE:  Francis Flute, the bellows mender.

FLUTE:  Here, Peter Quince.

QUINCE:  Flute, you must take Thisbe on you.                              35

FLUTE:  What is Thisbe? A wandering knight?

QUINCE:  It is the lady that Pyramus must love.

FLUTE:  Nay, faith, let not me play a woman. I have a beard coming.

QUINCE:  That's all one.° You shall play it in a mask, and you may speak as
small° as you will.                                                        40

BOTTOM:  An° I may hide my face, let me play Thisbe too. I'll speak in a
monstrous little voice: "Thisne, Thisne!" "Ah, Pyramus, my lover dear!
Thy Thisbe dear, and lady dear!"

QUINCE:  No, no, you must play Pyramus, and Flute, you Thisbe.

BOTTOM:  Well, proceed.                                                    45

QUINCE:  Robin Starveling, the tailor.

STARVELING:  Here, Peter Quince.

QUINCE:  Robin Starveling, you must play Thisbe's mother. Tom Snout,
the tinker.

SNOUT:  Here, Peter Quince.                                                50

QUINCE:  You, Pyramus' father; myself, Thisbe's father; Snug, the joiner,
you, the lion's part; and I hope here is a play fitted.

SNUG:  Have you the lion's part written? Pray you, if it be, give it me, for I
am slow of study.

QUINCE:  You may do it extempore, for it is nothing but roaring.          55

BOTTOM:  Let me play the lion too. I will roar that I will do any man's
heart good to hear me. I will roar that I will make the Duke say, "Let him
roar again, let him roar again."

QUINCE:  An you should do it too terribly, you would fright the Duchess
and the ladies, that they would shriek; and that were enough to hang     60
us all.

ALL:  That would hang us, every mother's son.

BOTTOM:  I grant you, friends, if you should fright the ladies out of their
wits, they would have no more discretion but to hang us; but I will
aggravate° my voice so that I will roar you° as gently as any sucking     65
dove;° I will roar you an 'twere° any nightingale.

QUINCE:  You can play no part but Pyramus; for Pyramus is a sweet-faced
man, a proper° man as one shall see in a summer's day, a most lovely
gentlemanlike man. Therefore you must needs play Pyramus.

---

**39. That's all one:** it makes no difference.    **40. small:** high-pitched.    **41. An:** if (also at
line 59).    **65. aggravate:** (Bottom's blunder for "moderate.")    **roar you:** i.e., roar for you.
**65–66. sucking dove:** (Bottom conflates *sitting dove* and *sucking lamb*, two proverbial images of
innocence.)    **66. an 'twere:** as if it were.    **68. proper:** handsome.

BOTTOM:  Well, I will undertake it. What beard were I best to play it in?  70
QUINCE:  Why, what you will.
BOTTOM:  I will discharge° it in either your° straw-color beard, your
orange-tawny beard, your purple-in-grain° beard, or your French-crown-
color° beard, your perfect yellow.
QUINCE:  Some of your French crowns° have no hair at all, and then you  75
will play barefaced. But, masters, here are your parts. [*He distributes
parts.*] And I am to entreat you, request you, and desire you to con°
them by tomorrow night, and meet me in the palace wood, a mile
without the town, by moonlight. There will we rehearse; for if we
meet in the city, we shall be dogged with company, and our devices°  80
known. In the meantime I will draw a bill° of properties, such as our
play wants. I pray you, fail me not.
BOTTOM:  We will meet, and there we may rehearse most obscenely° and
courageously. Take pains, be perfect.° Adieu.
QUINCE:  At the Duke's oak we meet.  85
BOTTOM:  Enough. Hold, or cut bowstrings.°                 *Exeunt.*


## ACT 2, SCENE 1°

*Enter a Fairy at one door, and Robin Goodfellow [Puck] at another.*

PUCK:
How now, spirit, whither wander you?
FAIRY:
Over hill, over dale,
    Thorough° bush, thorough brier,
Over park, over pale,°
    Thorough flood, thorough fire,
I do wander everywhere,                 5
Swifter than the moon's sphere;°
And I serve the Fairy Queen,
To dew° her orbs° upon the green.

---

72. **discharge:** perform.   **your:** i.e., you know the kind I mean.   73. **purple-in-grain:** dyed a
very deep red (from *grain*, the name applied to the dried insect used to make the dye).
73–74. **French-crown-color:** i.e., color of a French crown, a gold coin.   75. **crowns:** heads
bald from syphilis, the "French disease."   77. **con:** learn by heart.   80. **devices:** plans.
81. **draw a bill:** draw up a list.   83. **obscenely:** (An unintentionally funny blunder, whatever
Bottom meant to say.)   84. **perfect:** i.e., letter-perfect in memorizing your parts.
86. **Hold . . . bowstrings:** (An archer's expression, not definitely explained, but probably
meaning here "keep your promises, or give up the play.")   ACT 2, SCENE 1. **Location:** A wood
near Athens.   3. **Thorough:** through.   4. **pale:** enclosure.   7. **sphere:** orbit.   9. **dew:**
sprinkle with dew.   **orbs:** circles, i.e., fairy rings (circular bands of grass, darker than the surrounding area, caused by fungi enriching the soil).

The cowslips tall her pensioners° be.                                    10
In their gold coats spots you see;
Those be rubies, fairy favors;°
In those freckles live their savors.°
I must go seek some dewdrops here
And hang a pearl in every cowslip's ear.                                 15
Farewell, thou lob° of spirits; I'll be gone.
Our Queen and all her elves come here anon.°

PUCK:
The King doth keep his revels here tonight.
Take heed the Queen come not within his sight.
For Oberon is passing fell° and wrath,°                                  20
Because that she as her attendant hath
A lovely boy, stolen from an Indian king;
She never had so sweet a changeling.°
And jealous Oberon would have the child
Knight of his train, to trace° the forests wild.                        25
But she perforce° withholds the lovèd boy,
Crowns him with flowers, and makes him all her joy.
And now they never meet in grove or green,
By fountain° clear, or spangled starlight sheen,°
But they do square,° that all their elves for fear                      30
Creep into acorn cups and hide them there.

FAIRY:
Either I mistake your shape and making quite,
Or else you are that shrewd° and knavish sprite°
Called Robin Goodfellow. Are not you he
That frights the maidens of the villagery,°                             35
Skim milk,° and sometimes labor in the quern,°
And bootless° make the breathless huswife° churn,
And sometimes make the drink to bear no barm,°
Mislead night wanderers,° laughing at their harm?

---

10. **pensioners:** retainers, members of the royal bodyguard.   12. **favors:** love tokens.
13. **savors:** sweet smells.   16. **lob:** country bumpkin.   17. **anon:** at once.   20. **passing
fell:** exceedingly angry.   **wrath:** wrathful.   23. **changeling:** child exchanged for another
by the fairies.   25. **trace:** range through.   26. **perforce:** forcibly.   29. **fountain:** spring.
**starlight sheen:** shining starlight.   30. **square:** quarrel.   33. **shrewd:** mischievous.   **sprite:**
spirit.   35. **villagery:** village population.   36. **Skim milk:** i.e., steal the cream.   **quern:** hand
mill (where Puck presumably hampers the grinding of grain).   37. **bootless:** in vain. (Puck
prevents the cream from turning to butter.)   **huswife:** housewife.   38. **barm:** head on the
ale. (Puck prevents the barm or yeast from producing fermentation.)   39. **Mislead night
wanderers:** i.e., mislead with false fire those who walk abroad at night (hence earning Puck his
other names of Jack o' Lantern and Will o' the Wisp).

Those that "Hobgoblin" call you, and "Sweet Puck,"°      40
You do their work, and they shall have good luck.
Are you not he?
PUCK:          Thou speakest aright;
I am that merry wanderer of the night.
I jest to Oberon and make him smile
When I a fat and bean-fed° horse beguile,      45
Neighing in likeness of a filly foal;
And sometimes lurk I in a gossip's° bowl
In very likeness of a roasted crab,°
And when she drinks, against her lips I bob
And on her withered dewlap° pour the ale.      50
The wisest aunt,° telling the saddest° tale,
Sometimes for three-foot stool mistaketh me;
Then slip I from her bum, down topples she,
And "Tailor"° cries, and falls into a cough;
And then the whole choir° hold their hips and laugh,      55
And waxen° in their mirth, and neeze,° and swear
A merrier hour was never wasted° there.
But, room,° fairy! Here comes Oberon.
FAIRY:
And here my mistress. Would that he were gone!

*Enter [Oberon] the King of Fairies at one door, with his train, and [Titania]*
*the Queen at another, with hers.*

OBERON:
Ill met by moonlight, proud Titania.      60
TITANIA:
What, jealous Oberon? Fairies, skip hence.
I have forsworn his bed and company.
OBERON:
Tarry, rash wanton.° Am not I thy lord?
TITANIA:
Then I must be thy lady; but I know
When thou hast stolen away from Fairyland      65

---

**40. Those . . . Puck:** i.e., those who call you by the names you favor rather than those denoting the mischief you do.   **45. bean-fed:** well fed on field beans.   **47. gossip's:** old woman's.   **48. crab:** crab apple.   **50. dewlap:** loose skin on neck.   **51. aunt:** old woman. **saddest:** most serious.   **54. Tailor:** (Possibly because she ends up sitting cross-legged on the floor, looking like a tailor, or else referring to the *tail* or buttocks.)   **55. choir:** company. **56. waxen:** increase.  **neeze:** sneeze.   **57. wasted:** spent.   **58. room:** stand aside, make room. **63. wanton:** headstrong creature.

And in the shape of Corin° sat all day,
Playing on the pipes of corn° and versing love
To amorous Phillida.° Why art thou here
Come from the farthest step° of India,
But that, forsooth, the bouncing Amazon,                    70
Your buskined° mistress and your warrior love,
To Theseus must be wedded, and you come
To give their bed joy and prosperity.

OBERON:

How canst thou thus for shame, Titania,
Glance at my credit with Hippolyta,°                         75
Knowing I know thy love to Theseus?
Didst not thou lead him through the glimmering night
From Perigenia,° whom he ravishèd?
And make him with fair Aegles° break his faith,
With Ariadne° and Antiopa?°                                  80

TITANIA:

These are the forgeries of jealousy;
And never, since the middle summer's spring,°
Met we on hill, in dale, forest, or mead,°
By pavèd° fountain or by rushy° brook,
Or in° the beachèd margent° of the sea,                      85
To dance our ringlets° to° the whistling wind,
But with thy brawls thou hast disturbed our sport.
Therefore the winds, piping to us in vain,
As in revenge, have sucked up from the sea
Contagious° fogs which, falling in the land,                 90
Hath every pelting° river made so proud
That they have overborne their continents.°

---

66, 68. **Corin, Phillida:** (Conventional names of pastoral lovers.)  67. **corn:** (Here, oat stalks.)
69. **step:** farthest limit of travel, or, perhaps, *steep*, "mountain range."  71. **buskined:** wearing
half-boots called buskins.  75. **Glance . . . Hippolyta:** make insinuations about my favored
relationship with Hippolyta.  78. **Perigenia:** i.e., Perigouna, one of Theseus' conquests. (This
and the following women are named in Thomas North's translation of Plutarch's "Life of Theseus.")  79. **Aegles:** i.e., Aegle, for whom Theseus deserted Ariadne according to some
accounts.  80. **Ariadne:** the daughter of Minos, King of Crete, who helped Theseus to escape
the labyrinth after killing the Minotaur; later she was abandoned by Theseus. **Antiopa:**
Queen of the Amazons and wife of Theseus; elsewhere identified with Hippolyta, but
here thought of as a separate woman.  82. **middle summer's spring:** beginning of midsummer.  83. **mead:** meadow.  84. **pavèd:** with pebbled bottom. **rushy:** bordered with
rushes.  85. **in:** on. **margent:** edge, border.  86. **ringlets:** dances in a ring. (See *orbs* in
2.1.9.) **to:** to the sound of.  90. **Contagious:** noxious.  91. **pelting:** paltry.  92. **continents:** banks that contain them.

The ox hath therefore stretched his yoke° in vain,
The plowman lost his sweat, and the green corn°
Hath rotted ere his youth attained a beard;                    95
The fold° stands empty in the drownèd field,
And crows are fatted with the murrain° flock;
The nine-men's morris° is filled up with mud,
And the quaint mazes° in the wanton° green
For lack of tread are indistinguishable.                       100
The human mortals want° their winter° here;
No night is now with hymn or carol blessed.
Therefore° the moon, the governess of floods,
Pale in her anger, washes° all the air,
That rheumatic diseases° do abound.                            105
And thorough this distemperature° we see
The seasons alter: hoary-headed frosts
Fall in the fresh lap of the crimson rose,
And on old Hiems'° thin and icy crown
An odorous chaplet of sweet summer buds                        110
Is, as in mockery, set. The spring, the summer,
The childing° autumn, angry winter, change
Their wonted liveries,° and the mazèd° world
By their increase° now knows not which is which.
And this same progeny of evils comes                           115
From our debate,° from our dissension.
We are their parents and original.°

OBERON:
Do you amend it, then. It lies in you.
Why should Titania cross her Oberon?
I do but beg a little changeling boy                           120
To be my henchman.°

93. **stretched his yoke:** i.e., pulled at his yoke in plowing.   94. **corn:** grain of any kind.
96. **fold:** pen for sheep or cattle.   97. **murrain:** having died of the plague.   98. **nine-men's morris:** i.e., portion of the village green marked out in a square for a game played with nine pebbles or pegs.   99. **quaint mazes:** i.e., intricate paths marked out on the village green to be followed rapidly on foot as a kind of contest.   **wanton:** luxuriant.   101. **want:** lack.   **winter:** i.e., regular winter season; or, proper observances of winter, such as the *hymn* or *carol* in the next line (?).   103. **Therefore:** i.e., as a result of our quarrel.   104. **washes:** saturates with moisture.   105. **rheumatic diseases:** colds, flu, and other respiratory infections.   106. **distemperature:** disturbance in nature.   109. **Hiems':** the winter god's.   112. **childing:** fruitful, pregnant.   113. **wonted liveries:** usual apparel.   **mazèd:** bewildered.   114. **their increase:** their yield, what they produce.   116. **debate:** quarrel.   117. **original:** origin.   121. **henchman:** attendant, page.

TITANIA:                        Set your heart at rest.
 The fairy land buys not the child of me.
 His mother was a vot'ress of my order,°
 And in the spicèd Indian air by night
 Full often hath she gossiped by my side     125
 And sat with me on Neptune's yellow sands,
 Marking th' embarkèd traders° on the flood,°
 When we have laughed to see the sails conceive
 And grow big-bellied with the wanton° wind;
 Which she, with pretty and with swimming° gait,   130
 Following — her womb then rich with my young squire —
 Would imitate, and sail upon the land
 To fetch me trifles, and return again
 As from a voyage, rich with merchandise.
 But she, being mortal, of that boy did die;    135
 And for her sake do I rear up her boy,
 And for her sake I will not part with him.
OBERON:
 How long within this wood intend you stay?
TITANIA:
 Perchance till after Theseus' wedding day.
 If you will patiently dance in our round°    140
 And see our moonlight revels, go with us;
 If not, shun me, and I will spare° your haunts.
OBERON:
 Give me that boy, and I will go with thee.
TITANIA:
 Not for thy fairy kingdom. Fairies, away!
 We shall chide downright, if I longer stay. *Exeunt [Titania with her train].* 145
OBERON:
 Well, go thy way. Thou shalt not from° this grove
 Till I torment thee for this injury.
 My gentle Puck, come hither. Thou rememb'rest
 Since° once I sat upon a promontory,
 And heard a mermaid on a dolphin's back    150
 Uttering such dulcet° and harmonious breath°

---

123. **was . . . order:** had taken a vow to serve me. 127. **traders:** trading vessels. **flood:** flood tide. 129. **wanton:** (1) playful (2) amorous. 130. **swimming:** smooth, gliding. 140. **round:** circular dance. 142. **spare:** shun. 146. **from:** go from. 149. **Since:** when. 151. **dulcet:** sweet. **breath:** voice, song.

That the rude° sea grew civil at her song,
And certain stars shot madly from their spheres
To hear the sea-maid's music?

PUCK:                                    I remember.

OBERON:
That very time I saw, but thou couldst not,                    155
Flying between the cold moon and the earth
Cupid, all° armed. A certain° aim he took
At a fair vestal° thronèd by° the west,
And loosed° his love shaft smartly from his bow
As° it should pierce a hundred thousand hearts;              160
But I might° see young Cupid's fiery shaft
Quenched in the chaste beams of the watery moon,
And the imperial vot'ress passèd on,
In maiden meditation, fancy-free.°
Yet marked I where the bolt° of Cupid fell:                    165
It fell upon a little western flower,
Before milk-white, now purple with love's wound,
And maidens call it love-in-idleness.°
Fetch me that flower; the herb I showed thee once.
The juice of it on sleeping eyelids laid                        170
Will make or man or° woman madly dote
Upon the next live creature that it sees.
Fetch me this herb, and be thou here again
Ere the leviathan° can swim a league.

PUCK:
I'll put a girdle round about the earth                          175
In forty° minutes.                              [*Exit.*]

OBERON:                    Having once this juice,
I'll watch Titania when she is asleep
And drop the liquor of it in her eyes.
The next thing then she waking looks upon,
Be it on lion, bear, or wolf, or bull,                          180
On meddling monkey, or on busy ape,
She shall pursue it with the soul of love.

---

152. **rude:** rough.  157. **all:** fully.  **certain:** sure.  158. **vestal:** vestal virgin. (Contains a complimentary allusion to Queen Elizabeth as a votaress of Diana and probably refers to an actual entertainment in her honor at Elvetham in 1591.)  **by:** in the region of.  159. **loosed:** released.  160. **As:** as if.  161. **might:** could.  164. **fancy-free:** free of love's spell.  165. **bolt:** arrow.  168. **love-in-idleness:** pansy, heartsease.  171 **or . . . or:** either . . . or.  174. **leviathan:** sea monster, whale.  176. **forty:** (Used indefinitely.)

And ere I take this charm from off her sight,
As I can take it with another herb,
I'll make her render up her page to me.                              185
But who comes here? I am invisible,
And I will overhear their conference.

*Enter Demetrius, Helena following him.*

DEMETRIUS:
I love thee not; therefore pursue me not.
Where is Lysander and fair Hermia?
The one I'll slay; the other slayeth me.                             190
Thou toldst me they were stol'n unto this wood;
And here am I, and wood° within this wood
Because I cannot meet my Hermia.
Hence, get thee gone, and follow me no more.

HELENA:
You draw me, you hardhearted adamant!°                               195
But yet you draw not iron, for my heart
Is true as steel. Leave you° your power to draw,
And I shall have no power to follow you.

DEMETRIUS:
Do I entice you? Do I speak you fair?°
Or rather do I not in plainest truth                                 200
Tell you I do not nor I cannot love you?

HELENA:
And even for that do I love you the more.
I am your spaniel; and, Demetrius,
The more you beat me I will fawn on you.
Use me but as your spaniel, spurn me, strike me,                     205
Neglect me, lose me; only give me leave,
Unworthy as I am, to follow you.
What worser place can I beg in your love —
And yet a place of high respect with me —
Than to be usèd as you use your dog?                                 210

DEMETRIUS:
Tempt not too much the hatred of my spirit,
For I am sick when I do look on thee.

---

192. **and wood:** and mad, frantic (with an obvious wordplay on *wood,* meaning "woods").
195. **adamant:** lodestone, magnet (with pun on *hardhearted,* since adamant was also thought to
be the hardest of all stones and was confused with the diamond).   197. **Leave you:** give up.
199. **speak you fair:** speak courteously to you.

HELENA:
And I am sick when I look not on you.

DEMETRIUS:
You do impeach° your modesty too much
To leave° the city and commit yourself                    215
Into the hands of one that loves you not,
To trust the opportunity of night
And the ill counsel of a desert° place
With the rich worth of your virginity.

HELENA:
Your virtue° is my privilege.° For that°                   220
It is not night when I do see your face,
Therefore I think I am not in the night;
Nor doth this wood lack worlds of company,
For you, in my respect,° are all the world.
Then how can it be said I am alone                         225
When all the world is here to look on me?

DEMETRIUS:
I'll run from thee and hide me in the brakes,°
And leave thee to the mercy of wild beasts.

HELENA:
The wildest hath not such a heart as you.
Run when you will. The story shall be changed:            230
Apollo flies and Daphne holds the chase,°
The dove pursues the griffin,° the mild hind°
Makes speed to catch the tiger — bootless° speed,
When cowardice pursues and valor flies!

DEMETRIUS:
I will not stay thy questions.° Let me go!                 235
Or if thou follow me, do not believe
But I shall do thee mischief in the wood.

HELENA:
Ay, in the temple, in the town, the field,
You do me mischief. Fie, Demetrius!

---

214. **impeach:** call into question.   215. **To leave:** by leaving.   218. **desert:** deserted.
220 **virtue:** goodness or power to attract.   **privilege:** safeguard, warrant.   **For that:** because.
224. **in my respect:** as far as I am concerned, in my esteem.   227. **brakes:** thickets.
231. **Apollo . . . chase:** (In the ancient myth, Daphne fled from Apollo and was saved from rape by being transformed into a laurel tree; here it is the female who *holds the chase*, or pursues, instead of the male.)   232. **griffin:** a fabulous monster with the head and wings of an eagle and the body of a lion.   **hind:** female deer.   233. **bootless:** fruitless.   235. **stay thy questions:** wait for or put up with your talk or argument.

Your wrongs do set a scandal on my sex.°                                          240
We cannot fight for love, as men may do;
We should be wooed and were not made to woo.          [*Exit Demetrius.*]
I'll follow thee and make a heaven of hell,
To die upon° the hand I love so well.                              [*Exit.*]

OBERON:
Fare thee well, nymph. Ere he do leave this grove                                245
Thou shalt fly him, and he shall seek thy love.

*Enter Puck.*

Hast thou the flower there? Welcome, wanderer.

PUCK:
Ay, there it is.                                          [*He offers the flower.*]

OBERON:                I pray thee, give it me.
I know a bank where the wild thyme blows,°
Where oxlips° and the nodding violet grows,                                      250
Quite overcanopied with luscious woodbine,°
With sweet muskroses° and with eglantine.°
There sleeps Titania sometime of° the night,
Lulled in these flowers with dances and delight;
And there the snake throws° her enameled skin,                                  255
Weed° wide enough to wrap a fairy in.
And with the juice of this I'll streak° her eyes
And make her full of hateful fantasies.
Take thou some of it, and seek through this grove.

                                          [*He gives some love juice.*]

A sweet Athenian lady is in love                                                260
With a disdainful youth. Anoint his eyes,
But do it when the next thing he espies
May be the lady. Thou shalt know the man
By the Athenian garments he hath on.
Effect it with some care, that he may prove                                     265
More fond on° her than she upon her love;
And look thou meet me ere the first cock crow.

PUCK:
Fear not, my lord, your servant shall do so.          *Exeunt [separately].*

240. **Your . . . sex:** i.e., the wrongs that you do me cause me to act in a manner that disgraces my sex.   244. **upon:** by.   249. **blows:** blooms.   250. **oxlips:** flowers resembling cowslip and primrose.   251. **woodbine:** honeysuckle.   252. **muskroses:** a kind of large, sweet-scented rose.   **eglantine:** sweetbrier, another kind of rose.   253. **sometime of:** for part of.   255. **throws:** sloughs off, sheds.   256. **Weed:** garment.   257. **streak:** anoint, touch gently.   266. **fond on:** doting on.

## Act 2, Scene 2°

*Enter Titania, Queen of Fairies, with her train.*

TITANIA:
Come, now a roundel° and a fairy song;
Then, for the third part of a minute,° hence —
Some to kill cankers° in the muskrose buds,
Some war with reremice° for their leathern wings
To make my small elves coats, and some keep back          5
The clamorous owl, that nightly hoots and wonders
At our quaint° spirits. Sing me now asleep.
Then to your offices, and let me rest.

*Fairies sing.*

FIRST FAIRY:
You spotted snakes with double° tongue,
Thorny hedgehogs, be not seen;                            10
Newts° and blindworms, do no wrong;
Come not near our Fairy Queen.

CHORUS [*dancing*]:
Philomel,° with melody
Sing in our sweet lullaby;
Lulla, lulla, lullaby, lulla, lulla, lullaby.             15
Never harm
Nor spell nor charm
Come our lovely lady nigh.
So good night, with lullaby.

FIRST FAIRY:
Weaving spiders, come not here;                           20
Hence, you long-legged spinners, hence!
Beetles black, approach not near;
Worm nor snail, do no offense.°

CHORUS [*dancing*]:
Philomel, with melody
Sing in our sweet lullaby;                                25

ACT 2, SCENE 2. Location: The wood.  1. roundel: dance in a ring.  2. the third . . .
minute: (Indicative of the fairies' quickness.)  3. cankers: cankerworms (i.e., caterpillars or
grubs).  4. reremice: bats.  7. quaint: dainty.  9. double: forked.  11. Newts: water liz-
ards (considered poisonous, as were *blindworms* — small snakes with tiny eyes — and spiders).
13. Philomel: the nightingale. (Philomela, daughter of King Pandion, was transformed into a
nightingale, according to Ovid's *Metamorphoses* 6, after she had been raped by her sister
Procne's husband, Tereus.)  23. offense: harm.

> Lulla, lulla, lullaby, lulla, lulla, lullaby.
> Never harm
> Nor spell nor charm
> Come our lovely lady nigh.
> So good night, with lullaby.                    [*Titania sleeps.*]  30

SECOND FAIRY:
> Hence, away! Now all is well.
> One aloof stand sentinel.°         [*Exeunt Fairies, leaving one sentinel.*]

*Enter Oberon [and squeezes the flower on Titania's eyelids].*

OBERON:
> What thou seest when thou dost wake,
> Do it for thy true love take;
> Love and languish for his sake.                                    35
> Be it ounce,° or cat, or bear,
> Pard,° or boar with bristled hair,
> In thy eye that shall appear
> When thou wak'st, it is thy dear.
> Wake when some vile thing is near.                    [*Exit.*]  40

*Enter Lysander and Hermia.*

LYSANDER:
> Fair love, you faint with wandering in the wood;
>     And to speak truth, I have forgot our way.
> We'll rest us, Hermia, if you think it good,
>     And tarry for the comfort of the day.

HERMIA:
> Be it so, Lysander. Find you out a bed,                            45
> For I upon this bank will rest my head.

LYSANDER:
> One turf shall serve as pillow for us both;
> One heart, one bed, two bosoms, and one troth.°

HERMIA:
> Nay, good Lysander, for my sake, my dear,
> Lie further off yet. Do not lie so near.                          50

LYSANDER:
> O, take the sense, sweet, of my innocence!°
> Love takes the meaning in love's conference.°

---

32. **sentinel:** (Presumably Oberon is able to outwit or intimidate this guard.)   36. **ounce:** lynx.   37. **Pard:** leopard.   48. **troth:** faith, trothplight.   51. **take . . . innocence:** i.e., interpret my intention as innocent.   52. **Love . . . conference:** i.e., when lovers confer, love teaches each lover to interpret the other's meaning lovingly.

I mean that my heart unto yours is knit,
So that but one heart we can make of it;
Two bosoms interchainèd with an oath —                                            55
So then two bosoms and a single troth.
Then by your side no bed-room me deny,
For lying so, Hermia, I do not lie.°

HERMIA:
Lysander riddles very prettily.
Now much beshrew° my manners and my pride                                        60
If Hermia meant to say Lysander lied.
But, gentle friend, for love and courtesy
Lie further off, in human° modesty.
Such separation as may well be said
Becomes a virtuous bachelor and a maid,                                          65
So far be distant; and, good night, sweet friend.
Thy love ne'er alter till thy sweet life end!

LYSANDER:
Amen, amen, to that fair prayer, say I,
And then end life when I end loyalty!
Here is my bed. Sleep give thee all his rest!                                    70

HERMIA:
With half that wish the wisher's eyes be pressed!°

[*They sleep, separated by a short distance.*]

*Enter Puck.*

PUCK:
Through the forest have I gone,
But Athenian found I none
On whose eyes I might approve°
This flower's force in stirring love.                                            75
Night and silence. — Who is here?
Weeds of Athens he doth wear.
This is he, my master said,
Despisèd the Athenian maid;
And here the maiden, sleeping sound,                                             80
On the dank and dirty ground.
Pretty soul, she durst not lie

---

58. **lie**: tell a falsehood (with a riddling pun on *lie*, "recline"). 60. **beshrew**: curse (but mildly
meant). 63. **human**: courteous (and perhaps suggesting "humane," the Quarto spelling).
71. **With . . . pressed**: i.e., may we share your wish, so that your eyes too are *pressed*, closed,
in sleep. 74. **approve**: test.

Near this lack-love, this kill-courtesy.
Churl, upon thy eyes I throw
All the power this charm doth owe.°    [*He applies the love juice.*]  85
When thou wak'st, let love forbid
Sleep his seat on thy eyelid.
So awake when I am gone,
For I must now to Oberon.                                    *Exit.*

*Enter Demetrius and Helena, running.*

HELENA:
Stay, though thou kill me, sweet Demetrius!                      90
DEMETRIUS:
I charge thee, hence, and do not haunt me thus.
HELENA:
O, wilt thou darkling° leave me? Do not so.
DEMETRIUS:
Stay, on thy peril!° I alone will go.                        [*Exit.*]
HELENA:
O, I am out of breath in this fond° chase!
The more my prayer, the lesser is my grace.°                    95
Happy is Hermia, wheresoe'er she lies,°
For she hath blessèd and attractive eyes.
How came her eyes so bright? Not with salt tears;
If so, my eyes are oftener washed than hers.
No, no, I am as ugly as a bear,                                100
For beasts that meet me run away for fear.
Therefore no marvel though Demetrius
Do, as a monster, fly my presence thus.°
What wicked and dissembling glass of mine
Made me compare° with Hermia's sphery eyne?°                   105
But who is here? Lysander, on the ground?
Dead, or asleep? I see no blood, no wound.
Lysander, if you live, good sir, awake.
LYSANDER [*awaking*]:
And run through fire I will for thy sweet sake.
Transparent° Helena! Nature shows art,°                       110

---

85. owe: own.   92. darkling: in the dark.   93. on thy peril: i.e., on pain of danger to you
if you don't obey me and stay.   94. fond: doting.   95. my grace: the favor I obtain.   96. lies:
dwells.   102–03. no marvel . . . thus: i.e., no wonder that Demetrius flies from me as from
a monster.   105. compare: vie.   sphery eyne: eyes as bright as stars in their spheres.
110. Transparent: (1) radiant (2) able to be seen through, lacking in deceit.   art: skill, magic
power.

That through thy bosom makes me see thy heart.
Where is Demetrius? O, how fit a word
Is that vile name to perish on my sword!

HELENA:

Do not say so, Lysander; say not so.
What though he love your Hermia? Lord, what though?                    115
Yet Hermia still loves you. Then be content.

LYSANDER:

Content with Hermia? No! I do repent
The tedious minutes I with her have spent.
Not Hermia but Helena I love.
Who will not change a raven for a dove?                    120
The will° of man is by his reason swayed,
And reason says you are the worthier maid.
Things growing are not ripe until their season;
So I, being young, till now ripe not° to reason.
And, touching° now the point° of human skill,°                    125
Reason becomes the marshal to my will
And leads me to your eyes, where I o'erlook°
Love's stories written in love's richest book.

HELENA:

Wherefore° was I to this keen mockery born?
When at your hands did I deserve this scorn?                    130
Is 't not enough, is 't not enough, young man,
That I did never — no, nor never can —
Deserve a sweet look from Demetrius' eye,
But you must flout my insufficiency?
Good troth,° you do me wrong, good sooth,° you do,                    135
In such disdainful manner me to woo.
But fare you well. Perforce I must confess
I thought you lord of° more true gentleness.°
O, that a lady, of° one man refused,
Should of another therefore be abused!°                    *Exit.*  140

LYSANDER:

She sees not Hermia. Hermia, sleep thou there,
And never mayst thou come Lysander near!
For as a surfeit of the sweetest things

---

121. **will:** desire.    124. **ripe not:** (am) not ripened.    125. **touching:** reaching.    **point:** summit.    **skill:** judgment.    127. **o'erlook:** read.    129. **Wherefore:** why.    135. **Good troth, good sooth:** i.e., indeed, truly.    138. **lord of:** i.e., possessor of.    **gentleness:** courtesy.    139. **of:** by.    140. **abused:** ill treated.

The deepest loathing to the stomach brings,
Or as the heresies that men do leave                                            145
Are hated most of those they did deceive,°
So thou, my surfeit and my heresy,
Of all be hated, but the most of° me!
And, all my powers, address° your love and might
To honor Helen and to be her knight!                              *Exit.*   150
HERMIA [*awaking*]:
  Help me, Lysander, help me! Do thy best
  To pluck this crawling serpent from my breast!
  Ay me, for pity! What a dream was here!
  Lysander, look how I do quake with fear.
  Methought a serpent ate my heart away,                                    155
  And you sat smiling at his cruel prey.°
  Lysander! What, removed? Lysander! Lord!
  What, out of hearing? Gone? No sound, no word?
  Alack, where are you? Speak, an if° you hear;
  Speak, of all loves!° I swoon almost with fear.                          160
  No? Then I well perceive you are not nigh.
  Either death, or you, I'll find immediately.
                     *Exit.* [*The sleeping Titania remains.*]

## ACT 3, SCENE 1°

*Enter the clowns*° [*Quince, Snug, Bottom, Flute, Snout, and Starveling*].

BOTTOM:   Are we all met?
QUINCE:   Pat,° pat; and here's a marvelous convenient place for our rehearsal. This green plot shall be our stage, this hawthorn brake° our tiring-house,° and we will do it in action as we will do it before the Duke.                                                                                  5
BOTTOM:   Peter Quince?
QUINCE:   What sayest thou, bully° Bottom?
BOTTOM:   There are things in this comedy of Pyramus and Thisbe that will never please. First, Pyramus must draw a sword to kill himself, which the ladies cannot abide. How answer you that?                                     10

145–46. as . . . deceive: as renounced heresies are hated most by those persons who formerly were deceived by them.   148. Of . . . of: by . . . by.   149. address: direct, apply.   156. prey: act of preying.   159. an if: if.   160. of all loves: for love's sake.   ACT 3, SCENE 1. Location: The action is continuous.   s.d. *clowns:* rustics.   2. Pat: on the dot, punctually.   3. brake: thicket.   4. tiring-house: attiring area, hence backstage.   7. bully: i.e., worthy, jolly, fine fellow.

SNOUT:   By 'r lakin,° a parlous° fear.

STARVELING:   I believe we must leave the killing out, when all is done.°

BOTTOM:   Not a whit. I have a device to make all well. Write me° a prologue, and let the prologue seem to say, we will do no harm with our
swords, and that Pyramus is not killed indeed; and for the more better    15
assurance, tell them that I, Pyramus, am not Pyramus but Bottom the
weaver. This will put them out of fear.

QUINCE:   Well, we will have such a prologue, and it shall be written in
eight and six.°

BOTTOM:   No, make it two more: let it be written in eight and eight.    20

SNOUT:   Will not the ladies be afeard of the lion?

STARVELING:   I fear it, I promise you.

BOTTOM:   Masters, you ought to consider with yourself, to bring in —
God shield us! — a lion among ladies° is a most dreadful thing. For
there is not a more fearful° wildfowl than your lion living, and we ought    25
to look to 't.

SNOUT:   Therefore another prologue must tell he is not a lion.

BOTTOM:   Nay, you must name his name, and half his face must be seen
through the lion's neck, and he himself must speak through, saying
thus or to the same defect:° "Ladies," or "Fair ladies, I would wish    30
you," or "I would request you," or "I would entreat you, not to fear, not
to tremble; my life for yours.° If you think I come hither as a lion,
it were pity of my life.° No, I am no such thing; I am a man as other
men are." And there indeed let him name his name, and tell them
plainly he is Snug the joiner.    35

QUINCE:   Well, it shall be so. But there is two hard things: that is, to bring
the moonlight into a chamber; for, you know, Pyramus and Thisbe meet
by moonlight.

SNOUT:   Doth the moon shine that night we play our play?

BOTTOM:   A calendar, a calendar! Look in the almanac. Find out moon-    40
shine, find out moonshine.                                  [*They consult an almanac.*]

QUINCE:   Yes, it doth shine that night.

BOTTOM:   Why then may you leave a casement of the great chamber

---

11. **By 'r lakin:** by our ladykin, i.e., the Virgin Mary.   **parlous:** perilous, alarming.   12. **when all is done:** i.e., when all is said and done.   13. **Write me:** i.e., write at my suggestion (*me* is used colloquially).   19. **eight and six:** alternate lines of eight and six syllables, a common bal-lad measure.   24. **lion among ladies:** (A contemporary pamphlet tells how, at the christening in 1594 of Prince Henry, eldest son of King James VI of Scotland, later James I of England, a "blackamoor" instead of a lion drew the triumphal chariot, since the lion's presence might have "brought some fear to the nearest.")   25. **fearful:** fear-inspiring.   30. **defect:** (Bottom's blun-der for "effect.")   32. **my life for yours:** i.e., I pledge my life to make your lives safe.   33. **it were . . . life:** i.e., I should be sorry, by my life; or, my life would be endangered.

window where we play open, and the moon may shine in at the case-
ment.                                                                    45
QUINCE:   Ay; or else one must come in with a bush of thorns° and a
    lantern and say he comes to disfigure,° or to present,° the person of
    Moonshine. Then there is another thing: we must have a wall in
    the great chamber; for Pyramus and Thisbe, says the story, did talk
    through the chink of a wall.                                         50
SNOUT:   You can never bring in a wall. What say you, Bottom?
BOTTOM:   Some man or other must present Wall. And let him have some
    plaster, or some loam, or some roughcast° about him, to signify wall;
    or let him hold his fingers thus, and through that cranny shall Pyramus
    and Thisbe whisper.                                                  55
QUINCE:   If that may be, then all is well. Come, sit down, every mother's
    son, and rehearse your parts. Pyramus, you begin. When you have spo-
    ken your speech, enter into that brake, and so everyone according to his
    cue.

    *Enter Robin [Puck].*

PUCK [*aside*]:
    What hempen homespuns° have we swaggering here                       60
    So near the cradle° of the Fairy Queen?
    What, a play toward?° I'll be an auditor;
    An actor, too, perhaps, if I see cause.
QUINCE:   Speak, Pyramus. Thisbe, stand forth.
BOTTOM [*as Pyramus*]:
    "Thisbe, the flowers of odious savors sweet — "                      65
QUINCE:   Odors, odors.
BOTTOM:
    " — Odors savors sweet;
    So hath thy breath, my dearest Thisbe dear.
    But hark, a voice! Stay thou but here awhile,
    And by and by I will to thee appear."                    *Exit.*   70
PUCK:
    A stranger Pyramus than e'er played here.°              [*Exit.*]

46. **bush of thorns:** bundle of thornbush fagots (part of the accoutrements of the man in the
moon, according to the popular notions of the time, along with his lantern and his dog).
47. **disfigure:** (Quince's blunder for "figure.")   **present:** represent.   53. **roughcast:** a mixture
of lime and gravel used to plaster the outside of buildings.   60. **hempen homespuns:** i.e., rustics dressed in clothes woven of coarse, homespun fabric made from hemp.   61. **cradle:** i.e.,
Titania's bower.   62. **toward:** about to take place.   71. **A stranger . . . here:** (Either Puck
refers to an earlier dramatic version played in the same theater, or he has conceived of a plan to
present a "stranger" Pyramus than ever seen before.)

FLUTE: Must I speak now?

QUINCE: Ay, marry, must you; for you must understand he goes but to see a
noise that he heard, and is to come again.

FLUTE [*as Thisbe*]:

"Most radiant Pyramus, most lily-white of hue,          75
    Of color like the red rose on triumphant° brier,
Most brisky juvenal° and eke° most lovely Jew,°
    As true as truest horse that yet would never tire.
I'll meet thee, Pyramus, at Ninny's tomb."

QUINCE: "Ninus'° tomb," man. Why, you must not speak that yet. That   80
you answer to Pyramus. You speak all your part° at once, cues and all.
Pyramus, enter. Your cue is past; it is "never tire."

FLUTE:

O — "As true as truest horse, that yet would never tire."

[*Enter Puck, and Bottom as Pyramus with the ass head.°*]

BOTTOM:

"If I were fair,° Thisbe, I were° only thine."

QUINCE: O, monstrous! O, strange! We are haunted. Pray, masters! Fly,   85
masters! Help!          [*Exeunt Quince, Snug, Flute, Snout, and Starveling.*]

PUCK:

I'll follow you, I'll lead you about a round,°
    Thorough bog, thorough bush, thorough brake, thorough brier.
Sometimes a horse I'll be, sometimes a hound,
    A hog, a headless bear, sometimes a fire;°          90
And neigh, and bark, and grunt, and roar, and burn,
Like horse, hound, hog, bear, fire, at every turn.          *Exit.*

BOTTOM: Why do they run away? This is a knavery of them to make me
afeard.

*Enter Snout.*

SNOUT: O Bottom, thou art changed! What do I see on thee?          95

BOTTOM: What do you see? You see an ass head of your own, do you?

[*Exit Snout.*]

---

76. **triumphant:** magnificent.   77. **brisky juvenal:** lively youth.   **eke:** also.   **Jew:** (An absurd
repetition of the first syllable of *juvenal* and an indication of how desperately Quince searches
for his rhymes.)   80. **Ninus':** mythical founder of Nineveh (whose wife, Semiramis, was supposed to have built the walls of Babylon where the story of Pyramus and Thisbe takes place).
81. **part:** (An actor's *part* was a script consisting only of his speeches and their cues.)
s.d. ***with the ass head:*** (This stage direction, taken from the Folio, presumably refers to a standard stage property.)   84. **fair:** handsome.   **were:** would be.   87. **about a round:** round-
about.   90. **fire:** will-o'-the-wisp.

*Enter Quince.*

QUINCE:   Bless thee, Bottom, bless thee! Thou art translated.°          *Exit.*
BOTTOM:   I see their knavery. This is to make an ass of me, to fright me, if
    they could. But I will not stir from this place, do what they can. I will
    walk up and down here, and will sing, that they shall hear I am not   100
    afraid.                                                        [*He sings.*]
        The ouzel cock° so black of hue,
            With orange-tawny bill,
        The throstle° with his note so true,
            The wren with little quill° —                                  105
TITANIA [*awaking*]:
    What angel wakes me from my flowery bed?
BOTTOM [*sings*]:
        The finch, the sparrow, and the lark,
            The plainsong° cuckoo gray,
        Whose note full many a man doth mark,
            And dares not answer nay° —                                    110
    For indeed, who would set his wit to° so foolish a bird? Who would give
    a bird the lie,° though he cry "cuckoo" never so?°
TITANIA:
    I pray thee, gentle mortal, sing again.
    Mine ear is much enamored of thy note;
    So is mine eye enthrallèd to thy shape;                                115
    And thy fair virtue's force° perforce doth move me
    On the first view to say, to swear, I love thee.
BOTTOM:   Methinks, mistress, you should have little reason for that. And
    yet, to say the truth, reason and love keep little company together
    nowadays — the more the pity that some honest neighbors will not   120
    make them friends. Nay, I can gleek° upon occasion.
TITANIA:
    Thou art as wise as thou art beautiful.
BOTTOM:   Not so, neither. But if I had wit enough to get out of this wood,
    I have enough to serve mine own turn.°
TITANIA:
    Out of this wood do not desire to go.                                  125

---

97. **translated:** transformed.   102. **ouzel cock:** male blackbird.   104. **throstle:** song thrush.
105. **quill:** (Literally, a reed pipe; hence, the bird's piping song.)   108. **plainsong:** singing
a melody without variations.   110. **dares . . . nay:** i.e., cannot deny that he is a cuckold.
111. **set his wit to:** employ his intelligence to answer.   111–12. **give . . . lie:** call the bird a liar.
112. **never so:** ever so much.   116. **thy . . . force:** the power of your unblemished excellence.
121. **gleek:** jest.   124. **serve . . . turn:** answer my purpose.

Thou shalt remain here, whether thou wilt or no.
I am a spirit of no common rate.°
The summer still doth tend upon my state,°
And I do love thee. Therefore, go with me.
I'll give thee fairies to attend on thee,                                    130
And they shall fetch thee jewels from the deep,
And sing while thou on pressèd flowers dost sleep.
And I will purge thy mortal grossness° so
That thou shalt like an airy spirit go.
Peaseblossom, Cobweb, Mote,° and Mustardseed!                 135

*Enter four Fairies [Peaseblossom, Cobweb, Mote, and Mustardseed].*

PEASEBLOSSOM:   Ready.
COBWEB:
 And I.
MOTE:   And I.
MUSTARDSEED:   And I.
ALL:                              Where shall we go?
TITANIA:
 Be kind and courteous to this gentleman.
 Hop in his walks and gambol in his eyes;°
 Feed him with apricots and dewberries,°                               140
 With purple grapes, green figs, and mulberries;
 The honey bags steal from the humble-bees,
 And for night tapers crop their waxen thighs
 And light them at the fiery glowworms' eyes,
 To have my love to bed and to arise;                                    145
 And pluck the wings from painted butterflies
 To fan the moonbeams from his sleeping eyes.
 Nod to him, elves, and do him courtesies.
PEASEBLOSSOM:   Hail, mortal!
COBWEB:   Hail!                                                                    150
MOTE:   Hail!
MUSTARDSEED:   Hail!
BOTTOM:   I cry your worships mercy,° heartily. I beseech your worship's name.

127. **rate**: rank, value.   128. **still . . . state**: always waits upon me as a part of my royal retinue.   133. **mortal grossness**: materiality (i.e., the corporeal nature of a mortal being).   135. **Mote**: i.e., speck. (The two words *moth* and *mote* were pronounced alike, and both meanings may be present.)   139. **in his eyes**: in his sight (i.e., before him).   140. **dewberries**: blackberries.   153. **I cry . . . mercy**: I beg pardon of your worships (for presuming to ask a question).

COBWEB: Cobweb.

BOTTOM: I shall desire you of more acquaintance,° good Master Cobweb. 155
If I cut my finger, I shall make bold with you.° — Your name, honest
gentleman?

PEASEBLOSSOM: Peaseblossom.

BOTTOM: I pray you, commend me to Mistress Squash,° your mother, and
to Master Peascod,° your father. Good Master Peaseblossom, I shall 160
desire you of more acquaintance too. — Your name, I beseech you,
sir?

MUSTARDSEED: Mustardseed.

BOTTOM: Good Master Mustardseed, I know your patience° well. That
same cowardly, giantlike ox-beef hath devoured many a gentleman of 165
your house. I promise you, your kindred hath made my eyes water°
ere now. I desire you of more acquaintance, good Master Mustardseed.

TITANIA:
Come wait upon him; lead him to my bower.
The moon methinks looks with a watery eye;
And when she weeps,° weeps every little flower, 170
Lamenting some enforcèd° chastity.
Tie up my lover's tongue;° bring him silently.            *Exeunt.*

## Act 3, Scene 2°

*Enter [Oberon,] King of Fairies.*

OBERON:
I wonder if Titania be awaked;
Then, what it was that next came in her eye,
Which she must dote on in extremity.

*[Enter] Robin Goodfellow [Puck].*

Here comes my messenger. How now, mad spirit?
What night-rule° now about this haunted° grove?            5

---

155. I . . . acquaintance: I crave to be better acquainted with you.  156. If . . . you:
(Cobwebs were used to stanch bleeding.)  159. Squash: unripe pea pod.  160. Peascod:
ripe pea pod.  164. your patience: what you have endured (mustard is eaten with beef).
166. water: (1) weep for sympathy (2) smart, sting.  170. she weeps: i.e., she causes dew.
171. enforcèd: forced, violated; or, possibly, constrained (since Titania at this moment is hardly
concerned about chastity).  172. Tie . . . tongue: (Presumably Bottom is braying like an
ass.)  Act 3, Scene 2. Location: The wood.  5. night-rule: diversion or misrule for the
night.  haunted: much frequented.

PUCK:

My mistress with a monster is in love.
Near to her close° and consecrated bower,
While she was in her dull° and sleeping hour,
A crew of patches,° rude mechanicals,°
That work for bread upon Athenian stalls,°            10
Were met together to rehearse a play
Intended for great Theseus' nuptial day.
The shallowest thickskin of that barren sort,°
Who Pyramus presented,° in their sport
Forsook his scene° and entered in a brake.            15
When I did him at this advantage take,
An ass's noll° I fixèd on his head.
Anon his Thisbe must be answerèd,
And forth my mimic° comes. When they him spy,
As wild geese that the creeping fowler° eye,        20
Or russet-pated choughs,° many in sort,°
Rising and cawing at the gun's report,
Sever° themselves and madly sweep the sky,
So, at his sight, away his fellows fly;
And, at our stamp, here o'er and o'er one falls;    25
He "Murder!" cries and help from Athens calls.
Their sense thus weak, lost with their fears thus strong,
Made senseless things begin to do them wrong,
For briers and thorns at their apparel snatch;
Some, sleeves — some, hats; from yielders all things catch.°   30
I led them on in this distracted fear
And left sweet Pyramus translated there,
When in that moment, so it came to pass,
Titania waked and straightway loved an ass.

OBERON:

This falls out better than I could devise.          35
But hast thou yet latched° the Athenian's eyes
With the love juice, as I did bid thee do?

PUCK:

I took him sleeping — that is finished too —

---

7. **close:** secret, private.  8. **dull:** drowsy.  9. **patches:** clowns, fools.  **rude mechanicals:** ignorant artisans.  10. **stalls:** market booths.  13. **barren sort:** stupid company or crew. 14. **presented:** acted.  15. **scene:** playing area.  17. **noll:** noddle, head.  19. **mimic:** burlesque actor.  20. **fowler:** hunter of game birds.  21. **russet-pated choughs:** reddish brown or gray-headed jackdaws.  **in sort:** in a flock.  23. **Sever:** i.e., scatter.  30. **from . . . catch:** i.e., everything preys on those who yield to fear.  36. **latched:** fastened, snared.

And the Athenian woman by his side,
That, when he waked, of force° she must be eyed.                    40

*Enter Demetrius and Hermia.*

OBERON:
Stand close. This is the same Athenian.
PUCK:
This is the woman, but not this the man.            [*They stand aside.*]
DEMETRIUS:
O, why rebuke you him that loves you so?
Lay breath so bitter on your bitter foe.
HERMIA:
Now I but chide; but I should use thee worse,                      45
For thou, I fear, hast given me cause to curse.
If thou hast slain Lysander in his sleep,
Being o'er shoes° in blood, plunge in the deep,
And kill me too.
The sun was not so true unto the day                                50
As he to me. Would he have stolen away
From sleeping Hermia? I'll believe as soon
This whole° earth may be bored, and that the moon
May through the center creep, and so displease
Her brother's° noontide with th' Antipodes.°                        55
It cannot be but thou hast murdered him;
So should a murderer look, so dead,° so grim.
DEMETRIUS:
So should the murdered look, and so should I,
Pierced through the heart with your stern cruelty.
Yet you, the murderer, look as bright, as clear                     60
As yonder Venus in her glimmering sphere.
HERMIA:
What's this to° my Lysander? Where is he?
Ah, good Demetrius, wilt thou give him me?
DEMETRIUS:
I had rather give his carcass to my hounds.
HERMIA:
Out, dog! Out, cur! Thou driv'st me past the bounds                 65

---

40. **of force:** perforce.   48. **Being o'er shoes:** having waded in so far.   53. **whole:** solid.
55. **Her brother's:** i.e., the sun's.   **th' Antipodes:** the people on the opposite side of the earth
(where the moon is imagined bringing night to noontime).   57. **dead:** deadly, or deathly pale.
62. **to:** to do with.

Of maiden's patience. Hast thou slain him, then?
Henceforth be never numbered among men.
O, once° tell true, tell true, even for my sake:
Durst thou have looked upon him being awake?
And hast thou killed him sleeping? O brave touch!°          70
Could not a worm,° an adder, do so much?
An adder did it; for with doubler° tongue
Than thine, thou serpent, never adder stung.

DEMETRIUS:
You spend your passion° on a misprised mood.°
I am not guilty of Lysander's blood,                        75
Nor is he dead, for aught that I can tell.

HERMIA:
I pray thee, tell me then that he is well.

DEMETRIUS:
And if I could, what should I get therefor?°

HERMIA:
A privilege never to see me more.
And from thy hated presence part I so.                      80
See me no more, whether he be dead or no.          *Exit.*

DEMETRIUS:
There is no following her in this fierce vein.
Here therefore for a while I will remain.
So sorrow's heaviness doth heavier° grow
For debt that bankrupt° sleep doth sorrow owe,             85
Which now in some slight measure it will pay,
If for his tender here I make some stay.°   [*He*] *lie*[*s*] *down* [*and sleeps*].

OBERON:
What hast thou done? Thou hast mistaken quite
And laid the love juice on some true love's sight.
Of thy misprision° must perforce ensue                      90
Some true love turned, and not a false turned true.

___

68. **once:** once and for all.   70. **brave touch!:** fine stroke! (said ironically).   71. **worm:** serpent.   72. **doubler:** (1) more forked (2) more deceitful.   74. **passion:** violent feelings.   **misprised mood:** anger based on misconception.   78. **therefor:** in return for that.   84. **heavier:** (1) harder to bear (2) more drowsy.   85. **bankrupt:** (Demetrius is saying that his sleepiness adds to the weariness caused by sorrow.)   86–87. **Which . . . stay:** i.e., to a small extent, I will be able to "pay back" and hence find some relief from sorrow, if I pause here awhile (*make some stay*) while sleep "tenders" or offers itself by way of paying the debt owed to sorrow.   90. **misprision:** mistake.

PUCK:
Then fate o'errules, that, one man holding troth,°
A million fail, confounding oath on oath.°

OBERON:
About the wood go swifter than the wind,
And Helena of Athens look° thou find.                                    95
All fancy-sick° she is and pale of cheer°
With sighs of love, that cost the fresh blood° dear.
By some illusion see thou bring her here.
I'll charm his eyes against she do appear.°

PUCK:
I go, I go, look how I go,                                               100
Swifter than arrow from the Tartar's bow.°                    [*Exit.*]

OBERON [*applying love juice to Demetrius' eyes*]:
Flower of this purple dye,
Hit with Cupid's archery,
Sink in apple° of his eye.
When his love he doth espy,                                              105
Let her shine as gloriously
As the Venus of the sky.
When thou wak'st, if she be by,
Beg of her for remedy.

*Enter Puck.*

PUCK:
Captain of our fairy band,                                              110
Helena is here at hand,
And the youth, mistook by me,
Pleading for a lover's fee.°
Shall we their fond pageant° see?
Lord, what fools these mortals be!                                      115

OBERON:
Stand aside. The noise they make
Will cause Demetrius to awake.

PUCK:
Then will two at once woo one;

---

92. **that . . . troth:** in that, for each man keeping true faith in love.   93. **confounding . . . oath:** i.e., breaking oath after oath.   95. **look:** i.e., be sure.   96. **fancy-sick:** lovesick. **cheer:** face.   97. **sighs . . . blood:** (An allusion to the physiological theory that each sigh costs the heart a drop of blood.)   99. **against . . . appear:** in anticipation of her coming.   101. **Tartar's bow:** (Tartars were famed for their skill with the bow.)   104. **apple:** pupil.   113. **fee:** privilege, reward.   114. **fond pageant:** foolish spectacle.

That must needs be sport alone.°
And those things do best please me          120
That befall preposterously.°                        [*They stand aside.*]

*Enter Lysander and Helena.*

LYSANDER:
Why should you think that I should woo in scorn?
Scorn and derision never come in tears.
Look when° I vow, I weep; and vows so born,
In their nativity all truth appears.°          125
How can these things in me seem scorn to you,
Bearing the badge° of faith to prove them true?

HELENA:
You do advance° your cunning more and more.
When truth kills truth,° O, devilish-holy fray!
These vows are Hermia's. Will you give her o'er?          130
Weigh oath with oath, and you will nothing weigh.
Your vows to her and me, put in two scales,
Will even weigh, and both as light as tales.°

LYSANDER:
I had no judgment when to her I swore.

HELENA:
Nor none, in my mind, now you give her o'er.          135

LYSANDER:
Demetrius loves her, and he loves not you.

DEMETRIUS [*awaking*]:
O Helen, goddess, nymph, perfect, divine!
To what, my love, shall I compare thine eyne?
Crystal is muddy. O, how ripe in show°
Thy lips, those kissing cherries, tempting grow!          140
That pure congealèd white, high Taurus'° snow,
Fanned with the eastern wind, turns to a crow°
When thou hold'st up thy hand. O, let me kiss
This princess of pure white, this seal° of bliss!

---

119. **alone:** unequaled.  121. **preposterously:** out of the natural order.  124. **Look when:** whenever.  124–25. **vows . . . appears:** i.e., vows made by one who is weeping give evidence thereby of their sincerity.  127. **badge:** identifying device such as that worn on the servants' livery (here, his tears).  128. **advance:** carry forward, display.  129. **truth kills truth:** i.e., one of Lysander's vows must invalidate the other.  133. **tales:** lies.  139. **show:** appearance.  141. **Taurus:** a lofty mountain range in Asia Minor.  142. **turns to a crow:** i.e., seems black by contrast.  144. **seal:** pledge.

HELENA:
    O spite! O hell! I see you all are bent        145
    To set against° me for your merriment.
    If you were civil and knew courtesy,
    You would not do me thus much injury.
    Can you not hate me, as I know you do,
    But you must join in souls° to mock me too?    150
    If you were men, as men you are in show,
    You would not use a gentle lady so —
    To vow, and swear, and superpraise° my parts,°
    When I am sure you hate me with your hearts.
    You both are rivals, and love Hermia,    155
    And now both rivals to mock Helena.
    A trim° exploit, a manly enterprise,
    To conjure tears up in a poor maid's eyes
    With your derision! None of noble sort°
    Would so offend a virgin and extort°    160
    A poor soul's patience, all to make you sport.
LYSANDER:
    You are unkind, Demetrius. Be not so.
    For you love Hermia; this you know I know.
    And here, with all good will, with all my heart,
    In Hermia's love I yield you up my part;    165
    And yours of Helena to me bequeath,
    Whom I do love, and will do till my death.
HELENA:
    Never did mockers waste more idle breath.
DEMETRIUS:
    Lysander, keep thy Hermia; I will none.°
    If e'er I loved her, all that love is gone.    170
    My heart to her but as guestwise sojourned,°
    And now to Helen is it home returned,
    There to remain.
LYSANDER:        Helen, it is not so.
DEMETRIUS:
    Disparage not the faith thou dost not know,

146. **set against:** attack. 150. **in souls:** i.e., heart and soul. 153. **superpraise:** overpraise. **parts:** qualities. 157. **trim:** pretty, fine (said ironically). 159. **sort:** character, quality. 160. **extort:** twist, torture. 169. **will none:** i.e., want no part of her. 171. **to . . . sojourned:** only visited with her.

Lest, to thy peril, thou aby° it dear.                                    175
Look where thy love comes; yonder is thy dear.

*Enter Hermia.*

HERMIA:
Dark night, that from the eye his° function takes,
The ear more quick of apprehension makes;
Wherein it doth impair the seeing sense,
It pays the hearing double recompense.                                    180
Thou art not by mine eye, Lysander, found;
Mine ear, I thank it, brought me to thy sound.
But why unkindly didst thou leave me so?

LYSANDER:
Why should he stay, whom love doth press to go?

HERMIA:
What love could press Lysander from my side?                              185

LYSANDER:
Lysander's love, that would not let him bide —
Fair Helena, who more engilds° the night
Than all yon fiery oes° and eyes of light.
Why seek'st thou me? Could not this make thee know
The hate I bear thee made me leave thee so?                               190

HERMIA:
You speak not as you think. It cannot be.

HELENA:
Lo, she is one of this confederacy!
Now I perceive they have conjoined all three
To fashion this false sport, in spite of me.°
Injurious Hermia, most ungrateful maid!                                   195
Have you conspired, have you with these contrived°
To bait° me with this foul derision?
Is all the counsel° that we two have shared —
The sisters' vows, the hours that we have spent
When we have chid the hasty-footed time                                   200
For parting us — O, is all forgot?
All schooldays' friendship, childhood innocence?
We, Hermia, like two artificial° gods

---

175. **aby:** pay for.    177. **his:** its.    187. **engilds:** gilds, brightens with a golden light.    188. **oes:** spangles (here, stars).    194. **in spite of me:** to vex me.    196. **contrived:** plotted.    197. **bait:** torment, as one sets on dogs to bait a bear.    198. **counsel:** confidential talk.    203. **artificial:** skilled in art or creation.

Have with our needles created both one flower,
Both on one sampler, sitting on one cushion,                205
Both warbling of one song, both in one key,
As if our hands, our sides, voices, and minds
Had been incorporate.° So we grew together,
Like to a double cherry, seeming parted,
But yet an union in partition,                             210
Two lovely° berries molded on one stem;
So, with two seeming bodies but one heart,
Two of the first, like coats in heraldry,
Due but to one and crownèd with one crest.°
And will you rend our ancient love asunder,               215
To join with men in scorning your poor friend?
It is not friendly, 'tis not maidenly.
Our sex, as well as I, may chide you for it,
Though I alone do feel the injury.

HERMIA:
I am amazèd at your passionate words.                      220
I scorn you not. It seems that you scorn me.

HELENA:
Have you not set Lysander, as in scorn,
To follow me and praise my eyes and face?
And made your other love, Demetrius,
Who even but now did spurn me with his foot,              225
To call me goddess, nymph, divine, and rare,
Precious, celestial? Wherefore speaks he this
To her he hates? And wherefore doth Lysander
Deny your love, so rich within his soul,
And tender° me, forsooth, affection,                      230
But by your setting on, by your consent?
What though I be not so in grace° as you,
So hung upon with love, so fortunate,
But miserable most, to love unloved?
This you should pity rather than despise.                 235

HERMIA:
I understand not what you mean by this.

HELENA:
Ay, do! Persever, counterfeit sad° looks,

208. **incorporate:** of one body.  211. **lovely:** loving.  213–14. **Two . . . crest:** i.e., we have two separate bodies, just as a coat of arms in heraldry can be represented twice on a shield but surmounted by a single crest.  230. **tender:** offer.  232. **grace:** favor.  237. **sad:** grave, serious.

Make mouths° upon° me when I turn my back,
Wink each at other, hold the sweet jest up.°
This sport, well carried,° shall be chronicled.                    240
If you have any pity, grace, or manners,
You would not make me such an argument.°
But fare ye well. 'Tis partly my own fault,
Which death, or absence, soon shall remedy.

LYSANDER:
Stay, gentle Helena; hear my excuse,                              245
My love, my life, my soul, fair Helena!

HELENA:
O excellent!

HERMIA [*to Lysander*]:     Sweet, do not scorn her so.

DEMETRIUS [*to Lysander*]:
If she cannot entreat,° I can compel.

LYSANDER:
Thou canst compel no more than she entreat.
Thy threats have no more strength than her weak prayers.          250
Helen, I love thee, by my life, I do!
I swear by that which I will lose for thee,
To prove him false that says I love thee not.

DEMETRIUS [*to Helena*]:
I say I love thee more than he can do.

LYSANDER:
If thou say so, withdraw, and prove it too.°                      255

DEMETRIUS:
Quick, come!

HERMIA:          Lysander, whereto tends all this?

LYSANDER:
Away, you Ethiope!°               [*He tries to break away from Hermia.*]

DEMETRIUS:          No, no; he'll
Seem to break loose; take on as° you would follow,
But yet come not. You are a tame man. Go!

LYSANDER [*to Hermia*]:
Hang off,° thou cat, thou burr! Vile thing, let loose,            260
Or I will shake thee from me like a serpent!

---

238. **mouths:** i.e., mows, faces, grimaces.   **upon:** at.   239. **hold . . . up:** keep up the joke.
240. **carried:** managed.   242. **argument:** subject for a jest.   248. **entreat:** i.e., succeed by
entreaty.   255. **withdraw . . . too:** i.e., withdraw with me and prove your claim in a duel (the
two gentlemen are armed).   257. **Ethiope:** (Referring to Hermia's relatively dark hair and
complexion; see also *tawny Tartar* six lines later.)   258. **take on as:** act as if, make a fuss as if.
260. **Hang off:** let go.

HERMIA:
Why are you grown so rude? What change is this,
Sweet love?
LYSANDER:     Thy love? Out, tawny Tartar, out!
Out, loathèd med'cine!° O hated potion, hence!
HERMIA:
Do you not jest?
HELENA:          Yes, sooth,° and so do you.          265
LYSANDER:
Demetrius, I will keep my word with thee.
DEMETRIUS:
I would I had your bond, for I perceive
A weak bond° holds you. I'll not trust your word.
LYSANDER:
What, should I hurt her, strike her, kill her dead?
Although I hate her, I'll not harm her so.          270
HERMIA:
What, can you do me greater harm than hate?
Hate me? Wherefore? O me, what news,° my love?
Am not I Hermia? Are not you Lysander?
I am as fair now as I was erewhile.°
Since night you loved me; yet since night you left me.     275
Why, then you left me — O, the gods forbid! —
In earnest, shall I say?
LYSANDER:          Ay, by my life!
And never did desire to see thee more.
Therefore be out of hope, of question, of doubt;
Be certain, nothing truer. 'Tis no jest          280
That I do hate thee and love Helena.
HERMIA [to Helena]:
O me! You juggler! You cankerblossom!°
You thief of love! What, have you come by night
And stol'n my love's heart from him?
HELENA:                    Fine, i' faith!
Have you no modesty, no maiden shame,          285
No touch of bashfulness? What, will you tear

---

264. **med'cine:** i.e., poison.   265. **sooth:** truly.   268. **weak bond:** i.e., Hermia's arm (with a pun on *bond,* "oath," in the previous line).   272. **what news:** what is the matter.   274. **erewhile:** just now.   282. **cankerblossom:** worm that destroys the flower bud, or wild rose.

Impatient answers from my gentle tongue?
Fie, fie! You counterfeit, you puppet,° you!

HERMIA:
"Puppet"? Why, so!° Ay, that way goes the game.
Now I perceive that she hath made compare                    290
Between our statures; she hath urged her height,
And with her personage, her tall personage,
Her height, forsooth, she hath prevailed with him.
And are you grown so high in his esteem
Because I am so dwarfish and so low?                          295
How low am I, thou painted maypole? Speak!
How low am I? I am not yet so low
But that my nails can reach unto thine eyes.

[*She flails at Helena but is restrained.*]

HELENA:
I pray you, though you mock me, gentlemen,
Let her not hurt me. I was never curst;°                     300
I have no gift at all in shrewishness;
I am a right° maid for my cowardice.
Let her not strike me. You perhaps may think,
Because she is something° lower than myself,
That I can match her.

HERMIA:                    Lower? Hark, again!               305

HELENA:
Good Hermia, do not be so bitter with me.
I evermore did love you, Hermia,
Did ever keep your counsels, never wronged you,
Save that, in love unto Demetrius,
I told him of your stealth° unto this wood.                  310
He followed you; for love I followed him.
But he hath chid me hence° and threatened me
To strike me, spurn me, nay, to kill me too.
And now, so° you will let me quiet go,
To Athens will I bear my folly back                          315
And follow you no further. Let me go.
You see how simple and how fond° I am.

HERMIA:
Why, get you gone. Who is 't that hinders you?

288. **puppet:** (1) counterfeit (2) dwarfish woman (in reference to Hermia's smaller stature).
289. **Why, so:** i.e., Oh, so that's how it is. 300. **curst:** shrewish. 302. **right:** true.
304. **something:** somewhat. 310. **stealth:** stealing away. 312. **chid me hence:** driven me
away with his scolding. 314. **so:** if only. 317. **fond:** foolish.

HELENA:
A foolish heart, that I leave here behind.
HERMIA:
What, with Lysander?
HELENA:                    With Demetrius.                               320
LYSANDER:
Be not afraid; she shall not harm thee, Helena.
DEMETRIUS:
No, sir, she shall not, though you take her part.
HELENA:
O, when she is angry, she is keen° and shrewd.°
She was a vixen when she went to school;
And though she be but little, she is fierce.                            325
HERMIA:
"Little" again? Nothing but "low" and "little"?
Why will you suffer her to flout me thus?
Let me come to her.
LYSANDER:              Get you gone, you dwarf!
You minimus,° of hindering knotgrass° made!
You bead, you acorn!
DEMETRIUS:              You are too officious                           330
In her behalf that scorns your services.
Let her alone. Speak not of Helena;
Take not her part. For, if thou dost intend°
Never so little show of love to her,
Thou shalt aby° it.
LYSANDER:              Now she holds me not.                            335
Now follow, if thou dar'st, to try whose right,
Of thine or mine, is most in Helena.                    [Exit.]
DEMETRIUS:
Follow? Nay, I'll go with thee, cheek by jowl.°    [Exit, following Lysander.]
HERMIA:
You, mistress, all this coil° is 'long of° you.
Nay, go not back.°
HELENA:              I will not trust you, I,                           340
Nor longer stay in your curst company.
Your hands than mine are quicker for a fray;

---

323. **keen**: fierce, cruel. **shrewd**: shrewish. 329. **minimus**: diminutive creature. **knotgrass**: a weed, an infusion of which was thought to stunt the growth. 333. **intend**: give sign of. 335. **aby**: pay for. 338. **cheek by jowl**: i.e., side by side. 339. **coil**: turmoil, dissension. **'long of**: on account of. 340. **go not back**: i.e., don't retreat. (Hermia is again proposing a fight.)

My legs are longer, though, to run away.          *[Exit.]*

HERMIA:

    I am amazed and know not what to say.          *Exit.*

    [*Oberon and Puck come forward.*]

OBERON:

    This is thy negligence. Still thou mistak'st,     345
    Or else committ'st thy knaveries willfully.

PUCK:

    Believe me, king of shadows, I mistook.
    Did not you tell me I should know the man
    By the Athenian garments he had on?
    And so far blameless proves my enterprise     350
    That I have 'nointed an Athenian's eyes;
    And so far° am I glad it so did sort,°
    As° this their jangling I esteem a sport.

OBERON:

    Thou seest these lovers seek a place to fight.
    Hie° therefore, Robin, overcast the night;     355
    The starry welkin° cover thou anon
    With drooping fog as black as Acheron,°
    And lead these testy rivals so astray
    As° one come not within another's way.
    Like to Lysander sometimes frame thy tongue,     360
    Then stir Demetrius up with bitter wrong;°
    And sometimes rail thou like Demetrius.
    And from each other look thou lead them thus,
    Till o'er their brows death-counterfeiting sleep
    With leaden legs and batty° wings doth creep.     365
    Then crush this herb° into Lysander's eye,     *[giving herb]*
    Whose liquor hath this virtuous° property,
    To take from thence all error with his° might
    And make his eyeballs roll with wonted° sight.
    When they next wake, all this derision°     370
    Shall seem a dream and fruitless vision,
    And back to Athens shall the lovers wend

---

352. **so far:** at least to this extent.   **sort:** turn out.   353. **As:** in that.   355. **Hie:** hasten. 356. **welkin:** sky.   357. **Acheron:** river of Hades (here representing Hades itself). 359. **As:** that.   361. **wrong:** insults.   365. **batty:** batlike.   366. **this herb:** i.e., the antidote (mentioned in 2.1.184) to love-in-idleness.   367. **virtuous:** efficacious.   368. **his:** its. 369. **wonted:** accustomed.   370. **derision:** laughable business.

With league whose date° till death shall never end.
Whiles I in this affair do thee employ,
I'll to my queen and beg her Indian boy; 375
And then I will her charmèd eye release
From monster's view, and all things shall be peace.

PUCK:

My fairy lord, this must be done with haste,
For night's swift dragons° cut the clouds full fast,
And yonder shines Aurora's harbinger,° 380
At whose approach ghosts, wand'ring here and there,
Troop home to churchyards. Damnèd spirits all,
That in crossways and floods have burial,°
Already to their wormy beds are gone.
For fear lest day should look their shames upon, 385
They willfully themselves exile from light
And must for aye° consort with black-browed night.

OBERON:

But we are spirits of another sort.
I with the Morning's love° have oft made sport,
And, like a forester,° the groves may tread 390
Even till the eastern gate, all fiery red,
Opening on Neptune with fair blessèd beams,
Turns into yellow gold his salt green streams.
But notwithstanding, haste, make no delay.
We may effect this business yet ere day.      [*Exit.*] 395

PUCK:

Up and down, up and down,
I will lead them up and down.
I am feared in field and town.
Goblin,° lead them up and down.
Here comes one. 400

*Enter Lysander.*

LYSANDER:

Where art thou, proud Demetrius? Speak thou now.

373. **date:** term of existence.   379. **dragons:** (Supposed by Shakespeare to be yoked to the car of the goddess of night or the moon.)   380. **Aurora's harbinger:** the morning star, precursor of dawn.   383. **crossways . . . burial:** [Those who had committed suicide were buried at crossways, with a stake driven through them; those who intentionally or accidentally drowned (in *floods* or deep water) would be condemned to wander disconsolately for lack of burial rights.]   387. **for aye:** forever.   389. **the Morning's love:** Cephalus, a beautiful youth beloved by Aurora; or perhaps the goddess of the dawn herself.   390. **forester:** keeper of a royal forest.   399. **Goblin:** Hobgoblin. (Puck refers to himself.)

PUCK [*mimicking Demetrius*]:
Here, villain, drawn° and ready. Where art thou?

LYSANDER:
I will be with thee straight.°

PUCK:                    Follow me, then,
To plainer° ground.          [*Lysander wanders about,° following the voice.*]

*Enter Demetrius.*

DEMETRIUS:          Lysander! Speak again!
Thou runaway, thou coward, art thou fled?          405
Speak! In some bush? Where dost thou hide thy head?

PUCK [*mimicking Lysander*]:
Thou coward, art thou bragging to the stars,
Telling the bushes that thou look'st for wars,
And wilt not come? Come, recreant;° come, thou child,
I'll whip thee with a rod. He is defiled          410
That draws a sword on thee.

DEMETRIUS:                    Yea, art thou there?

PUCK:
Follow my voice. We'll try° no manhood here.          *Exeunt.*

[*Lysander returns.*]

LYSANDER:
He goes before me and still dares me on.
When I come where he calls, then he is gone.
The villain is much lighter-heeled than I.          415
I followed fast, but faster he did fly,
That fallen am I in dark uneven way,
And here will rest me. [*He lies down.*] Come, thou gentle day!
For if but once thou show me thy gray light,
I'll find Demetrius and revenge this spite. [*He sleeps.*]          420

[*Enter*] Robin [*Puck*] *and Demetrius.*

PUCK:
Ho, ho, ho! Coward, why com'st thou not?

DEMETRIUS:
Abide° me, if thou dar'st; for well I wot°
Thou runn'st before me, shifting every place,

402. **drawn:** with drawn sword.  403. **straight:** immediately.  404. **plainer:** more open. s.d. *Lysander wanders about:* (Lysander may exit here, but perhaps not; neither exit nor re-entrance is indicated in the early texts.)  409. **recreant:** cowardly wretch.  412. **try:** test. 422. **Abide:** confront, face.  **wot:** know.

And dar'st not stand nor look me in the face.
Where art thou now?

PUCK:                              Come hither. I am here.                    425

DEMETRIUS:
Nay, then, thou mock'st me. Thou shalt buy° this dear,°
If ever I thy face by daylight see.
Now go thy way. Faintness constraineth me
To measure out my length on this cold bed.
By day's approach look to be visited.          [*He lies down and sleeps.*]  430

*Enter Helena.*

HELENA:
O weary night, O long and tedious night,
    Abate° thy hours! Shine comforts from the east,
That I may back to Athens by daylight
    From these that my poor company detest;
And sleep, that sometimes shuts up sorrow's eye,                            435
Steal me awhile from mine own company.      [*She lies down and*] sleep[*s*].

PUCK:
    Yet but three? Come one more;
    Two of both kinds makes up four.
    Here she comes, curst° and sad.
    Cupid is a knavish lad,                                                  440
    Thus to make poor females mad.

[*Enter Hermia.*]

HERMIA:
Never so weary, never so in woe,
    Bedabbled with the dew and torn with briers,
I can no further crawl, no further go;
    My legs can keep no pace with my desires.                               445
Here will I rest me till the break of day.
Heavens shield Lysander, if they mean a fray!   [*She lies down and sleeps.*]

PUCK:
        On the ground
        Sleep sound.
        I'll apply                                                          450
        To your eye,

---

426. **buy**: aby, pay for. **dear**: dearly.  432. **Abate**: lessen, shorten.  439. **curst**: ill-
tempered.

Gentle lover, remedy.        [*He squeezes the juice on Lysander's eyes.*]
  When thou wak'st,
  Thou tak'st
  True delight                                  455
  In the sight
Of thy former lady's eye;
And the country proverb known,
That every man should take his own,
In your waking shall be shown:                    460
  Jack shall have Jill;°
  Naught shall go ill;
The man shall have his mare again, and all shall be well.
               [*Exit. The four sleeping lovers remain.*]

## ACT 4, SCENE 1°

*Enter* [*Titania,*] *Queen of Fairies, and* [*Bottom the*] *clown, and Fairies; and* [*Oberon,*] *the King, behind them.*

TITANIA:
Come, sit thee down upon this flowery bed,
  While I thy amiable° cheeks do coy,°
And stick muskroses in thy sleek smooth head,
  And kiss thy fair large ears, my gentle joy.      [*They recline.*]
BOTTOM:    Where's Peaseblossom?                     5
PEASEBLOSSOM:    Ready.
BOTTOM:    Scratch my head, Peaseblossom. Where's Monsieur Cobweb?
COBWEB:    Ready.
BOTTOM:    Monsieur Cobweb, good monsieur, get you your weapons in
your hand, and kill me a red-hipped humble-bee on the top of a thistle;  10
and, good monsieur, bring me the honey bag. Do not fret yourself too
much in the action, monsieur; and, good monsieur, have a care the honey
bag break not. I would be loath to have you overflown with a honey bag,
signor. [*Exit Cobweb.*] Where's Monsieur Mustardseed?
MUSTARDSEED:    Ready.                             15
BOTTOM:    Give me your neaf,° Monsieur Mustardseed. Pray you, leave
your courtesy,° good monsieur.
MUSTARDSEED:    What's your will?

---

461. **Jack shall have Jill:** (Proverbial for "boy gets girl.") ACT 4, SCENE 1. Location: The action is continuous. The four lovers are still asleep onstage. (Compare with the Folio stage direction: "They sleep all the act.") 2. **amiable:** lovely.  **coy:** caress.  16. **neaf:** fist. 16–17. **leave your courtesy:** i.e., stop bowing, or put on your hat.

BOTTOM:    Nothing, good monsieur, but to help Cavalery° Cobweb° to
scratch. I must to the barber's, monsieur, for methinks I am marvelous    20
hairy about the face; and I am such a tender ass, if my hair do
but tickle me I must scratch.

TITANIA:
What, wilt thou hear some music, my sweet love?

BOTTOM:    I have a reasonable good ear in music. Let's have the tongs and
the bones.°                                    *[Music: tongs, rural music.°]*    25

TITANIA:
Or say, sweet love, what thou desirest to eat.

BOTTOM:    Truly, a peck of provender.° I could munch your good dry oats.
Methinks I have a great desire to a bottle° of hay. Good hay, sweet hay,
hath no fellow.°

TITANIA:
I have a venturous fairy that shall seek                              30
The squirrel's hoard, and fetch thee new nuts.

BOTTOM:    I had rather have a handful or two of dried peas. But, I pray you,
let none of your people stir° me. I have an exposition of° sleep come
upon me.

TITANIA:
Sleep thou, and I will wind thee in my arms.                         35
Fairies, begone, and be all ways° away.              *[Exeunt Fairies.]*
So doth the woodbine° the sweet honeysuckle
Gently entwist; the female ivy so
Enrings the barky fingers of the elm.
O, how I love thee! How I dote on thee!              *[They sleep.]*    40

*Enter Robin Goodfellow [Puck].*

OBERON *[coming forward]:*
Welcome, good Robin. Seest thou this sweet sight?
Her dotage now I do begin to pity.
For, meeting her of late behind the wood
Seeking sweet favors° for this hateful fool,
I did upbraid her and fall out with her.                             45

19. **Cavalery:** cavalier (form of address for a gentleman).    **Cobweb:** (Seemingly an error, since
Cobweb has been sent to bring honey, while Peaseblossom has been asked to scratch.)    **24–
25. tongs . . . bones:** instruments for rustic music (the tongs were played like a triangle,
whereas the bones were held between the fingers and used as clappers).    **s.d. Music . . .
music:** (This stage direction is added from the Folio.)    **27. peck of provender:** one-quarter
bushel of grain.    **28. bottle:** bundle.    **29. fellow:** equal.    **33. stir:** disturb.    **exposition of:**
(Bottom's phrase for "disposition to.")    **36. all ways:** in all directions.    **37. woodbine:**
bindweed, a climbing plant that twines in the opposite direction from that of honeysuckle.
**44. favors:** i.e., gifts of flowers.

For she his hairy temples then had rounded
With coronet of fresh and fragrant flowers;
And that same dew, which sometime° on the buds
Was wont to swell like round and orient pearls,°
Stood now within the pretty flowerets' eyes                    50
Like tears that did their own disgrace bewail.
When I had at my pleasure taunted her,
And she in mild terms begged my patience,
I then did ask of her her changeling child,
Which straight she gave me, and her fairy sent              55
To bear him to my bower in Fairyland.
And, now I have the boy, I will undo
This hateful imperfection of her eyes.
And, gentle Puck, take this transformèd scalp
From off the head of this Athenian swain,                      60
That he, awaking when the other° do,
May all to Athens back again repair,°
And think no more of this night's accidents
But as the fierce vexation of a dream.
But first I will release the Fairy Queen.        [*He squeezes an herb on her eyes.*]   65
    Be as thou wast wont to be;
    See as thou wast wont to see.
    Dian's bud° o'er Cupid's flower
    Hath such force and blessèd power.
Now, my Titania, wake you, my sweet queen.                  70
TITANIA [*awaking*]:
My Oberon! What visions have I seen!
Methought I was enamored of an ass.
OBERON:
There lies your love.
TITANIA:                    How came these things to pass?
O, how mine eyes do loathe his visage now!
OBERON:
Silence awhile. Robin, take off this head.                      75
Titania, music call, and strike more dead
Than common sleep of all these five° the sense.

48. **sometime:** formerly.   49. **orient pearls:** i.e., the most beautiful of all pearls, those coming from the Orient.   61. **other:** others.   62. **repair:** return.   68. **Dian's bud:** (Perhaps the flower of the *agnus castus* or chaste-tree, supposed to preserve chastity; or perhaps referring simply to Oberon's herb by which he can undo the effects of "Cupid's flower," the love-in-idleness of 2.1.166–68.)   77. **these five:** i.e., the four lovers and Bottom.

TITANIA:
Music, ho! Music, such as charmeth° sleep!                          [*Music.*]

PUCK [*removing the ass head*]:
Now, when thou wak'st, with thine own fool's eyes peep.

OBERON:
Sound, music! Come, my queen, take hands with me,            80
And rock the ground whereon these sleepers be.        [*They dance.*]
Now thou and I are new in amity,
And will tomorrow midnight solemnly°
Dance in Duke Theseus' house triumphantly,
And bless it to all fair prosperity.                                          85
There shall the pairs of faithful lovers be
Wedded, with Theseus, all in jollity.

PUCK:
Fairy King, attend, and mark:
I do hear the morning lark.

OBERON:
Then, my queen, in silence sad,°                                          90
Trip we after night's shade.
We the globe can compass soon,
Swifter than the wandering moon.

TITANIA:
Come, my lord, and in our flight
Tell me how it came this night                                            95
That I sleeping here was found
With these mortals on the ground.
                    *Exeunt [Oberon, Titania, and Puck]. Wind horn [within].*


*Enter Theseus and all his train; [Hippolyta, Egeus].*

THESEUS:
Go, one of you, find out the forester,
For now our observation° is performed;
And since we have the vaward° of the day,                         100
My love shall hear the music of my hounds.
Uncouple° in the western valley; let them go.
Dispatch, I say, and find the forester.              [*Exit an Attendant.*]
We will, fair queen, up to the mountain's top

---

78. **charmeth:** brings about, as though by a charm.   83. **solemnly:** ceremoniously.   90. **sad:** sober.   99. **observation:** i.e., observance to a morn of May (1.1.167).   100. **vaward:** vanguard, i.e., earliest part.   102. **Uncouple:** set free for the hunt.

And mark the musical confusion                                    105
Of hounds and echo in conjunction.

HIPPOLYTA:
  I was with Hercules and Cadmus° once
  When in a wood of Crete they bayed° the bear
  With hounds of Sparta.° Never did I hear
  Such gallant chiding;° for, besides the groves,            110
  The skies, the fountains, every region near
  Seemed all one mutual cry. I never heard
  So musical a discord, such sweet thunder.

THESEUS:
  My hounds are bred out of the Spartan kind,°
  So flewed,° so sanded;° and their heads are hung    115
  With ears that sweep away the morning dew;
  Crook-kneed, and dewlapped° like Thessalian bulls;
  Slow in pursuit, but matched in mouth like bells,
  Each under each.° A cry° more tunable°
  Was never holloed to nor cheered° with horn          120
  In Crete, in Sparta, nor in Thessaly.
  Judge when you hear. [He sees the sleepers.] But soft!° What nymphs are
      these?

EGEUS:
  My lord, this is my daughter here asleep,
  And this Lysander; this Demetrius is;
  This Helena, old Nedar's Helena.                            125
  I wonder of° their being here together.

THESEUS:
  No doubt they rose up early to observe
  The rite of May, and hearing our intent,
  Came here in grace of our solemnity.°
  But speak, Egeus. Is not this the day                       130
  That Hermia should give answer of her choice?
EGEUS:    It is, my lord.

---

107. **Cadmus:** mythical founder of Thebes. (This story about him is unknown.)   108. **bayed:** brought to bay.   109. **hounds of Sparta:** (A breed famous in antiquity for their hunting skill.)   110. **chiding:** i.e., yelping.   114. **kind:** strain, breed.   115. **So flewed:** similarly having large hanging chaps or fleshy covering of the jaw.   **sanded:** of sandy color.   117. **dewlapped:** having pendulous folds of skin under the neck.   118–19. **matched . . . each:** i.e., harmoniously matched in their various cries like a set of bells, from treble down to bass.   119. **cry:** pack of hounds.   **tunable:** well tuned, melodious.   120. **cheered:** encouraged.   122. **soft:** i.e., gently, wait a minute.   126. **wonder of:** wonder at.   129. **in . . . solemnity:** in honor of our wedding ceremony.

THESEUS:
Go bid the huntsmen wake them with their horns.     [*Exit an Attendant.*]

*Shout within. Wind horns. They all start up.*

Good morrow, friends. Saint Valentine° is past.
Begin these woodbirds but to couple now?                                                   135
LYSANDER:
Pardon, my lord.                                                                  [*They kneel.*]
THESEUS:              I pray you all, stand up.                  [*They stand.*]
I know you two are rival enemies;
How comes this gentle concord in the world,
That hatred is so far from jealousy°
To sleep by hate and fear no enmity?                                                       140
LYSANDER:
My lord, I shall reply amazedly,
Half sleep, half waking; but as yet, I swear,
I cannot truly say how I came here.
But, as I think — for truly would I speak,
And now I do bethink me, so it is —                                                        145
I came with Hermia hither. Our intent
Was to be gone from Athens, where° we might,
Without° the peril of the Athenian law —
EGEUS:
Enough, enough, my lord; you have enough.
I beg the law, the law, upon his head.
They would have stol'n away; they would, Demetrius,                                        150
Thereby to have defeated° you and me,
You of your wife and me of my consent,
Of my consent that she should be your wife.
DEMETRIUS:
My lord, fair Helen told me of their stealth,                                              155
Of this their purpose hither° to this wood,
And I in fury hither followed them,
Fair Helena in fancy° following me.
But, my good lord, I wot not by what power —
But by some power it is — my love to Hermia,                                               160
Melted as the snow, seems to me now

---

134. **Saint Valentine:** (Birds were supposed to choose their mates on Saint Valentine's Day.)
139. **jealousy:** suspicion.   147. **where:** wherever; or, to where.   148. **Without:** outside of,
beyond.   152. **defeated:** defrauded.   156. **hither:** in coming hither.   158. **in fancy:** driven by
love.

As the remembrance of an idle gaud°
Which in my childhood I did dote upon;
And all the faith, the virtue of my heart,
The object and the pleasure of mine eye,                    165
Is only Helena. To her, my lord,
Was I betrothed ere I saw Hermia,
But like a sickness did I loathe this food;
But, as in health, come to my natural taste,
Now I do wish it, love it, long for it,                     170
And will forevermore be true to it.

THESEUS:
Fair lovers, you are fortunately met.
Of this discourse we more will hear anon.
Egeus, I will overbear your will;
For in the temple, by and by, with us                       175
These couples shall eternally be knit.
And, for° the morning now is something° worn,
Our purposed hunting shall be set aside.
Away with us to Athens. Three and three,
We'll hold a feast in great solemnity.°                     180
Come Hippolyta.            [*Exeunt Theseus, Hippolyta, Egeus, and train.*]

DEMETRIUS:
These things seem small and undistinguishable,
Like far-off mountains turnèd into clouds.

HERMIA:
Methinks I see these things with parted° eye,
When everything seems double.

HELENA:                            So methinks;            185
And I have found Demetrius like a jewel,
Mine own, and not mine own.°

DEMETRIUS:                            Are you sure
That we are awake? It seems to me
That yet we sleep, we dream. Do not you think
The Duke was here, and bid us follow him?                   190

HERMIA:
Yea, and my father.

HELENA:                    And Hippolyta.

162. **idle gaud:** worthless trinket.   177. **for:** since.   **something:** somewhat.   180. **in great
solemnity:** with great ceremony.   184. **parted:** i.e., improperly focused.   186–87. **like . . .
mine own:** i.e., like a jewel that one finds by chance and therefore possesses but cannot certainly
consider one's own property.

LYSANDER:
And he did bid us follow to the temple.

DEMETRIUS:
Why, then, we are awake. Let's follow him,
And by the way let us recount our dreams.          [*Exeunt the lovers.*]

BOTTOM [*awaking*]:   When my cue comes, call me, and I will answer. My   195
next is "Most fair Pyramus." Heigh-ho! Peter Quince! Flute, the bellows
mender! Snout, the tinker! Starveling! God's° my life, stolen hence
and left me asleep! I have had a most rare vision. I have had a dream,
past the wit of man to say what dream it was. Man is but an ass if
he go about° to expound this dream. Methought I was — there is no   200
man can tell what. Methought I was — and methought I had — but
man is but a patched° fool if he will offer° to say what methought I
had. The eye of man hath not heard, the ear of man hath not seen,
man's hand is not able to taste, his tongue to conceive, nor his heart
to report° what my dream was. I will get Peter Quince to write a ballad°   205
of this dream. It shall be called "Bottom's Dream," because it hath
no bottom;° and I will sing it in the latter end of a play, before
the Duke. Peradventure, to make it the more gracious, I shall sing it at
her° death.          [*Exit.*]

## ACT 4, SCENE 2°

*Enter Quince, Flute, [Snout, and Starveling].*

QUINCE:   Have you sent to Bottom's house? Is he come home yet?

STARVELING:   He cannot be heard of. Out of doubt he is transported.°

FLUTE:   If he come not, then the play is marred. It goes not forward.
Doth it?

QUINCE:   It is not possible. You have not a man in all Athens able to   5
discharge° Pyramus but he.

FLUTE:   No, he hath simply the best wit° of any handicraft man in Athens.

QUINCE:   Yea, and the best person° too, and he is a very paramour for a
sweet voice.

FLUTE:   You must say "paragon." A paramour is, God bless us, a thing of   10
naught.°

---

197. **God's:** may God save.   200. **go about:** attempt.   202. **patched:** wearing motley, i.e.,
a dress of various colors.   **offer:** venture.   203–05. **The eye . . . report:** (Bottom garbles the
terms of 1 Corinthians 2:9.)   205. **ballad:** (The proper medium for relating sensational stories
and preposterous events.)   206–07. **hath no bottom:** is unfathomable.   209. **her:** Thisbe's (?).
ACT 4, SCENE 2. **Location:** Athens.   2. **transported:** carried off by fairies; or, possibly, transformed.   6. **discharge:** perform.   7. **wit:** intellect.   8. **person:** appearance.   10–11. **a . . .
naught:** a shameful thing.

*Enter Snug the joiner.*

SNUG: Masters, the Duke is coming from the temple, and there is two or three lords and ladies more married. If our sport had gone forward, we had all been made men.°

FLUTE: O sweet bully Bottom! Thus hath he lost sixpence a day° during his life; he could not have scaped sixpence a day. An the Duke had not given him sixpence a day for playing Pyramus, I'll be hanged. He would have deserved it. Sixpence a day in Pyramus, or nothing.

*Enter Bottom.*

BOTTOM: Where are these lads? Where are these hearts?°

QUINCE: Bottom! O most courageous day! O most happy hour!

BOTTOM: Masters, I am to discourse wonders.° But ask me not what; for if I tell you, I am no true Athenian. I will tell you everything, right as it fell out.

QUINCE: Let us hear, sweet Bottom.

BOTTOM: Not a word of° me. All that I will tell you is that the Duke hath dined. Get your apparel together, good strings° to your beards, new ribbons to your pumps;° meet presently° at the palace; every man look o'er his part; for the short and the long is, our play is preferred.° In any case, let Thisbe have clean linen; and let not him that plays the lion pare his nails, for they shall hang out for the lion's claws. And, most dear actors, eat no onions nor garlic, for we are to utter sweet breath; and I do not doubt but to hear them say it is a sweet comedy. No more words. Away! Go, away! [*Exeunt.*]

## ACT 5, SCENE 1°

*Enter Theseus, Hippolyta, and Philostrate, [lords, and attendants].*

HIPPOLYTA:
'Tis strange, my Theseus, that° these lovers speak of.

THESEUS:
More strange than true. I never may° believe
These antique° fables nor these fairy toys.°

---

14. **we . . . men:** i.e., we would have had our fortunes made. 15. **sixpence a day:** i.e., as a royal pension. 19. **hearts:** good fellows. 21. **am . . . wonders:** have wonders to relate. 25. **of:** out of. 26. **strings:** (To attach the beards.) 27. **pumps:** light shoes or slippers. **presently:** immediately. 28. **preferred:** selected for consideration. ACT 5, SCENE 1. Location: Athens. The palace of Theseus. 1. **that:** that which. 2. **may:** can. 3. **antique:** old-fashioned (punning, too, on *antic*, "strange," "grotesque"). **fairy toys:** trifling stories about fairies.

Lovers and madmen have such seething brains,
Such shaping fantasies,° that apprehend°                                    5
More than cool reason ever comprehends.°
The lunatic, the lover, and the poet
Are of imagination all compact.°
One sees more devils than vast hell can hold;
That is the madman. The lover, all as frantic,                              10
Sees Helen's° beauty in a brow of Egypt.°
The poet's eye, in a fine frenzy rolling,
Doth glance from heaven to earth, from earth to heaven;
And as imagination bodies forth
The forms of things unknown, the poet's pen                                 15
Turns them to shapes and gives to airy nothing
A local habitation and a name.
Such tricks hath strong imagination
That, if it would but apprehend some joy,
It comprehends some bringer° of that joy;                                   20
Or in the night, imagining some fear,°
How easy is a bush supposed a bear!

HIPPOLYTA:
But all the story of the night told over,
And all their minds transfigured so together,
More witnesseth than fancy's images°                                       25
And grows to something of great constancy;°
But, howsoever,° strange and admirable.°

*Enter lovers: Lysander, Demetrius, Hermia, and Helena.*

THESEUS:
Here come the lovers, full of joy and mirth.
Joy, gentle friends! Joy and fresh days of love
Accompany your hearts!

LYSANDER:                            More than to us                        30
Wait in your royal walks, your board, your bed!

THESEUS:
Come now, what masques,° what dances shall we have,

---

5. **fantasies:** imaginations. **apprehend:** conceive, imagine.  6. **comprehends:** understands.
8. **compact:** formed, composed.  11. **Helen's:** i.e., of Helen of Troy, pattern of beauty.
**brow of Egypt:** i.e., face of a gypsy.  20. **bringer:** i.e., source.  21. **fear:** object of fear.
25. **More . . . images:** testifies to something more substantial than mere imaginings.
26. **constancy:** certainty.  27. **howsoever:** in any case.  **admirable:** a source of wonder.
32. **masques:** courtly entertainments.

To wear away this long age of three hours
Between our after-supper and bedtime?
Where is our usual manager of mirth?                                    35
What revels are in hand? Is there no play
To ease the anguish of a torturing hour?
Call Philostrate.
PHILOSTRATE:        Here, mighty Theseus.
THESEUS:
Say, what abridgment° have you for this evening?
What masque? What music? How shall we beguile                          40
The lazy time, if not with some delight?
PHILOSTRATE [ *giving him a paper*]:
There is a brief° how many sports are ripe.
Make choice of which Your Highness will see first.
THESEUS [*reads*]:
"The battle with the Centaurs,° to be sung
By an Athenian eunuch to the harp"?                                    45
We'll none of that. That have I told my love,
In glory of my kinsman° Hercules.
[*He reads.*] "The riot of the tipsy Bacchanals,
Tearing the Thracian singer in their rage"?°
That is an old device;° and it was played                              50
When I from Thebes came last a conqueror.
[*He reads.*] "The thrice three Muses mourning for the death
Of Learning, late deceased in beggary"?°
That is some satire, keen and critical,
Not sorting with° a nuptial ceremony.                                  55
[*He reads.*] "A tedious brief scene of young Pyramus
And his love Thisbe; very tragical mirth"?
Merry and tragical? Tedious and brief?
That is, hot ice and wondrous strange° snow.
How shall we find the concord of this discord?                         60

---

39. **abridgment:** pastime (to abridge or shorten the evening).   42. **brief:** short written state-
ment, summary.   44. **battle . . . Centaurs:** (Probably refers to the battle of the Centaurs
and the Lapithae, when the Centaurs attempted to carry off Hippodamia, bride of Theseus's
friend Pirothous. The story is told in Ovid's *Metamorphoses* 12.)   47. **kinsman:** (Plutarch's
"Life of Theseus" states that Hercules and Theseus were near kinsmen. Theseus is referring to a
version of the battle of the Centaurs in which Hercules was said to be present.)   48–49. **The
riot . . . rage:** (This was the story of the death of Orpheus, as told in *Metamorphoses* 11.)
50. **device:** show, performance.   52–53. **The thrice . . . beggary:** (Possibly an allusion to
Spenser's *Teares of the Muses*, 1591, though "satires" deploring the neglect of learning and the
creative arts were commonplace.)   55. **sorting with:** befitting.   59. **strange:** (Sometimes
emended to an adjective that would contrast with *snow*, just as *hot* contrasts with *ice*.)

PHILOSTRATE:

   A play there is, my lord, some ten words long,
   Which is as brief as I have known a play;
   But by ten words, my lord, it is too long,
   Which makes it tedious. For in all the play
   There is not one word apt, one player fitted.       65
   And tragical, my noble lord, it is,
   For Pyramus therein doth kill himself.
   Which, when I saw rehearsed, I must confess,
   Made mine eyes water; but more merry tears
   The passion of loud laughter never shed.       70

THESEUS:   What are they that do play it?

PHILOSTRATE:

   Hardhanded men that work in Athens here,
   Which never labored in their minds till now,
   And now have toiled° their unbreathed° memories
   With this same play, against° your nuptial.       75

THESEUS:

   And we will hear it.

PHILOSTRATE:         No, my noble lord,
   It is not for you. I have heard it over,
   And it is nothing, nothing in the world;
   Unless you can find sport in their intents,
   Extremely stretched° and conned° with cruel pain       80
   To do you service.

THESEUS:         I will hear that play;
   For never anything can be amiss
   When simpleness° and duty tender it.
   Go, bring them in; and take your places, ladies.

                       *[Philostrate goes to summon the players.]*

HIPPOLYTA:

   I love not to see wretchedness o'ercharged,°       85
   And duty in his service° perishing.

THESEUS:

   Why, gentle sweet, you shall see no such thing.

HIPPOLYTA:

   He says they can do nothing in this kind.°

---

74. **toiled:** taxed. **unbreathed:** unexercised. 75. **against:** in preparation for. 80. **stretched:** strained. **conned:** memorized. 83. **simpleness:** simplicity. 85. **wretchedness o'ercharged:** social or intellectual inferiors overburdened. 86. **his service:** its attempt to serve. 88. **kind:** kind of thing.

THESEUS:
The kinder we, to give them thanks for nothing.
Our sport shall be to take what they mistake;                    90
And what poor duty cannot do, noble respect°
Takes it in might, not merit.°
Where I have come, great clerks° have purposèd
To greet me with premeditated welcomes;
Where I have seen them shiver and look pale,                     95
Make periods in the midst of sentences,
Throttle their practiced accent° in their fears,
And in conclusion dumbly have broke off,
Not paying me a welcome. Trust me, sweet,
Out of this silence yet I picked a welcome;                     100
And in the modesty of fearful duty
I read as much as from the rattling tongue
Of saucy and audacious eloquence.
Love, therefore, and tongue-tied simplicity
In least° speak most, to my capacity.°                          105

[*Philostrate returns.*]

PHILOSTRATE:
So please Your Grace, the Prologue° is addressed.°
THESEUS:    Let him approach.                    [*A flourish of trumpets.*]

*Enter the Prologue [Quince].*

PROLOGUE:
If we offend, it is with our good will.
    That you should think, we come not to offend,
But with good will. To show our simple skill,                   110
    That is the true beginning of our end.
Consider, then, we come but in despite.
    We do not come, as minding° to content you,
Our true intent is. All for your delight
    We are not here. That you should here repent you,           115
The actors are at hand; and, by their show,
You shall know all that you are like to know.

91. **respect:** evaluation, consideration.  92. **Takes . . . merit:** values it for the effort made rather than for the excellence achieved.  93. **clerks:** learned men.  97. **practiced accent:** i.e., rehearsed speech; or, usual way of speaking.  105. **least:** i.e., saying least.  **to my capacity:** in my judgment and understanding.  106. **Prologue:** speaker of the prologue.  **addressed:** ready.  113. **minding:** intending.

THESEUS:   This fellow doth not stand upon points.°

LYSANDER:   He hath rid° his prologue like a rough° colt; he knows not the
stop.° A good moral, my lord: it is not enough to speak, but to speak   120
true.

HIPPOLYTA:   Indeed, he hath played on his prologue like a child on a
recorder:° a sound, but not in government.°

THESEUS:   His speech was like a tangled chain: nothing° impaired, but all
disordered. Who is next?   125

*Enter Pyramus [Bottom], and Thisbe [Flute], and Wall [Snout], and Moonshine
[Starveling], and Lion [Snug].*

PROLOGUE:

Gentles, perchance you wonder at this show;
But wonder on, till truth make all things plain.
This man is Pyramus, if you would know;
This beauteous lady Thisbe is, certain.
This man with lime and roughcast doth present   130
Wall, that vile wall which did these lovers sunder;
And through Wall's chink, poor souls, they are content
To whisper. At the which let no man wonder.
This man, with lantern, dog, and bush of thorn,
Presenteth Moonshine; for, if you will know,   135
By moonshine did these lovers think no scorn°
To meet at Ninus' tomb, there, there to woo.
This grisly beast, which Lion hight° by name,
The trusty Thisbe coming first by night
Did scare away, or rather did affright;   140
And as she fled, her mantle she did fall,°
Which Lion vile with bloody mouth did stain.
Anon comes Pyramus, sweet youth and tall,°
And finds his trusty Thisbe's mantle slain;
Whereat, with blade, with bloody, blameful blade,   145
He bravely broached° his boiling bloody breast.
And Thisbe, tarrying in mulberry shade,
His dagger drew, and died. For all the rest,

118. **stand upon points:** (1) heed niceties or small points (2) pay attention to punctuation in his reading. (The humor of Quince's speech is in the blunders of its punctuation.)   119. **rid:** ridden.   **rough:** unbroken.   120. **stop:** (1) stopping of a colt by reining it in (2) punctuation mark.   123. **recorder:** wind instrument like a flute.   **government:** control.   124. **nothing:** not at all.   136. **think no scorn:** think it no disgraceful matter.   138. **hight:** is called.   141. **fall:** let fall.   143. **tall:** courageous.   146. **broached:** stabbed.

Let Lion, Moonshine, Wall, and lovers twain
At large° discourse, while here they do remain.                    150
*Exeunt Lion, Thisbe, and Moonshine.*
THESEUS:    I wonder if the lion be to speak.
DEMETRIUS:    No wonder, my lord. One lion may, when many asses do.
WALL:
  In this same interlude° it doth befall
  That I, one Snout by name, present a wall;
  And such a wall as I would have you think                         155
  That had in it a crannied hole or chink,
  Through which the lovers, Pyramus and Thisbe,
  Did whisper often, very secretly.
  This loam, this roughcast, and this stone doth show
  That I am that same wall; the truth is so.                        160
  And this the cranny is, right and sinister,°
  Through which the fearful lovers are to whisper.
THESEUS:    Would you desire lime and hair to speak better?
DEMETRIUS:    It is the wittiest partition° that ever I heard discourse, my lord.

*[Pyramus comes forward.]*

THESEUS:    Pyramus draws near the wall. Silence!                   165
PYRAMUS:
  O grim-looked° night! O night with hue so black!
    O night, which ever art when day is not!
  O night, O night! Alack, alack, alack,
    I fear my Thisbe's promise is forgot.
  And thou, O wall, O sweet, O lovely wall,                         170
    That stand'st between her father's ground and mine,
  Thou wall, O wall, O sweet and lovely wall,
    Show me thy chink, to blink through with mine eyne.

*[Wall makes a chink with his fingers.]*

  Thanks, courteous wall. Jove shield thee well for this.
    But what see I? No Thisbe do I see.                             175
  O wicked wall, through whom I see no bliss!
    Cursed be thy stones for thus deceiving me!
THESEUS:    The wall, methinks, being sensible,° should curse again.°

---

150. **At large:** in full, at length.   153. **interlude:** play.   161. **right and sinister:** i.e., the right side of it and the left; or, running from right to left, horizontally.   164. **partition:** (1) wall (2) section of a learned treatise or oration.   166. **grim-looked:** grim-looking.   178. **sensible:** capable of feeling.   **again:** in return.

PYRAMUS:     No, in truth, sir, he should not. "Deceiving me" is Thisbe's cue:
she is to enter now, and I am to spy her through the wall. You shall see,     180
it will fall pat° as I told you. Yonder she comes.

*Enter Thisbe.*

THISBE:
O wall, full often hast thou heard my moans
    For parting my fair Pyramus and me.
My cherry lips have often kissed thy stones,
    Thy stones with lime and hair knit up in thee.     185
PYRAMUS:
I see a voice. Now will I to the chink,
    To spy an° I can hear my Thisbe's face.
Thisbe!
THISBE:     My love! Thou art my love, I think.
PYRAMUS:
    Think what thou wilt, I am thy lover's grace,°
And like Limander° am I trusty still.     190
THISBE:
And I like Helen,° till the Fates me kill.
PYRAMUS:
Not Shafalus to Procrus° was so true.
THISBE:
As Shafalus to Procrus, I to you.
PYRAMUS:
O, kiss me through the hole of this vile wall!
THISBE:
I kiss the wall's hole, not your lips at all.     195
PYRAMUS:
Wilt thou at Ninny's tomb meet me straightway?
THISBE:
'Tide life, 'tide° death, I come without delay.     [*Exeunt Pyramus and Thisbe.*]
WALL:
Thus have I, Wall, my part dischargèd so;
And, being done, thus Wall away doth go.     [*Exit.*]
THESEUS:     Now is the mural down between the two neighbors.     200

---

181. **pat:** exactly.   187. **an:** if.   189. **lover's grace:** i.e., gracious lover.   190, 191. **Limander, Helen:** (Blunders for "Leander" and "Hero.")   192. **Shafalus, Procrus:** (Blunders for "Cephalus" and "Procris," also famous lovers.)   197. **'tide:** betide, come.

DEMETRIUS:   No remedy, my lord, when walls are so willful° to hear without warning.°

HIPPOLYTA:   This is the silliest stuff that ever I heard.

THESEUS:   The best in this kind° are but shadows,° and the worst are no
worse, if imagination amend them.                                                    205

HIPPOLYTA:   It must be your imagination then, and not theirs.

THESEUS:   If we imagine no worse of them than they of themselves, they
may pass for excellent men. Here come two noble beasts in, a man
and a lion.

*Enter Lion and Moonshine.*

LION:

You, ladies, you, whose gentle hearts do fear                                     210
   The smallest monstrous mouse that creeps on floor,
May now perchance both quake and tremble here,
   When lion rough in wildest rage doth roar.
Then know that I, as Snug the joiner, am
A lion fell,° nor else no lion's dam;                                              215
For, if I should as lion come in strife
Into this place, 'twere pity on my life.

THESEUS:   A very gentle beast, and of a good conscience.

DEMETRIUS:   The very best at a beast, my lord, that e'er I saw.

LYSANDER:   This lion is a very fox for his valor.°                                220

THESEUS:   True; and a goose for his discretion.°

DEMETRIUS:   Not so, my lord, for his valor cannot carry his discretion, and
the fox carries the goose.

THESEUS:   His discretion, I am sure, cannot carry his valor; for the goose
carries not the fox. It is well. Leave it to his discretion, and let us listen   225
to the moon.

MOON:

This lanthorn° doth the hornèd moon present —

DEMETRIUS:   He should have worn the horns on his head.°

---

**201. willful:** willing.   **201–02. without warning:** i.e., without warning the parents. (Demetrius
makes a joke on the proverb "Walls have ears.")   **204. in this kind:** of this sort.   **shadows:**
likenesses, representations.   **215. lion fell:** fierce lion (with a play on the idea of "lion skin").
**220. is . . . valor:** i.e., his valor consists of craftiness and discretion.   **221. a goose . . .
discretion:** i.e., as discreet as a goose, that is, more foolish than discreet.   **227. lanthorn:** (This
original spelling, *lanthorn*, may suggest a play on the *horn* of which lanterns were made and
also on a cuckold's horns; however, the spelling *lanthorn* is not used consistently for comic
effect in this play or elsewhere. At 5.1.134, for example, the word is *lantern* in the original.)
**228. on his head:** (As a sign of cuckoldry.)

THESEUS:   He is no crescent,° and his horns are invisible within the circumference.                    230

MOON:
This lanthorn doth the hornèd moon present;
Myself the man i' the moon do seem to be.

THESEUS:   This is the greatest error of all the rest. The man should be put into the lanthorn. How is it else the man i' the moon?

DEMETRIUS:   He dares not come there for° the candle, for you see it is   235
already in snuff.°

HIPPOLYTA:   I am weary of this moon. Would he would change!

THESEUS:   It appears, by his small light of discretion, that he is in the wane; but yet, in courtesy, in all reason, we must stay the time.

LYSANDER:   Proceed, Moon.                    240

MOON:   All that I have to say is to tell you that the lanthorn is the moon, I, the man i' the moon, this thornbush my thornbush, and this dog my dog.

DEMETRIUS:   Why, all these should be in the lanthorn, for all these are in the moon. But silence! Here comes Thisbe.                    245

*Enter Thisbe.*

THISBE:
This is old Ninny's tomb. Where is my love?

LION [*roaring*]:   O!

DEMETRIUS:   Well roared, Lion.          [*Thisbe runs off, dropping her mantle.*]

THESEUS:   Well run, Thisbe.

HIPPOLYTA:   Well shone, Moon. Truly, the moon shines with a good grace.   250
          [*The Lion worries Thisbe's mantle.*]

THESEUS:   Well moused,° Lion.

[*Enter Pyramus; exit Lion.*]

DEMETRIUS:   And then came Pyramus.

LYSANDER:   And so the lion vanished.

PYRAMUS:
Sweet Moon, I thank thee for thy sunny beams;
I thank thee, Moon, for shining now so bright;                    255
For, by thy gracious, golden, glittering gleams,
I trust to take of truest Thisbe sight.
But stay, O spite!
But mark, poor knight,

229. **crescent:** a waxing moon.   235. **for:** because of, for fear of.   236. **in snuff:** (1) offended (2) in need of snuffing or trimming.   251. **moused:** shaken, torn, bitten.

What dreadful dole° is here?  260
   Eyes, do you see?
   How can it be?
O dainty duck! O dear!
   Thy mantle good,
   What, stained with blood?  265
Approach, ye Furies° fell!°
   O Fates,° come, come,
   Cut thread and thrum;°
Quail,° crush, conclude, and quell!°

THESEUS:  This passion, and the death of a dear friend, would go near to  270
make a man look sad.°

HIPPOLYTA:  Beshrew my heart, but I pity the man.

PYRAMUS:
O, wherefore, Nature, didst thou lions frame?
Since lion vile hath here deflowered my dear,
Which is — no, no, which was — the fairest dame  275
That lived, that loved, that liked, that looked with cheer.°
   Come, tears, confound,
   Out, sword, and wound
The pap° of Pyramus;
   Ay, that left pap,  280
   Where heart doth hop.            [He stabs himself.]
Thus die I, thus, thus, thus.
   Now am I dead,
   Now am I fled;
My soul is in the sky.  285
   Tongue, lose thy light;
   Moon, take thy flight.           [Exit Moonshine.]
Now die, die, die, die, die.         [Pyramus dies.]

DEMETRIUS:  No die, but an ace,° for him; for he is but one.°

LYSANDER:  Less than an ace, man; for he is dead, he is nothing.  290

---

260. dole: grievous event.  266. Furies: avenging goddesses of Greek myth.  fell: fierce.
267. Fates: the three goddesses (Clotho, Lachesis, Atropos) of Greek myth who spun, drew,
and cut the thread of human life.  268. thread and thrum: i.e., everything — the good and
bad alike; literally, the warp in weaving and the loose end of the warp.  269. Quail: over-
power.  quell: kill, destroy.  270–71. This . . . sad: i.e., if one had other reason to grieve,
one might be sad, but not from this absurd portrayal of passion.  276. cheer: countenance.
279. pap: breast.  289. ace: the side of the die featuring the single pip, or spot. (The pun is on
die as a singular of dice; Bottom's performance is not worth a whole die but rather one single
face of it, one small portion.)  one: (1) an individual person (2) unique.

THESEUS:   With the help of a surgeon he might yet recover, and yet prove an ass.°

HIPPOLYTA:   How chance Moonshine is gone before Thisbe comes back and finds her lover?

THESEUS:   She will find him by starlight.                                    295

[*Enter Thisbe.*]

Here she comes; and her passion ends the play.

HIPPOLYTA:   Methinks she should not use a long one for such a Pyramus. I hope she will be brief.

DEMETRIUS:   A mote° will turn the balance, which Pyramus, which° Thisbe, is the better: he for a man, God warrant us; she for a woman,  300 God bless us.

LYSANDER:   She hath spied him already with those sweet eyes.

DEMETRIUS:   And thus she means,° videlicet:°

THISBE:

    Asleep, my love?
    What, dead, my dove?
O Pyramus, arise!                                                            305
    Speak, speak. Quite dumb?
    Dead, dead? A tomb
Must cover thy sweet eyes.
    These lily lips,                                                  310
    This cherry nose,
These yellow cowslip cheeks,
    Are gone, are gone!
    Lovers, make moan.
His eyes were green as leeks.                                                 315
    O Sisters Three,°
    Come, come to me,
With hands as pale as milk;
    Lay them in gore,
    Since you have shore°                                            320
With shears his thread of silk.
    Tongue, not a word.
    Come, trusty sword,
Come, blade, my breast imbrue!°                          [*She stabs herself.*]

---

292. **ass:** (With a pun on *ace.*)  299. **mote:** small particle.  **which . . . which:** whether . . . or.  303. **means:** moans, laments (with a pun on the meaning "lodge a formal complaint"). **videlicet:** to wit.  316. **Sisters Three:** the Fates.  320. **shore:** shorn.  324. **imbrue:** stain with blood.

And farewell, friends.                                             325
Thus Thisbe ends.
Adieu, adieu, adieu.                                    [*She dies.*]
THESEUS:   Moonshine and Lion are left to bury the dead.
DEMETRIUS:   Ay, and Wall too.
BOTTOM [*starting up, as Flute does also*]:   No, I assure you, the wall is down that  330
parted their fathers. Will it please you to see the epilogue, or to hear a
Bergomask dance° between two of our company?

[*The other players enter.*]

THESEUS:   No epilogue, I pray you; for your play needs no excuse. Never
excuse; for when the players are all dead, there need none to be
blamed. Marry, if he that writ it had played Pyramus and hanged him-  335
self in Thisbe's garter, it would have been a fine tragedy; and so it is, truly,
and very notably discharged. But, come, your Bergomask. Let your
epilogue alone.                                         [*A dance.*]
The iron tongue° of midnight hath told° twelve.
Lovers, to bed, 'tis almost fairy time.                            340
I fear we shall outsleep the coming morn
As much as we this night have overwatched.°
This palpable-gross° play hath well beguiled
The heavy° gait of night. Sweet friends, to bed.
A fortnight hold we this solemnity,                                345
In nightly revels and new jollity.                      *Exeunt.*

*Enter Puck [carrying a broom].*

PUCK:
Now the hungry lion roars,
    And the wolf behowls the moon,
Whilst the heavy° plowman snores,
    All with weary task fordone.°                                  350
Now the wasted brands° do glow,
    Whilst the screech owl, screeching loud,
Puts the wretch that lies in woe
    In remembrance of a shroud.
Now it is the time of night                                        355

---

332. **Bergomask dance:** a rustic dance named from Bergamo, a province in the state of Venice.
339. **iron tongue:** i.e., of a bell.  **told:** counted, struck ("tolled").   342. **overwatched:** stayed
up too late.   343. **palpable-gross:** palpably gross, obviously crude.   344. **heavy:** drowsy, dull.
349. **heavy:** tired.   350. **fordone:** exhausted.   351. **wasted brands:** burned-out logs.

That the graves, all gaping wide,
Every one lets forth his sprite,°
    In the church-way paths to glide.
And we fairies, that do run
    By the triple Hecate's° team                               360
From the presence of the sun,
    Following darkness like a dream,
Now are frolic.° Not a mouse
    Shall disturb this hallowed house.
I am sent with broom before,                                   365
To sweep the dust behind° the door.

*Enter [Oberon and Titania,] King and Queen of Fairies, with all their train.*

OBERON:
Through the house give glimmering light,
    By the dead and drowsy fire;
Every elf and fairy sprite
    Hop as light as bird from brier;                           370
And this ditty, after me,
Sing, and dance it trippingly.

TITANIA:
First, rehearse° your song by rote,
To each word a warbling note.
Hand in hand, with fairy grace,                                375
Will we sing, and bless this place.      *[Song and dance.]*

OBERON:
Now, until the break of day,
Through this house each fairy stray.
To the best bride-bed will we,
Which by us shall blessèd be;                                  38o
And the issue there create°
Ever shall be fortunate.
So shall all the couples three
Ever true in loving be;
And the blots of Nature's hand                                 38
Shall not in their issue stand;

---

357. **Every . . . sprite:** every grave lets forth its ghost.    360. **triple Hecate's:** (Hecate ruled in three capacities: as Luna or Cynthia in heaven, as Diana on earth, and as Proserpina in hell.) 363. **frolic:** merry.    366. **behind:** from behind, or else like sweeping the dirt under the carpet. (Robin Goodfellow was a household spirit who helped good housemaids and punished lazy ones, but he could, of course, be mischievous.)    373. **rehearse:** recite.    381. **create:** created.

Never mole, harelip, nor scar,
Nor mark prodigious,° such as are
Despisèd in nativity,
Shall upon their children be.                                             390
With this field dew consecrate,°
Every fairy take his gait,°
And each several° chamber bless,
Through this palace, with sweet peace;
And the owner of it blest                                                  395
Ever shall in safety rest.
Trip away; make no stay;
Meet me all by break of day.          *Exeunt [Oberon, Titania, and train].*

PUCK [*to the audience*]:
   If we shadows have offended,
   Think but this, and all is mended,                          400
   That you have but slumbered here°
   While these visions did appear.
   And this weak and idle theme,
   No more yielding but° a dream,
   Gentles, do not reprehend.                                   405
   If you pardon, we will mend.°
   And, as I am an honest Puck,
   If we have unearnèd luck
   Now to scape the serpent's tongue,°
   We will make amends ere long;                                410
   Else the Puck a liar call.
   So, good night unto you all.
   Give me your hands,° if we be friends,
   And Robin shall restore amends.°                  [*Exit.*]

---

388. **prodigious:** monstrous, unnatural.    391. **consecrate:** consecrated.    392. **take his gait:** go his way.    393. **several:** separate.    401. **That . . . here:** i.e., that it is a "midsummer night's dream."    404. **No . . . but:** yielding no more than.    406. **mend:** improve.    409. **serpent's tongue:** i.e., hissing.    413. **Give . . . hands:** applaud.    414. **restore amends:** give satisfaction in return.

# Textual Notes for
# A Midsummer Night's Dream

Copy text: the First Quarto of 1600. The act and scene divisions are absent from the Quarto; the Folio provides act divisions only.

**Act 1, Scene 1.** 4. wanes: waues. 10. New: now. 19. s.d. *Lysander:* Lysander *and* Helena. 24. **Stand forth, Demetrius:** [printed as s.d. in Q] 26. **Stand forth, Lysander:** [printed as s.d. in Q] 74. **their:** there. 132. Ay: Eigh. 136. low: loue. 187. **Yours would:** Your words. 191. I'd: ile. 216. sweet: sweld. 219. stranger companies: strange companions. 224. s.d. *Exit Hermia:* [after line 223 in Q].

**Act 2, Scene 1.** 1. s.p. [and elsewhere] Puck: *Robin.* 61. s.p. [and elsewhere] Titania: *Qu.* 61. Fairies: Fairy. 79. Aegles: Eagles. 109. thin: chinne 158. the west: west. 183. off: of. 190. slay: stay. slayeth: stayeth. 194. thee: the. 201. not nor: not, not. 206. lose: loose. 246. s.d.: [at line 247 in Q].

**Act 2, Scene 2.** 4. leathern: lethen. 9. s.p. First Fairy: [not in Q; also at line 20] 13. s.p. Chorus: [not in Q; also at line 24] 44. comfort: comfor. 45. Be: Bet. 49. good: god. 53. is: it. 155. ate: eate.

**Act 3, Scene 1.** 52. s.p. Bottom: *Cet.* 60. s.p. Puck: *Ro.* 65. s.p. bottom: *Pyra.* [also at lines 67 and 84] 66. Odors, odors: Odors, odorous. 71. s.p. Puck: *Quin.* 72. s.p. Flute: *Thys.* [also at lines 75 and 83] 124. own: owe. 136–37. Ready . . . go: [assigned to Fairies in Q] 149. s.p. Peaseblossom: *1. Fai.* 150. s.p. Cobweb: *1. Fai.* 151. s.p. Mote: *2. Fair.* 152. s.p. Mustardseed: *3 Fai.* 167. you of: you. 172. s.d. Exeunt: *Exit.*

**Act 3, Scene 2.** s.d. [Q: *Enter King of Fairies, and Robin Goodfellow*] 3. s.d.: [See previous note.] 6–7. love. / Near . . . bower: loue, / Neere . . . bower. 15-16. brake. / When . . . take,: brake, / When . . . take:. 19. mimic: Minnick. 38. s.p. [and elsewhere] Puck: *Rob.* 80. I so: I 85. sleep: slippe. 213. like: life. 215. rend: rent. 220. passionate words: words. 250. prayers: praise. 260. off: of. 299. gentlemen: gentleman. 326. but: hut. 344. s.d. Exit: *Exeunt.* 406. Speak! In some bush?: Speake in some bush. 426. shalt: shat. 451. To your: your.

**Act 4, Scene 1.** 5. s.p. [and elsewhere] Bottom: *Clown.* 17. courtesy: curtsie. 21. marvelous: maruailes. 50. flowerets': flouriets. 60. off: of. 68. o'er: or. 77. five: fine. 78. ho: howe. 112. Seemed: Seeme. 123. this is: this. 133. s.d. Wind . . . up: *they all start vp. Winde hornes.* 167. saw: see. 186. found: fonnd. 194. let us: lets. 200. to expound: expound. 202. a patched: patcht a. 205. ballad: Ballet.

**Act 4, Scene 2.** s.d. [*Snout, and Starveling*]: Thisby *and the rabble.* 3. s.p. Starveling: *Flut.* 5. s.p. Flute: *Thys.* [and at lines 9, 13, 19]. 29. no: not.

**Act 5, Scene 1.** 34. our: Or. 107. s.p. [and elsewhere] Theseus: *Duke.* 121. his: this. 150. s.d. Exeunt: *Exit* [and at line 153 in Q]. 154. Snout: *Flute.* 185. up in thee: now againe. 188. love! thou art my: loue thou art, my. 200. mural down: Moon vsed. 203. s.p. [and elsewhere] Hippolyta: *Dutch.* 208. beasts in, a: beasts, in a. 256. gleams: beames. 293. before: before?. 299. mote: moth. 300. warrant: warnd. 330. s.p. Bottom: *Lyon.* 347. lion: Lyons. 348. behowls: beholds. 395-96. And . . . rest: [these lines are transposed in Q].

# PART TWO

---✦---

## *Contextual Readings*

FIGURE 2 *City and woods. These woodcuts, probably from the late seventeenth century, contrast the worlds of everyday and holiday that are encompassed by* A Midsummer Night's Dream. *City denizens are occupied in the fundamental activities of human society — work and play, conflict and teamwork, digestion and excretion — while the couples in the arboreal domain of an anatomically correct Cupid outside the city enjoy the various stages of courtship. As in* Midsummer Night's Dream, *the two realms are mutually permeable, with elements of the fantastic infiltrating the everyday world in the form of an ass–headed man looming in the doorway of the inn. Ballad woodcuts were primarily decorative, the same woodcut often embellishing many different ballads.*

# CHAPTER I

## *Popular Festivals and Court Celebrations*

───────────────── ✦ ─────────────────

Intoxicated by the holiday ambiance of *A Midsummer Night's Dream,* and enthralled by the preposterous yet all-too-familiar amorous plights of the play's lovers, readers and playgoers may not be aware of the intricate relationship between forms of celebration and the social changes taking place in early modern England, or of the intense controversy surrounding holiday customs. The action of *A Midsummer Night's Dream* is propelled by two celebrations, the popular holiday of Midsummer's Eve, and the elite ceremony of a royal marriage. Each was a significant and resonant occasion for Shakespeare's audience, and the sights, sounds, sentiments, and fantasies associated with these popular and court celebrations are crucial to the play. But these occasions have long vanished from our cultural memory and today most of us have no knowledge of how they looked or what they signified.

As the play begins, Duke Theseus and Hippolyta anticipate a court wedding of pomp, triumph, and reveling (1.1.19), and the young lovers Hermia and Lysander flee into the woods where the popular holiday of May Day is observed (1.1.165–67), evoking the contrast between elite and popular festivity that by the 1590s had become progressively marked. The increasing distinction between popular and elite festivity in early modern England confirmed and strengthened the corresponding hierarchies of ruler and ruled, gentlemen and common people, and men and women, social hierarchies that expedited the formation of the modern family and nation. The following selections on the Maygames enjoyed on Midsummer's Eve and the court entertainments staged in Elizabethan England (in place of the royal wedding that the queen never celebrated) explore the many ways in which traditional and court festivities were understood and the manner in which these cultural practices, and their representations, reflected and shaped the society that produced them.

We might imagine the Maygame as an all-embracing bucolic idyll, part of a shared rural heritage universally enjoyed by all ranks and conditions in a "merry England"; but this communal Maygame, if it ever existed, had certainly vanished by Shakespeare's time. Instead, there were many "Maydays" in the collective imagination, contradictory and associated with specific social interests, which ranged from John Stow's vision of a unifying celebration in *A Survey of London* (1603) to Philip Stubbes's nightmare of destructive license in *The Anatomy of Abuses* (1583). In traditional critical readings of the play, the ending of *A Midsummer Night's Dream* stages the absorption of a human world of conflict into the cyclical eternity of a great creating nature that is part fairyland, part holiday. However, even in Shakespeare's time, May Day as an unchanging festival of national immortality, self-renewing like spring vegetation, was already a fantasy, and the Maygame a contested historical space.

In medieval Europe, largely agrarian and united by a common belief system under the Roman Catholic Church, popular culture *was* the culture (Burke, *Europe* 28), its religious and seasonal festivals celebrated outdoors by the whole community. By the late fourteenth century, however, the continental nobility had begun to withdraw into banquet halls and private gardens and devise their own, more refined entertainments. The festive customs of the continental Renaissance were imported to a culturally backward England — which had been occupied with the dynastic struggles between the Lancaster and York families called the Wars of the Roses — when the Tudor Henry VII (1485–1509), a descendant of both families and the grandfather of Queen Elizabeth, returned from exile in France (Kipling 97–115). Throughout the sixteenth century, the elite fashions in music and dancing were brought up to date by young English gentlemen returning from their "educational" sojourns in Italy (Ascham B2v). In early modern England as on the continent, two separate and socially linked cultures began to take shape — the popular culture of the humble majority that was oral, inherited, and communal, and an elite culture of the wealthy and educated minority that was literate, continental, and exclusive. Both popular and elite cultures, however, included a wide range of practices and were mutually influential, with classical deities infiltrating stage plays and ballads, folk customs included in court entertainments, and outmoded elite fashions passing into popular shows.

Although widely enjoyed in their respective social spheres, both popular customs and courtly diversions were controversial, for nearly all of the most captivating festive practices of post-Reformation England were associated with the Roman Church. New continental fashions were suspect for their origins in Catholic France, Italy, and Spain, and seasonal festivals like May Day and Midsummer's Eve, nominally saints' days, were associated with England's Catholic past. Accordingly, after the break with the Roman Church under Henry VIII (1509–1547), old holiday customs, although they were still practiced, gradually fell from favor during the Protestant reign of his son Edward VI (1547–1553), were revived under his Catholic daughter Queen Mary (1553–1558), and were enjoyed but gradually replaced by state occasions under Queen Elizabeth (1558–1603).

## The Rites of May

Early on Midsummer's day, when Theseus and Hippolyta stumble across the four lovers sleeping in the woods, Theseus observes tactfully, "No doubt they rose up early to observe / The rite of May" (4.1.127–28). In *A Midsummer Night's Dream*, Shakespeare blends elements of two popular holidays, May Day and Midsummer's Eve, which, though six weeks apart, were not distinct occasions as holidays are in our Hallmark times. Instead, Maygames were celebrated throughout the months of May and June, and the two holidays overlapped, encompassing the whole season of warm weather, long days, fertility, and growth. How were the rites of May performed? Since a defining feature of popular culture is the absence of written records, to imagine these practices we must rely on the observations and descriptions of the literate elite. The selections that follow from John Stow's *Survey of London* (1603), Henry Machyn's *Diary of a Resident in London* (1550–1563), and Philip Stubbes's *The Anatomy of Abuses* (1583) present conflicting contemporary pictures of the Maygame, which probably informed the play, and certainly influenced later scholars — John Brand, E. K. Chambers, C. L. Barber, and most recently, Ronald Hutton — whose work has shaped our image of popular festivity in England.

The "bringing home of May" is recorded as early as 1240 (Hutton, *Sun* 226), but the Maygame performed throughout the spring and early summer, believed to have been a hybrid of ancient urban festivals and agricultural celebrations superimposed with the feast days of the Christian calendar, took shape in the fifteenth and sixteenth centuries. May Day, perhaps an offshoot of the Roman Floralia and Celtic vernal festivals, had become the feast of Saints Philip and James, and Midsummer Day, the summer solstice marked in Roman times by a feast of the household gods, was celebrated as the feast day of St. John the Baptist. As Christian celebrations, the holidays retained the imprint of agricultural origins, with spring fertility incarnated in the green-leafed branches carried home from the forest and the floral Maypole erected on the common, and the growth season of long, sunny days honored by the fires and watches of St. John's Eve.

On May Day, the return of spring was celebrated with a collective return to the woods at daybreak to gather branches of sycamore and hawthorn to trim doorways, church, and street, and to collect the Maydew believed to confer eternal beauty. On the village green, a tree or bush was adorned or a flower-decked Maypole set up around which the celebrants joyfully danced. A Puck-like Lord of Misrule (sometimes in the person of Robin Hood, seasonally attired in green or yellow) played tricks on the revelers, a feast sponsored by parish or town was hosted by a Lord and Lady of May, a procession of musicians and morris dancers enlivened the proceedings, and a play might be performed. Since May Day was a fertility feast and therefore a suitable occasion for sexual license, sooner or later young women might return from the woods wearing grass-stained "green gowns."

If May Day celebrated the natural world and the light of day, Midsummer's Eve celebrated the supernatural and the night. Midsummer's Eve was a time of fantasy, magic, and heat-driven madness, when apparitions could be summoned foretelling marriage and death. Monstrous shapes danced by the light of bonfires, sometimes made of bones since the resulting stench was thought to banish evil spirits (Hutton, *England* 38). In London, elaborate torchlight processions wound through the city, with "great and ugly giants marching as if they were alive, and armed at all points, but within . . . stuffed full of brown paper and tow [hemp fibers], which the shrewd boys underpeering [did] guilefully discover and turn to great derision" (Puttenham, *Poesie* 165). Flowers with magical properties like St. John's wort were gathered by young women and carefully arrayed for the purposes of bewitchment or prophecy, and in the woods, couples performing the rites of May might encounter fairies dancing in rounds on green meadows, pinching untidy maids in their sleep, or misleading poor travelers (Nashe, *Terrors of the Night* B2v).

In *A Midsummer Night's Dream*, these vernal festivals are not, of course, pedantically reconstructed point by point, although fairies do dance in

rounds and travelers are misled. Instead, familiar images flicker "momentany as a sound, / Swift as a shadow, short as any dream" (1.1.143–44) and
vanish as soon as they are glimpsed. In the spirit of festive inversion, the play
upends traditional customs: May was the time of female fertility over which
the moon presided, but the play begins with an image of lunar age and
sterility, a "dowager," a "cold fruitless moon" (1.1.5,73). The young lovers Hermia and Lysander set out not *to* the romantic May Day wood but *through* it
to the barren domicile of Lysander's spinster aunt (1.1.157–60). Oberon and
Titania, kindred of the cheerful and sunny Lord and Lady of May, are "ill
met by moonlight" (2.1.60). Bottom is "translated" to a hobbyhorse (3.1.97),
which traditionally accompanied the morris dancers (Figure 3), and Robin
Hood's arrows to Cupid's fiery shafts. The "painted Maypole" that traditionally signified male fertility becomes an epithet of ill-favored femininity
hurled at Helena by an angry Hermia (3.2.296), and the magical Maydew
that made ladies beautiful is replaced by the enchanting fairy juice that
makes Oberon powerful (2.1.166–85). These dream-like fragments of popular holiday practices in *A Midsummer Night's Dream* are not merely festive
play with "antique fables," but evoke the play's "local habitation," a society in
the midst of radical cultural transformation.

In *A Survey of London*, John Stow offers accounts of the Maygame and
the Midsummer Watch that emphasize the merriment, harmony, richness,
and variety of these traditional celebrations in the City of London. Stow's
London is a model of hierarchy and civic rule in which the social conflicts of
his day are reduced to "warlike shows," and holidays are a fantasy of
medieval hospitality that erases the contemporary spectre of dearth with
vigil tables "furnished with sweet bread and good drink, and meats and
drinks plentifully." His vigorous, confident portrait of festive London confirms the image of England as a fruitful commonwealth whose birthright is
concord and order — an image that has endured far longer than the festivals
he described, and informed later notions of English festivity.

Stow's *Survey* participated in the project of national self-definition in
which Elizabethan England was engaged. Detached from the spiritual and
political authority of the Roman Church, England was suddenly free to
consolidate its national identity. Every conceivable aspect of the isle of
England was studied and charted: William Harrison and others (see Chapter 2) analyzed English social structure; Richard Grafton, Edward Hall, and
John Stow wrote and rewrote English history; the English *Book of Common
Prayer* replaced Latin devotions; John Speed mapped the English land,
Michael Drayton celebrated it in *Poly-Olbion* (Figure 4), and English poets
and playwrights created "a kingdom of our own language."

FIGURE 3 *Morris dancers. The "Ancient Window in the House of George Tollet, Esq. at Henley in Staffordshire" shows the customary personages of the pantomime version of the morris dance — a Fool, a piper, a Friar, Maid Marian, St. George mounted on a hobbyhorse, morris dancers with ribbons flying from their arms, and at the center, a Maypole. The appealing vigor of the figures serves to erase the controversy surrounding popular practices like the morris dance, and their symmetrical arrangement in separate panels articulates the framing of popular culture for the delight of the elite.*

In the dedication to the Lord Mayor of London in the 1603 edition, Stow emphasizes his national purpose:

> I have attempted the discovery of London, my native soil and country, at the desire and persuasion of some of my good friends, as well as because I have seen sundry antiquities myself touching that place, as also for that through search of records to other purposes divers written helps are come to my hands, which few others have fortuned to meet withal . . . it is a duty that I willingly owe to my native mother and country, and an office that of right I hold myself bound in love to bestow upon the politic body and members of the same. What London hath been of ancient time men may here see, as what it is now every man doth behold.

FIGURE 4 *Maypole dance. In Michael Drayton's* Poly-Olbion, *traditional festivity is mapped into the English landscape in the form of morris men who dance around a Maypole, framed by feasting countryfolk, a watchful shepherd, and grazing Cotswold sheep.*

Topography and history, two emerging disciplines crucial to the construction of English identity, inform the *Survey*. Ward by ward, Stow "walks" through the city of London, examining its architecture and monuments, describing its social institutions of learning, worship, charity, government, and trade, and praising its sports, pastimes, and royal spectacles. In the course of his perambulations, Stow recounts the history of the city from Roman times, recalling the achievements of its notable citizens and the circumstances of important events as he "passes" the places where they occurred.

Although Stow's nationalist sentiments and reliance upon documentary authority are typical of the early modern era, his omissions in recording what "every man doth behold" reveal his nostalgia for the past, and his desire to preserve it. Profoundly conservative, Stow was dismayed by the destruction and misuse of old monuments since the Reformation and retaliates by neglecting to mention the new ones; distressed by increasing poverty and tumult in the city, he virtually ignores many sites of disorder, including the stage (Kingsford 1: xl–xli). Although Stow clearly specifies that his May Day and Midsummer's Eve are "of old time" and describes them in the past tense, he nevertheless infuses them with a sense of immediacy, as if to keep alive the harmonious holiday customs that (as he admits at the end of both selections) were already a thing of the past.

If Stow's account is a conservative fantasy of "merry England," the flat, eyewitness reports taken from Henry Machyn's diary entries for the months of May and June (1552–61) may more closely approximate the lived reality. Machyn places holiday celebrations within a context of daily life, only one of the many kinds of spectacles — of execution, civic celebration, punishment, royal procession, and mourning — that were staged and observed in public. The social harmony Stow emphasizes is contradicted by Machyn's reports of contention and hostility: servants attempting to poison their masters, a pregnant woman killed in a drive-by shooting, heretics dismembered, consumers and merchants profiting from adulterated food, pickpockets and other urban criminals exercising their trades. More important, the diary entries undermine Stow's festive absolutism by demonstrating that holiday practices, far from being a stable core of Englishness, were provisional and strongly dependent on shifting power relations.

Machyn's diary is filled with descriptions of holiday pageants and (since he was an ardent Catholic) records of important events in the post-Reformation religious struggles. Spanning the reigns of three monarchs, Edward VI, Mary Tudor, and Elizabeth I, the diary disrupts the identification of popular festivity with an unchanging natural order by documenting the fluctuating fortunes of traditional holidays as the nation oscillated from Protestant to Catholic and back again. Under the Protestant Edward VI, Machyn records, civic authorities expressed the pervasive disapproval of the old festivals by ordering the Maypole taken down and broken; during Queen Mary's restoration of Catholicism, however, the Maygame and other holiday pastimes thrived amid the public executions of Protestant martyrs (by whose sympathizers she was called "Bloody Mary"). Unexpectedly, outdoor Maygames and midsummer pageants continued under the Protestant Queen Elizabeth, who, as Machyn attests, not only permitted them but also participated in them, in spite of reformist opposition to the old festivals.

During the course of Elizabeth's long reign, however, traditional religious observances like the Corpus Christi ("Body of Christ") celebration, in which townspeople carried the wafers and wine of the Communion sacrament in a procession through the streets and the trade guilds enacted biblical scenes, were gradually discontinued. They were replaced by national holidays like the Queen's Accession Day, which honored sovereign and state, and civic celebrations like the Lord Mayor's procession (Montrose, *Purpose* 25), which confirmed the power of urban leaders. The transition from religious to secular festivity was not sharply defined, though, and elements of both often coexisted, as in the civic Corpus Christi procession that Machyn records (see p. 104) in which the rites of the Catholic past merged with the customs of the secular, urban future.

Even as the queen graced traditional celebrations and crowds of her subjects apparently enjoyed them, the festivities aroused the censure of many others. The disapproval of strict Protestants was vigorously expressed in a voluminous inventory of pamphlets — John Northbrooke's *A Treatise wherein Dicing, Dancing, Vain Plays and Interludes . . . are Reproved* (1577), Stephen Gosson's *The School of Abuse* (1579), and Stubbes's *Anatomy of Abuses* among them. Better known to us for their condemnation of the stage and its scurrilous dissemblers, these antifestive pamphleteers typically identified the Maypole with the idolatrous Golden Calf, invoked identical biblical reproofs, used the same discourse of infection and monstrosity, and cited similar instances of contemporary depravity and anarchy, all to prove that holiday pastimes were the repository of every vice that impeded the foundation of a godly nation.

If conservatives like Stow envisioned the festivals of the past as a socially beneficial model of harmony, order, and generosity, and a personally salutary celebration of good fellowship and forgiveness, for Puritans like Stubbes, holiday practices shredded the social fabric, substituted pleasure for godliness, and encouraged wickedness. Up to a point, the reformists were correct:

May Day was potentially dangerous. On a designated "independence day," in the relative seclusion of the woods beyond familial and civic control, more than sexual liberties might be taken, and May Day had long been associated with rebellion and youthful violence (Hutton, *England* 89).

Although many Protestant extremists were outraged by the old holiday practices, opposition to festivity was neither consistent nor uniformly observed, for the reformist movement included moderate Anglicans as well as stringent Puritans, and the latter included gentry and merchants as well as craftsmen and the poor. According to the extremists, dancing was "an introduction to whoredom, a preparative to wantonness, a provocative to uncleanness, an entry to all kind of lewdness" (Stubbes, *Anatomy* MSv), but many Protestants, like the earl of Leicester, danced anyway. Most likely, popular holidays inspired a variety of sentiments in addition to pleasure or outrage, including, perhaps, indifference or irritation. However, Stow's nostalgic descriptions and Stubbes's acrimonious ones convey the wide range of attitudes toward holiday pastimes and the social divisions that these attitudes articulated and intensified.

The morris, which Stubbes calls the "devil's dance," was a favored target of antifestive legislation and prosecution, especially when it was performed on Sundays. The morris was believed to be of pagan or Moorish origin (though perhaps actually a court cast-off [Hutton, *Sun* 265]) and was therefore regarded as multiply idolatrous. A staple of seasonal holidays, weddings, and wakes, the dance was usually, but not always, performed by men. Frenetic and raucous, with jerky kicks and jumps ("let us jerk it over the green," says the morris dancer in Anthony Munday's *John a Kent and John a Cumber*, c. 1594), its spirited movements were amplified by jangling bells on the dancer's legs and scarves fluttering from his arms. The morris was, in fact, the epitome of a communal pleasure in unruly physicality that was wholly incompatible with the serene private devotions advocated by the Puritans. But ironically, when the Puritans came to power in 1642, the morris and other "country" dances became fashionable with the erstwhile enemies of holiday (Baskerville 351), and in later centuries, the disruptive, vilified, foreign dance gradually became the "English national dance," emblem of village heritage and cultural unity.

The morris dance took several forms, the best known a pantomime enacted by morris dancer, hobbyhorse, friar, fool, St. George, dragon, minstrel, Robin Hood, and a Maid Marian played by a boy — or for greater mischief, a heavily bearded man (Hutton, *England* 118). Alternately, it might be a great, amorphous procession, like the inebriated revel that Stubbes describes, which disrupted civic order and Sabbath services. The morris was also one of the earliest theatrical dances, performed as a solo to entertain and astonish an audience. Will Kempe, who played Bottom in the first *A Midsummer Night's Dream,* was as well known to his contemporaries as a dancer as he was as a clown; he was even celebrated in a ballad for his skill and verve. After he left the Lord Chamberlain's Men in 1599, not only did he perform a record-breaking morris from London to Norwich, but he immediately published an account of his triumph, modestly titled *Kempe's Nine Days Wonder.* We will probably never know if Kempe danced in *A Midsummer Night's Dream,* either at the conclusion of "Pyramus" (5.1.338) or after the play, but we may speculate that his association with disorderly dancing (emphasized for the obtuse by his hobbyhorse head) added interesting resonances to those first performances of the play.

→ JOHN STOW

# *From* A Survey of London                                                1603

If the modern historian is defined by his use of documentary evidence rather than myth, hearsay, and conjecture, John Stow (1525?–1605), or Stowe (as the name is sometimes spelled), who drew his account of London from civic, parish, and guild records as well as from medieval chronicles, was the city's first modern historian. Born in London into a family of candlemakers, he was apprenticed to a tailor and admitted to the Merchant Taylors' Company in 1547. Although he continued to work as a tailor throughout his life, his true vocation, in spite of little formal education, was history. A prodigious collector of old manuscripts, he produced three influential works on English history — the *Summary of English Chronicles* (1566), *The Chronicles of England* (1580), and the *Annals of England* (1592). The *Survey of London* (1598, 1603) was Stow's final work; though written for his own enjoyment, it became the best known.

John Stow, *A Survey of London. Containing the Original, Antiquity, Increase, Modern estate, and description of that City, written in the year 1598 by John Stow, Citizen of London. Since by the same author increased, with divers rare notes of antiquity, and published in the year 1603* (London: John Windet, 1603) STC 23343. "Sports and Pastimes of Old Time Used in This City," H1v–H2v; and "Of Watches in this City," H3v–H4v.

## *From* SPORTS AND PASTIMES OF OLD TIME USED IN THIS CITY

In the month of May, namely on May Day in the morning, every man, except impediment,[1] would walk into the sweet meadows and green woods, there to rejoice their spirits with the beauty and savor of sweet flowers, and with the harmony of birds, praising God in their kind, and for example hereof, Edward Hall[2] hath noted, that King Henry VIII, as in the third [year] of his reign and divers other years, so namely in the seventh of his reign, on May Day in the morning with Queen Katherine his wife, accompanied with many lords and ladies, rode a-Maying from Greenwich to the high ground of Shooter's Hill, where as they passed by the way they espied a company of tall yeomen,[3] clothed all in green, with green hoods, and with bows and arrows to the number of two hundred. One being their chieftain was called Robin Hood, who requireth the king and his company to stay and see his men shoot; whereunto the king granting, Robin Hood whistled, and all the two hundred archers shot off, loosing all at once; and when he whistled again they likewise shot again, their arrows whistled by craft of the head[4] so that the noise was strange and loud, which greatly delighted the king, queen, and their company. Moreover, this Robin Hood desired the king and queen with their retinue to enter the green wood, where, in arbors made of boughs, and decked with flowers, they were set and served plentifully with venison and wine, by Robin Hood and his [company], to their great contentment, and had other pageants and pastimes as ye may read in my said author.

I find also that in the month of May, the citizens of London of all estates, lightly[5] in every parish, or sometimes two or three parishes joining together, had their several[6] Mayings, and did fetch in Maypoles, with divers warlike shows, with good archers, morris[7] dancers, and other devices, for pastime all the day long, and towards the evening they had stage plays, and bonfires in the streets. . . .These great Mayings and Maygames, made by the governors and masters of this city, with the triumphant setting up of the great shaft[8] (a principal Maypole in Cornhill before[9] the parish church of St. Andrew) therefore called Undershaft,[10] by means of[11] an insurrection of youths against aliens on May Day, 1517, the ninth [year] of Henry VIII, [Maygames]

---

[1] **impediment:** i.e., person with a physical defect or malady.   [2] **Edward Hall:** English chronicler, author of *The Union of the Noble and Illustrious Families of Lancaster and York* (1548), or *Hall's Chronicle.*   [3] **yeomen:** attendants in a noble household; or small landowners who cultivate their own land.   [4] **craft of the head:** arrowheads skillfully made.   [5] **lightly:** commonly.   [6] **several:** separate.   [7] **morris:** a lively dance performed at many seasonal celebrations (see p. 98).   [8] **shaft:** pole, column; Maypole.   [9] **before:** in front of.   [10] **called Undershaft:** the Church of St. Andrew Undershaft.   [11] **by means of:** because of.

have not been as freely used as afore, and therefore I leave them, and will somewhat touch of watches[12] as also of shows in the night.

## From OF WATCHES IN THIS CITY

In the months of June, and July, on the vigils[13] of festival days, and on the same festival days in the evenings after the sun setting, there were usually made bonfires in the streets, every man bestowing wood or labor towards them: the wealthier sort also, before their doors near to the said bonfires, would set out tables on the vigils, furnished with sweet bread, and good drink, and on the festival days with meats[14] and drinks plentifully, whereunto they would invite their neighbors and passengers[15] also to sit, and be merry with them in great familiarity,[16] praising God for his benefits bestowed on them. These were called bonfires as well of good amity among neighbors that being before at controversy,[17] were there, by the labor of others, reconciled, and made of bitter enemies, loving friends; and also for the virtue[18] that a great fire hath to purge the infection of the air. On the vigil of St. John [the] Baptist,[19] and on St. Peter and Paul the Apostles,[20] every man's door being shadowed with green birch, long fennel, St. John's wort, orpin,[21] white lilies, and such like, garnished upon with garlands of beautiful flowers, had also lamps of glass, with oil burning in them all the night; some hung out branches of iron curiously wrought, containing hundreds of lamps alight at once, which made a goodly show. . . . Then had ye besides the standing watches[22] all in bright harness,[23] in every ward and street of this city and suburbs, a marching watch that passed through the principal streets. . . . The whole way ordered for this marching watch extendeth to 3200 tailors yards of assize;[24] for the furniture[25] whereof with lights, there were appointed 700 cressets,[26] 500 of them being found[27] by the companies,[28] the other 200 by the Chamber of London. Besides the which lights, every constable[29] in London, in number more than 240, had his cresset; the charge of every cresset was in light two shillings and four pence, and every cresset had two men, one to bear or hold it, another to bear a bag with light, and to serve it, so that the poor men pertaining to[30] the cressets [were]

---

[12] **watches:** night guard-duty; here, the wakes or revels held on St. John's Eve. [13] **vigils:** the nights preceding festival or holy days. [14] **meats:** food. [15] **passengers:** travelers. [16] **familiarity:** intimacy, friendliness. [17] **controversy:** dispute, contention. [18] **virtue:** power or ability. [19] **the vigil of St. John [the] Baptist:** June 23. [20] **St. Peter and Paul the Apostles:** June 28. [21] **orpin:** a ground cover of the succulent family. [22] **standing watches:** stationary guards. [23] **harness:** armor or military equipment for man and horse; suit of mail. [24] **assize:** regulated measure. [25] **furniture:** supplies, equipment, provision. [26] **cressets:** iron oil-lamps, torches. [27] **found:** provided. [28] **companies:** trade or craft associations of the City of London. [29] **constable:** peace officer. [30] **pertaining to:** concerned with.

taking wages, besides that every one had a straw hat with a badge painted,[31] and his breakfast in the morning, amounted in number to almost 2,000. The marching watch contained in number about 2,000 men, part of them being old soldiers, of skill to be captains, lieutenants, sergeants, corporals, etc., whistlers,[32] drummers, and fifes, standard and ensign bearers, sword players, trumpeters on horseback, demilances[33] on great horses, gunners with hand guns or half hakes,[34] archers in coats of white fustian,[35] signed on the breast and back with the arms[36] of the city, their bows bent in their hands with sheaves of arrows by their sides, pikemen in bright corslets[37] . . . there were also divers pageants[38] [and] morris dancers . . . [The mayor's] henchmen[39] following him, his minstrels before him, and his cresset light passing by him, the waits of the city, the mayor's officers for his guard before him . . . the mayor himself well mounted on horseback, the swordbearer before him in fair armor well mounted also, the mayor's footmen, and the like torch-bearers about him, henchmen twain,[40] upon great stirring[41] horses, following him. The sheriffs' watches came one after another in like order, but not so large in number as the mayor's, for where the mayor had besides his giant[42] three pageants, each of the sheriffs had besides their giants but two pageants, each their morris dance, and one henchman, their officers in jackets of worsted or, say, parti-colored,[43] differing from the mayor's, and from each other, but having harnessed men a great many, etc.

This Midsummer Watch was thus accustomed yearly, time out of mind, until the year 1539, the thirty-first [year] of Henry VIII, in which year, on the eighth of May, a great muster[44] was made by the citizens, at the Mile's End, all in bright harness with coats of white silk, or cloth and chains of gold, in three great battailes,[45] to the number of 15,000, which passed through London to Westminster, and so through the Sanctuary, and round about the park of St. James, and returned home through Holborn. King Henry then considering the great charges[46] of the citizens for the furniture[47] of this unusual muster, forbade the marching watch provided for, at Mid-summer for that year, which being once laid down, was not raised again until the year 1548, the second [year] of Edward VI, Sir John Gresham, then being mayor, who caused the marching watch both on the eve of St. John the Baptist, and of St. Peter the Apostle, to be revived and set forth,

---

[31] **badge painted:** colored emblem.    [32] **whistlers:** pipers.    [33] **demilances:** short lance (bearers).    [34] **hakes:** a short fire-arm used in the sixteenth century.    [35] **fustian:** coarse cloth of cotton or flax.    [36] **arms:** emblem.    [37] **corslets:** body armor.    [38] **pageants:** wagons on which scenes were played in religious cycles and city festivals.    [39] **henchmen:** grooms or squires.    [40] **twain:** both.    [41] **stirring:** lively, energetic.    [42] **giant:** monstrous human figure traditional to spring and summer procession.    [43] **parti-colored:** patches of contrasting color.    [44] **muster:** assembly, display.    [45] **battailes:** battalions.    [46] **charges:** costs.    [47] **furniture:** furnishing, provision.

in as comely order as it hath been accustomed. . . . [S]ince this mayor's time, the like marching watch in this city hath not been used, though some attempts have been made thereunto; as in the year 1585 [when] a book was . . . dedicated to Sir Thomas Pullison, then Lord Mayor, and his brethren the aldermen, containing the manner and order of a marching watch in the city upon the even[ing]s accustomed, in commendation whereof, namely, in times of peace to be used, he hath words to this effect: "The artificers[48] of sundry sorts were thereby well set a-work, none but rich men charged, poor men helped, old soldiers, trumpeters, drummers, fifes, and ensign bearers, with such like men, meet for prince's service kept in ure,[49] wherein the safety and defense of every commonweal consisteth. Armor and weapon being yearly occupied in this wise, the citizens had of their own readily prepared for any need; whereas by intermission[50] hereof, armorers are out of work, soldiers out of pay, weapons overgrown with foulness,[51] [and] few or none good being provided," etc.

[48] **artificers**: craftsmen.   [49] **in ure**: in practice, in operation.   [50] **intermission**: pause, break in continuity.   [51] **foulness**: rust.

→ HENRY MACHYN

## *From* Diary of a Resident in London          *1550–63*

Henry Machyn (1498?-1563?), citizen of London, identifies himself in his diary as a merchant-tailor; apparently, he specialized in supplying funerals and started the diary as a business record. Soon, though, he began to vary descriptions of his funerals with brief reports of the significant or striking events of the day, recounted in flat, detached prose, which for the modern reader seems to confirm their veracity. Nevertheless, Machyn's reliability (or vigilance) as a narrator may certainly be questioned in light of the fact that in 1554, he gives his age as fifty-six, and in 1562, as sixty-six. The manuscript of the diary, which was not printed until the Camden edition in 1848, is in the British Library.

### [1552   REIGN OF KING EDWARD VI][1]

The 26 day of May came into Fenchurch parish a goodly Maypole as you have seen. It was painted white and green, and there the men and women

[1] Editorial changes or additions are bracketed; Camden additions have been subsumed into the text. Roman numerals have been changed to arabic numerals throughout.

Henry Machyn, *Diary of a Resident in London (1550–1563)*, Camden Society, vol. 42 (London, 1848) 20, 88–89, 136–37, 140–41, 196–201, 261.

did wear about their neck baldricks[2] of white and green, [and there was a] giant,[3] [and a] morris dance . . . and the same day the lord mayor by counsel caused it to be taken down and broken. . . .

The 17 day of June there were set on the pillory[4] a man and a woman; the woman bought a piece of mutton and when she had it, she took a piece of tile and thrust it into the midst of the mutton, and she said she had it of[5] the butcher and would have him punished. [But] it was hanged over her head in the pillory, and so there were they set both.

## [1555   REIGN OF QUEEN MARY]

The 17 day of May was buried the Countess of Westmorland[6] at Shoreditch, for there was a goodly hearse with four banners . . . and many mourners . . . and after all was done a great dinner.

The 25 day of May were arraigned at St. Paul's [Cathedral] for heresy, before the Bishop, Master Cardmaker[7] [and] some-time Vicar of St. Bride's [Church] in Fleet Street, and one John Warren a clothworker in Walbrook, and another . . . and cast[8] to be burned, and carried back to Newgate [Prison].

The 29 day of May was a goodly procession of the children of the hospital[9] and of all the schools in London.

The 30 day of May was burned in Smithfield Master Cardmaker and some-time Vicar of St. Bride's and Master Warren, clothworker dwelling against[10] St. John's in Walbrook, an upholsterer, and his wife being in Newgate.

The 27 day of May was the Clerk's procession from Guildhall college,[11] and there was a goodly Mass be heard, and every clerk having a cope[12] and garland[13] with one hundred streamers borne, and the waits[14] playing round Cheap,[15] and so to Ledenhall unto St. Ethelburga Church, and there they put off their gear, and there was the Blessed Sacrament borne[16] with torchlight about, and from thence unto the Barber Hall[17] to dinner.

---

[2] **baldricks:** necklaces, or belts worn diagonally across the shoulder.    [3] **giant:** monstrous figure carried in processions.    [4] **pillory:** punitive device that held criminals by the neck and hands, exposing them to public ridicule and abuse.    [5] **of:** from.    [6] **Countess of Westmorland:** Lady Catherine, wife of Ralph Neville, fourth earl of Westmorland, privy councellor under Henry VIII.    [7] **Master Cardmaker:** John Cardmaker (or Taylor), a friar before the dissolution of the monasteries in the late 1530s, later a married minister and reader at St. Paul's, was arrested and executed for heresy under the Marian restoration. Craftsmen often took the name of their trade as a surname: a cardmaker made implements for combing wool.    [8] **cast:** condemned.    [9] **hospital:** children of Christ's Hospital, an orphanage.    [10] **against:** directly opposite.    [11] **college:** society; meeting place of the society.    [12] **cope:** long cope or cape.    [13] **garland:** wreath of flowers or leaves.    [14] **waits:** band of musicians and singers; wind instruments.    [15] **Cheap:** a ward, or administrative division, of the City of London.    [16] **Blessed Sacrament borne:** on the Feast of Corpus Christi (Body of Christ), the sacrament was carried in a procession around the town.    [17] **Barber Hall:** guild hall of the Barber-Surgeons.

The 26 day of May was a goodly Maygame at Saint Martin's-in-the-Field, with giant and hobbyhorses, with drums and guns and morris dances and with other minstrels.

The 3 day of June came a goodly procession from St. Peter's in Cornhill with the Fishmongers, and my Lord Mayor, with a hundred [men in] copes unto Paul's,[18] and there they offered, with the waits, playing and singing.

The same day was a goodly Maygame at Westminster as has been seen, with giants, morris-pikes,[19] guns and drums, and devils, and three morris dances, and bagpipes and viols,[20] and many disguised, and the Lord and Lady of May rode gorgeously, with [diverse minstrels] playing. . . .

The 10 day of June was delivered out of Newgate seven men to be carried[21] into Essex and Suffolk to be burned.

## [1557]

The 14 day of May was burned in Cheapside and other places in London certain meal that was not sweet; and they said that [the merchant] had put in lime and sand to deceive the people, and he was had to the counter.[22]

The 27 day of May at afternoon was a woman great with child was slain going in Finsbury Field with her husband, with an arrow shot in the neck. . . .

The 22 day of May came out of the Tower . . . six prisoners, one Thomas Stafford,[23] and Captain Sanders, Seywell, and Prowther, and a Frenchman, and one other; were cast five, and so [were] carried to the Tower again through London by land. . . .

The 25 day of May was arraigned at Westminster one, a Frenchman, that was taken at Scarborough when that Thomas Stafford was taken with his adherents, and cast to die, and so carried to the Tower again. The same day was hanged at Tyburn seventeen [people]; one was an old woman of sixty years, the strongest cut-purse[24] a woman that has been heard of, and a lad [also] a cut-purse: for his time he began well.

The 27 day of May, the which was the Ascension Day, the King's and Queen's Grace[25] rode unto Westminster with all the lords and knights

---

[18] **Paul's:** St. Paul's Cathedral.    [19] **morris-pikes:** weapon with a metal head, sometimes hooked, on a long stick; believed to be of Moorish origin.    [20] **viols:** early stringed instruments played with a bow.    [21] **carried:** conveyed by cart or wagon.    [22] **counter:** prison attached to the city court.    [23] **Thomas Stafford:** a rebel of royal descent on both sides of his family, Stafford claimed the succession after Queen Mary, asserting that she had forfeited her rights by marrying a Spaniard. With French aid, he seized Scarborough Castle, but was defeated by militia forces under Henry Neville, fifth earl of Westmorland, and was hanged and quartered.    [24] **cut-purse:** pickpocket.    [25] **King and Queen's Grace:** Queen Mary and her husband, Philip II of Spain.

and gentlemen, and their . . . graces went [in] procession about the cloister, and so they heard Mass.

The 28 day of May, Thomas Stafford was beheaded on Tower Hill, by nine of the clock, Master Wode being his ghostly father;[26] and after there were three more drawn from the Tower and through London into Tyburn, and there they were hanged and quartered; and the morrow after was Master Stafford quartered, and hanged on a [cart], and so [taken] to Newgate to boil. . . .

The 29 day of May was the four heads set upon London Bridge, and their 16 quarters set up, 3 and 2, on every gate of London; the same morning was Thomas Stafford's body quartered.

The 30 day of May was a jolly Maygame in Fenchurch Street, with drums and guns and pikes, and the Nine Worthies[27] did read, and they had speeches every man, and the morris dance . . . and the Sultan and young [Moors] with targets[28] and darts,[29] and the Lord and Lady of May.

## [1559  REIGN OF QUEEN ELIZABETH I]

The 25 day of April was St. Mark's Day, the Queen's Grace[30] supped at Baynard Castle at my Lord Pembroke's place, and after supper the Queen's Grace [was] rowed up and down [the] Thames, and [a] hundred boats about her Grace, with trumpets and drums and flutes and guns, and squibs hurling[31] on high to and fro till ten at night [when] Her Grace departed, and all [along] the water side . . . a thousand people looking on Her Grace.

The first day of May there was two pinnaces[32] was decked with streamers, banners, and flags, and trumpets and drums and guns, going a-Maying, and against[33] the Queen's Palace at Westminster; and there they shot and threw eggs and oranges one against another, and with squibs, and by chance one fell on a bag of gunpowder and set divers men afire, and so the men drew to one side of the pinnace, and it did overwhelm the [boat], and many fell in the Thames, but thank be God, there was but one man drowned, and a hundred boats about here, and the Queen's Grace and her lords and ladies looking out of windows; this was done by nine of the clock on May even[ing] last.

---

[26] **ghostly father:** father confessor.    [27] **Nine Worthies:** familiar personages in civic celebrations, the Nine Worthies were famous persons of antiquity and legend — three Jews (Joshua, David, and Judas Maccabeus), three Gentiles (Hector, Alexander, and Julius Caesar), and three Christians (Arthur, Charlemagne, and Godfrey of Bouillon).    [28] **targets:** light shields.    [29] **darts:** light spears or javelins.    [30] **the Queen's Grace:** i.e., Queen Elizabeth.    [31] **squibs hurling:** fireworks flying.    [32] **pinnace:** a light, two-masted boat.    [33] **against:** opposite.

The 29 day of April at [Downgate Ward] in London, there was a maid dwelling with Master Cottingham, one of the Queen's poulterers;[34] the maid put into a pot of [food] certain poison, and brought them unto her masters and to four of [their] servants, and they did eat them, and as soon as they had eaten them they began to swell and vomit piteously. And there came a good woman [who] caused to be fetched certain dole[35] of salad oil to drink, and thank be to God, they began to mend, and never any one died of it. . . . These two [sic] persons [who] have devilishly given poison to their masters and their household . . . [had their] hands cut off.

The 10 day of May the Parliament was ended, and the Queen's Grace went to the Parliament House.

The 11 day of May, the same fellow and the maid was set on the pillory again, and their other hands cut off for the same offense.

The 12 day of May began the English Service[36] in the Queen's Chapel. . . .

The sixth day of June, St. George's Feast was kept at Windsor, the Earl of Pembroke was the Queen's substitute . . . there was installed at that time the Duke of Norfolk, my lord Marquis of Northhampton, the Earl of Rutland, and my lord Robert Dudley,[37] the Master of the Queen's Horse, new-made Knights of the Garter, and there was great feasting there, and there began the Communion that day and English[38]. . . .

The 24 day of June there was a Maygame . . . with a giant, and drums and guns, and the Nine Worthies, with speeches and a goodly pageant with a queen . . . and divers other, with speeches; and then St. George and the dragon, the morris dance, and after Robin Hood and Little John and Maid Marian and Friar Tuck, and they had speeches round about London.

The 25 day of June, the same Maygame went unto the palace at Greenwich, playing before the Queen and the council.

## [1561]

The 24 day of June was Midsummer Day; at Greenwich was great triumph[39] of the river against the Court. There was a goodly castle made upon

---

[34] **poulterers:** persons in charge of the purchase of poultry and game.     [35] **dole:** portion.     [36] **English Service:** the order of worship of the Anglican Church was formalized in the *Book of Common Prayer* (1549, 1552). To emphasize the break with Rome and the national character of the new religion, worship was conducted in English; the Latin service was briefly restored under Mary, but with the Act of Uniformity (1559), the English rite was reinstated gradually, first in the queen's chapel, then in more public settings.     [37] **Robert Dudley:** later the earl of Leicester.     [38] **Communion that day and English:** the sacrament of the Lord's Supper was called the Mass in the Catholic Church, Holy Communion in the Anglican; Holy Communion was one of the two sacraments recognized in the *Book of Common Prayer*, that is, the "English" service.     [39] **triumph:** public festivity, celebration.

Thames, and men-of-arms within it, with guns and spears for to defend the same, and about it there were certain small pinnaces with . . . great shooting of guns and hurling of balls of wildfire, and there was a bark[40] . . . for the Queen's Grace to [sit] in for to see the pastime, the which was very late ere it was done.

[40] bark: boat.

➜ PHILIP STUBBES

## *From* The Anatomy of Abuses                                    *1583*

Phillip Stubbes (1555?-1593), Puritan pamphleteer, was educated at Cambridge but never graduated, instead passing "seven winters travailing from place to place, even all the land over" in order to "see fashions, acquaint myself with natures, qualities, properties, and conditions of all men" (Furnivall, *Anatomy* 22). His moralistic inclinations were evident from his first publication, a ballad titled "A Fearful and Terrible Example of God's Just Judgment upon a Lewd Fellow Who Usually Accustomed to Swear by God's Blood" (c. 1581). *The Anatomy of Abuses* appeared in 1583 and was a rousing success, with a second edition in the same year, a third in 1584–85, and a fourth in 1595, testifying to the wide appeal (or entertainment value) of Stubbes's views.

### A MORRIS DANCE

[T]hey bedeck themselves with scarves, ribbons, and laces hanged all over with gold rings, precious stones, and other jewels; this done, they tie about either leg twenty or forty bells, with rich handkerchiefs in their hands, and sometimes laid across over their shoulders and necks, borrowed for the most part of[1] their pretty Mopsies and loving Bessies, for bussing[2] them in the dark. Thus all things set in order, then have they their hobby-horses, dragons, and other antiques,[3] together with their bawdy pipers and thundering drummers to strike up the devil's dance

The monstrous attiring of my Lord of Misrule's Men.

The rabble . . . with devil's guard.

[1] of: from.    [2] bussing: kissing.    [3] antiques: pagan figures.

Philip Stubbes, *The Anatomy of Abuses, Containing a Discovery of Vices in a Very Famous Island Called Ailgna* [Stubbes's anagram for England], (London: J. Kingston for R. Jones, 1583) STC 23376. Description of a morris dance and a Maygame from "Lords of Misrule in Ailgna," M2r–v and M3v.

withal.[4] Then march this heathen company towards the Church and Churchyard, their pipers piping, their drummers thundering, their stumps[5] dancing, their bells jingling, their handkerchiefs swinging about their heads like madmen, their hobby-horses and other monsters skirmishing[6] amongst the rout:[7] in this sort, they go to the Church (I say) and into the Church (though the Minister be at prayer or preaching) dancing and swinging their handkerchiefs over their heads, in the Church, like devils incarnate, with such a confused noise, that no man can hear his own voice. Then the foolish people, they look, they stare, they laugh, they fleer,[8] and mount upon forms[9] and pews to see these goodly pageants solemnized in this sort. Then after this, about the Church they go again and again, and so forth into the churchyard, where they have commonly[10] their summer-halls, their bowers, arbors, and banqueting houses set up, wherein they feast, banquet, and dance all that day, and (peradventure)[12] all the night, too. And thus these terrestrial furies spend the Sabbath day.

*The behavior of the Devil's band in the temple of God.*

*Receptacles[11] in the cemeteries or churchyards for the devil's agents.*

## The Fruits of Maygames

Against[13] May[day], Whitsunday,[14] or other time, all the young men and maids, old men and wives, run gadding over night to the woods, groves, hills, and mountains, where they spend all the night in pleasant pastimes, and in the morning they return, bringing with them birch and branches of trees, to deck their assemblies withal, and no marvel, for there is a great Lord present among them, as superintendent and lord over their pastimes and sports, namely Satan, Prince of Hell. But the chiefest jewel they bring from thence is their Maypole, which they bring home with great veneration, as thus. They have twenty or forty yoke of oxen, every ox having a sweet nosegay of flowers placed on the tip of his horns, and these oxen draw home this Maypole (this stinking idol, rather)

*The order of their Maygames.*

*A great Lord present in Maygames, as superintendent thereof.*

---

[4] **withal:** with them. [5] **stumps:** legs. [6] **skirmishing:** colliding. [7] **rout:** confusion. [8] **fleer:** jest rudely. [9] **forms:** blocks. [10] **commonly:** usually; together. [11] **Receptacles:** places, spaces. [12] **peradventure:** sometimes (always). [13] **Against:** approaching. [14] **Whitsunday:** Pentecost, the seventh Sunday after Easter.

which is covered all over with flowers, and herbs bound round about with strings from the top to the bottom, and sometimes painted with variable colors, with two or three hundred men, women, and children following it with great devotion. And thus being reared up with handkerchiefs and flags hovering on the top, they straw[15] the ground round about, bind green boughs about it, set up summer halls, bowers, and arbors hard by it, and then they fall to dance about it like as the heathen people did at the dedication of the idols, whereof this is a perfect pattern, or rather the thing itself. I have heard it credibly reported . . . by men of great gravity and reputation, that of forty, threescore, or a hundred maids going to the wood over night, there have scarcely the third part of them returned home again undefiled. These be the fruits which these cursed pastimes bring forth.

*The manner of bringing their Maypoles.*

*Maypoles a pattern of the heathen idols.*

*The fruit of Maygames.*

[15] **straw:** put down a layer of straw.

## The Ballad

The broadside ballad, like the public playhouse, was enjoyed by the full spectrum of English society, and the category of "ballad" encompassed both traditional songs of unknown authorship and lyric poems by distinguished writers. Ballads might be romantic, religious, satirical, or topical; their audiences were rural, urban, or both; their subjects ranged from the general (courtship, faithless lovers, defiant wives) to the particular (the Armada victory), from the myths of Robin Hood and King Arthur to historical events like the execution of Essex; they celebrated seasonal, national, and religious occasions and warned against fornication or overeating.

Broadside ballads were so called because they were printed on one side of a sheet of coarse paper, or "broadside"; the ballads were illustrated with woodcuts that might or might not be relevant to the ballad's topic, and, since knowledge of familiar tunes was assumed, the title of a similar song was often substituted for musical notation. Broadsides sold at two or three for a penny (the cost of the cheapest admission to the public theater), and so were available to apprentices, artisans, and people of modest means. Posted in taverns and shops, they could even be enjoyed *gratis,* and when they were sung in the streets, the illiterate could learn them as well. However, their audience was not restricted to the poor or uneducated: the same ballad that was sung in the street or in an alehouse might also be played by minstrels in the country houses of the nobility or in the court of the monarch. Both song and poem, the ballad spanned the imprecise boundary between oral and print cultures, medieval and modern customs, village and city life — a paradigm of a society in transition.

## ⤳ The Fetching Home of May

Traditional songs are often difficult to date with accuracy; however, the publisher of this ballad, of which there is only one copy extant, flourished in and after 1635 (Chappell 3: 311), so it may postdate *A Midsummer Night's Dream.* Like the play, "The Fetching Home of May" is a mingling of popular and elite elements in a nominally popular form: the rites of May celebrated by English youth are framed and ratified by the kindred actions of classical figures, and the English procession into the woods is transformed into a classical "love-chase" spiced with intimations of metamorphosis and monstrosity. Spring's rampant fertility, demonstrated in *A Midsummer Night's Dream* in the oscillating pairings of Theseus with Hippolyta (and the past liaisons of Theseus with Ariadne, and Hippolyta with Oberon), of Oberon with Titania (Oberon with Phillida, and Titania with Theseus), of Titania with Bottom, of Hermia with Lysander (and also Demetrius), and of Helena with Demetrius (and also Lysander), is rendered in the ballad by the impetuous couplings of the ballad's many Jacks and Jills.

Unlike *A Midsummer Night's Dream*, which insists on maidenly chastity, the ballad explicitly recognizes that May Day is first and last about female sexuality — that each lass *strives* to have a green gown. May was the month of female fecundity, May Day a fertility feast, and the "green gowns" acquired by the maidens as they plummeted onto the grass with their lovers were legend. In Thomas Nashe's *Summer's Last Will and Testament,* Spring ranks the sports that are proper to the season as "giving wenches green gowns, making garlands for fencers, and tricking up children gay" (235–38). Of course, it was always possible for green gowns to be acquired during harmless activities like picnicking.

In *A Midsummer Night's Dream*, no one gets her gown green (except possibly Titania, offstage): "gentle friend, for love and courtesy / Lie further off, in human modesty," Hermia entreats Lysander (2.2.62–63), and later the exhausted Demetrius lies down alone "on this cold bed" (3.2.429). Female sexuality is dramatically safeguarded as well as generically regulated in *A Midsummer Night's Dream*, which concludes with multiple marriages and with Titania's rehabilitation. In contrast, the ballad both acknowledges and celebrates female sexuality, conclusively revealing the activities of the revelers by associating them with

---

"The Fetching Home of May, or, A Pretty new Ditty wherein is made known, / How each lass doth strive to have a green gown," in *The Roxburghe Ballads,* vol. 3, part 1, edited and with notes by William Chappell (Hertford: Stephen Austin and Sons, 1875) 312–17.

FIGURE 5 *The woodcut accompanying the ballad "The Crost Couple, Or a Good Misfortune" shows a couple in late seventeenth-century dress reclining vigorously on the grass under the watchful eyes of a speechless Cupid and the monitory surveillance of a concerned tree and demonstrates one way in which a girl might acquire a "green gown."*

"Dame Venus [who] did burn in desire" (2.67). However, neither the lusty Venus nor the green-gowned maidens are ever censured or reformed: Venus's wronged husband Vulcan ignores his disheveled wife and glares at her lover instead, and the ballad singer simply winks at the maidens — "from Cupid few are free." In *A Midsummer Night's Dream*, female desire is contained in universal wedlock, but in the ballad, desire remains unfettered by matrimony or even moral injunction, championing the resistance, which the play has only intimated (Montrose *Purpose* 117), to the dominant ideology of marriage.

## *"The Fetching Home of May"*

### *To the Tune of "Room for Company"*

Now Pan leaves piping,
The gods have done feasting,
    There's never a goddess a hunting today:
Mortals do marvel at Coridon's jesting,
    That lends them assisting to entertain May.
The lads and the lasses,
With scarves on their faces,

So lively it passes,
   Trip over the downs:
Much mirth and sport they make,                10
Running at Barley-break:[1]
Good lack! what pains they take
   For their green gowns.

Fine John and Gillian,
Henry with Frances,                      15
   Meg with Mary, and Robin with Will:
George and Margery set all the dances,
   For they were reported to have the best skill.
Cicely and Nannie,
The fairest of many,                  20
That came last of any
   From out of the town,
Quickly got in among
The midst of the throng,
Thus they did so much long          25
   For the green gown.

Blanch and Beatrice,
Both of a family,
   Came very lazily, lagging behind:
Annise and Annabel noted their policy,[2]
   Cupid is cunning although he be blind.     30
Winny the witty,
That came from the city,
With Parnell the pretty,
   And Bessie the brown,          35
Clem, Joan and Isabell
Sue, Alice and bonny Nell,
Liked of their journeys well
   For the green gown.

But wanton Deborah                40
Whispered to Dorothy,
   That she should wink upon Richard and Sim;
Now mincing Maudlin showed her authority,

[1] **Barley-break:** an old country game played in couples combining features of "tag" and "Red Rover." [2] **policy:** strategy.

And in the quarrel did venture a limb.[3]
Sibyl was sickly,                                                   45
And could not come quickly,
And therefore was likely
    To fall in a swoon.
There was none would tarry
For Hugh or for Harry,                                              50
Lest Christian should carry
    Away the green gown.

Thus all the youngsters
Had reached the green meadows
    Where they appointed to gather their May;                       55
Some in the sunshine, and some in the shadows,
    Singled in couples did fall to their play:
Constant Penelope,
Faith, Hope and Charity,
Looked very modestly,                                               60
    Yet they sat down;
Prudence prevented
What Rachel repented
And Kate was contented
    To take the green gown.                                         65

*The Second Part.*
*to the same tune*

This Maying so pleased
Most of the fine lasses,
    That they much desired to fetch in May flowers,
For to strew the windows and such like places,
Besides they'll have May bows, fit for shady bowers.               5
    But most of all they go
To find where Love doth grow,
Each young man knows 'tis so,
    Else he's a clown:
For 'tis an old saying,                                            10
"There is a great joying,
When maids go a Maying,"
    They'll have a green gown.

---

[3] **venture a limb:** take a risk.

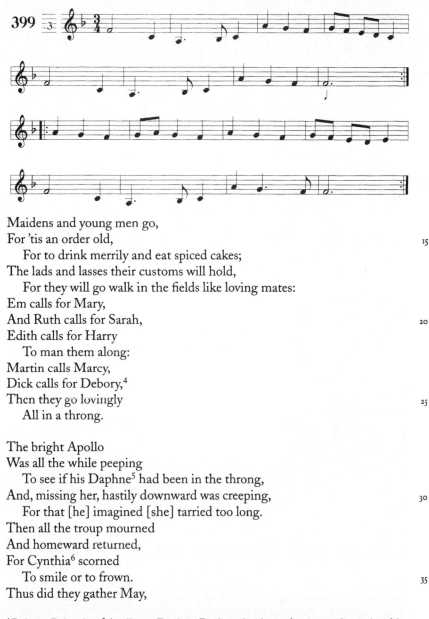

Maidens and young men go,
For 'tis an order old,                                          15
    For to drink merrily and eat spiced cakes;
The lads and lasses their customs will hold,
    For they will go walk in the fields like loving mates:
Em calls for Mary,
And Ruth calls for Sarah,                                       20
Edith calls for Harry
    To man them along:
Martin calls Marcy,
Dick calls for Debory,[4]
Then they go lovingly                                           25
    All in a throng.

The bright Apollo
Was all the while peeping
    To see if his Daphne[5] had been in the throng,
And, missing her, hastily downward was creeping,               30
    For that [he] imagined [she] tarried too long.
Then all the troup mourned
And homeward returned,
For Cynthia[6] scorned
    To smile or to frown.                                       35
Thus did they gather May,

---

[4] **Debory:** Deborah.   [5] **Apollo . . . Daphne:** Daphne, daughter of a river god, was loved by Apollo and Leucippus. Leucippus followed her disguised as a woman and was discovered and slain by the nymphs. Apollo continued to pursue her, and finally, at her request, changed her into a bay tree.   [6] **Cynthia:** Diana; also, the moon.

All the long summer's day,
And went at night away,
    With a green gown.

Bright Venus still glisters,                                              40
Out-shining of Luna;
    Saturn[7] was present, as right did require;
And he called Jupiter with his Queen Juno,
    To see how Dame Venus did burn in desire:
Now Jove sent Mercury[8]                                                  45
To Vulcan[9] hastily,
Because he should descry[10]
    Dame Venus[11] down:
Vulcan came running,
On Mars he stood frowning,                                               50
Yet for all his cunning,
    Venus had a green gown.

Cupid shoots arrows
At Venus her darlings
    For they are nearest unto him by kind:[12]                           55
Diana he hits not, nor can he pierce worldings,
    For they have strong armor his darts to defend:
The one hath chastity,
And Cupid doth defy;[13]
The other's cruelty                                                      60
    Makes him a clown.
But leaving this, I see,
From Cupid few are free,
And there's much courtesy[14]
    In a green gown.

FINIS[15]

Printed at London for J. Wright junior, dwelling at the upper end of the Old Bailey.[16]

---

[7] **Saturn:** Roman god of agriculture, early king of Rome, his reign was regarded as the age of gold.   [8] **Mercury:** messenger of the gods, analogous to the Greek Hermes.   [9] **Vulcan:** Roman god of fire and patron of blacksmiths.   [10] **descry:** discover; announce.   [11] **Venus:** Roman goddess of love, analogous to the Greek Aphrodite, who betrayed her husband Vulcan (Hephaestos) with Mars (Aries).   [12] **kind:** birth; inclination.   [13] **defy:** repudiate.   [14] **courtesy:** ceremony; nobility.   [15] **FINIS:** THE END.   [16] **Old Bailey:** the criminal court in London.

## Court Entertainments

While festive enchantment and romance suffuse *A Midsummer Night's Dream,* the play is not only a holiday escape from the daily world of work and rank; after all, a royal marriage such as that of Theseus and Hippolyta was usually impelled less by romance and more by a practical concern for the consolidation of power and property. But in Elizabethan England, the royal marriage had never occurred, and its absence had hovered over the queen and her subjects for most of her reign. By the mid-1590s, Queen Elizabeth I (1533–1603) was long past marriageable age; she had not married and had not therefore borne an heir who would free England from another succession crisis — though parliament had insistently pressed for it and diplomats had made many attempts to arrange it. Therefore, the play's royal marriage of Theseus, which the mechanicals celebrate and for which the fairy king promises flawless heirs (5.1.385–90), was perhaps a wishful refashioning of a troubling national experience.

Instead of celebrating a wedding, and the ensuing ceremonies of a woman's married life like baptisms and churchings (the ritual of thanksgiving after childbirth), the queen remained a single woman throughout her life, surrounded by her ladies in waiting, wooed by striving courtiers, and honored by entertainments such as those at the aristocratic country estates of Kenilworth (1575) and Elvetham (1591) that celebrated her singularity. If May and June were the season of popular holiday, high summer was the season of the royal progress. The summer progress was a kind of Maying writ large, when the queen and her court sojourned to the countryside, stopping at one estate or another for recreation and entertainment. The progress placed the queen, actually and imaginatively, at the center of the national landscape; the entertainments presented to her both celebrated her reign and defused the ideological challenge that a woman ruler posed in an era that proclaimed absolute masculine dominance; and the popular shows incorporated within these entertainments staged the relations between elite and common folk that informed *A Midsummer Night's Dream* and structured the society.

In theory, hosting the queen on her summer progresses was an exquisite honor, and ambitious men welcomed this royal favor. But while some sought the honor of entertaining the queen — those eager to compete for royal benevolence and to enhance their reputations with a spectacle of courtly display — it was by no means a universal aspiration. Sheltering the queen and her household of courtiers, retainers, servants, horses, vehicles, and trunks was an appalling expense; simply feeding everyone was a monumental undertaking. One requisition for the royal household included a hundred veals, fifty lambs, sixteen dozen capons, ten dozen hens, five dozen geese, and one hundred dozen chickens. To a few, a royal visit was a dreaded inconvenience: knowing that a visit "shall be a great trouble and hindrance," Anthony Wingfield, one of the queen's ushers, assured his friend Sir William More that he had warned the Lord Chamberlain "what few small rooms and how unmeet your house was for the Queen's Majesty" and advised More himself to emphasize the discomfort and ignominy of his estate. This strategy of deprecation worked for the season, but, alas, a few years later, Sir William was again alerted to expect a visit from Her Majesty, instructed to make his house "sweet and meet," and send his family away to make room for her entourage (Wingfield 265–66).

Though the festivities at Kenilworth and Elvetham have been credited with inspiring the play's images of mermaid, dolphin, fireworks, and dancing fairy queen (Brooks lxviii), the connections between private parties at Kenilworth in 1575 and Elvetham in 1591 and representations on the public stage in 1595 may seem tenuous. However, the diversions presented to the queen by her courtier-hosts were not, in fact, such private affairs. Since power and reputation depended on monarchical proximity and favor, which lavishly entertaining the queen affirmed, it was in the interest of the host and others involved to ensure that their success was well publicized — and indeed, accounts of the revels at both Kenilworth and Elvetham were printed soon after they occurred. Moreover, many outside the courtly circle experienced or knew about these summer entertainments, including the players who performed in them and the functionaries, servants, and country folk who supplied comestibles and services. The festivities thus were part of the heritage of the many Londoners who, like Shakespeare, had provincial roots.

The links between Kenilworth and the London playhouse, in fact, are striking. In 1575, Shakespeare was a boy living nearby in Stratford and may have heard tales of the lavish entertainments at Kenilworth or seen the religious plays presented by the craft guilds at the nearby town of Coventry. Additionally, when the Earl of Leicester's Men, a company of professional players, performed at Kenilworth in 1575, their numbers probably included James Burbage, father of Richard Burbage (Montrose, *Purpose* 183–84) who first played Hamlet, Richard III, and other leading Shakespearean roles. The entertainments at Kenilworth may well have become part of the players' oral history, preserved and handed down in the old-timers' lore of the playhouse. However, as fragments of courtly practices and old representations were reproduced on the public stage in *A Midsummer Night's Dream*, they were transformed by the interests of players and spectators of a variety of origins and ranks — law students, wealthy merchants, ambitious mechanicals, wives and servants, illiterate laborers, petty criminals — all with conflicting attitudes towards the elite customs that subordinated them or allowed them to rise.

## KENILWORTH AND COVENTRY

The entertainments at Kenilworth described in Robert Laneham's *Letter* (1575) mark the rise of a national, festive focus on the queen (Montrose, *Purpose* 182–84), the finale of the local, amateur tradition of playing, and the formal staging of popular culture for elite amusement. Throughout the Elizabethan era, as state and civic occasions that glorified the body politic replaced local, religious festivals that celebrated the Body of Christ, the Virgin Queen replaced the Virgin Mary as an object of veneration (Montrose, "Eliza" 43–45). Among the traditional observances gradually suppressed after the Reformation were the religious cycle plays like the Coventry Corpus Christi, which had its final performance in 1579, four years after the queen's visit to Kenilworth. Likewise, amateur plays like Hock Tuesday, which commemorated a local event — the defeat of the Danish invaders in the eleventh century — were replaced by London stagings of recent English history that exalted the rise of the Tudors.

Kenilworth stands as a paradigm of the rewards and demands of courtiership under a female ruler. In early modern ideology, the woman was the "weaker vessel" whose deficiencies demanded that she be ruled by men. Women could not (until widowed) hold property, which traditionally passed from man to man, either from father to first son or from king to lord. However, during Elizabeth's reign, all men were ruled by one woman who controlled property and titles; and since the era of the warrior had given way to the era of the courtier and the bureaucrat, men no longer won honors with brave deeds in battle, but by behaving correctly and delighting the queen.

The country estate was a nexus of the intricate new economic and political exchanges between monarch and subject, exchanges that were much more complex than the feudal relationship of ruler and lord. Unlike the imaginary wood of *A Midsummer Night's Dream*, an uncultivated no-man's-land, the estate was private property. But much of this private property was under the control of the Crown, which had acquired vast tracts of land and habitable structures with the dissolution of the monasteries in the late 1530s. Crown property might be awarded for loyalty or service, and ultimately, the "new men" resided there at the pleasure of the monarch and without the established claim enjoyed by the old aristocracies. Moreover, unlike the medieval castle, the estates were vulnerable to force, for they were not fortified for defense but designed for courtly leisure (Berry 88) and the monarch's pleasure.

The queen's host at Kenilworth, Robert Dudley, earl of Leicester, was, like his estate, somewhat vulnerable. Long a "favorite" of the queen, he began his rise with his installation as Master of the Horse (noted by Machyn, see p. 107), and came to full flower in 1566 when the queen awarded him the estate of Kenilworth and his title. But by 1575, Leicester was being replaced in the queen's affections by another courtier and was secretly embroiled in an amorous liaison that if publicized would certainly displease the monarch. Seeking to secure himself in the queen's good graces, as well as to enhance his political power as a Protestant leader, Leicester, who as Master of the Horse organized the queen's summer progresses, scheduled an opportune visit to Kenilworth. Here, she might be reminded of happy old times and be assured with a lavish display of gratitude and hospitality of his enduring loyalty. How fitting it was that the estate she had given him became a kind of stage (Smith, "Landscape" 60–61) on which Leicester's devoted subjection might be enacted on a grand scale.

To entertain the queen at Kenilworth, Leicester offered three kinds of pastimes: literary masques, aristocratic hunts, and popular shows (Kuin 7). The masques, written by George Gascoigne and printed in 1576, were performed by the professional players. Unfortunately, they were apparently the first diversions to fall to weather or overbooking: "Unto this banquet there was appointed a masque, for riches of array, of an incredible cost: but the time so far spent and very late in the night now, was cause that it came not forth to the show" (see p. 134) — providing a convenient precedent for their omission in this volume. Instead, our selections focus on the setting itself, the "chase" (a favorite gentlemanly pastime particularly enjoyed by the queen), and the diversions presented by the common people, the "solemn bride-ale" and the Coventry play.

On the summer progress, the riches of the courtier — the "natural grace" of Kenilworth described in the first section of Laneham's letter, and the "great art, cost, and diligence" (see p. 128) with which it was decorated — were placed on display for the queen as she, in turn, displayed herself to her people as beloved supervisor. The welcoming ceremonies with music, fireworks, and elaborate speeches which honored the queen at Kenilworth were marked, like *A Midsummer Night's Dream*, by an intermingling of popular and courtly elements, with classical sibyls greeting the queen in "English rhyme and meter" before the Lady of the Lake of Arthurian legend conveyed her to the estate. The cultural eclecticism of the spectacles focused on

FIGURE 6  *Queen Elizabeth on a hunt. An engraving in Turberville's* The Book of Falconry *represents the queen as a Diana, goddess of the hunt, a role she played at Kenilworth.*

the queen both affirmed her cultural dominance and revealed the need for a unifying myth in a nation of increasing cultural disparity.

The "chase" was the paramount activity of the Kenilworth entertainments (Berry 96). The queen loved to hunt and was often likened to the chaste huntress Diana, who personified a militant virginity (Montrose, *Purpose* 168). The figure of Diana was but one facet of the "cult of Elizabeth" (Berry 63), the collection of imaginative identities with which the queen was endowed in an attempt to manage the power differential between her female status as virgin and her political function of prince. ("Prince" was the queen's favored term for "ruler," and perhaps it was no accident that she chose a word so redolent of the strategies of modern statecraft set forth in Machiavelli's *The Prince*.) The goddess Diana was one of the more virile identities associated with the queen; both excelled at manly skills and possessed life-and-death power over men (according to myth, Diana transformed the impertinent Acteon into a stag that was hunted and killed by his own dogs). Although in other entertainments, as at Elvetham, the queen's radiant femininity was complimented with a masque of a fairy queen and her ladies, at Kenilworth, Leicester sought to enhance his own power by honoring the queen's masculine strength.

During her stay, Leicester provided several occasions for the queen to demonstrate her gentlemanly skills in the chase, and explicit tributes to her strength and courage were incorporated into the entertainments. As the queen returns on the evening of the first chase, out of the woods jumps an incarnation of the primitive wild man, the *"Hombre Salvagio,"* the paradigm of savage masculine virility "forgrown all in moss and ivy" and carrying an uprooted oak. In a gesture of "submission" to the queen, this Savage "broke his tree asunder," a well-intentioned gesture that causes her horse to start, providing the queen with an opportunity to display a regal composure, and Laneham with what he calls the best part of the play (see p. 130). The Coventry Men, too, compliment the queen's martial mastery when, requesting permission to perform their play, they suggest that its display of female bravery and patriotism (perhaps enacted by the women of Coventry themselves [Fletcher 264]) might especially please her.

Hunting for sport as conducted at Kenilworth was an important practice of gentlemanly self-fashioning, one that displayed breeding, wealth, and social mastery and separated the landed elite from the subsistence poacher. George Gascoigne, who wrote the masques for Kenilworth, also composed a prefatory "Commendation" for George Turberville's *Noble Art of Venery, or Hunting* (1575), one of a thriving genre of instructional works on gentlemanly refinements. The "Commendation" praises hunting as a social stratifier, "A sport for noble peers, a sport for gentle bloods, / The pain I leave for servants such as beat the bushy woods." The basis of the gentleman's physical fitness program, hunting was supposed to teach manly courage and prepare the hunter for the hardships of war (Fletcher 132–34). Advocates of the sport emphasized the skill involved, though as Laneham observes (see p. 127–28), the wild wood was well supplied with game ahead of time, preparations that almost ensured a kill — something to remember during the "love chase" of *A Midsummer Night's Dream.*

In *A Midsummer Night's Dream,* the hunt never happens, but references to hunting articulate the mixture of scorn and admiration that elite practices evoked in city dwellers. In the play, hunting serves both as an object of mockery and as a means by which elite ideals are ratified. The sport that affirmed the martial and moral nobility of the gentleman is reduced to the hormone-driven love-chase of the four young Athenians. The hunting hounds "bred out of the Spartan kind" (4.1.114) of which Theseus is so proud are "[s]low in pursuit, but matched in mouth like bells" (118), perhaps, like the aristocracy itself, overbred for aesthetics at the expense of function. But these jokes on the elite are double-edged, for the play also confirms the social hierarchies inherent in the sport. The love-chase ends with women silent and subdued; and most poignantly, it is Hippolyta's memories of her former hunting days (4.1.107–13) that emphasize her present subjection. In sharp contrast with the Virgin Queen, Hippolyta, like a good post-Reformation wife, distances herself from the Amazonian life of war and agency by placing manly activities firmly in the past tense.

At Kenilworth, the Hock Tuesday play performed by the local artisans and the "solemn bride-ale" that precedes it are, like the mechanicals' "Pyramus and Thisbe" in *A Midsummer Night's Dream,* rustic shows enclosed in an elite entertainment for the amusement of courtly spectators. In comparison with the Maying of Henry VIII described by Stow (see p. 100), both the Kenilworth entertainment and Shakespeare's play witness a distinct change in the way in which popular practices are incorporated into elite shows. In the Henrician Maygame the royals and the archers share the same world, the courtiers conversing with Robin Hood and his men and admiring the archers' displays of skill. However, at Kenilworth and in *A Midsummer Night's Dream,* a barrier is raised between the elite and the common people as the rustics are placed on display as a courtly diversion (Montrose, *Purpose* 183) and regarded with detachment and mirth.

The Athenians' responses to the mechanicals' play and Laneham's representation of the country wedding emphasize the difference between gentlemen and common people and the superiority of the former, by ridiculing the attempts of common folk to imitate their betters. During "Pyramus," the Athenians of *A Midsummer Night's Dream* entertain each other with displays of wit at the mechanicals' expense: "This is the silliest stuff that ever I heard," remarks Hippolyta (5.1.204), "I am aweary of this moon. Would he would change" (238). But their jokes are mild compared to Laneham's mockery of the wedding party in which the young men are half-dressed, village girls simper like "a mare cropping a thistle," the bride is compared to a sluttish old nag, the bridecup swarms with flies, and sexually excited horses thwart the village boys as they attempt a gallant tilt.

Laneham's Coventry Men, in contrast, are shown to be quite clever — not surprising since Laneham, as a member of the Mercers' Company, was a guildsman too. In fact, guildsmen, particularly in a mercantile town like Coventry, were usually men of power and status (Davidson 87), more like the erudite and versatile Captain Cox described by Laneham than Bottom and the mechanicals, and their dramatic offerings were displays of power, not spectacles of incompetence. In requesting permission to perform their play, the Coventry Men adroitly appeal to the full range of contemporary political, religious, local, and personal interests. They invoke tradition: the play was "wont to be played in our city yearly . . . had an ancient beginning and a long continuance, till now of late laid down" (see p. 132). They appeal to the new nationalism: their "old storial show" enacts the battle during which "the Danes . . . were all dispatched, and the realm rid" (see p. 131–32). They flatter the queen's persona of chaste warrior: "the matter mentioneth how valiantly our English women for love of their country behaved themselves." They appease potential Protestant opposition: unlike the old religious plays, theirs is "without ill example of manners, papistry, or any superstition." And, most important, they defer to power, making a "humble petition unto Her Highness, that they might have their plays up again" (see p. 132).

The sophistication of the Coventry Men, however, is not equalled by the mechanicals in *A Midsummer Night's Dream,* their ostensible counterparts. Instead, the mechanicals are childish, theatrically naive, pathetically fearful of giving offense, and nearly as inept as Laneham's bumbling villagers. This portrayal might seem puzzling, since most players, like Shakespeare himself, were of artisan origins. However, just as the awkwardness of the country folk sets off the elegance of the landed courtier in Laneham's letter, the mechanicals' clumsy theatrics emphasize the smooth expertise of the professional players who perform *A Midsummer Night's Dream.* Both Laneham's letter and *A Midsummer Night's Dream* reinforce social hierarchies by reproducing the elite disparagement of the common, but Laneham supports the old landed elite and craft guilds, while Shakespeare's play supports the new professional elite — like his own company — whose property was the representations that earned them a living. And even as *A Midsummer Night's Dream* reinforced social hierarchies it also subverted them, since the players who represented the elite so convincingly were mechanicals themselves.

Many plays of Shakespeare's time show players playing for an onstage audience, but *A Midsummer Night's Dream* is unusual in showing the process of staging from beginning to end. The mechanicals' subplot affords a unique view of theatrical production from backstage: the players are (mis)cast in "Pyramus and Thisbe" (1.2), rehearse and rewrite the script to excise elements that "will never please" (3.1.9), dress for performance and plan to abstain from garlic (4.2), and perform (5.1). Although the result of the mechanicals' efforts is endearingly comic and patently inferior to the refined impersonations of the professionals, the essential elements of the profession are present in embryonic form, including organization ("call forth your actors by the scroll," 1.2.12), a passion for playing ("An I may hide my face, let me play Thisbe too," 41), versatility ("Let me play the lion too," 56), a wardrobe of disguises (72–74), theatrical illusions ("if we meet in the city, we shall be dogged with company, and our devices known," 79–81), and diligence ("rehearse your parts," 3.1.57).

The Coventry records afford another backstage glimpse, one that is less amusing but equally revealing, into the amateur artisan tradition. The records deal primarily with the expenditures of several craft guilds for wages and materials for the Hock Tuesday play performed at Kenilworth, with the Cappers' payment records for the revival of 1576 merging into the "charges of the pageant" that was presumably the Corpus Christi, since the records mention the traditional personages of the medieval religious play — spirits, Marys, bishops, a devil, and a Pilate. The Coventry records offer evidence of a playing tradition of dedication and competence, and a serious dramatic association characterized by formal rehearsals, a system of compensation, close attention to the visual details of presentation, and careful maintenance of equipment, costumes, and properties — an organization with surprising similarities to that of the mechanicals.

→ ROBERT LANEHAM

## *From* A Letter Describing the Entertainment of the Queen at Kenilworth
*1575*

Robert Laneham's letter, ostensibly to a young friend, Humfrey Martin, recounting the flamboyant hospitality extended to the queen by the earl of Leicester, may have been written as a satire rather than a celebration of court entertainments. Perhaps it was not written by Laneham at all but by another courtier as a burlesque of Laneham's characteristic effusions (Frye, *Elizabeth I* 63–64). Whatever the truth of the matter, a Robert Laneham (c. 1535–1580) or Langham (Kuin 10–15), native of Nottinghamshire, attended grammar school, was apprenticed to a mercer, and was admitted to the Mercers' Company in 1557. The languages he acquired during his business travels were helpful in his position as a minor court functionary, the Keeper of the Council Chamber: "my languages now and then stand me in good stead," he wrote, "my French, my Spanish, my Dutch, and my Latin: sometime among ambassadors' men, if their master be within the Council, sometime with the Ambassador himself if he bids me call his lacky or asks me what's a clock" (Laneham, *A Letter* 83).

Eclectic in form, the letter's classical salutation identified it with the epistolary tradition of the elite (Kuin 12, 80) while its intemperate length (eighty-seven pages), euphoric style, colloquial language, and spelling that was bizarre even for its day were more characteristic of a popular pamphlet. Printed (where and by whom is unknown) without authorial attribution soon after it was written, Laneham's letter, along with the texts of masques and poems printed in George Gascoigne's *Princely Pleasures at the Court at Kenilworth* (1576), has provided an important record of the queen's summer progresses.

Unto my good friend, Master Humphrey Martin, Mercer.[1]

After my hearty commendations, I commend me heartily to you. Understand ye, that since through God and good friends I am placed at Court here (as ye wot)[2] in a worshipful room,[3] whereby I am not only acquainted

---

[1] **Mercer:** dealer in fabrics, especially silk, velvet, and other costly materials; Laneham and Martin were members of the Mercers' Company of London. [2] **wot:** know. [3] **worshipful room:** honorable position.

---

Robert Laneham, *A Letter: Wherein part of the entertainment unto the Queens Majesty at Killingworth Castle in Warwickshire in this Summer's Progress, 1575, is signified, from a friend officer attendant in the Court unto his friend a Citizen and Merchant of London* (London, c. 1575) STC 15191. Description of Kenilworth, 1–5; the queen's arrival, 7–8, 9–11, 15; the entertainments, 15–18, 20–25; the bride-ale, 26–32; the Hock Tuesday play, 32–40.

with the most, and well known to the best, and every officer glad of my company, but also have power [on] days (while the Council[4] sits not) to go and to see things sightworthy, and to be present at any show or spectacle only where this Progress[5] represented[6] unto her Highness. And of part of which sports,[7] having taken some notes and observations (for I cannot be idle at any hand[8] in the world) as well to put from me suspicion of sluggardy[9] as to pluck from you doubt[10] of any [of] my forgetfulness of friendship, I have thought it meet to impart them unto you, as frankly, as friendly, and as fully as I can. . . .

But herein, the better for conceiving of my mind and instruction of yours, ye must give me leave a little as well to preface unto my matter as to discourse somewhat of Killingworth Castle. A territory of the right honorable, my singular good Lord, my Lord the Earl of Leicester,[11] of whose incomparable cheering, and entertainment there unto her Majesty now, I will [show] them you a part here, that could not see all, nor had I seen all could well report the half: where things for the persons, for the place, time, cost, device,[12] strangeness,[13] and abundance of all that ever I saw . . . I saw none anywhere so memorable, I tell you plain.

The Castle hath name of Killingworth, but of truth grounded upon faithful[14] story, Kenilworth. It stands in Warwickshire, seventy-four miles northwest from London, and . . . four mile somewhat south from Coventry[15] (a proper city), and a like distance from Warwick, a fair shire[16] town on the north. In air sweet and wholesome, raised on an easy[17] mounted hill, is set evenly coasted[18] with the front straight into the east, hath the tenants and town about it, that pleasantly shifts from dale to hill, sundry where[19] with sweet springs bursting forth, and is so plentifully well sorted[20] on every side into arable,[21] meadow, pasture, wood, water, and good air as it appeareth to have need of nothing that may pertain to living or pleasure. . . . North and west, a goodly chase,[22] vast, wide, large, and full of red deer and other stately games[23] for hunting, beautified with many delectable, fresh,

---

[4] the Council: Laneham was Keeper of the [Privy] Council Chamber.   [5] Progress: state or ceremonial journey.   [6] represented: presented.   [7] sports: diversions.   [8] at any hand: under any circumstances.   [9] sluggardy: laziness.   [10] pluck from you doubt: disabuse you.   [11] Earl of Leicester: Robert Dudley, the queen's host and erstwhile "favorite."   [12] device: ingenuity. [13] strangeness: originality.   [14] faithful: credible.   [15] Coventry: a religious center and market town, important in the cloth and wool trade, located near Stratford, Shakespeare's birthplace. Before the Reformation, Coventry was well known for its cycle of biblical plays performed by the craft guilds and trading companies on June 14, Corpus Christi day, which drew many visitors from nearby towns.   [16] shire: county seat.   [17] easy: easily.   [18] evenly coasted: parallel to the road.   [19] sundry where: dotted.   [20] sorted: arranged.   [21] arable: farmland.   [22] chase: hunting ground, enclosed park land.   [23] stately games: majestic wild animals.

and umbrageous[24] bowers, arbors, seats, and walks, that with great art, cost, and diligence were very pleasantly appointed,[25] which also the natural grace by[26] the tall and fresh fragrant trees and soil did so far forth commend[27] as Diana[28] herself might have deigned[29] the air well enough to range[30] for her pastime.[31] . . .

On Saturday, the ninth of July . . . it was eight o'clock in the evening ere Her Highness came to Killingworth. Where in the park, about a flight-shoot[32] from the braize[33] and first gate of the castle, one of the ten Sibyls,[34] . . . comely clad in a pall[35] of white silk, pronounced a proper poesy in English rhyme and meter of effect how[36] great gladness Her Highness' presence brought into every stead[37] where it pleased her to come, and especially now into that place that had so long longed after the same. [The poem] ended with prophecy certain of much and long prosperity, health, and felicity: this Her Majesty benignly accepting, passed forth unto the next gate of the braize. . . .

. . . Trumpeters . . . stood upon the wall of the gate there to sound up a tune of welcome . . . this music maintained from them very delectably while Her Highness all along this tiltyard[38] rode into the inner gate next [to] the base court[39] of the castle: where the Lady of the Lake (famous in King Arthur's book) with two Nymphs waiting upon her, arrayed all in silks, attending Her Highness' coming. . . .

This pageant was closed up with a delectable harmony of hautboys,[40] shawms,[41] cornets, and such other loud music, that held on while Her Majesty pleasantly so passed from thence toward the castle gate: whereunto, from the base court over a dry valley cast into a good form, was there framed a fair bridge of a twenty foot wide and seventy foot long. . . .

So passing into the inner court, Her Majesty (that never rides but alone) there set down from her palfrey,[42] was conveyed up to chamber: when after, did follow so great a peal of guns and such lightning by firework a long space together, as Jupiter would show himself to be no further behind with his welcome than the rest of his gods: and that would he have all the country

---

[24] umbrageous: shaded.  [25] appointed: equipped, prepared.  [26] by: of.  [27] forth commend: recommend itself.  [28] Diana: Roman goddess associated with the moon, the hunt, female community, and chastity; often linked with Queen Elizabeth.  [29] deigned: judged.  [30] range: stroll.  [31] pastime: recreation.  [32] flight-shoot: distance which an arrow is shot.  [33] braize: military outwork with guard towers.  [34] Sibyls: prophetesses of antiquity.  [35] pall: mantle.  [36] of effect how: to the effect that.  [37] stead: place.  [38] tiltyard: enclosed space for tournaments.  [39] base court: the lower or outer court of a castle, occupied by servants.  [40] hautboys: oboes.  [41] shawms: medieval wind instruments related to the oboe.  [42] palfrey: small saddle horse for ladies.

to know: for indeed the noise and flame were heard and seen a twenty mile off. . . .

On Sunday, the forenoon occupied (as for the Sabbath day) in quiet and vacation from work, and in divine service and preaching at the parish church; the afternoon in excellent music of sundry sweet instruments, and in dancing of lords and ladies,[43] and other worshipful degrees,[44] uttered[45] with such lively agility and commendable grace. . . .

At night late, as though Jupiter the last night, had forgot for business,[46] or forborn for courtesy and quiet, part of his welcome unto Her Highness appointed . . . displays me his main power: with blazes of burning darts, flying to and fro, . . . streams and hail of fiery sparks, lightnings of wildfire, . . . thunderbolts, all with such countenance,[47] terror, and vehemency that the heavens thundered, the waters surged, the earth shook. . . . This ado lasted while the midnight was past. . . .

Monday was hot, and therefore Her Highness kept in till five o'clock in the evening, what time it pleased her to ride forth into the chase to hunt the hart of force,[48] which, found anon and after sore[49] chased, and chased by the hot pursuit of the hounds, was fain of fine force,[50] at last to take soil[51] . . . with the stately carriage of his head in his swimming . . . like the sail of a ship, the hounds harrowing[52] after as . . . to the spoil of a caravel.[53] . . . Well the hart was killed, a goodly deer, but so ceased not the game yet.

For about nine o'clock at the hither[54] part of the chase, where torchlight attended: out of the woods in Her Majesty's return, roughly came there forth *Hombre Salvagio*,[55] with an oaken plant plucked up by the roots in his hand, himself forgrown[56] all in moss and ivy, who [greeted the company and] called he upon all his familiars and companions, the Fauns, the Satyrs,[57] the Nymphs, the Dryads,[58] and the Hamadryads,[59] but none making answer . . . [except] his old friend Echo[60] [to whom he recounts the events of the preceding days]. . . . as this Savage for the more submission [to the Queen], broke his tree[61] asunder, cast the top from him, it had almost

[43] **dancing of lords and ladies:** dancing on the sabbath was forbidden to Puritans, of whom Leicester was one, but the queen loved to dance.  [44] **worshipful degrees:** distinguished social ranks.  [45] **uttered:** expressed, displayed.  [46] **business:** anxiety; excessive occupation.  [47] **countenance:** appearance.  [48] **hunt the hart of force:** hunt on horseback by running the deer to ground.  [49] **sore:** grievously.  [50] **fain of fine force:** required.  [51] **take soil:** take to marshy ground or water.  [52] **harrowing:** plundering.  [53] **caravel:** a kind of ship.  [54] **hither:** nearer.  [55] *Hombre Salvagio:* wild man, woodman; a human figure naked or enveloped in foliage, representing the antithesis of civilization, often seen in heraldry and pageants.  [56] **forgrown:** overgrown.  [57] **Satyrs:** woodland gods or demons, partly human and partly bestial, supposedly the companions of Bacchus.  [58] **Dryads:** wood nymphs.  [59] **Hamadryads:** wood nymphs who live within a tree.  [60] **Echo:** mythological wood nymph who rejected the advances of Pan and was transformed into a voice that could only repeat the last words spoken to her.  [61] **tree:** oaken stick.

light upon Her Highness' horse's head, whereat he started and the gentleman [playing the Savage was] much dismayed. Seeing the benignity[62] of the
Prince,[63] as the footmen looked well to the horse, and [the horse] of generosity[64] soon calmed of himself, "[N]o hurt, no hurt," quoth Her Highness.
Which words, I promise you, we were all glad to hear, and took them to be
the best part of the play. . . .

A Sunday opportunely the weather broke up again, and after divine service in the parish church for the Sabbath day . . . a solemn bride-ale[65] of a
proper couple was appointed, set in order in the tiltyard, to come and make
their show before the castle in the great court, where as was pight[66] a comely
quintain[67] for feats of arms, which when they had done, to march out at the
north gate of the castle homeward again into the town.

And thus were they marshalled. First, all the lusty lads and bold bache-
lors of the parish, suitably every wight[68] with his blue buckram[69] bridelace[70]
with a branch of green broom (because rosemary[71] is scant there) tied on his
left arm (for on that side lies the heart) . . . some with a hat, some in a cap,
some a coat some a jerkin,[72] some for lightness in his doublet[73] and his
hose . . . some [with] boots and no spurs, [some with] spurs and no boots,
[and some with] neither nother.[74] . . . [T]he bridegroom foremost, in his
father's tawny[75] worsted jacket (for his friends were fain that he should be a
bridegroom before the Queen) . . . a bridegroom indeed: with this special
grace by the way, that ever as he would have framed him [with] the better
countenance, with the worse face he looked.

Well, sir, after these horsemen [came] a lively morris dance according to
the ancient manner, six dancers, Maid Marian, and the fool. Then, three
pretty pucelles[76] as bright as a breast of bacon, of a thirty year old apiece,
that carried three special spicecakes . . . before the bride, sizely[77] with set
countenance, and lips so demurely simpering as it had been a mare cropping
a thistle. After these, a lovely lubberworts,[78] freckle-faced and red headed . . .
to bear the bride-cup. . . . This gentle cupbearer yet had his freckled phys-
iognomy somewhat unhappily infested as he went by the busy flies that
flocked about the bride-cup . . . but he like a tall[79] fellow withstood their

[62] **benignity:** amiability, kindness.   [63] **Prince:** the ruler, i.e., Queen Elizabeth.   [64] **generosity:**
high spirits, excitement.   [65] **bride-ale:** wedding feast, a wedding ale-drinking.   [66] **pight:**
pitched, set up.   [67] **quintain:** a board for tilting with lances, darts, or poles.   [68] **wight:** strong
fellow.   [69] **buckram:** coarse cloth or linen stiffened with paste.   [70] **bridelace:** laces, sometimes
gold, used to tie on sprigs of rosemary, an early kind of wedding favor.   [71] **rosemary:** herb
linked with memory, traditional to both weddings and funerals.   [72] **jerkin:** close-fitting jacket.
[73] **doublet:** jacket or vest; doublet-and-hose was a state of partial undress, the equivalent of
rolled-up sleeves.   [74] **neither nother:** neither the one nor the other.   [75] **tawny:** brownish-
yellow.   [76] **pucelles:** maidens.   [77] **sizely:** daintily.   [78] **lubberworts:** great oaf.   [79] **tall:** valiant.

malice stoutly[80] (see what manhood may do) beat them away, killed them by scores, stood to his charge and marched on in good order.

Then followed the worshipful[81] bride led (after the country manner) between two ancient parishioners, honest townsmen. But a stale stallion[82] and a well spread, (hot as the weather was) God wot,[83] and an ill smelling was she: a thirty-five year old, of color brown-bay, not very beautiful indeed but ugly, foul, ill favored,[84] yet marvelous fain of the office,[85] because she heard say she should dance before the Queen, in which feat she thought she would foot it as finely as the best. Well, after this bride came there two by two a dozen damsels for bridesmaids, that for favor, attire, for fashion and cleanliness, were as meet for such a bride as a treen[86] ladle for a porridge pot. . . .

As the company in this order were come into the court, marvelous were the martial acts that were done this day. . . . [A]fter the bridegroom had made his course, ran the rest of the band awhile in some order . . . [one] would run his race bias[87] among the thickest of the throng, that down came they together, hand over head; another, while he directed his course to the quintain, his jument[88] would carry him to a mare among the people, so his horse as amorous as himself adventurous. Another to run and miss the quintain with his staff and hit the board with his head.

Many such gay games were there among these riders, who by and by after, upon a greater courage, left their quintaining and ran at one another. There to see the stern countenances, the grim looks, the courageous attempts, the desperate adventures, the dangerous curves,[89] the fierce encounters, whereby the buff[90] at the man and the counterbuff at the horse that both sometime came toppling to the ground. . . .

And hereto followed as good a sport (me thought) presented in an historical cue[91] by certain good-hearted men of Coventry, my lord's neighbors there . . . [who] made petition that they might renew now their old storial show,[92] of argument how the Danes whilom[93] here in a troublous season[94]

---

[80] **stoutly:** bravely.  [81] **worshipful:** distinguished.  [82] **stale stallion:** unchaste woman, also called a hobby-horse.  [83] **God wot:** God knows.  [84] **ill favored:** unattractive.  [85] **fain of the office:** eager for the ceremony.  [86] **treen:** wooden.  [87] **bias:** crossways.  [88] **jument:** stallion.  [89] **curves:** maneuvers.  [90] **buff:** blow.  [91] **cue:** style.  [92] **old storial show:** old historical show, the Hock Tuesday play. On Hock Tuesday, the second Tuesday after Easter, Coventry celebrated the battle that ended Danish rule in the eleventh century. This was a holiday on which female aggression was sanctioned — women chased men to the ground and tied them up ("hock" is believed to derive from the German "hocken," binding) — and was manifested in the Coventry play by the English women who fought against the Danes. Michaelmas and Hock Tuesday divided the calendar year into winter and summer halves; on the latter, rents were paid and money collected for the parish, so the holiday served a variety of social and economic functions.  [93] **whilom:** long ago.  [94] **troublous season:** unsettled time.

were for quietness[95] borne withal and suffered in peace, that anon by[96] outrage and importable[97] insolency, abusing both Ethelred, the king then and all estates[98] everywhere beside, at the grievous complaint and counsel of Huna, the king's chieftain in war, on St. Brice's night Anno Domini 1012 (as the book says) that falleth yearly on the thirteenth of November, were all dispatched, and the realm rid. And for because the matter mentioneth how valiantly our English women for love of their country behaved themselves, expressed in action and rhymes after their manner, [the Coventry men] thought it might move some mirth to Her Majesty the rather.

The thing,[99] said they, is grounded on story,[100] and for pastime wont to be played in our city yearly, without ill[101] example of manners, papistry, or any superstition, and else[102] did so occupy the heads of a number, that likely enough would have had worse meditations. It had an ancient beginning and a long continuance, till now of late laid down,[103] [and] they knew of no cause why, unless it were by the zeal of certain [of] their preachers, men very commendable for their behavior and learning, and sweet in their sermons, but somewhat too sour in preaching away their pastime: [the Coventry men] wished, therefore, that as [the preachers] should continue their good doctrine in pulpit, so, for matters of policy and governance of the city, they would permit[104] them to the mayor and magistrates, and said . . . they would make their humble petition unto Her Highness, that they might have their plays up again.

But aware,[105] keep back, make room[106] now, here they come. And first, Captain Cox, an odd man, I promise you: by profession a mason, and that right skillful, very cunning in fence,[107] and hardy as Gawain, for his tonsword[108] hangs at his table end. Great oversight[109] hath he in matters of story, for as[110] *King Arthur's Book,*[111] *Huon of Bordeaux,*[112] . . . *Bevis of Hampton,*[113] *The Squire of Low Degree,*[114] . . . *Sir Gawain,*[115] *Oliver of the Castle,*[116] . . . *Virgil's Life, The Castle of Ladies,*[117] . . . *Gargantua,*[118] *Robin*

---

[95] **quietness:** civic peace.   [96] **anon by:** ultimately because of.   [97] **importable:** unbearable.   [98] **estates:** social ranks.   [99] **The thing:** i.e., the play.   [100] **story:** history.   [101] **ill:** bad.   [102] **else:** otherwise.   [103] **laid down:** forbidden.   [104] **permit:** leave.   [105] **aware:** look out.   [106] **make room:** the traditional announcement of the players' arrival.   [107] **fence:** fencing.   [108] **tonsword:** long sword; two-handed sword.   [109] **oversight:** knowledge.   [110] **for as:** for example.   [111] *King Arthur's Book:* Malory, *Le Morte d'Arthur,* 1485.   [112] *Huon of Bordeaux:* French romance, with a fairy king named Oberon.   [113] *Bevis of Hampton:* popular fourteenth-century romance.   [114] *The Squire of Low Degree:* romance of a squire in love with a Princess of Hungary.   [115] *Sir Gawain:* the English romance of Arthur's court.   [116] *Oliver of the Castle: Oliver of Castile,* a Spanish romance.   [117] *The Castle of Ladies:* probably Christine de Pizan's *City of Ladies.*   [118] *Gargantua:* the Rabelais work, or perhaps a French folktale.

Hood,[119] ... *The Wife Lapped in Morel's Skin,*[120] ... *Colin Clout,*[121] ...
*Eleanor Rumming*[122] ... with many more than I rehearse here: I believe he
have them all at his fingers' ends. ... Besides this in the field a good marshall at musters,[123] of very great credit and trust in the town here, for he has
been chosen alecunner[124] many a year ... his judgment will be taken above
the best, be his nose ne'er so red.

Captain Cox came marching on valiantly before ... flourishing with his
tonsword, and another fencemaster with him, thus in the forward making
room for the rest. After them proudly pricked on[125] foremost the Danish
lance-knights on horseback, and then the English, each with their alderpole[126] martially in their hand. Even at the first entry the meeting waxed
somewhat warm, that by and by kindled with courage a[127] both sides, grew
from a hot skirmish unto a blazing battle, first by spear and shield ... with
furious encounters that together they tumbled to the dust, sometimes
[both] horse and man: and after fall to it with sword and target,[128] good
bangs a both sides. The fight so ceasing, but the battle not so ended, followed the footmen, both the hosts,[129] ton after tother,[130] first marching in
ranks, then warlike turning, then from ranks into squadrons, then into two
triangles, from that into rings, and so winding out again. ... Twice the
Danes had the better, but at the last conflict, beaten down, overcome and
many led captive for triumph by English women.

This was the effect of this show, that as it was handled, made much matter of good pastime, brought all indeed into the great court, even under Her
Highness' window to be seen: but (as unhappy it was for the bride) that
came thither too soon. ... Her Highness [was] beholding in her chamber
delectable dancing indeed ... and but a little of the Coventry play Her
Highness also saw, [and] commanded therefore on the Tuesday following to
have it full out, as accordingly it was presented, whereat Her Majesty
laughed well, [the Coventry men] were the jocunder,[131] and so much the
more because Her Highness had given them two bucks[132] and five marks in
money to make merry together; they prayed for Her Majesty, long, happily

---

[119] **Robin Hood:** one of the many ballads.   [120] *The Wife Lapped in Morel's Skin: Here Beginneth
a Merry Jest of a Shrewd and Curst Wife Lapped in Morel's Skin* (c. 1580), perhaps a source for
*The Taming of the Shrew.*   [121] **Colin Clout:** John Skelton's satire on Cardinal Wolsey and the
clergy. Skelton was a poet, priest, and tutor to Henry VIII, known for his satire.   [122] *Eleanor
Rumming: The Tunning of Eleanor Rumming,* Skelton's satire of an alewife and her gossips. In
the Middle Ages, women (alewives) brewed the ale, but the trade was gradually taken over by
men and moved out of the household.   [123] **marshall at musters:** militia officer.   [124] **alecunner:**
ale taster.   [125] **pricked on:** spurred on.   [126] **alderpole:** stick made of alder, a wood that resists
rot.   [127] **a:** on.   [128] **target:** small, round shield.   [129] **hosts:** forces.   [130] **ton after tother:** the one
after the other.   [131] **jocunder:** merrier.   [132] **bucks:** male deer.

to reign, and oft to come thither that oft they might see her: and what,[133] rejoicing upon their ample reward, and what, triumphing upon the good acceptance,[134] they vaunted[135] that their play was never so dignified,[136] nor ever any players afore so beatified.[137]

Thus though the day took an end, yet slipped not the night all sleeping away: for as neither office[138] nor obsequy[139] ceased at any time to the full, to perform the plot[140] his Honor[141] had appointed. So after supper was there a play presented of a very good theme,[142] but so set forth by the actors' well handling[143] that pleasure and mirth made it seem very short, though it lasted two good hours and more. . . . After the play out of hand,[144] followed a most delicious and (if I may so term it) an ambrosial banquet. . . . Unto this banquet there was appointed a masque,[145] for riches of array, of an incredible cost: but the time so far spent and very late in the night now, was cause that it came not forth to the show.

[The next day, the queen again hunted in the late afternoon, and on her return was welcomed with a water-pageant featuring Triton on a Mermaid's back, and Arion (an "excellent and famous musician") riding on a Dolphin, from whose belly issued lovely music. After an additional nine days of recreation, including the repeat performance of the Hock Tuesday play with the queen paying attention, the queen departed.]

[133]what: whatever, so forth.   [134]acceptance: reception.   [135]vaunted: boasted.   [136]dignified: honored.   [137]beatified: blessed.   [138]office: duty.   [139]obsequy: ceremony.   [140]plot: entertainment.   [141]his Honor: Leicester.   [142]very good theme: worthwhile.   [143]handling: execution.   [144]out of hand: was done.   [145]appointed a masque: George Gascoigne had written an elaborate masque that was not performed but was printed in *The Princely Pleasures of the Court at Kenilworth* (London, 1576).

→ ## Coventry Records
of the Hock Tuesday Play

*1575, 1576, 1591*

The *Records of Early English Drama* (REED) series, a compilation of all records of music, drama, and public ceremony between 1392 and the closure of the theaters under the Commonwealth in 1642, testifies to the vigorous tradition of playing and festival in the English countryside. Each volume is devoted to one county or region, draws from both original sources (civic, county, parish, house-

Coventry Records of the Hock Tuesday Play, in *Records of Early English Drama: Coventry*, edited by W. Ingram (Toronto and Buffalo: U of Toronto P, 1981) 1575, 271–72; 1576, 277–78; and 1591, 332.

hold records) and nineteenth-century antiquarian accounts, and presents the records chronologically and with a minimum of commentary. The records cited below include the City Annals (not kept contemporaneously), which list the mayors of Coventry and the "historical and memorable events" that occurred during their tenure (Ingram xxx); the Council Book (1555–1640), primarily concerned with city property but sometimes noting payments for city celebrations (xxxiv); and the records of the craft and trade guilds that sponsored the Corpus Christi plays since their inception in the late Middle Ages. The Drapers, who with the Mercers were the most affluent of the guilds, were the pageants' most generous supporters, and the Cappers, who remain active into the present, were meticulous recorders of their pageant. The Weavers' Corpus Christi play is one of two from the cycle that has been preserved (xliii).

The payments listed in the records might best be understood in relation to the wages and working conditions of the semi-skilled laborer established in the "Statute of Artificers" in 1563. For a workday that began, between March and September, at or before five in the morning and ended at eight at night, with not more than two hours taken for food and drink, the worker received nine pence, if he were fed by employers (fol. 19). For the wages of skilled workers, see Proclamation 778, "Regulating Chester Wages" (see p. 186–87). In Shakespeare's London, a penny would buy a mug of beer, a ballad, or a "groundling's" admission to stand in the playhouse yard to watch a play (Smith, "Reading Lists" 129).

## City Annals                                                                        *1575*

Simon Cotton, butcher, mayor 1574 and ended in 1575 . . . In his year the Queen came to Killingworth Castle again and recreated[1] herself there twelve or thirteen days. At which time Coventry men went to make her merry with their play of Hock Tuesday, and for their pains had a reward and venison also to make them merry.

## Cappers' Records (Payments)

paid to the players for one rehearse,[2] 18d[3]
paid for breakfast for the company at the same rehearse, 18d
paid for hiring of one harness[4] and for scouring the same, 6d
paid for carrying 2 harnesses and for points,[5] 6d
paid to master mayor, 22s[6] 8d

---

[1]recreated: refreshed.   [2]rehearse: rehearsal.   [3]d: abbreviation for pence, plural of penny.
[4]harness: body armor.   [5]points: laces or cords used to fasten clothing.   [6]s: abbreviation for shilling, a unit of the English monetary system used from the Norman Conquest until 1971; the shilling was worth twelve pence, and twenty shillings were worth one pound sterling.

*Weavers' Accounts (Payments)*

> In primis for one rehearse, 12d
>
> Item paid to master mayor for the pageants, 22s

*Drapers' Accounts (Payments)*

> paid for the pageant,[7] 26s 8d
>
> paid for a cord and mending the pageant, 6d
>
> paid for bearing harness[8] at the fair, 15d

*City Annals*                                                                1576

Thomas Nicklyn, Mayor. This year the said mayor caused Hock Tuesday, whereby is mentioned[9] an overthrow of the Danes by the inhabitants of this city to be again set up and showed forth to his great commendation and the city's great commodity, which said Hock Tuesday was the year before played before the Queen at Kenilworth in the time of her progress by the commandment of the Queen's Council.

This year the pageants or Hock Tuesday that had been laid down eight years were played again.

*Cappers' Records (Payments)*

> paid for hire of 2 harnesses on Hock Tuesday, 8d
>
> paid for wearing the same harnesses and for points, 8d
>
> paid for wearing 2 harnesses on the fair day and for points, 6d
>
> paid to the minstrels and singers, 20d

*Charges of the Pageant*

> paid to the players at the first rehearse, 18d
>
> spent at Mr. Walden's at the same rehearse, 2s
>
> paid to the players at the second rehearse, 20d
>
> spent at William Ashburn's at the same rehearse, 2s

---

[7] **pageant:** pageant wagon.   [8] **bearing harness:** wearing armor.   [9] **mentioned:** recounted.

spent at the setting forth of the pageant, 6d

paid to Mr. Pixley for boards and ledges,[10] 3s

paid for cart nails and other nails, 2s 6d

paid 2 carpenters for one day's work, 18d

paid for 2½ yards of buckram to make the spirit's coat, 2s 1d

paid for making the same coat, 8d

paid for mending the Mary's hair, 8d

paid for a door and hinges and nails behind the pageant, 12d

paid for mending Pilate's club, 3d

paid for dressing[11] the pageant, 6d

paid for points for our harness, 12d

paid for gloves, 3s 6d

paid for soap for the wheels, 4d

paid for driving the pageant, 6s 8d

paid for tenter hooks[12] and lathe nails, 2d ob.[13]

paid for small cord, 1d ob.

paid for 4 iron clips for the wheels and shutting the hooks for the ladder 2s

paid for painting the bishop's miters and the devil's club, 2s

paid for mending the devil's coat and making the devil's head, 4s 6d

*Payments*

paid for rushes,[14] 4d

paid for hire of 4 harnesses and weapons, 20d

paid for washing 2 surplices, 1d ob.

spent at repairing the pageant, 12d

paid for a skein of green silk and mending Pilate's gown, 6d

*Payments to the Players*

paid for the prologue,[15] 4d

paid God and dead man, 20d

---

[10] **ledges:** wooden traverse bars attached to furniture or door. [11] **dressing:** decorating. [12] **tenter hooks:** metal hooks for hanging articles. [13] **ob.:** abbreviation for *obolus*, or halfpenny. [14] **rushes:** grasses used to cover the ground or the floor of the pageant wagon. [15] **prologue:** player who speaks the prologue.

paid the 2 bishops, 2s

paid Pilate, 4s 4d

paid the 4 knights, 6s 8d

paid 3 Marys, 2s

paid 2 angels, 8d

paid the devil, 16d

paid the players for their supper, 2s 8d

paid Pilate, the bishops, and knights to drink between the stages,[16] 9d

paid for drink in the pageant, 10d

paid the singers, 2s

paid the minstrel, 10d

paid for our supper, 4s

*Council Book*                                                                                                    *1591*

It is also agreed by the whole consent of this house that the Destruction of Jerusalem, the Conquest of the Danes, or the History of King Edward IV, at the request of the Commons of this city shall be played on the pageants on Midsummer Day and St. Peter's Day next in this city and none other plays. And that all the Maypoles that now are standing in this city shall be taken down before Whitsunday next, none hereafter to be set up in this city.

[16]**stages:** locations where the pageant was performed.

### THE FAIRY QUEEN

Titania, the Fairy Queen, is not Queen Elizabeth I; however, the figure of the fairy queen was often linked with the queen, as in Sir Edmund Spenser's epic poem *The Faerie Queene,* and fascinated Elizabethan poets and playwrights. Occasionally, the fairy queen was even represented parodically, as in Ben Jonson's play *The Alchemist* (1610) when Doll Common appears as the Queen of Faery ("Here she is come," another character whispers, "Down o' your knees and wriggle: / She has a stately presence," [5.4.21–24]). Representations of Queen Elizabeth I, in fact, occupied nearly every possible gender position (Goldberg 39) — Prince, milkmaid, Petrarchan beloved to her courtiers, mother to her people — and the corresponding array of her royal personae enabled her to move back and forth across boundaries of gender, rank, and culture, ultimately transcending them (Fletcher 79). If the queen's manly strength was personified in Diana, her sagacity was embodied in Astraea, imperial virgin of the Golden Age, unique woman in a man's world wise enough to rely on her male councillors (Berry 64, 78). Alternately, her power was mystified by identifying her with shepherdesses (Montrose, "Eliza" 34), fairies, and other pastoral maidens.

Both Maiden and Prince, the queen was also the head of a household, which was customarily the prerogative of a married man; and disconcertingly, her household was a female one. During the reign of a king, the members of the Privy Chamber who performed domestic services for the monarch (the Groom of the Bedchamber, the Groom of the Stool) were men, but during the reign of a queen, these same functions were, of course, performed by women. The reign of a queen unsettled social hierarchies by subordinating all men to a woman, and a female court further ensured that relatively fewer men and more women had the power conferred by proximity to the monarch. Consequently, courtiers and diplomats not only had a queen to please and placate, but they also were often forced to gain access to her through powerful ladies in waiting who operated a "free market of favors" (Pam Wright 161). The embarrassing challenge to masculine supremacy posed by a powerful female community was managed by the extreme portrayals of women that either exaggerated female power to the monstrous proportions of fierce warrior maidens, or reduced it to the dainty dimensions of ingenuous fairies, nymphs, or shepherds like the little fairies and adorable queen of Elvetham and *A Midsummer Night's Dream* and Elisa and her nymphs in *The Shepheardes Calendar*.

In "The Fourth Day's Entertainment" at Elvetham (1591), a Fairy Queen dances rounds and carols Titania-like with her maidens in a garden while the queen watches the diversion from an upper window. Nearly contemporaneous with *A Midsummer Night's Dream*, the entertainment has been cited as a "source" of the play, for during the dance, the Fairy Queen presents Queen Elizabeth with a wreath of golden flowers from Auberon, the Fairy King. More subtly, the entertainment evokes another, more threatening, image of the Fairy Queen, of Circe, also called "Titania" in Ovid's *Metamorphoses*, who reduced men to beasts with her wand. Queen Elizabeth not only enjoyed watching this covert festive tribute to her power, she commanded that it be repeated three times for the "delight" of her lords and ladies.

The image of queen and court in the "Aprill" eclogue of *The Shepheardes Calendar* (1579) is more complex and foregrounds a feminine intimacy that in *A Midsummer Night's Dream* occurs offstage and in the past. As in the entertainment at Elvetham, feminine power is reduced to simplicity (Montrose, "Eliza" 34); however, in Spenser's "Aprill" eclogue, the female community is directed inward, wholly centered on Elisa. The scene celebrates the emotional and physical intimacy among women, with naked nymphs admiring the spectacle of an Elisa unclothed save for the floral wreathes that crown her, and her natural "red and white" blush (Berry 70–80). And the image of Elisa tenderly decked with flowers by her nymphs both recalls an idolatrous standing Maypole and anticipates the scene in which the fairies crown Bottom with flowers in *A Midsummer Night's Dream*.

→ *From* Entertainment at Elvetham                    *1591*

Compared to Kenilworth, the estate of the earl of Hereford was miniscule, but unlike Sir William More, Hereford did not attempt to shirk his hospitable duties. Instead, he set three hundred carpenters to work building new rooms, offices, and kitchens for the queen and her court, and since he had insufficient land to accommodate the chase, he ordered a lake constructed for elaborate pageants and water sports. Within a week of the queen's departure from Elvetham, the first description of the events there was entered in the Stationer's Register on October 1, 1591, quickly followed by four more printings of three or four editions (Jean Wilson 99). The popularity of this account testifies to the singular inventiveness of this entertainment, the self-promotion of its inventors, or to a vicarious pleasure in, and market for, accounts of the revels of the nobility.

### *From* THE FOURTH DAY'S ENTERTAINMENT

On Thursday morning, Her Majesty was no sooner ready and at her gallery window looking into the garden, but there began three cornets[1] to play certain fantastic[2] dances, at the measure[3] whereof the Fairy Queen came into the garden, dancing with her maids about her. She brought with her a garland, made in form of an imperial crown; within the sight of Her Majesty, she fixed upon a silvered staff, and sticking the staff into the ground, spake as followeth:

[1] cornets: wind instruments resembling horns or clarinets, probably the latter. [2] fantastic: imaginative; extravagant. [3] measure: melody.

"The Honorable Entertainment given to the Queen's Majesty in a Progress, at Elvetham in Hampshire, by the Right Honorable Earl of Hereford, 1591," in *Entertainments for Elizabeth I*, edited by Jean Wilson (Woodbridge: Brewer, 1980), from "The Fourth Day's Entertainment," 115–16.

FIGURE 7 *Elvetham. This engraving shows an idealized rendition of the* Nau- *machia, or sea battle, the centerpiece of the entertainment at Elvetham offered to Queen Elizabeth on her summer progress in 1591 by the earl of Hereford. Since Elvetham was not surrounded with expansive forests in which the queen might hunt, the earl ingeniously and prodigally excavated an artificial lake on which was staged an extravagant water spectacle.*

*The Speech of the Fairy Queen to Her Majesty.*

I that abide in places underground,
Aureola,[4] the Queen of Fairy Land,
That every night in rings of painted[5] flowers
Turn round and carol out Elisa's name:
Hearing that Nereus[6] and the Sylvan gods[7]
Have lately welcomed your Imperial Grace,
[I opened] the earth with this enchanting[8] wand,
To do my duty to Your Majesty,
And humbly to salute you with this chaplet,[9]
Given to me by Auberon, the Fairy King.

---

[4] **Aureola:** allegorical name meaning golden crown or halo.   [5] **painted:** colorful.   [6] **Nereus:** Homeric god of the sea.   [7] **Sylvan gods:** forest gods.   [8] **enchanting:** magical.   [9] **chaplet:** wreath of flowers or gold.

Bright, shining Phoebe,[10] that in human shape
Hid'st Heaven's perfection, vouchsafe to[11] accept it;
And I Aureola, beloved in heaven,
(For amorous stars fall nightly in my lap)
Will cause that Heavens enlarge thy golden days,
And cut them short, that envy at thy praise.

After this speech, the Fairy Queen and her maids danced about the garden, singing a song of six parts, with the music of an exquisite consort,[12] wherein was the lute, bandora,[13] bass-viol, cittern,[14] treble-viol, and flute. And this was the Fairies' song:

Elisa is the fairest Queen
That ever trod upon this green.
Elisa's eyes are blessed stars,
Inducing peace, subduing wars.
Elisa's hand is crystal bright,
Her words are balm, her looks are light.
Elisa's breast is that fair hill,
Where Virtue dwells, and sacred skill.
O blessed be each day and hour,
Where sweet Elisa builds her bower.

This spectacle and music so delighted Her Majesty that she commanded to hear it sung and danced three times over and called for diverse lords and ladies to behold it; and then dismissed the actors with thanks, and with a gracious largess,[15] which of her exceeding goodness she bestowed upon them.

[10]**Phoebe:** "bright, shining one," associated, like Diana, with the moon.    [11]**vouchsafe to:** deign to; be willing to.    [12]**consort:** company of musicians.    [13]**bandora:** stringed instrument like a guitar or lute.    [14]**cittern:** stringed instrument like a guitar.    [15]**largess:** generous gift.

→ EDMUND SPENSER

## From The Shepheardes Calendar                    1579

The paradigm of the "made man" who rose from humble beginnings to courtiership, Edmund Spenser (1552–1599) was born in London, attended Richard Mulcaster's Merchant Taylor's School and went to Cambridge as a scholarship student. His Cambridge degree brought him into the circles of the elite, and he

Edmund Spenser, *The Shepheardes Calendar conteyning twelve Aeglogues proportional to the twelve monethes* (London, 1579), from "Aprill," 13–15.

FIGURE 8 *The queen and her court. The engraving accompanying the "Aprill" eclogue in Spenser's* The Shepheardes Calendar *shows another of the queen's royal identities, the persona of "pastoral simplicity," with the queen in an idealized country setting surrounded by ladies playing harp, lute, and flute, shepherds piping and tending contented sheep.*

was a secretary to several important men, including the earl of Leicester. While he was in Leicester's employ he met other courtier-poets interested in the development of a national poetry, including Sir Philip Sidney, to whom Spenser dedicated *The Shepheardes Calendar,* published in 1579. Spenser's marriage poems *Epithalamion* and *Prothalamion* are roughly contemporaneous with *A Midsummer Night's Dream* and similarly evoke the world of popular festivity. Spenser spent most of an undistinguished civil service career in Ireland, presented his *View of the Present State of Ireland* (1596), but never significantly influenced national policy. Constantly attempting to win royal favor, he dedicated his monumental national epic, *The Faerie Queene* (1590, 1596), to Queen Elizabeth I.

## *From* APRILL

### *Argument*

This Æglogue[1] is purposely intended to the honor and prayse of our most gracious sovereigne, Queene Elizabeth. The speakers herein be Hobbinoll and Thenott, two shepheardes: the which Hobbinoll being before mentioned,

---

[1] **Æglogue:** the Roman poet Virgil was known for his eclogues, and this form of pastoral dialogue was revived in the Renaissance.

greatly to have loved Colin, is here set forth more largely,[2] complayning[3] him of that boyes great misadventure in Love, whereby his mynd was alienate[4] and with drawen not onely from him, who moste loved him, but also from all former delightes and studies, aswell in pleasaunt pyping, as conning[5] ryming and singing, and other his laudable exercises. Whereby he taketh occasion, for proofe of his more excellencie and skill in poetrie, to recorde a songe, which the sayd Colin sometime made in honor of her Majestie, whom abruptely[6] he termeth Elysa.

. . . . . . . . . . . . .

HOBBINOLL
Contented I: then will I singe his laye[7]
Of fayre *Elisa*, Queene of shepheardes all:
Which once he made, as by a spring he laye,          35
And tuned it unto the Waters fall.

Ye dayntye Nymphs, that in this blessed Brooke
    doe bathe your brest,
For sake your watry bowres, and hether looke,
    at my request:                                    40
And eke[8] you Virgins,[9] that on *Parnasse* dwell,
Whence floweth *Helicon*[10] the learned well,
    Helpe me to blaze[11]
    Her worthy praise,
Which in her sexe doth all excell.                    45

Of fayre *Elisa* be your silver song,
    that blessed wight:[12]
The flowre of Virgins, may shee florish long,
    In princely plight.[13]
For shee is *Syrinx* daughter without spotte,         50
Which *Pan* the shepheards God of her begot:[14]
    So sprong her grace
    Of heavenly race,
No mortall blemishe may her blotte.

---

[2] **largely:** fully.   [3] **complayning:** lamenting.   [4] **alienate:** estranged, isolated.   [5] **conning:** learning.   [6] **abruptely:** suddenly.   [7] **laye:** song.   [8] **eke:** also.   [9] **you Virgins:** the nine Muses, daughters of the Greek gods Apollo and Memory, who lived on Mount Parnassus in Greece.   [10] *Helicon:* a spring at the foot of Parnassus.   [11] **blaze:** praise, used especially of feminine beauty.   [12] **wight:** being.   [13] **plight:** condition.   [14] *Syrinx . . . Pan:* Syrinx, a nymph of Arcadia, signifies to Queen Elizabeth's mother Anne Boleyn, and Pan stands for Henry VIII.

See, where she sits upon the grassie greene,                    55
   (O seemely[15] sight)
Yclad in Scarlot like a mayden Queene,
   And Ermines white.
Upon her head a Cremosin coronet,
With Damaske roses and Daffadillies[16] set:                    60
   Bayleaves betweene,
   And Primroses greene,
Embellish[17] the sweete Violet.

Tell me, have ye seene her angelick face,
   Like *Phoebe*[18] fayre?                              65
Her heavenly haveour, her princely grace
   can you well compare?
The Redde rose medled[19] with the White yfere,[20]
In either cheeke depeincten[21] lively chere.
   Her modest eye,                                      70
   Her Majestie,
Where have you seene the like, but there?

I sawe *Phoebus* thrust out his golden hedde,
   upon her to gaze:
But when he sawe, how broade her beames did spredde,            75
   it did him amaze.
He blusht to see another Sunne belowe,
Ne durst[22] againe his fyrye face out showe:[23]
   Let him, if he dare,
   His brightnesse compare                              80
With hers, to have the overthrowe.[24]

---

[15] **seemely:** pleasant, lovely.  [16] **Daffadillies:** daffodils.  [17] **Embellish:** set off, contrast with.
[18] *Phoebe:* the moon, sister to Phoebus, the sun.  [19] **medled:** mingled.  [20] **Redde rose . . .
White yfere:** a red and white complexion was the poetic ideal of female beauty. Red and white
roses also refer to Elizabeth's grandfather, Henry VII, descended from the families of both York
(symbolized by the white rose) and Lancaster (symbolized by the red); he reconciled the dynastic conflicts of the Wars of the Roses. The implication is that the queen is an image of perfectly
balanced beauty and political harmony.  [21] **depeincten:** depicted.  [22] **Ne durst:** never dared.
[23] **out showe:** display.  [24] **overthrowe:** victory.

Shewe thy selfe *Cynthia*[25] with thy silver rayes,
  and be not abasht:
When shee the beames of her beauty displayes,
  O how art thou dasht?                                         85
But I will not match her with *Latonaes*[26] seede,
Such follie, great sorow to *Niobe* did breede.
    Now she is a stone,
    And makes dayly mone,
Warning all other to take heede.                            90

*Pan* may be proud, that ever he begot
  such a Bellibone,[27]
And *Syrinx* rejoyse, that ever was her lot
  to beare such an one.
Soone as my younglings cryen for the dam,               95
To her will I offer a milkwhite Lamb:
    Shee is my goddesse plaine,[28]
    And I her shepherds swayne,[29]
Albee forswonck and forswatt[30] I am.

I see *Calliope*[31] speede her to the place,          100
  where my Goddesse shines:
And after her the other Muses trace,[32]
  with their Violines.
Bene they not Bay braunches,[33] which they doe beare,
All for *Elisa* in her hand to weare?                 105
    So sweetely they play,
    And sing all the way,
That it a heaven is to heare.

Lo how finely the graces can it foote[34]
  to the Instrument:                                   110
They dauncen deffly, and singen soote,[35]
  in their meriment.

---

[25] *Cynthia:* a name given to the Greek goddess Artemis, associated, like Phoebe and Diana, with the moon.   [26] *Latonaes* seede: in Greek myth, Niobe bragged of her seven sons and seven daughters, so Latona's two children, Apollo and Diana, killed them. Niobe was turned to stone while she wept for her children.   [27] **Bellibone:** *belle bonne,* pretty maid.   [28] **plain:** absolute.   [29] **swayne:** servant.   [30] **Albee forswonck and forswatt:** although overworked and sunburned.   [31] *Calliope:* the muse of epic poetry.   [32] **trace:** dance.   [33] **Bene:** are; **Bay braunches:** sign of military victory and of poetry.   [34] **foote:** dance.   [35] **dauncen deffly, and singen soote:** dance skillfully and sing sweetly.

Wants not a fourth grace, to make the daunce even?
Let that rowme to my Lady be yeven:
   She shalbe a grace,                        115
   To fyll the fourth place,
And reigne with the rest in heaven.


And whither rennes this bevie of Ladies bright,
   raunged in a rowe?
They bene all Ladyes of the lake behight,[36]        120
   that unto her goe.
*Chloris,*[37] that is the chiefest Nymph of al,
Of Olive braunches beares a Coronall:[38]
   Olives bene[39] for peace,
   When wars doe surcease:              125
Such for a Princesse bene principall.[40]


Ye shepheards daughters, that dwell on the greene,
   hye you there apace:[41]
Let none come there, but that Virgins bene,
   to adorne her grace.                 130
And when you come, whereas shee is in place,
See, that your rudenesse doe not you disgrace:
   Binde your fillets[42] faste,
   And gird in your waste,
For more finesse, with a tawdrie lace.[43]       135


Bring hether the Pincke and purple Cullambine,
   With Gelliflowres:[44]
Bring Coronations, and Sops in wine,[45]
   worne of Paramoures.[46]
Strowe me the ground with Daffadowndillies,[47]      140
And Cowslips, and Kingcups, and loved Lillies:

---

[36] **behight:** called.   [37] *Chloris:* nymph of vegetation, flowers, and herbs.   [38] **Coronall:** crown.
[39] **bene:** are.   [40] **principall:** princely; foremost. Peace is paramount to this distinctly unmartial maiden.   [41] **apace:** quickly.   [42] **fillets:** hair ribbons.   [43] **tawdrie lace:** silk lace necktie worn in the sixteenth and seventeenth centuries in honor of St. Audrey, who reputedly believed that she was punished for wearing jewels, and thereafter wore only lace.   [44] **Gelliflowres:** clove-scented flowers like dianthus.   [45] **Sops in wine:** clove pinks, a flower.   [46] **Paramoures:** lovers.   [47] **Daffadowndillies:** daffodils.

The pretie Pawnce,[48]
And the Chevisaunce,[49]
Shall match with the fayre flowre Delice.[50]
Now ryse up *Elisa*, decked as thou art,                               145
    in royall aray:[51]
And now ye daintie Damsells may depart
    echeone her way.
I feare, I have troubled your troupes to longe:
Let dame *Eliza* thanke you for her song.                              150
    And if you come hether,
    When Damsines[52] I gether,
I will part them all you among.

---

[48] **Pawnce:** pansy.    [49] **Chevisaunce:** wallflower.    [50] **flowre Delice:** *fleur de lis,* lily; the heraldic emblem of the French monarch.    [51] **aray:** array.    [52] **Damsines:** damson plums.

# CHAPTER 2

## *The Making of Men*

‑‑‑‑‑‑‑‑‑‑‑‑‑‑‑‑‑‑‑ ✦✦ ‑‑‑‑‑‑‑‑‑‑‑‑‑‑‑‑‑‑‑

In the first scene of *A Midsummer Night's Dream,* a jubilant Theseus dispatches Philostrate, his household Master of Revels, to "stir up the Athenian youth to merriments" (1.1.12) in celebration of his upcoming nuptials. The second scene shows an immediate response to this call for city-wide celebration as Peter Quince and his fellow workingmen (or "mechanicals") meet to cast and rehearse the play that they will enter into competition. But while Theseus's idea of a city tuned to a single key of pomp, triumph, and reveling may imply social harmony, social harmony here is something of an illusion. Theseus has no sooner made his announcement than old Egeus enters "full of vexation" (1.1.22) to reveal a bitter dispute over who has the right to choose his daughter Hermia's husband. Egeus himself would choose Demetrius, but Hermia prefers the equally suitable Lysander — "as well derived as he, / As well possessed" (99–100). Here is a quarrel between the sexes and the generations, but perhaps most of all a quarrel between men, which threatens the joyousness of Theseus's own marriage.

The image of Athenian unity is more profoundly dispelled, however, by the social organization of the play itself, which resolutely keeps the wellborn courtly lovers and the baseborn mechanicals in complete social and physical isolation from one another until Act 5. Both lovers and mechanicals pursue their different goals in the same extra-urban location, the fairy-haunted forest just outside Athens. But in social terms they have no reason to know about each other's existence or to regard their destinies as intertwined. The larger question — why Shakespeare should have organized his play so as to require the separation of lovers from mechanicals — has at least two possibly overlapping answers. One is the class stratification that was increasingly a feature of late sixteenth-century English society. Before that time, events like the religious plays performed on the holiday of Corpus Christi or processions on saints' days and other feast days had brought townsmen and villagers together in one communal body. Suppressing such events as part of the Protestant Reformation had the (perhaps unintended) effect of weakening civic life and communal feeling (Montrose, "Kingdom" 72). Theseus's call for general theatrical merriment would have reminded the Elizabethan audience of holidays past and playfully acknowledged the professional public theater that, encouraged by the Crown, had supplanted the earlier theatricals. When Shakespeare makes fun of the mechanicals as amateur actors, he seems to be pointing (whether fairly or not) to the great difference between their acting skill and that of his own consummately professional company of players. Though his joke is not entirely at the mechanicals' expense (the aristocrats are not, after all, a very kind or sympathetic audience), it is one based upon the obviousness of social differences.

Another reason Shakespeare kept the social classes separate in this play is that every Shakespeare play, no matter where or when it is set, reproduces a creative abstraction of contemporary English social structures. *A Midsummer Night's Dream* represents a city made up, apparently, of only two kinds of male subjects — a governing elite attached to Duke Theseus's court and workingmen who moonlight as amateur actors. They are overseen, at a distance, by fairies who haunt their woodlands and intervene from time to time in their destinies. The key social contrast is between the courtly lovers and the mechanicals, between aristocratic young men whose exclusive preoccupation appears to be intensely competitive wooing of the same woman and the manual laborers, their social inferiors, who here seek social advancement by putting on a play before their duke. The thematic connection between the two groups is oblique, taking the form of Titania's godson, the Indian boy raised in a fairy court whom Oberon wishes to have as page and for whom Bottom is a substitute. The fairies' quarrel over the boy's nurture reflects the kind of quarrel that might have erupted in an upper-class household when parents disagreed over when the boy should leave the mother's care and be sent to the harsher environment of school.

At the end of the play, Theseus rewards the mechanicals with praise, thanks, and remuneration. The lovers are rewarded not only with an invitation to repair to their wedding beds but, after all the human characters have exited the play, with Oberon's blessing upon their issue. We are left with an image of social harmony, but the image is problematic if we remember the physical and social separation between the ranks of men that the comic ending has not altered.

## The Ranks of Men: William Harrison's *Of Degrees of People*

When Englishmen theorized their social order, they did so entirely in male terms. This means that a normative description of English society, such as the excerpt from William Harrison's *Description of England* reproduced below, mentions a king rather than a queen, despite the inconvenient fact of their own monarch's sex. In a patriarchal order, a ruling queen is a default monarch, succeeding to the throne only in the absence of a male heir. What Harrison offers is a conventional description of the English social ranks that drastically simplifies the more complex, more fluid social reality. In part this simplification results from a lack of what we would consider to be reliable empirical data. But it also results from Harrison's received understanding of which people counted for purposes of social classification. He would have seen no reason, for example, to leave space for a description of social differences among Englishwomen since their differences, while complicating his scheme, could only derive from men's anyway. An Englishwoman's rank depended, almost entirely, first on that of her father and then on that of her husband. Harrison's labels, furthermore, describe only the achieved status of adult men. He leaves out all those in this relatively young society — boys, students, apprentices, and servants, for example — who were on their way to an adult place in the social order but lacked an official rank in the meantime. For an Elizabethan male, full manhood could only be achieved with the financial and sexual arrangements of marriage, with the assumption of patriarchal authority over a wife and a household: "The real man was household head, a little patriarch ruling over wife, children, servants, journeymen, and apprentices. . . . What gave access to the world of brothers was one's mastery of a woman which guaranteed one's sexual status" (Roper 46).

At the very top, there was an unbridgeable distance between the monarch and all of his subjects. Below that, Harrison describes a four-fold division of "gentlemen, citizens or burgesses, yeomen, which are artificers, or laborers" (see p. 153). In the conventional definition of the term, gentlemen derived their status primarily from hereditary ownership of land and from not having to work for a living. The term "citizens" refers to townsmen engaged in trade; London-born Harrison was himself the son of a citizen. "Yeomen" refers to respectable countrymen, especially small rural landholders or those who cultivated their own land. "Artificers" or handicraftsmen belonged to city, town, and country village alike; they were the men, like Peter Quince and his fellows, who wove and cut cloth, built houses, made furniture, mended bellows. The greatest division in rank, at least theoretically, came between gentlemen and everyone below them, which is why Harrison classifies all aristocrats as gentlemen. These he defines as "those whom their race and blood, or at the least their virtues do make noble and known" (see p. 153).

But Harrison's structure, while helpful in its normativeness, is much too tidy. It does not really describe all the adult men of England even on its own terms because it minimizes the real possibility of movement between the classes and obscures the great extremes of wealth and poverty that separated them. The basic social division between gentlemen and the baseborn was constantly bridged in the late sixteenth century by large numbers of "new men" who were not born gentlemen but became so by education and the adoption of a profession. Such new men would include the physician Simon Forman, whose dreams of Queen Elizabeth we reproduce below, and William Shakespeare himself. William Harrison, however, describes social mobility and the attainment of gentle status not as an expansion of numbers but rather as an exchange between merchants and gentlemen: "they often change estate with gentlemen, as gentlemen do with them, by a mutual conversion of the one into the other" (see p. 154). Individuals may change places in this closed structure, but the difference in rank remains. In fact, what was required to be a "real" gentleman in late sixteenth-century England became increasingly ambiguous as the wealth and prominence of London's mercantile citizenry grew and as its social competition with the great rural landowners accelerated.

→ WILLIAM HARRISON

## *From* The Description of England                                   *1587*

William Harrison (1534–1593) first wrote his *Description of England* in the 1560s as part of a description of the nations of the world begun, but never completed, by Queen Elizabeth's printer, Reginald Wolfe. Much of the material of this chapter first saw print in Sir Thomas Smith's *De republica Anglorum* (1583). Harrison later re-borrowed from Smith when his own work was published in 1587 as

William Harrison, *The Description of England* in Raphael Holinshed, *Chronicles of England, Scotland, and Ireland*, Vol. 2 (London, 1587) 156, 162–64.

the second part of the revised and expanded edition of Raphael Holinshed's *Chronicles of England, Scotland and Ireland.*

## OF DEGREES OF PEOPLE IN THE COMMONWEALTH OF ENGLAND

We in England divide our people commonly into four sorts, as gentlemen, citizens or burgesses, yeomen, which are artificers,[1] or laborers. Of gentlemen the first and chief (next the king) be the prince, dukes, marquesses, earls, viscounts, and barons. And these are called gentlemen of the greater sort or (as our common usage of speech is) lords and noblemen. And next unto them be knights, esquires, and, last of all, they that are simply called gentlemen. So that in effect our gentlemen are divided into their conditions[2] whereof in this chapter I will make particular rehearsal.[3]

[Harrison describes the titles of the Prince of Wales and of the great peers. He differentiates among the peers in terms of the classical or Germanic origins of their titles and military responsibilities. He includes the peers of the church, since they sit with the noblemen in the House of Lords, and praises them for being the most learned clergymen in Europe.]

Gentlemen be those whom their race and blood,[4] or at the least their virtues,[5] do make noble and known. The Latins call them *nobiles et generosus,* as the French do *nobles* or *gentilhommes.* The etymology of the name expoundeth the efficacy[6] of the word; for as *gens* in Latin betokeneth the race and surname, so the Romans had Cornelios, Sergios, Appios, Curios, Papyrios, Scipiones, Fabios, Aemilios, Julios, Brutos,[7] etc., of which who were *Agnati*[8] and therefore kept the name were also called *Gentiles,* gentlemen of that or that house and race.

Moreover, as the king doth dub[9] knights and createth the barons and higher degrees, so gentlemen whose ancestors are not known to come in with William, duke of Normandy[10] (for of the Saxon races[11] yet remaining we now make none account much less of the British issue[12]), do take their beginning in England after this manner in our times. Whosoever studieth the laws of the realm, who so abideth in the university giving his mind to his book, or professeth physic[13] and the liberal sciences, or, beside his service in

---

[1] **artificers:** skilled workmen, handicraftsmen.   [2] **conditions:** qualifications.   [3] **particular rehearsal:** one-by-one account.   [4] **race and blood:** ancestry and lineage.   [5] **virtues:** abilities. [6] **efficacy:** purpose.   [7] **Cornelios ... Brutos:** surnames of ancient Roman patrician families. [8] **Agnati:** Latin for blood relatives on the father's side.   [9] **dub:** confer rank on.   [10] **William, duke of Normandy:** William the Conqueror (1027?–87), reigned as William I (1066–1087). [11] **Saxon races:** descendants of invaders of Germanic ancestry.   [12] **British issue:** descendants of original Celtic inhabitants of southern England.   [13] **professeth physic:** studies or practices medicine.

the room of a captain in the wars, or good counsel given at home, whereby his commonwealth be benefited, can live without manual labor, and thereto is able and will bear the post,[14] charge,[15] and countenance[16] of a gentleman, he shall for money have a coat and arms bestowed upon him by heralds[17] (who in the charter[18] of the same do of custom pretend antiquity[19] and service, and many gay things[20]) and thereunto being made so good cheap[21] be called master, which is the title that men give to esquires and gentlemen, and reputed for a gentleman ever after.

[Harrison regards this purchase of gentlemanly status pragmatically as a net gain for the state, since gentlemen pay more in taxes and, when called to war, are obliged to serve. What he does object to in current practice is sending young gentlemen into Italy, where they come to disrespect their native faith and to adopt proud and disdainful behaviors.]

Citizens and burgesses have next place to gentlemen, who be those that are free[22] within the cities and are of some likely substance[23] to bear office in the same. But these citizens or burgesses are to serve the commonwealth in their cities and boroughs or in corporate towns where they dwell. And in the common assembly of the realm, wherein our laws are made (for in the counties they bear but little sway[24]) which assembly is called the high court of Parliament, the ancient cities appoint four and the boroughs two burgesses to have voices in it and give their consent or dissent unto such things as pass or stay there, in the name of the city or borough for which they are appointed.

In this place also are our merchants to be installed, as amongst the citizens (although they often change estate with gentlemen, as gentlemen do with them, by a mutual conversion of the one into the other), whose number is so increased in these our days that their only maintenance[25] is the cause of the exceeding prices of foreign wares, which otherwise when every nation was permitted to bring in her own commodities were far better cheap[26] and more plentifully to be had.

[Harrison complains about the importation of foreign goods into England and the inflation of prices that results. The rise in English exports and the

---

[14] **post:** position.  [15] **charge:** expenses.  [16] **countenance:** reputation, standing.  [17] **heralds:** officials of the Heralds' College or College of Arms, appointed to oversee granting arms, tracing genealogies, and recording honors.  [18] **charter:** official document (granting arms).  [19] **antiquity:** ancient lineage.  [20] **gay things:** splendid accomplishments.  [21] **made so good cheap:** made [a gentleman] so easily.  [22] **free:** licensed to engage in trade.  [23] **substance:** net worth.  [24] **bear but little sway:** have little power.  [25] **their only maintenance:** i.e., only in order to support them.  [26] **better cheap:** cheaper.

expansion of trade into the East and West Indies has not resulted in any lowering of prices.]

Yeomen are those which by our law are called *legales homines*, freemen born English and may dispend of[27] their own free land in yearly revenue to the sum of forty shillings sterling or six pounds as money goeth in our times. [Though the origin of the word *yeoman* is in dispute, it] signifieth (as I have read) a settled or staid man, such, I mean, as being married and of some years, betaketh[28] himself to stay in the place of his abode for the better maintenance of himself and his family, whereof the single sort have no regard, but are likely to be still fleeting, now hither, now thither, which argueth want[29] of stability in determination and resolution in judgment, for the execution of things of any importance. This sort of people have a certain preeminence and more estimation[30] than laborers and the common sort of artificers, and these commonly live wealthily, keep good houses, and travail[31] to get riches. They are also for the most part farmers to[32] gentlemen . . . or at the leastwise artificers; and with grazing, frequenting of markets, and keeping of servants (not idle servants as the gentlemen do, but such as get both their own and part of their master's living) do come to great wealth, insomuch that many of them are able and do buy the lands of unthrifty gentlemen, and often, setting their sons to the schools, to the universities, and to the Inns of the Court, or otherwise leaving them sufficient lands whereupon they may live without labor, do make them by those means to become gentlemen. These were they that in times past made all France afraid.[33] And albeit they be not called master as gentlemen are, or sir as to knights appertaineth,[34] but only John and Thomas, etc., yet have they been found to have done very good service. [Often such people, having fought for the king, stayed with him as footmen.]

The fourth and last sort of people in England are day laborers, poor husbandmen, and some retailers[35] (which have no free land), copyholders,[36] and all artificers, as tailors, shoemakers, carpenters, brickmakers, masons, etc. As for slaves and bondmen, we have none. [When bondmen do come to England from elsewhere, they are made free.] This fourth and last sort of people therefore have neither voice nor authority in the commonwealth, but are to be ruled and not to rule other. Yet they are not altogether neglected,[37] for in cities and corporate towns, for default of yeomen, they are fain to

---

[27] **dispend of:** have an income from.   [28] **betaketh:** commits.   [29] **want:** lack.   [30] **estimation:** reputation.   [31] **travail:** work hard.   [32] **to:** employed by.   [33] **made all France afraid:** i.e., during the Hundred Years' War (1337–1453).   [34] **appertaineth:** belongs by right.   [35] **retailers:** traders, dealers.   [36] **copyholders:** those whose lands are granted by manorial records (copy).   [37] **neglected:** disregarded.

make up their inquests[38] of such manner of people. And in villages they are commonly made churchwardens, sidemen,[39] aleconners,[40] now and then constables, and many times enjoy the name of headboroughs.[41]

## The Formation of the Ruler: Plutarch's "Life of Theseus"

With his marriage to the Amazonian queen in prospect, the Duke of Athens calls attention to himself as a man embarked on a major transition.

Shakespeare found the general outlines for the figure of Theseus in Plutarch's *The Lives of the Noble Grecians and Romans,* in several passages of Ovid's *Metamorphoses,* and in Geoffrey Chaucer's "Knight's Tale." His Duke of Athens is a complex construction of his gleanings from these and other texts. Compared to Chaucer's Theseus, who is noted for his compassion and pity, Shakespeare's Duke — unmoved by Hermia's plight, willing to uphold a severe marital law, and dismissively skeptical about poetry and the imagination — seems a stern and imposing figure. As it is, we don't see him much, since he appears only in three scenes and speaks fewer than two hundred lines (Mowat 335–51).

For anyone interested in early modern English culture, all of Plutarch's "Life of Theseus" repays study, as does his comparison between Theseus as founder of Athens and Romulus as founder of Rome. Because of *A Midsummer Night's Dream*'s thematic focus on male development, however, we have excerpted passages only from the early parts of Theseus's life story up to the war of the Amazons. But even this partial narrative suggests how rich in implication Theseus's life would have been for the playwright and his audience.

Plutarch's retelling offers in complex legendary form much of what early modern patriarchy feared and what it wished to promote as the character of a ruler. On the positive side, Theseus appears in the idealized guise of savior for an Athens beset — as was England in the 1590s — with a host of problems, both natural and man-made. His sudden, unheralded appearance as the king's hitherto unknown son and heir solves the Athenian succession crisis and the bitter factionalism it had caused. His bravery in leading a group of Athenian youth to confront the Cretan Minotaur rescues Athens from its debilitating, demoralizing subjection to Crete. For Elizabethan readers, Theseus's youth, energy, and timely arrival offered a startling contrast to

---

[38] **inquests:** juries.    [39] **sidemen:** assistant churchwardens.    [40] **aleconners:** inspectors appointed to assess the wholesomeness of bread and ale.    [41] **headboroughs:** petty constables.

their political situation marked by an aging queen still refusing to name her heir. Once king, Theseus reinvigorates the commonwealth with his youth and stabilizes it through his political vision and statesmanship. He even reconfigures the political structure of the Athenian monarchy into a republic in order to enlarge the Athenian citizenry and secure the city's hold over surrounding territories.

But this clear picture of heroic military and political leadership is troubled by details of Theseus's life and character that compromise his usefulness as a masculine role model for early modern English patriarchy. In the circumstances of his conception, for example, readers would have found an image of sexual entanglement that demonstrates the anxieties and risks surrounding paternity. Aethra, the mother of Theseus, tricks Aegeus, the king of Athens, into sex — against the enigmatic advice of an oracle. (It is interesting to note that the name of Theseus's father returns, in Shakespeare's play, as the name of another father.) Aethra proves not only Aegeus's weakness in the face of sexual desire but also the importance of interpretive skills: she and her father understand the meaning of the oracle but Aegeus does not. Just as the oracle had hinted, succumbing to this sexual temptation prevents Aegeus from fathering any other children. Hence, by making Aegeus a childless king, Aethra represents a threat both to his masculinity and to its corollary — the future security of Athens. Aethra compounds this political danger by keeping her son ignorant of his father's identity until Theseus demands the right to claim that recognition as the sign of his own independent manhood.

But the relation between father and son, once established, makes the story of Theseus even more complicated and troubling. Given the nine months between conception and birth, proof of virility and paternity (for suspicious or anxious patriarchs) was never more than conjectural. Theseus, announcing himself years after the event, is dangerously belated proof of his father's virility; as successor, he proves to be just as much a threat to Athens as its salvation. He is, both symbolically and literally, Aegeus's rescuer and killer: not content to subordinate himself to Aegeus or avoid risk in order to ensure succession, he undertakes the hazardous journey to Crete against his father's wishes. Then, overjoyed by his triumph, Theseus forgets his promise to signal his miraculous victory to his father by changing black sails to white when he rounds the Athenian headland. In mistaken despair over the loss of his heir and the other Athenian youth, Aegeus throws himself into the sea. Theseus, now king and parricide, will at the end of his own life complete the tragic circle by mistakenly killing his son Hippolytus.

Other material of Theseus's life could have resonated in complicated ways for Elizabethan male readers. His difficult journey to Athens, undertaken at his own initiative in emulation of his cousin Hercules, lives out the kind of heroic adventures that formed the backbone of popular romantic fiction for young male readers (Ben-Amos 24–25). His journey to Crete as sacrificial tribute for the Minotaur is a combination of self-sacrifice, physical courage, and guile. He carries it off by resorting to theatrical means: rather than lead a group composed of equal numbers of boys and girls as sacrificial victims of the Minotaur, he disguises two of the boys as girls so skillfully that they cannot be detected. The group he leads to Crete is thus physically stronger — because more male — than it would otherwise have been; for Elizabethan readers used to male actors playing women, such a group would have seemed distinctly theatricalized. Plutarch's Theseus is also marked by the romantic treacheries, personal disloyalties, and dependence on women that figure elsewhere in the Theseus mythography. The Minotaur legend highlights Theseus's dependence on Ariadne, who gives him the skein of thread that allows him to escape from the labyrinth. On his homeward journey to Athens, Theseus abandons her, grieving and pregnant, on the island of Naxos. In Shakespeare's play, Theseus's flaws as a lover are remembered only briefly, when Oberon lists the women whom Theseus has betrayed (2.1.78–80).

Apart from its length and complexity, there is also a certain incoherence to Plutarch's "Life of Theseus" and to the character of its hero. Plutarch found the stories that circulated around his legend irreconcilable and refused to decide between them in order to produce a tidier narrative (Mowat 337). Yet it is probably not the irreconcilability of Plutarch's sources that produces the real threat of incoherence in the character of Theseus. What is far more troubling is that the ambiguities of Theseus's life and deeds may indicate an incoherence at the heart of heroic masculinity itself.

→ PLUTARCH

## *From* The Lives of the Noble Grecians and Romans  1579
*Translated by Sir Thomas North*

The writings of Plutarch (c. 50–c. 120) could only have been known in the original to educated Elizabethans able to read Greek. Even Sir Thomas North, the English translator of *The Lives of the Noble Grecians and Romans* (1579), used Jacques Amyot's French translation of the work as the basis of his own transla-

Plutarch's *The Lives of the Noble Grecians and Romans*, Vol. 1, translated by Sir Thomas North (1579; rpt. London: David Nutt, 1895), "The Life of Theseus," 29–58.

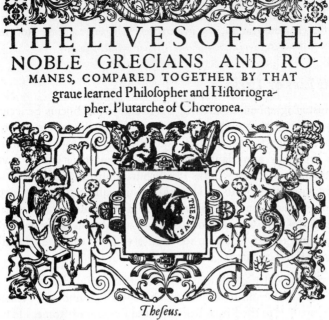

## THE LIVES OF THE
### NOBLE GRECIANS AND RO-
MANES, COMPARED TOGETHER BY THAT
graue learned Philofopher and Hiftoriogra-
pher, Plutarche of Chœronea.

*Thefeus.*

**A**     IKE as hiftoriographers defcribing the world(frende *Sofsius Senecio*) doe of purpofe referre to the vttermoft partes of their mappes the farre diftant regions whereof they be ignorant,with this note:thefe contries are by meanes of fandes and drowthes vnnauigable, rude, full of venimous beaftes , S c y t h i a n ife , and frofen feas . Euen fo may l (which in comparinge noble mens liues haue already gone fo farre into antiquitie , as the true and certaine hiftorie could lead me) of the reft, being thinges paft all proofe or chalenge , very well fay: that beyonde this time all is full of fufpicion and dout, being deliue-red vs by Poets and Tragedy makers,fometimes without trueth and likelihoode, and alwayes **B** without certainty. Howbeit, hauing heretofore fet foorth the liues of *Lycurgus* ( which efta-blifhed the lawes of the L a c e d æ m o n i a n s)and of king *Numa Pompilius*:me thought I might goa litle further to the life of *Romulus*, fence I was come fo nere him. But confidering my felfe as the Poet *AEfchilus* did:

*VVhat champion may vvith fuch a man compare?*
*or vvho(thinke I)fhalbe againft him fet?*
*VVho is fo bold? or vvho is he that dare*
*defend his force,in fuch encounter met?*

**A**

*Sofsius Sene-
cio a Senator
of Rome.*

FIGURE 9 *Page from Plutarch's* The Lives of the Noble Grecians and Romans.

159

tion. It is North's Plutarch to which Shakespeare turned again and again — for research, for characterization, for inspiration — in representing Roman and Greek heroes onstage.

## *From* THE LIFE OF THESEUS

Like as historiographers describing the world, friend Socius Senecio,[1] do of purpose refer to the uttermost part of their maps, the far distant regions whereof they be ignorant, with this note: these countries are by means of sands and droughts[2] unnavigable, rude,[3] full of venomous beasts, Scythian ice,[4] and frozen seas. Even so, may I (which in comparing noble men's lives have already gone so far into antiquity as the true and certain history could lead me) of the rest, being things past all proof[5] or challenge, very well say: that beyond[6] this time all is full of suspicion[7] and doubt, being delivered to us by poets and tragedy-makers, sometimes without truth and likelihood and always without certainty.

[Despite the difficulty of dealing with contradictory materials of great antiquity, Plutarch recounts the life of Theseus, the founder of Athens, in order to compare it to the life of Romulus, the founder of Rome. He begins with Theseus's lineage and the circumstances of his conception whereby Aegeus, childless king of Athens, is tricked into sexual intercourse with Aethra, one of the many children of Pittheus, king of Troezen.]

But Aegeus desiring (as they say) to know how he might have children went unto the city of Delphos to the oracle of Apollo, where, by Apollo's nun, that notable prophecy was given him for an answer. The which did forbid him to touch or know[8] any woman until he was returned again to Athens. And because the words of his prophecy were somewhat dark and hard,[9] he took his way by the city of Troezen to tell it unto Pittheus. The words of the prophecy were these:

O thou which art a gem of perfect grace,
    pluck not the tap[10] out of thy trusty tun.[11]
Before thou do, return unto thy place,
    in Athens town from whence thy race[12] doth run.

[1] **Socius Senecio:** consul of Rome in 98 and 107 B.C., friend of Plutarch to whom the historian dedicates this and several other *Lives.*  [2] **droughts:** deserts.  [3] **rude:** uncivilized.  [4] **Scythian ice:** i.e., extreme coldness. Scythia, an ancient region of Asia and southeastern Russia, was shorthand for remote and inhospitable territory.  [5] **proof:** verification.  [6] **beyond:** before.  [7] **suspicion:** conjecture.  [8] **know:** have sexual intercourse with.  [9] **dark and hard:** obscure and difficult to interpret.  [10] **tap:** stopper.  [11] **tun:** cask, barrel.  [12] **race:** lineage.

Pittheus, understanding the meaning, persuaded him or rather cunningly by some device deceived him in such sort that he made him to lie with his daughter called Aethra. Aegeus, after he had accompanied[13] with her, knowing that she was Pittheus' daughter with whom he had lain and doubting[14] that he had gotten her with child, left her a sword and a pair of shoes the which he hid under a great hollow stone; the hollowness whereof served just to receive those things which he laid under it; and made no living creature privy to it but her alone, straightly[15] charging her that if she happened to have a son, when he were come to man's state and of strength to remove the stone, and to take those things from under it which he left there, that she should then send him unto him by those tokens, as secretly as she could that nobody else might know of it. For he did greatly fear the children of one called Pallas,[16] the which lay in wait and spial[17] by all the means they could to kill him, only of despite because he had no children, they being fifty brethren and all begotten of one father. This done, he departed from her. And Aethra within few months after was delivered of a goodly son, the which from that time was called Theseus: and, as some say, so called because of the tokens of knowledge his father had laid under the stone. Yet some others write that it was afterwards at Athens when his father knew him and avowed him for his son.[18]

[Learning of his real parentage, Theseus determines to journey to Athens by the perilous overland route in order to emulate the heroic exploits of his cousin Hercules. He finds Athens to be a city suffering from barrenness, plague, and drought. It is filled with dissension because of the king's childlessness and because the Athenians must pay a yearly tribute of children to Minos, king of Crete, as reparation for a crime committed against him.]

He found the commonwealth turmoiled with seditions, factions, and divisions, and particularly the house of Aegeus in very ill terms also, because that Medea[19] (being banished out of the city of Corinth) was come to dwell in Athens and remained with Aegeus, whom she had promised by virtue of certain medicines to make him to get children. But when she heard tell that Theseus was come, before that the good king Aegeus (who was now become old, suspicious, and afraid of sedition . . .) knew what he was, she persuaded

---

[13] **accompanied:** had sexual intercourse.   [14] **doubting:** suspecting.   [15] **straightly:** directly, strictly.
[16] **Pallas:** Aegeus's brother.   [17] **spial:** espial, surveillance.   [18] **some others . . . son:** Theseus's name contains a many-layered pun on the Greek word *thesin*, referring to the act of placing the tokens in a hiding place and to the progenitor who both makes and acknowledges his son. Hence he might have been named at his birthplace or later by his father at Athens.   [19] **Medea:** tragic heroine, famous for magical powers. After killing her two sons by Jason (whom she had helped to get the Golden Fleece), she seeks refuge in Athens and marries Aegeus.

him to poison him at a feast which they would make him as a stranger that passed by. Theseus failed not to go to this prepared feast whereto he was bidden, but yet thought it good not to disclose himself. And the rather to give Aegeus occasion and mean to know him, when they brought the meat to the board, he drew out his sword as though he would have cut it withal and showed it unto him. Aegeus, seeing it, knew it straight and forthwith overthrew the cup with poison which was prepared for him and after he had inquired of him, and asked things, he embraced him as his son. Afterwards in the common assembly of inhabitants of the city, he declared how he avowed him for his son. Then all the people received him with exceeding joy for the renown of his valiantness and manhood.

[To Aegeus's dismay, Theseus volunteers to lead to Crete a group of seven boys and seven girls, chosen by lot for the sacrifice. He prays to Apollo for a successful outcome.]

[A]fter he was arrived in Crete, he slew there the Minotaur[20] (as the most part of ancient authors do write) by the means and help of Ariadne who, being fallen in fancy with him, did give him a clue[21] of thread by the help whereof she taught him how he might easily wind out of the turnings and cranks[22] of the labyrinth. And they say that, having killed this Minotaur, he returned back again the same way he went, bringing with him those other young children of Athens whom with Ariadne also he carried afterwards away. . . . Theseus made league with her, and carried away the young children of Athens which were kept as hostages and concluded peace and amity between the Athenians and the Cretans who promised and swore they would never make wars against them. They report many other things touching this matter, and specially of Ariadne. But there is no truth or certainty in it [as Plutarch demonstrates by retelling several contradictory legends of Ariadne's actions after leaving Crete with Theseus].

[W]hen they drew near the coast of Attica,[23] they were so joyful, he and his master,[24] that they forgot to set up their white sail by which they should have given knowledge of their health and safety to Aegeus. Who, seeing the black sail afar off, being out of all hope and sorrow to see his son again, took such a grief at his heart that he threw himself headlong from the top of a cliff and killed himself. So soon as Theseus was arrived at the port named Phalerum, he performed the sacrifices which he had vowed to the gods at

---

[20] **Minotaur:** monstrous offspring, half-man and half-bull, of Pasiphaë, Queen of Crete, who was infatuated with a bull. It lived within a labyrinth and devoured the Athenian children. [21] **clue:** skein. [22] **cranks:** windings. [23] **Attica:** countryside around Athens. [24] **master:** ship captain.

his departure and sent an herald of his before unto the city to carry news of his safe arrival. The herald found many of the city mourning the death of king Aegeus. Many other received him with great joy as may be supposed. They would have crowned him also with a garland of flowers for that he had brought so good tidings that the children of the city were returned in safety. The herald was content to take the garland[25] yet would he not in any wise put it on his head but did wind it about his herald's rod he bore in his hand and so returneth forthwith to the sea where Theseus made his sacrifices. Who, perceiving they were not yet done, did refuse to enter into the temple and stayed without[26] for troubling[27] of the sacrifices. Afterwards, all ceremonies finished, he went in and told him the news of his father's death. Then he and his company, mourning for sorrow, hasted with speed towards the city.

[Their ceremonies to the gods are efficacious and cure infertility from that day forward in Athens.] [Some] hold opinion also that the feast of boughs[28] which is celebrated at Athens at this time was then first of all instituted by Theseus. It is said, moreover, that he did not carry [to Crete] all the wenches upon whom the lots did fall, but chose two fair young boys whose faces were sweet and delicate as maidens be, that otherwise were hardy and quick-sprighted. But he made them so oft bathe themselves in hot baths and kept them in from the heat of the sun and so many times to wash, anoint, and rub themselves with oils which serve to supple and smooth their skins to keep fresh and fair the color to make yellow and bright their hairs. And withal did teach them so to counterfeit their speech, countenance, and fashion of young maids that they seemed to be like them rather than young boys. For there was no manner of difference to be perceived outwardly, and he mingled them with the girls without the knowledge of any man. Afterwards, when he was returned, he made a procession in which both he and the other young boys were apparelled then as they be now, which carry boughs on the day of the feast in their hands. They carry them in the honor of Bacchus and Ariadne,[29] following the fable that is told of them: or rather because they returned home just, at the time and season, when they gather the fruit of those trees.

[In gratitude for his accomplishments the Athenians build a temple in his honor, and Theseus sets about the tasks of rebuilding the city-state.]

---

[25] **garland:** token of victory.   [26] **without:** outside.   [27] **for troubling:** for fear of disturbing. [28] **feast of boughs:** the Oschophoria, Athenian festival in which celebrants carried branches of grape-laden vines.   [29] **Bacchus and Ariadne:** the god falls in love with the Cretan princess, who has been abandoned on the isle of Naxos by Theseus. Upon her death, the god transforms her into a constellation.

Furthermore, after the death of his father Aegeus, he undertook a marvelous great enterprise. For he brought all the inhabitants of the whole province of Attica to be within the city of Athens, and made them all one corporation, which were before dispersed into diverse villages, and by reason thereof were very hard to be assembled together, when occasion was offered to establish any order concerning the common state. Many times also they were at variance together and by the ears, making wars one upon another. But Theseus took the pains to go from village to village, and from family to family, to let them understand the reasons why they should consent unto it. So he found the poor people and private men,[30] ready to obey and follow his will, but the rich, and such as had authority in every village, all against it. Nevertheless he won them, promising that it should be a commonwealth, and not subject to the power of any sole prince, but rather a popular state. In which he would only reserve to himself the charge of the wars and the preservation of the laws: for the rest, he was content that every citizen in all and for all should bear a like sway and authority. So there were some that willingly granted thereto. Other who had no liking thereof yielded notwithstanding, for fear of his displeasure and power which then was very great. So they thought it better to consent with good will unto that he required than to tarry[31] his forcible compulsion. Then he caused all the places where justice was ministered and all their halls of assembly to be overthrown and pulled down. He removed straight all judges and officers and built a town house[32] and a council hall, in the place where the city now standeth, which the Athenians call Asty,[33] but he called the whole corporation of them all, Athens. Afterwards he instituted the great feast and common sacrifice for all of the country of Attica, which they call Panatheneia. Then he ordained another feast also upon the sixteenth day of the month of June, for all strangers which should come to dwell in Athens, which is called Metoecia and is kept even to this day. That done, he gave over his regal power according to his promise and began to set up an estate[34] or policy[35] of a commonwealth, beginning first with the service of the gods.

[Theseus seeks out the oracles of Apollo to find out the fortunes of the city.]

Moreover, because he would further yet augment his people and enlarge his city, he enticed many to come and dwell there by offering them the selfsame freedom and privileges which the natural-born citizens had. So that many judge that these words which are in use at this day in Athens when

---

[30] **private men:** ordinary citizens.   [31] **tarry:** wait for.   [32] **town house:** town hall.   [33] **Asty:** upper town.   [34] **estate:** form of government.   [35] **policy:** political structure.

any open proclamation is made — "All people, come ye hither" — be the self-same [proclamation] which Theseus then caused to be proclaimed when he in that sort did gather a people together of all nations. Yet for all that, he suffered not the great multitude that came thither, tag and rag,[36] to be without distinction of degrees[37] and orders. For he first divided the noblemen from husbandmen and artificers, appointing the noblemen as judges and magistrates to judge upon matters of religion and touching the service of the gods. And of them also he did choose rulers to bear civil office in the common weal to determine the law and to tell[38] all holy and divine things. By this means he made the noblemen and the two other estates equal in voice. And as the noblemen did pass the other in honor, even so the artificers exceeded them in number, and the husbandmen them in profit. Now that Theseus was the first who of all others yielded to have a common weal or popular estate (as Aristotle sayeth) and did give over his regal power. Homer himself seemeth to testify it, in numbering the ships which were in the Grecians' army before the city of Troy. For amongst all the Grecians, he only calleth the Athenians people.[39]

[Theseus coins money and establishes games, including games in honor of Neptune and games played at night with the character rather of sacrifices or mysteries than games.]

Touching the voyage he made by the Sea Major,[40] Philochorus and some other hold opinion that he went thither with Hercules against the Amazons and that, to honor his valiantness, Hercules gave him Antiopa the Amazon. But the more part of the other historiographers, namely Hellanicus, Phere-cydes, and Herodotus, do write that Theseus went thither alone after Hercules' voyage and that he took this Amazon prisoner, which is likeliest to be true. For we do not find that any other who went this journey with him had taken any Amazon prisoner besides himself. Bion also, the historiographer, this notwithstanding, sayeth that he brought her away by deceit and stealth. For the Amazons (sayeth he) naturally loving men, did not fly at all when they saw them land in their country but sent them presents and that Theseus enticed her to come into his ship who brought him a present and so soon as she was aboard, he hoisted his sail and so carried her away.

[Plutarch summarizes the divergent historical accounts of Theseus's wars against the Amazons, including a detailed account of fighting within the city of Athens, and the story of Antiopa.]

[36] tag and rag: contemptuous description of the people.    [37] degrees: ranks.    [38] tell: pronounce upon.    [39] people: i.e., a nation.    [40] Sea Major: Black Sea.

Afterwards at the end of four months, peace was taken between them by means of one of the women called Hippolyta. For this historiographer calleth the Amazon which Theseus married Hippolyta and not Antiopa. . . . We are not to marvel if the history of things so ancient be found so diversely written. For there are also that write that Queen Antiopa sent those secretly which were hurt then into the city of Chalcis where some of them recovered and were healed. And others also died which were buried near to the place called Amazoneum. Howsoever it was, it is most certain that this war was ended by agreement. . . . And this is that which is worthy memory (in mine opinion) touching the wars of these Amazons.

## The Formation of the Gentleman: Sir Thomas Elyot and Roger Ascham

As Harrison's two-fold division of society into gentlemen and everyone else implies, the social formation of the young gentleman was a major preoccupation of sixteenth-century patriarchy. Many of the humanist texts devoted to the subject share with *A Midsummer Night's Dream* a sense that male childhood is marked by an inevitable struggle between mothers and fathers over a boy's nurture. One of patriarchy's major tasks was to take the young boy from the tender care of women and to inculcate in him the repressive self-control and desire for mastery that he would need in order to take up the obligations of his adult station.

Most Elizabethan fathers had little interest in or say about the lives of the very young child. A boy, wearing children's gender-neutral dresses and in outward appearance barely distinguishable from his sister, began his life in the company of women. His world was dominated by his mother or mother-surrogate, her female servants and/or attendants. But Sir Thomas Elyot's *The Book Named the Governor* betrays considerable anxiety about the nursery world as the first environment for a future ruling-class male. Accepting the common belief that the qualities of the wet nurse passed directly in the milk to the sucking child, Elyot lays downs strict criteria of age, rank, and temperament for the nurse and for the older woman who supervises her. He recommends a strict exclusion of men from the nursery, "except physicians only" (see p. 170), apparently fearing the effects of the wanton language that might pass between a lowborn nurse and a male visitor, decrying the sexual atmosphere they might create. He pictures the damage for the child as a "tache" or blemish or, worse yet, as an infection within (see p. 170). It seems almost as if, after a child survives the risks of congenital defect in the mother's womb, he must then face the possible corruptions of the female-controlled nursery world. Yet, despite such anxiety, fathers were not encouraged to play with or fondle their babies, since these behaviors were regarded as effeminate (Crawford, "Sucking Child" 41–42).

Infancy ended and boyhood began with a ceremonial first pair of breeches, at around the age of six. Within a year, the upper-class boy was taken from the world of his mother, where he could be "spoiled" by maternal permissiveness and coddling, and introduced to an emotionally much harsher, male-only world of tutors and schoolmasters. Girls too could receive single-sex schooling at what were called dame schools, but this was an environment with a radically different, far less rigorous curriculum. According to Anthony Fletcher, gentry families usually opted for schooling outside the home rather than hiring in-house tutors, probably because sending the boy away made it easier to separate him from his mother (Fletcher 297–98). If the young boy at school absolutely required a female servant, Elyot wants her to be elderly and gloomy ("ancient and sad") and forbids her the companionship of young women lest the boy's reason be inflamed by "sparks of volptuosity." The choice of an elderly tutor ("ancient and worshipful") is to be preferred altogether, so that the boy may grow up to be like Achilles or better yet Alexander (see p. 173).

*A Midsummer Night's Dream* also alludes to the major stages from boyhood to adulthood in a wellborn youth's life in Titania and Oberon's quarrel over the changeling boy. Neither fairy is birth parent to the child, but, like many an Elizabethan grownup, is eager to serve as foster parent. Aristocratic households routinely sent children back and forth to one another, recommending children to the care and nurture of an admired relative or powerful future patron. Children were like gifts, passed along in complex rituals of alliance and exchange as a way of promoting or maintaining ties between the families involved in the transfer. At the center of the gift-giving exchanges was the queen, who participated by accepting aristocratic girls as maids of honor, often after several prior exchanges (Fumerton 36–44). In the play, Titania, the Indian boy's godmother, has provided his early rearing; Oberon wishes to take over at a second stage and train the boy as his own court page. The key question arises for the fairies, as for Elizabethan parents generally, over just when a transfer in supervision ought to take place. The play identifies the emotional violence of this radical separation of mother and son with Titania and her ferocious refusal to let her godson go. Oberon parodies and ridicules her maternal attachment and care by putting the monstrous Bottom in the boy's place. Perhaps, for adult gentlemen in Shakespeare's audience, the memory of these separations was difficult and needed to be distanced through complex ridicule. Perhaps this is why Titania's godchild does not appear onstage and why it is Bottom, the lowborn weaver, who can be left to "spoil" in the indulgent care of women and fairies.

What young males of all ranks had in common was dependency: young servants and apprentices were dependent on their masters, the noble youth on his parents or guardians. The apprentice was forbidden to marry (and financially could not have done so anyway). The young gentleman might have been entered into apprenticeship with a merchant. Otherwise, barred by his status from taking up a trade or doing work, he had little to do after his education but travel abroad or wait — for marriage, for inheritance, for office — before assuming the privileges of adult malehood. In prescribing the activities fit for this time of life, Roger Ascham's *The Schoolmaster* recommended courtly pastimes. These included quasi-martial activities like sports and hunting, which were thought to be a kind of training for warfare, and civilizing activities like foreign travel and learning languages. The young gentleman's idleness, however, should not be unsupervised, according to Ascham, because it led to independent notions, even to rebellion in that prime matter of parental concern — marital choice. It is ironic that Ascham regards Athenian education as a model for Elizabethan imitation, given the romantic freedom in Theseus's Athens which has allowed Demetrius to court and jilt Helena and Lysander to woo Hermia behind her father's back.

→   SIR THOMAS ELYOT

## *From* The Book Named the Governor                                    *1531*

Sir Thomas Elyot (1490?-1546), a statesman of enormous learning, served as a diplomat for Henry VIII, to whom he dedicated *The Book Named the Governor* (1531). His other important works include the popular manual *The Castle of Health* (1534) and Elyot's *Dictionary* (1538), the first Latin-English dictionary based on the new humanistic learning. *The Book Named the Governor,* principally focusing upon the education requisite for young men of the ruling classes, is an orthodox restatement of social and political order in which rank was determined, by and large, by birthright.

Of particular interest for the social differences between male characters in *A Midsummer Night's Dream* is Elyot's functional analogy between the different members of a commonwealth and the furnishings of a house:

> for the pans and pots garnisheth well the kitchen, and yet they should be to the chamber none ornament. Also the beds, testers, and pillows beseemeth

---

Sir Thomas Elyot, *The Book Named the Governor* (London, 1531) 15v–21v.

not the hall, no more than the carpets and cushions becometh the stable. Semblably the potter and tinker, only perfect in their craft, shall little do in the ministration of justice. A ploughman or carter shall make but a feeble answer to an ambassador. Also a weaver or fuller should be an unmeet captain of an army, or in another other office of a governor. (5v)

For Elyot, perhaps, the mechanicals' performance of "Pyramus and Thisbe" at the wedding celebration of Duke Theseus and Queen Hippolyta is equivalent to the pots and pans escaping from the kitchen and presuming to decorate the hall.

## THE EDUCATION OR FORM OF BRINGING UP OF THE CHILD OF A GENTLEMAN WHICH IS TO HAVE AUTHORITY IN A PUBLIC WEAL

Forasmuch as all noble authors do conclude, and also common experience proveth, that where the governors of realms and cities be found adorned with virtues and do employ their study and mind to the public weal,[1] as well to the augmentation thereof as to the establishing and long continuance of the same, there a public weal must needs be both honorable and wealthy. To the intent that I will declare how such personages may be prepared, I will use the policy of a wise and cunning gardener who, purposing to have in his garden a fine and precious herb[2] that should be to him and all other repairing thereto excellently commodious[3] or pleasant, he will first search throughout his garden where he can find the most mellow and fertile earth and therein will he put the seed of the herb to grow and be nourished and, in most diligent wise,[4] attend[5] that no weed be suffered to grow or approach nigh unto it. And to the intent it may thrive the faster, as soon as the form of an herb once appeareth, he will set a vessel of water by it in such wise that it may continually distill on the root sweet drops and, as it springeth in stalk, underset it with something that it break not and always keep it clear from weeds. Semblable[6] order will I ensue[7] in the forming of gentle wits of noblemen's children who from the wombs of their mother shall be made propise[8] or apt to the governance of a public weal.

First, they unto whom the bringing up of such children appertaineth ought against[9] the time that their mother shall be of them delivered, to be sure of a nurse which should be of no servile condition[10] or vice notable. For as some ancient writers do suppose, often times the child sucketh the vice of

---

[1] **public weal:** state, community, or (as below) general good. [2] **herb:** generic term for plant. [3] **commodious:** beneficial. [4] **wise:** manner. [5] **attend:** make sure. [6] **semblable:** similar. [7] **ensue:** follow. [8] **propise:** fit. [9] **against:** in preparation for. [10] **servile condition:** very low rank.

his nurse with the milk of her pap.[11] And also observe that she be of mature or ripe age, not under twenty years or above thirty, her body also being clean from all sickness or deformity and having her complexion most of the right and pure sanguine,[12] forasmuch as the milk thereof coming excelleth all other both in sweetness and substance. Moreover, to the nurse should be appointed another woman of approved virtue, discretion, and gravity who shall not suffer in the child's presence to be showed any act or tache[13] dishonest or any wanton or unclean word to be spoken. And for that cause, all men except physicians only should be excluded and kept out of the nursery. Perchance some will scorn me for that I am so serious, saying that there is no such damage to be feared in an infant who for tenderness of years hath not the understanding to discern good from evil. And yet no man will deny but, in that innocency, he will discern milk from butter and bread from pap[14] and ere he can speak he will with his hand or countenance signify which he desireth. And I verily do suppose that in the brains and hearts of children, which be members spiritual,[15] whiles they be tender and the little slips[16] of reason begin in them to burgeon, there may hap by evil custom some pestiferous dew of vice to pierce the said members and infect and corrupt the soft and tender buds, whereby the fruit may grow wild and some time contain in it fervent and mortal poison to the utter destruction of a realm.

And we have in daily experience that little infants assayeth to follow, not only the words, but also the facts[17] and gestures of them that be provect[18] in years. For we daily hear, to our great heaviness, children swear great oaths and speak lascivious and unclean words by the example of other whom they hear; whereat the lewd[19] parents do rejoice, soon after, or in this world or elsewhere, to their great pain and torment. Contrariwise, we behold some children, kneeling in their game before images and holding up their little white hands, do move their pretty mouths as[20] they were praying; other going and singing as it were in procession. Whereby they do express their disposition to the imitation of those things, be they good or evil, which they usually do see or hear. Wherefore not only princes, but also all other children, from their nurses' paps are to be kept diligently from the hearing or seeing of any vice or evil tache. And incontinent[21] as soon as they can speak, it behoveth with most pleasant allurings to instill in them sweet manners and virtuous custom. Also to provide for them such companions and playfellows which shall not do in his presence any reproachable act or speak

---

[11] pap: breast.  [12] complexion . . . sanguine: bodily constitution of the healthiest kind.  [13] tache: fault.  [14] pap: gruel.  [15] members spiritual: parts of the body endowed with higher faculties.  [16] slips: figuratively, sprouts, sprigs.  [17] facts: deeds.  [18] provect: mature.  [19] lewd: ignorant, silly.  [20] as: as if.  [21] incontinent: immediately.

any unclean word or oath, nor to advaunt him[22] with flattery, remembering his nobility or any other like thing wherein he might glory. Only as it be to persuade him to virtue or to withdraw him from vice in the remembering to him the danger of his evil example. For noblemen more grievously offend by their example than by their deed. Yet often remembrance to them of their estate may happen to radicate[23] in their hearts intolerable pride, the most dangerous poison to nobleness. Wherefore there is required to be therein much cautel[24] and soberness.

## The Order of Learning That a Nobleman Should Be Trained In Before He Be Come to the Age of Seven Years

Some old authors hold opinion that before the age of seven years a child should not be instructed in letters; but those writers were either Greeks or Latins among whom all doctrine and sciences were in their maternal tongues, by reason whereof they saved all that long time which at this day is spent in understanding perfectly the Greek or Latin. Wherefore it requireth now a longer time to the understanding of both. Therefore that infelicity of our time and country compelleth us to encroach somewhat upon the years of children, and specially of noblemen, that they may sooner attain to wisdom and gravity than private persons, considering, as I have said, their charge and example, which above all things is most to be esteemed. Notwithstanding, I would not have them enforced by violence to learn but, according to the counsel of Quintilian,[25] to be sweetly allured thereto with praises and such pretty gifts as children delight in. And their first letters to be painted or limned in a pleasant manner, wherein children of gentle courage[26] have much delectation. And also there is no better allective[27] to noble wits than to induce them into a contention with their inferior companions, they sometime purposely suffering the more noble children to vanquish and, as it were, giving them place and sovereignty, though indeed the inferior children have more learning. But there can be nothing more convenient than by little and little to train and exercise them in speaking of Latin, informing them to know first the names in Latin of all things that cometh in sight and to name all the parts of their bodies, and giving them somewhat that they covet or desire in most gentle manner to teach them to ask it again in Latin. And if by this means they may be induced to understand and speak Latin, it shall afterwards be less grief to them, in a manner, to learn anything

---

[22] advaunt him: make him boastful.    [23] radicate: implant.    [24] cautel: caution.    [25] Quintilian: Marcus Fabius Quintilianus (born c. 30 A.D.), Roman rhetorician and teacher, author of the influential *Institutio Oratoria*.    [26] gentle courage: noble disposition.    [27] allective: enticement.

where they understand the language wherein it is written. And, as touching grammar, there is at this day no better introductions, and more facile, than ever before were made, concerning as well Greek as Latin, if they be wisely chosen. And it shall be no reproach to a nobleman to instruct his own children or at the leastways to examine them by the way of dalliance[28] or solace, considering that the emperor Octavius Augustus disdained not to read the words of Cicero[29] and Virgil[30] to his children and nephews. And why should not noblemen rather so do than teach their children how at dice and cards they may cunningly lose and consume their own treasure and substance? Moreover teaching representeth the authority of a prince: wherefore Dionysius,[31] king of Sicily, when he was for tyranny expelled by his people, he came in to Italy and there in a common school taught grammar, wherewith, when he was of his enemies embraided[32] and called a schoolmaster, he answered them that although Sicilians had exiled him, yet in despite of them all he reigned, noting thereby the authority that he had over his scholars. Also when it was of him demanded what availed him, Plato or philosophy, wherein he had been studious, he answered that they caused him to sustain adversity patiently and made his exile to be to him more facile and easy. Which courage and wisdom considered of his people, they eftsoons[33] restored him unto his realm and estate royal, where if he had procured against them hostility or wars, or had returned into Sicily with any violence, I suppose the people would have always resisted him and have kept him in perpetual exile, as the Romans did the proud king Tarquin[34] whose son ravished Lucrece. But to return to my purpose: it shall be expedient that a nobleman's son in his infancy have with him continually only such as may accustom him by little and little to speak pure and elegant Latin. Semblably the nurses and other women about him if it be possible to do the same, or at the leastways that they speak none English but that which is clean, polite, perfectly and articulately pronounced, omitting no letter or syllable, as foolish women often times do of a wantonness, whereby divers noblemen and gentlemen's children (as I do at this day know) have attained corrupt and foul pronunciation. This industry used in forming little infants, who shall doubt but that they (not lacking natural wit) shall be apt to receive learning when they come to more years? And in this wise may they be instructed without any violence or enforcing, using the most part of the time until they

---

[28] **dalliance:** pastime, amusement.   [29] **Cicero:** Marcus Tullius Cicero (106–43 B.C.), Roman republican and acclaimed orator.   [30] **Virgil:** Publius Vergilius Maro (70–19 B.C.), Roman pastoral and epic poet, author of the *Aeneid.*   [31] **Dionysius:** Dionysius II, ruler (367–344 B.C.) of Syracuse (on the island of Sicily).   [32] **embraided:** mocked.   [33] **eftsoons:** soon again.   [34] **Tarquin:** legendary last (534–510 B.C.) king of Rome.

come to the age of seven years in such disports as do appertain to children wherein is no resemblance or similitude of vice.

## At What Age a Tutor Should Be Provided and What Shall Appertain to His Office to Do

After that a child is come to seven years of age, I hold it expedient that he be taken from the company of women, saving that he may have, one year or two at the most, an ancient and sad[35] matron attending on him in his chamber which shall not have any young woman in her company. For though there be no peril of offence in that tender and innocent age, yet in some children nature is more prone to vice than to virtue; and in the tender wits be sparks of voluptuosity[36] which, nourished by any occasion or object, increase often times into so terrible a fire that therewith all virtue and reason is consumed. Wherefore to eschew that danger, the most sure counsel is to withdraw him from all company of women and to assign unto him a tutor which should be an ancient and worshipful[37] man in whom is approved to be much gentleness mixed with gravity and, as nigh as can be, such one as the child by imitation following may grow to be excellent. And if he be also learned, he is the more commendable. Peleus, the father of Achilles, committed the governance of his son to Phenix, which was a stranger born, who, as well in speaking elegantly as in doing valiantly, was master to Achilles (as Homer saith). How much profited it to king Philip,[38] father to the great Alexander,[39] that he was delivered in hostage to the Thebans? Where he was kept and brought up under the governance of Epaminondas,[40] a noble and valiant captain of whom he received such learning, as well in acts martial as in other liberal sciences, that he excelled all other kings that were before his time in Greece, and finally as well by wisdom as prowess subdued all that country.

Semblably he ordained for his son Alexander a noble tutor called Leonidas[41] unto whom, for his wisdom, humanity, and learning, he committed the rule and preeminence over all the masters and servants of Alexander. In whom, notwithstanding, was such a familiar vice which Alexander apprehending in childhood could never abandon. Some suppose it to be fury and hastiness, other superfluous drinking of wine. Which of

---

[35] sad: serious.  [36] voluptuosity: sensuality.  [37] worshipful: honorable.  [38] Philip: King of Macedon, 359–336 B.C.; his military and diplomatic gifts laid the foundations of Macedonia's greatness.  [39] Alexander: Alexander the Great (356–323 B.C.), conqueror of Greece, Persia, and Egypt.  [40] Epaminondas: (d. 362 B.C.), known for his nobility of character.  [41] Leonidas: according to Plutarch, a kinsman of Alexander's mother Olympias and his head schoolmaster.

them it were, it is a good warning for gentlemen to be the more serious in searching not only for the virtues but also for the vices of them unto whose tuition and governance they will commit their children.

The office of a tutor is first to know the nature of his pupil, that is to say, whereto he is most inclined or disposed and in what thing he setteth his most delectation or appetite. If he be of nature courteous, piteous,[42] and of a free and liberal[43] heart, it is a principal token of grace (as it is by all scripture determined). Then shall a wise tutor purposely commend those virtues, extolling also his pupil for having of them. And therewithal he shall declare them to be of all men most fortunate, which shall happen to have such a master. And moreover shall declare to him what honor, what love, what commodity shall happen to him by these virtues. And if any have been of disposition contrary, then to express the enormity of their vice, with as much detestation as may be. And if any danger have thereby ensued, misfortune, or punishment, to aggrieve[44] it in such wise, with so vehement words, as the child may abhor it and fear the semblable adventure.[45]

[42] **piteous:** compassionate.   [43] **liberal:** generous.   [44] **aggrieve:** show its seriousness.   [45] **semblable adventure:** similar result.

→ ROGER ASCHAM

## *From* The Schoolmaster     *1570*

Roger Ascham (1515–1568), scholar and humanist, served Elizabeth I as Greek and Latin tutor and official Latin Secretary. His treatise on education, though left unfinished at his death, was enormously influential.

[In antiquity, a young man had little freedom to go where he wanted and, until he was married or held public office, was under the watchful eye of a governor. English youth, complains Ascham, are so free that they even dare to marry without first seeking the consent of their parents.]

Our time is so far from that old discipline and obedience, as now, not only young gentlemen but even very girls dare without all fear, though not without open shame, where they list,[1] and how they list, marry themselves

[1] **list:** please.

Roger Ascham, *The Schoolmaster, or plain and perfect way of teaching children the Latin tongue. The first book teaching the bringing up of youth* (London, 1570) 13–20.

FIGURE 10  *Title page from* A Catechism, *a Latin primer (1571). This is the all-male environment to which the Elizabethan boy was sent upon leaving his mother's care. Note the bundle of switches beside the schoolmaster's raised and throne-like chair.*

in spite of father, mother, God, good order, and all. The cause of this evil is, that youth is least looked unto, when they stand [in] most need of good keep and regard. It availeth not to see them well taught in young years, and after, when they come to lust and youthful days, to give them license to live as they lust themselves. For if ye suffer the eye of a young gentleman once to be entangled with vain[2] sights, and the ear to be corrupted with fond[3] or filthy talk, the mind shall quickly fall sick, and soon vomit and cast up all the wholesome doctrine that he received in childhood, though he were never so well brought up before. And being once glutted with vanity,[4] he will straightway loathe all learning, and all good counsel to the same. And the

---

[2] **vain:** foolish.    [3] **fond:** foolish.    [4] **vanity:** worthless pursuits.

parents, for all their great cost and charge, reap only, in the end, the fruit of grief and care.

This evil is not common to poor men, as God will have it, but proper to rich and great men's children, as they deserve it. Indeed, from seven to seventeen, young gentlemen commonly be carefully enough brought up. But from seventeen to seven and twenty (the most dangerous time of all a man's life, and most slippery to stay well in), they have commonly the rein of all license in their own hand, and specially such as do live in the Court. And that which is most to be marveled at commonly, [is that] the wisest and also best men be found the fondest[5] fathers in this behalf. And if some good father would seek some remedy herein, yet the mother (if the house hold of our Lady) had rather, yea, & will, too, have her son cunning & bold, in making him to live trimly[6] when he is young, [and] then by learning and travel, to be able to serve his Prince and his country, both wisely in peace and stoutly in war, when he is old.

The fault is in yourselves, ye noble men's sons, and therefore ye deserve the greater blame, that commonly the meaner men's children come to be the wisest counselors and greatest doers in the weighty affairs of this Realm. And why? for God will have it so, of his providence: because he will have it no otherwise, by your negligence. . . .

For wisdom and virtue, there be many fair examples in this Court, for young gentlemen to follow. But they be, like fair marks[7] in the field, out of a man's reach, too far off, to shoot at well. The best and worthiest men, indeed, be sometimes seen but seldom talked withal: a young gentleman may sometime kneel to their person, [but] smally[8] use their company, for their better instruction.

But young gentlemen are feign commonly to do in the court as young archers do in the field: that is, take such marks as be nigh them, although they be never so foul to shoot at. I mean, they be driven to keep company with the worst: and what force ill company hath to corrupt good wits, the wisest men know best.

And not ill company only, but the ill opinion also of the most part, doth much harm, and namely of those which should be wise in the true deciphering of the good disposition of nature, of comeliness in courtly manners, and all right doings of men.

But error and fantasy do commonly occupy the place of truth and judgment. For if a young gentleman be demure and still of nature, they say he is simple and lacketh wit. If he be bashful,[9] and will soon blush, they call him a

---

[5] fondest: most permissive.    [6] trimly: properly.    [7] marks: archery targets.    [8] smally: rarely.
[9] bashful: sensitive, modest.

babyish and ill-brought-up thing. If he be innocent and ignorant of ill, they say he is rude[10] and hath no grace, so ungraciously do some graceless men misuse the fair and godly word *grace*.

[The graceless young men at court blush at nothing, claim to know everything, fawn over the powerful, thrust themselves aggressively into groups of people, and behave rudely to newcomers. In the military there is the same contrast between worthy soldiers and ruffians; and among servants there are some of staid disposition and some who do their masters great mischief.]

But I marvel the less, that these misorders be amongst some in the Court, for commonly in the country also everywhere, innocence is gone; bashfulness is banished; much presumption in youth; small authority in age. Reverence is neglected; duties be confounded; and to be short, disobedience doth overflow the banks of good order, almost in every place, almost in every degree of man. . . .

The remedy of this doth not stand only in making good common laws for the whole realm, but also (and perchance chiefly) in observing private discipline, every man carefully in his own house. And namely, if special regard be had to youth, and that not so much in teaching them what is good as in keeping them from that that is ill.

Therefore, if wise fathers be not as well ware in weeding from their children ill things and ill company, as they were before, in grafting them learning, and providing for them good schoolmasters, what fruit they shall reap of all their cost and care, common experience doth tell. [Though the past provides many examples of the proper training of excellent soldiers and matchless men of learning, the noblest example is that of ancient Athens. The lasting fame of the commonwealth proves the value of much learning as the way to wisdom and worthiness.]

And to say all in short, though I lack authority to give counsel, yet I lack not good will to wish that the youth in England, especially gentlemen, and namely nobility, should be by good bringing up, so grounded in judgment of learning, so founded in love of honesty, as, when they should be called forth to the execution of great affairs, in service of their Prince and country, they might be able to use and to order all experiences, were they good, were they bad; and that, according to the square, rule, and line of wisdom, learning, and virtue.

---

[10] **rude:** uncultivated.

FIGURE II *Title page from Turberville's* The Noble Art of Venery, or Hunting. *The queen is shown with her courtiers, resting in the woods during a day of hunting. A gentleman kneels in front of her gesturing toward the magnificent repast prepared by the serving women, a man fills a chalice, courtiers relax in conversation, and two young male pages disport themselves in the foreground.*

And I do not mean by all this talk that young gentlemen should always be poring on a book, and by using good studies should leese[11] honest pleasure, and haunt no good pastime. I mean nothing less. For it is well known that I both like and love, and have always and do yet still use, all exercises and pastimes that be fit for my nature and ability. And beside natural disposition, in judgment also, I was never either Stoic in doctrine or Anabaptist[12] in religion to mislike a merry, pleasant, and playful nature, if no outrage be committed against law, measure, and good order. . . .

Therefore, to ride comely, to run fair at the tilt or ring, to play at all weapons, to shoot fair in bow, or surely in gun, to vault lustily, to run, to leap, to wrestle, to swim, to dance comely, to sing, and play of instruments cunningly, to hawk, to hunt, to play at tennis, and all pastimes generally, which be joined with labor, used in open place, and [in] the daylight, containing either some fit exercise for war, or some pleasant pastime for peace, be not only comely and decent, but also very necessary for a courtly gentleman to use.

[11] **leese:** lose.    [12] **Stoic . . . Anabaptist:** Stoic philosophy professed indifference to pleasure or pain. The Anabaptists, a strict Protestant sect, disavowed all earthly pleasure.

## Working Men

This section deals with men below the rank of gentlemen in the Elizabethan social order, beginning with those whom Harrison describes as artificers and who are represented in *A Midsummer Night's Dream* by Peter Quince, Bottom, and the rest of the amateur actors. As skilled workers, such men do not represent the Elizabethan poor but rather belong to what was called "the middling sort" — a large and varied group of people, between the abject poor and the gentleborn, whom modern historians have found difficult to classify. They were householders, small property-holders, and independent craftsmen (Leinwand, "Middling Sort" 290–91); even if such men were relatively affluent, they were not considered gentlemen. As members of the middling sort, Shakespeare's mechanicals are respectable people with real, if modest, social standing who, barring personal catastrophe or a general economic collapse, could expect to live their lives free from want.

We should note that most of the fictive Athenian artificers, like some of their Elizabethan counterparts, can read. Peter Quince distributes acting parts at the first cast meeting of "Pyramus and Thisbe" and expects his players to have their lines memorized by the next rehearsal. (Snout, the joiner, being slow of study, has only to roar.) Such literacy among workingmen reflects the expansion of education in the mid-sixteenth century. Town boys — the children of merchants and even of some artisans — could attend the many new elementary and grammar schools built in large market towns between 1560 and 1660, just as William Shakespeare probably did at King's New School in Stratford-upon-Avon. The grammar school hours of study were long and the curriculum was dominated by close study of Latin texts related only slightly, if at all, to the work that most of the boys would take up after leaving school to become apprentices. But supporting the curriculum, and justifying its content, were social values inculcating renunciation of instinct, respect for rules, and above all obedience to authority. Until they left grammar school, boys from gentry and middling families mixed freely. Thereafter, however, their lives diverged significantly; the upper class youth moved on to more years of education, the lower class youth moved into the labor market through the apprenticeship system until, like Bottom and his fellows, they became independent craftsmen or shopkeepers.

According to historian Ilana Krausman Ben-Amos, what boys took from school into the world of apprenticeship and work was a confusion of values from two conflicting sets of norms. The orthodox patriarchal ideal stressed deference and obedience to authority, even as their own nuclear families prized maturity and independence. This conflict of expectations and values — of submission versus autonomy, passivity in the face of discipline versus initiative-taking and maturity of judgment — is basic to the Elizabethan social structure. And it is responsible for the anxiety about the young that is so often voiced in early modern English texts (Ben-Amos 238–39). A society that wanted everyone to have a place and to stay in it expected authority from its masters and employers, but required deference and submission from boys and young men as they prepared to become masters and employers. In *A Midsummer Night's Dream*, this mixed message creates some of the difficulties faced by Peter Quince's players. They take the initiative to promote themselves before their prince in the hope of being "made men" but badly handicap their efforts at playmaking for fear of seeming too bold, especially in front of the ladies.

## THE STATUTE OF ARTIFICERS

Regulating the terms and conditions of labor in Elizabethan England was a responsibility of the central government. The history of its efforts at doing so, a major preoccupation of labor and economic historians, is not our focus here. Rather, we reproduce portions of the first Elizabethan Statute of Artificers in order to note the social principles that underlie it, social principles in which masterlessness and vagabondage are abhorrent and the free movement of workers from place to place or from occupation to occupation is to be avoided.

The Statute of Artificers was passed by the House of Commons in 1563 and established the legal framework of English labor for the next two hundred years. The pressure for its passage came when the government realized that price inflation had made the wage rates passed early in the century unworkable and unrealistic. Besides the upward pressure on wages due to inflation, there was also a short-term labor shortage, thanks to the epidemics of plague in 1558 and 1559. The statute refers only obliquely, however, to a shortage of workers, speaking rather of Parliament's hope that passage of the statute will "banish idleness" and "advance husbandry." The statute attempts to create stability in the labor market and to avoid worker uprisings by imposing mutual obligations on employers and their workers: workers shall work for a fixed term of service of one year and their hours and wages are to be determined yearly by local authorities. Not only could laborers be brought before the authorities for leaving their masters without testimonials (that is, without specific written permission to do so), but employment itself was also a matter of enforcement. Justices of the peace told the unemployed to present themselves for day or seasonal work at a specified time and place and these men could not refuse employment. Most important, perhaps, the statute sought to prevent excessive social mobility and balance tensions between agricultural and urban employers by insisting upon property qualifications for the parents of apprentices. The law required parents of adolescents seeking apprenticeships in large market towns to hold land yielding £3 of income per year, while parents of adolescents seeking apprenticeships in smaller towns were required to have land yielding £2 of income per year. The provision was intended to ensure a fixed supply of agricultural laborers. It prevented poor rural families from seeking to improve their children's chances in life by apprenticing them in skilled urban occupations.

What follows the text of the 1563 Statute of Artificers is a list of wages for different occupations published and posted publicly in the city of Chester in April 1596. With this list, which is similar to ones from localities all over England, we hope to suggest something of the range of manual occupations in Elizabethan England, both for agricultural workers and for craftsmen, and something of the basic value attached to their skills. It is also worth noting that workers could be paid several different ways — by taking their pay yearly or daily, and in straight wages or by a mixture of wages and food and drink. Day labor, as for example in haying season when extra hands were needed, was primarily seasonal and not to be preferred to steady yearly employment. Wage rates are given for the year and for the day. How many and who chose which options must have varied greatly from locality to locality, from year to year. But the difference in the basic wage rates suggests something, as well, of how much it cost an employer to provide basic subsistence to his workers.

## ✦ *From* The Statute of Artificers $\qquad$ *1563*

When originally introduced, this important piece of legislation was a small bill which, in its passage through the House of Commons and its committees, grew to its final massive proportions of forty provisions. We include only the first few of them below.

### AN ACT TOUCHING[1] DIVERS ORDERS FOR ARTIFICERS, LABORERS, SERVANTS OF HUSBANDRY,[2] AND APPRENTICES

Although there remain and stand in force presently a great number of acts and statutes concerning the retaining, departing, wages, and orders of apprentices, servants, and laborers, as well in husbandry, as in divers other arts, mysteries,[3] and occupations: yet partly for the imperfection and contrariety[4] that is found and doth appear in sundry of the said laws, and for the variety and number of them, and chiefly for that the wages and allowances limited and rated[5] in many of the said statutes are in divers places too small, and not answerable to this time, respecting the advancement of prices of all things belonging to the said servants and laborers, the said laws cannot conveniently without the great grief and burden of the poor laborer and hired man be put in good and due execution. And as the said several acts and statutes were at the time of the making of them thought to be very good and beneficial for the commonwealth of this realm (as divers of them yet are): So if the substance of the many of the said laws as are meet[6] to be continued shall be digested[7] and reduced into one sole law and statute, and in the same an uniform order prescribed and limited concerning the wages and other

---

[1] **touching:** concerning.　[2] **husbandry:** farming.　[3] **mysteries:** trades, crafts.　[4] **imperfection and contrariety:** omissions and contradictions.　[5] **rated:** allotted, apportioned.　[6] **meet:** worthy.　[7] **digested:** arranged systematically.

"The Statute of Artificers (5 Eliz. c. 4), 1563: At the Parliament holden at Westminster the xii. of January in the fifth year of the reign of our Sovereign Lady Elizabeth," reprinted from *Tudor Economic Documents: Being Select Documents Illustrating the Economic and Social History of Tudor England,* Vol. 1, edited by R. H. Tawney and Eileen Power (London: Longmans, Green, 1924) 338–41.

orders for apprentices, servants, and laborers, there is good hope that it will come to pass that the same law (being duly executed) should banish idleness, advance husbandry, and yield unto the hired person, both in the time of scarcity and in the time of plenty, a convenient[8] proportion of wages.

I. Be it therefore enacted . . . that as much of all the estatutes heretofore made and every branch of them as touch or concern the hiring, keeping, departing, working, wages, or order of servants, workmen, artificers, apprentices, and laborers, or any of them, and the penalties and forfeitures concerning the same shall be from and after the last day of September next ensuing repealed [but all other statutes remain in effect].

II. And be it further enacted . . . that no manner of person or persons after [the same date] shall retain, hire, or take into service or cause to be retained, hired, or taken into service, nor any person shall be retained, hired, or taken into service by any means or color[9] to work for any less time or term than for one whole year in any of the sciences, crafts, mysteries, or arts of clothiers, woolen cloth weavers, tuckers,[10] fullers,[11] cloth workers, shearmen,[12] dyers, hosiers, tailors, shoemakers, tanners, pewterers, bakers, brewers, glovers, cutlers,[13] smiths, farriers,[14] curriers,[15] saddlers, spurriers,[16] turners,[17] cappers,[18] hatmakers or feltmakers, bowyers,[19] fletchers,[20] arrowhead makers, butchers, cooks, or millers.

III. . . . [T]hat every person being unmarried and every other person being under the age of thirty years that after the feast of Easter next shall marry, and having been brought up in any of the said arts, crafts, or sciences, or that hath used or exercised any of them by the space of three years or more and not having lands, tenements,[21] rents, or hereditaments,[22] copyhold,[23] or freehold[24] of one estate of inheritance, or for term of any life or lives, of clear yearly value of forty shillings, nor being worth of his own goods the clear value of ten pounds and so allowed by two justices of the peace of the county where he hath most commonly inhabited by the space of one whole year [or by other municipal officials] nor being retained with any person in husbandry or in any of the aforesaid arts and sciences, according to this statute; nor lawfully retained in any other art or science, nor being lawfully retained in household or in any office with any nobleman, gentleman, or others, according to the laws of this realm, nor having a convenient

---

[8] **convenient:** suitable, just.   [9] **color:** reason, excuse.   [10] **tuckers:** cloth-finishers.   [11] **fullers:** those who cleanse and thicken cloth.   [12] **shearmen:** those who shear woolen cloth.   [13] **cutlers:** knife-makers.   [14] **farriers:** those who shoe horses.   [15] **curriers:** those who dress and color tanned leather.   [16] **spurriers:** spurmakers.   [17] **turners:** those who make objects on a lathe.   [18] **cappers:** capmakers.   [19] **bowyers:** bow-makers.   [20] **fletchers:** arrow-makers.   [21] **tenements:** real estate holdings.   [22] **hereditaments:** properties to inherit.   [23] **copyhold:** land held by right granted on manorial court-rolls.   [24] **freehold:** land held for life (one's own or another's).

farm or other holding in tillage, whereupon he may employ his labor shall (during the time that he or they shall so be unmarried, or under the said age of 30 years, upon request made by any person using the art or mystery wherein the said person so required hath been exercised,[25] as is aforesaid) be retained, and shall not refuse to serve according to the tenor of this statute upon the pain[26] and penalty hereafter mentioned.

**IV.** . . . [T]hat no person which shall retain any servant shall put away his or her said servant and that no person retained according to this statute shall depart from his master, mistress, or dame, before the end of his or her term upon the pain hereafter mentioned, unless it be for some reasonable and sufficient cause or matter to be allowed before two justices of peace [or other municipal official] to whom any of the parties grieved shall complain. Which said justices [etc.] shall have and take upon them or him the hearing and ordering of the matter betwixt the said master, mistress, or dame, and servant according to the equity of the cause. And that no such master, mistress, or dame shall put away any such servant at the end of his term or that any such servant shall depart from this said master, mistress, or dame at the end of his term without one quarter[27] warning given before the end of his said term either by the said master, mistress, or dame, or servant, the one to the other, upon the pain hereafter ensuing.

**V.** . . . [That] every person between the age of twelve years and the age of threescore years not being lawfully retained nor apprentice[d] with any fisherman or mariner haunting the seas, nor being in service with any kiddier[28] or carrier of any corn, grain, or meal for provision of the city of London, nor with any husbandman in husbandry, nor in any city, town corporate, or market town, in any of the arts or sciences . . . appointed by this statute to have or take apprentices, nor being retained by the year or half the year at the least, for the digging, seeking, finding, getting, melting, fining,[29] working, trying,[30] making of any silver, tin, lead, iron, copper, stone, sea-coal,[31] stone-coal,[32] moor-coal,[33] or charcoal, nor being occupied in or about the making of any glass, nor being a gentleman born, nor being a student or scholar in any of the universities or in any school, nor having lands [etc. as in section III] . . . nor having a father or mother then living or other ancestor whose heir apparent he is, then having lands [etc.] of the yearly value of ten pounds or above or goods or cattles[34] of the value of forty pounds nor being a necessary or convenient officer or servant, lawfully

[25] **exercised:** occupied.  [26] **pain:** punishment.  [27] **one quarter:** of a year; three months.  [28] **kiddier:** one who buys provisions and brings them to market for resale.  [29] **fining:** refining.  [30] **trying:** purifying, separating.  [31] **sea-coal:** coal mined from the seacoast.  [32] **stone-coal:** hard coal.  [33] **moor-coal:** peat.  [34] **cattles:** property.

retained as is aforesaid, nor having a convenient farm or holding whereupon he may or shall employ his labor, nor being otherwise lawfully retained, according to the true meaning of this statute, shall . . . by virtue of this estatute, be compelled to be retained to serve in husbandry by the year with any person that keepeth husbandry and will require any such person to serve within the same shire where he shall be so required.

[Section VI specifies the penalty for masters unduly dismissing servants to be forty shillings and for servants unduly leaving or refusing service to be imprisonment. In all, the statute consisted of forty sections seeking to limit the mobility of workers, to prevent unemployment and vagabondage, to control the hours and conditions of work, to adjust wages for every locality according to local conditions, to punish employers for infractions of wage rates, and to ensure a sufficient supply of agricultural workers for harvests.]

## → Royal Proclamation Regulating Chester Wages    *1596*

The following comes from a royal proclamation establishing laborers' wages for the town of Chester in 1596. Other such proclamations establish wages elsewhere in England. We include this document to suggest the variety and relative wage scale for the working trades and also to show that workers, by the year or the day, could be paid with or without an allotment for food and drink. The penny earned daily by a weaver, thatcher, hosier, tanner, glover, or cook was also the price for standing room at a London public playhouse.

| | *Wages by the year with meat and drink* | *Wages by the year without meat and drink* | *Wages by the day with meat and drink* |
|---|---|---|---|
| Smith | 26s.[1] 8d.[2] | £5[3] | 2d. |
| Wheelwright | 40s. | £5 10s. | 2¼ d. |
| Plowwright | 30s. | £5 | 2d. |
| Millwright | 23s. 4d. | £5 10s. | 3d. |
| Master carpenter | 53s. 4d. | £5 13s. 4d. | 4d. |
| Servant, carpenter's | 20s. | £3 10s. | 1d. |
| Joiner | 30s. | £4 | 2d. |
| Rough mason | 26s. 8d. | £5 | 2¼ d. |
| Plasterer | 20s. | £5 | 2d. |
| Sawyer | 28s. | £4 10s. | 2d. |
| Linemaker | 23s. | £4 6s. 8d. | 2d. |
| Bricklayer | 20s. | £4 | 2¼ d. |
| Brickman | 26s. | £4 10s. | 2d. |
| Tiler | 25s. | £3 13s. 4d. | 2d. |
| Slater | 26s. | £4 | 1½ d. |
| Tilemaker | 30s. | £4 | 2d. |
| Linen weaver | 20s. | £4 | 1d. |
| Turner | 16s. | £3 | 1d. |
| Woolen weaver | 28s. | £3 13s. 4d. | 1d. |

[1] s.: abbreviation for shilling, coin equivalent to 12 pennies or 1/26 of a pound.
[2] d.: abbreviation for *denarius*, Latin for penny.
[3] £: abbreviation, from Latin *libra*, of the pound, weighing 16 ounces of gold or silver.

Proclamation 778; Chester, April 1596, 38 Elizabeth I. British Museum, ms. Harleian 2091, 215.

| | | | |
|---|---|---|---|
| Cooper | 30s. | £4 | 2d. |
| Miller | 30s. | £4 | 2d. |
| Fuller | 26s. | £3 13s. 4d. | 1½d. |
| Walker | 23s. 4d. | £4 | 1¼d. |
| Thatcher | 20s. | £4 | 1d. |
| Shingler | 30s. | £4 | 2d. |
| Shearman | 20s. | £3 13s. 4d. | 1½d. |
| Dyer | 26s. 8d. | £3 13s. 4d. | 1½d. |
| Hosiers | 23s. | £3 10s. | 1d. |
| Shoemakers | 30s. | £4 | 2d. |
| Tanners | 26s. | £4 | 1d. |
| Pewterers | 20s. | £3 13s. 4d. | 2½d. |
| Bakers | 16s. | £3 10s. | 1d. |
| Brewers | 20s. | £3 10s. | 1¼d. |
| Glovers | 26s. 8d. | £3 16s. | 1d. |
| Cutlers | 27s. | £4 10s. | 1½d. |
| Saddlers | 25s. | £4 | 1½d. |
| Spurriers | 25s. | £4 | 1½d. |
| Cappers | 20s. | £3 10s. | 2d. |
| Hatmakers | 30s. | £4 10s. | 2d. |
| Bowyers | 28s. | £4 | 2d. |
| Fletchers | 20s. | £3 10s. | 2d. |
| Arrowheadmakers | 15s. | £3 10s. | 1d. |
| Butchers | 26s. 8d. | £3 10s. | 2d. |
| Cooks | 20s. | £3 5s. | 1d. |
| Bailiff of husbandry | 40s. | £4 | 3d. |
| Mowers of grass | | | 4d. |
| Taskers | | | 4d. |
| Reapers | | | 2d. |
| Mowers of corn | | | 4[d.] |
| of the best sort | 20s. | £3 10[s.] | |
| of the second sort | 10s. | 50s. | |
| of the third sort | 8s. | 36[s.] | |

## The New Man: Simon Forman's Dreams

Central to understanding how the codes of Elizabethan masculinity operate in *A Midsummer Night's Dream* is the somewhat scandalous image of Bottom lying in Titania's lap. She is a queen and he is only a weaver. That such an image was produced before the theatergoing public implies that, by the mid-1590s, the eroticized language of Elizabethan courtiership had thoroughly pervaded English, or certainly London, society.

This suggestion is reinforced by the texts of three dreams about Queen Elizabeth that astrological physician Simon Forman recorded in his remarkable *Autobiography*. As we have seen in Harrison's normative *Description of England*, there was a structural tension at the heart of Elizabethan society: it was anomalous for a patriarchal society, founded upon and organized around the subordination of women, to be ruled by a female monarch. Forman's dream relations with the queen reenact this tension in capsule form as the queen's image appears and changes in the abrupt transitions characteristic of dreams.

At the time of the dreams in 1597–98, Forman was forty-five and the queen, at sixty-four, was old enough to be his mother. Elizabeth, as an unmarried woman, tended to avoid maternal imagery in her political self-presentation, preferring to be figured more powerfully as a prince or more mystically as a Virgin Queen. As the years of her reign went on and as the queen herself aged visibly, her iconography as Virgin Queen remained the same. Her image in portraits was frozen as that of a youngish maiden immune to the decay of age. Forman's two short dreams figure the queen as a patient, seeking him out in his professional capacity and interceding for him in his recurrent struggles with the London College of Physicians. Perhaps the queen enters these dreams as a kind of magical protector, defending against the professional vulnerability Forman must have experienced as an ambitious but unlicensed physician with a powerful clientele. The longest of the three dreams speaks powerfully of how courtly discourse spread into social realms inhabited by aspirants like Forman. Elizabeth's courtiers were encouraged to use erotic terms of address, to supplicate her in a lover's language, as Forman does here. In the figure of the tall, presumptuous, red-bearded weaver, Forman's dream intersects almost magically with the imagery and action of *A Midsummer Night's Dream*. (It's fun to imagine that Forman, who did go to the theater and mentions plays in his diary, might have seen this play, but, alas, no evidence exists.)

In this third dream, Forman's imagination reenacts the eroticism at the heart of Elizabethan political discourse and gives Forman the sought-after place as wooer at the queen's side. They walk in the garden, talking and "reasoning of many matters." But the dreamer adopts the submissiveness and abjection requisite for a courtly lover only in part. Protected by the private fantasy of dream, freed from the self-censorship of daily social life, Forman the dreamer does not relinquish the privileges of his gender, which here includes the privileged position of the voyeur. The dream-narrator enjoys the power of the male gaze, unfettered, to represent the female object in view without flattery: Elizabeth becomes a little elderly woman, stripped of royalty right down to her petticoat, but oddly retaining her role as female beloved. Forman also takes the privilege of the dream to split himself in two. In the first person, the dreamer is the queen's favorite, protecting her from the unseemly and inappropriate attentions of his surrogate in the third person, the tall, red-bearded weaver distract of his wits. And perhaps it is the dominance established by this rescue that emboldens the dreamer to remake himself finally not as royal subject but as progenitor — swelling the royal belly with magical issue, solving the nation's political crisis through his own act of implantation.

→  SIMON FORMAN

## *From* The Autobiography of Simon Forman        *1597–98*

Simon Forman (1552–1611) made his living as a doctor, practicing astrological medicine in London from 1583 until his death. As an unlicensed practitioner, he was continually at odds with the London College of Physicians, who examined him on medical knowledge and forced him to pay fines and occasionally serve time in jail. But Forman had powerful friends, especially the noblewomen who consulted him for their ailments. He was finally awarded a medical degree in 1603 by Jesus College, Cambridge. Among Forman's surviving manuscript volumes now at the Bodleian Library, Oxford, are medical casebooks, a famous *Autobiography*, and a diary for the years 1564–1602. The diary contains Forman's responses to seeing *Macbeth, Cymbeline, Richard II*, and *The Winter's Tale*, as well as these three dreams about himself and Queen Elizabeth I.

### DREAM 1

Anno 1597 the 23 January about 3 AM I dreamt that I was with the queen, and that she was a little elderly woman in a coarse white petticoat, all unready.[1] & she & I walked up and down through lanes and closes,[2] talking

---

[1] all unready: undressed, partially dressed.    [2] closes: fields.

---

Simon Forman, *The Autobiography of Simon Forman*, Ashmole ms. 226, 44R–V, 310r.

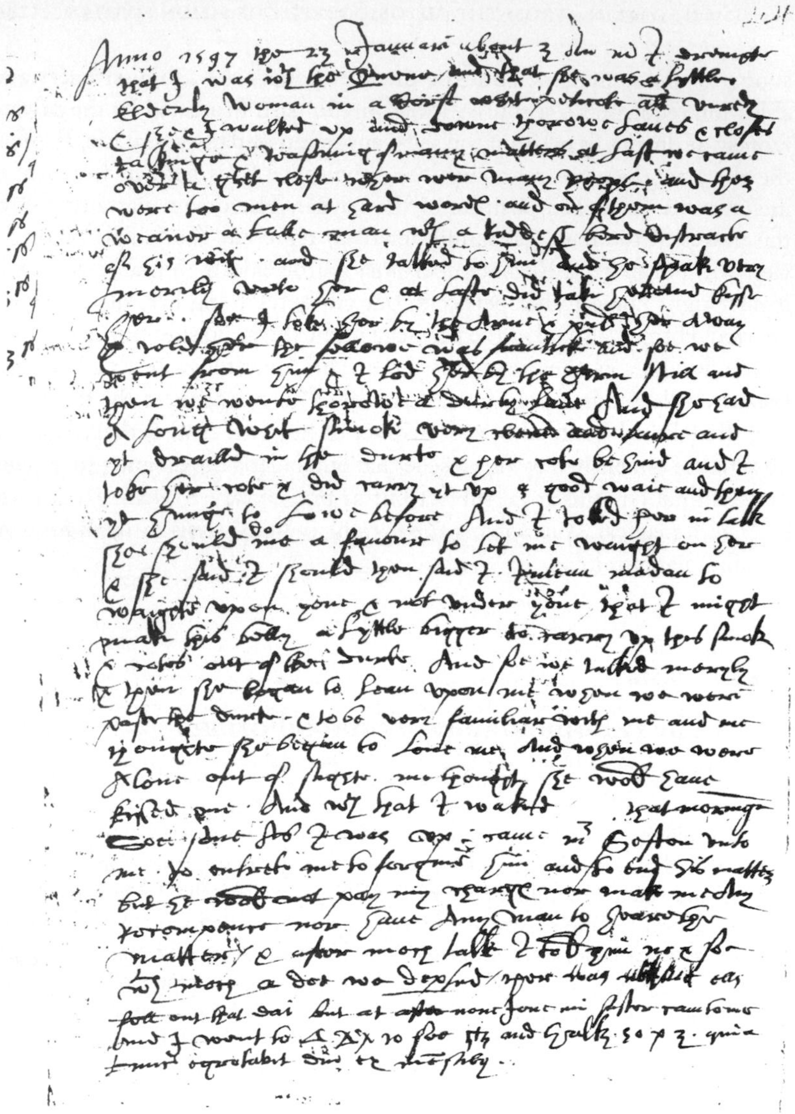

FIGURE 12 *Manuscript page from* The Autobiography of Simon Forman, *recalling his dream as suitor to the queen. Transcribing such a document requires knowledge of Elizabethan handwriting.*

and reasoning of many matters. At last we came over a great close where were many people and there were two men at hard words.[3] And one of them was a weaver, a tall man with a reddish beard, distract of his wits. And she talked to him and he spake very merrily unto her & at last did take her and kiss her. So I took her by the arm & pulled her away & told her the fellow was frantic[4] and so we went from him. & I led her by the arm still and then we went through a dirty lane. And she had a long white smock,[5] very clean and fair, and it trailed in the dirt & her coat behind. And I took her coat & did carry it up a good way and then it hung too low before and I told her in talk she should do me a favor to let me wait on her. & she said I should. Then said I, I mean, madam, to wait upon[6] you & not under you that I might make this belly a little bigger to carry up this smock & coats out of the dirt. And so we talked merrily & then she began to lean upon me when we were past the dirt & to be very familiar with me. And methought she began to love me and when we were alone out of sight, methought she would have kissed me. And with that I waked.

## DREAM 2

Item, the 21 of February [1597] I dreamt of the Queen that she came to me all in black & a French hood. That day I had anger by Dorothy and Mrs. Pennington that came to me about words my man spake.

## DREAM 3

Item 1598, the 9 of January AM at 3 I dreamt that the Queen did commend me much for my skill & judgment in physic[7] & chid with the doctors and railed on them much for troubling me.

---

[3] at hard words: arguing.   [4] frantic: insane.   [5] smock: woman's undergarment, shift.   [6]wait upon: with sexual pun on "weight upon."   [7] physic: medicine.

# CHAPTER 3

## *Female Attachments and Family Ties*

✕

The royal marriage in prospect at the opening of *A Midsummer Night's Dream* is predicated not on one woman's submission to a man, but on the submission of an entire community of self-governing women: the community of the Amazons. The Amazons were warrior women of classical legend who lived entirely apart from men and who were still reported to exist in remote new world lands. Unlike Shakespeare's *The Tempest*, in which characters powerfully evoke and obsessively remember a political prehistory of usurpation and betrayal, *A Midsummer Night's Dream* seeks to divert attention from and defuse potentially explosive memories of a past event: the battle between male and female warriors in which Amazons, led by their queen, Hippolyta, are defeated by Athenian soldiers, led by their king, Theseus. Contemporary interpretation of this epic battle and these legendary women drew upon conflicting traditions, one that celebrated the idealized figure of the female warrior and another that portrayed the Amazon as the paradigm of the unruly woman. While iconography of Queen Elizabeth I as an Amazon seeks to draw unproblematically on the first tradition, the monstrous specter of the female dominatrix can never be fully assuaged in a patriarchal society with a female head of state.

The play's opening allusion to female communal self-rule might also have evoked deep cultural memories of the religious institutions under Roman Catholicism in which women could live apart from and independent of men. The English Reformation formally began when Henry VIII, Elizabeth's father, broke with the Roman Church over the refusal of Pope Clement VII to sanction his divorce from Katherine of Aragon, who had borne him one daughter, Mary, and no sons. Prior to the official break in 1534, when the Act of Supremacy declared the king to be the head of the church, there had been religious reformers in England influenced by those on the continent, especially Martin Luther; the king, however, was not in sympathy with reformist ideas and, in response to Martin Luther, had even written a book on the sacraments for which he received the title of "Defender of the Faith" from the pope.

The deciding factor in the break with Rome was not religious but political — Henry's compelling desire for a son to secure the succession, and his passion for Anne Boleyn, who might produce one. The king declared himself Protector and Supreme Head of the Church of England, ordered a new English translation of the Bible, and when in 1536 the state needed money he ordered the dissolution of the monasteries and the annexation of church lands. Anne Boleyn, having produced only a daughter, the future Queen Elizabeth I, was quickly beheaded, and her successor, Jane Seymour, bore a son who ascended the throne at the age of ten as Edward VI. During Edward's six-year reign, the country was ruled by his protectors, the duke of Somerset and the Archbishop Cranmer, who transformed England into a Protestant state.

After the dissolution of monastic life in the 1530s, there remained cultural institutions for young men, since the scholastic institutions for males (see Chapter 2) escaped the satiric attacks against monasteries and convents and, indeed, produced the nation's ruling elite. But for ordinary women in post-Reformation England, only one recognized path remained — marriage, motherhood, and eventually, perhaps, widowhood. The image of an institutionally sanctioned community of single women, headed by a woman, had been ruled out of order — except, of course, in the case of the queen's household. In *A Midsummer Night's Dream*, the disapproval of female community may be glimpsed in the awful fate held out to Hermia if she persists in refusing to marry her father's choice of mate, "to be in shady cloister mew'd, / To live a barren sister all your life" (1.1.71–72), itself apparently rebellion in another form, is a fate only slightly less dreadful than that of summary execution.

*A Midsummer Night's Dream* begins with the end of Amazonian rule, and over the course of the play, as the male-female couples move inexorably toward marriage, female attachments are gradually erased: the threat of the convent fades, Titania and her fairy court are absorbed back into Oberon's domain, and the intimacy between Hermia and Helena dissolves. Likewise, in the England of 1595, institutional female community was in decline: the independence of convent life was long past or far away, and with the queen in her sixties, the future of her female household was limited. Societies of Amazons, however, though they were extinct in the old world, had been sighted in the new, as Sir Walter Raleigh reported in *The History of the World* (1614), and once again, Amazons potentially posed a threat. Likewise, female talk and fellowship, although subject to continuous assault in marriage manuals and sermons, persistently defied masculine disapproval.

The alternatives to marriage posed within *A Midsummer Night's Dream*, although they are finally dismissed, suggest that the feminine impulse toward marriage was less stable and consistent than the ending of the play suggests. The selections below are intended to challenge the comic resolution in which marriage is universally desired, female communities vanquished, and female attachments dissolved. They amplify the resistances to marriage and masculine domination — refusal of the designated husband, disobedience in marriage, longing for female friendship — that the play suppresses, offering conflicting versions of female rule, and of women's desire to share their experiences with other women and exist spiritually, physically, and intellectually apart from men.

## Amazons

The existence and habits of Amazons were something of a cultural preoccupation in early modern England. The customs of the Amazons inverted all the traditions of patriarchal society: Amazons usurped masculine martial and administrative functions, lived apart from men but used them for procreation, cherished and educated their daughters and disposed of their sons, and (in an emblematic rejection of both maternity and sexual allure)

FIGURE 13 *Lascivious and threatening Amazons, in Hulsius's engravings from a German edition of Sir Walter Raleigh's* The Discovery of Guiana, *illustrate the behavior that challenged the norms of patriarchal society. The top engraving on p. 195 shows the Amazons (here, not noticeably breastless) provocatively luring and lasciviously embracing male warriors, presumably to become pregnant and produce their own heirs; below, the Amazons attack and conquer the warriors, occupy their lands, then brutally slay, roast (and perhaps even devour) the men.*

burned off a breast in the interests of martial efficiency. Contemporary anxieties over threats to the social order and the dangers of the new world were displaced onto the Amazons, formerly denizens of India, Asia, and Africa and recently discovered in the Americas. However, narratives of the Amazons defused these threats: although they vividly portrayed Amazonian aggressiveness, they usually ended with the extinction or taming of the Amazons.

Since tales of the legendary Amazons served to allay current fears, whatever they might be, specific details of their rise and fall varied with the social circumstances in which their story was retold. In an England darkened by memories of civil strife and peasant uprisings, William Painter in *The Palace of Pleasure* (1567) explained their advent as a response of "manly courage" to the decimation of Scythian men by civil war and peasant revolt. Thomas Heywood, in *The Exemplary Lives and Memorable Acts of the Nine Most Worthy Women in the World* (1640), writing during an unsettled, prerevolutionary era during which concerns over the corrupt state were displaced onto women, emphasized the licentiousness and cruelty of the Amazons. Heywood's Amazons are menacing even before their men are killed in battle, imperiously warning their husbands, off at war, that "if they made not speedy home, they would provide themselves of issue of their neighbors" (O2r). When their men are slain, the wives take arms, and, "finding the sweetness of liberty and sovereignty added, refuse to take husbands . . . holding the masculine sex in great contempt," they kill "all those husbands which yet remained among them," and strangle the sons they bear.

In Plutarch's "Life of Theseus," long considered one of Shakespeare's sources for *A Midsummer Night's Dream,* the Amazons pose little threat to masculine dominance: Athenian forces led by Theseus easily vanquish a society of "man-loving" Amazons, who greet the Athenians with gifts upon their landing. Before they attack, the invaders confidently relax awhile as if on holiday and after four months of fighting, during which many Amazons are killed, they conclude a peace treaty with the cooperation of Hippolyta, whom Theseus had captured by luring her aboard his ship. Thereafter, the fate of Hippolyta is unclear: either she was slain, leaving Theseus to marry Antiopa, or she lived and married Theseus. Plutarch's account gives no sense whatever of a female community (unlike Painter, Heywood, and Raleigh, he does not attempt to explain the rise of the Amazons), and he represents the women warriors as credulous and ineffectual plunder.

At the beginning of *The Book of the City of Ladies* (1405), Christine de Pizan resolves to counter men's negative portrayals of women with narratives that reflect her own experience of women's integrity. As if to support her, three personifications, the ladies Reason, Justice, and Rectitude, appear and vow to found a City of Ladies that, unlike the society of Amazons, will be strong enough to last forever. Whether or not Shakespeare knew Pizan's work in Brian Anslay's English translation (1521), *A Midsummer Night's Dream* raises the possibilities of female attachments and female agency absent from Plutarch and fully realized by Pizan; for this reason, and to include in our contextual readings an early modern feminist perspective, we have chosen Pizan over Plutarch as the Amazons' primary advocate.

In her City of Ladies, Pizan did not seek to overturn traditional social hierarchies, but to create a space for women within them: mindful of the distinction between gentle and common, her Amazons remove their breasts according to their social rank: "the noble women . . . their left paps were cut off . . . that they should not be cumbered to bear the shield. And to them that were not gentlewomen, their right paps were cut away to shoot the more easily" (see p. 202). Pizan's Amazons did not seek rule, but forced by the loss of their men in battle to assume their own governance, demonstrated female courage and resourcefulness in the face of necessity. Moreover, these Amazons possess the virtues, reason, justice, and rectitude, traditionally designated as masculine: their administration is consensual, their sexuality procreative, and their rule merciful (they chase men away rather than kill them, and return sons to their fathers to raise).

As they honorably avenge their murdered male relations, Pizan's Amazons win fame and territory in their valiant battles. So formidable is their reputation that the Greek forces, led by Theseus and Hercules, approach them stealthily and launch a surprise attack; the women warriors, though decimated by the assault, fight with such skill and bravery that they nearly vanquish the great heroes. When the most courageous warriors, Menalippe and Hippolyta, are finally taken and their queen makes a treaty for their return, the Athenians back home are greatly relieved. But having been treated respectfully after her capture, Hippolyta prefers to stay, and Theseus and Hippolyta marry for love.

In *The Book of the City of Ladies*, Pizan imagines female agency both within their own community and in their relations with men. Hippolyta is nearly the equal of the great warrior, and when captured she is treated honorably "with great joy and pleasance." Unlike Shakespeare's Theseus, who woos and wins Hippolyta with his sword (1.1.16–17), Pizan's Theseus wins Hippolyta with his admiration, ardor, and deference, acknowledging her right to accept or reject him by soliciting her queen's permission to marry. The Amazon queen approves the marriage of the two mighty opposites, and Hippolyta is not tamed by Theseus, as is Shakespeare's Hippolyta, but chooses him.

If Pizan enlisted the Amazonian legend to affirm female agency, in *The History of the World* (1614), Sir Walter Raleigh uses the tale to stage a virtuosic display of masculine learning, and where Shakespeare's Theseus subdued unruly femininity with the sword, Raleigh contains it within the lances of erudition. Raleigh's intent, he claims, is simply scientific — to prove that "such Amazons have been and are." His underlying preoccupation, however, is with female sexuality — he immediately defines the Amazons by their reputed exploitation of masculine virility, beginning his account with the Amazon queen who visits Alexander the Great to become pregnant, and having achieved her purpose, goes on her way.

With a seemingly endless list of classical and modern authorities, Raleigh establishes the existence of Amazons in the ancient world, and having demonstrated the veracity of past observations, itemizes recent sightings of women with customs "agreeable to the reports of elder times." The Amazons who challenged patriarchal structures, believed to have been extinct, have surfaced again in the new world. But Raleigh's new world Amazons, unlike Pizan's, do not threaten to colonize masculine territory, instead, like the rich, virgin lands in which they live (Raleigh, *Guiana* 96), Raleigh's Amazons generously offer their riches and invite colonization.

If the Amazons personified the female unruliness which needed to be tamed in the interests of domestic order and national expansion, they also represented the "monstrous" female reigns afflicting England and the continent which needed to be terminated. When John Knox published his attack on female rule, *The First Blast of the Trumpet against the Monstrous Regiment of Women* (1558), there were several powerful European queens — Catherine de' Medici in France, Mary of Guise (wife of James V of Scotland and mother of Mary, Queen of Scots), and Mary Tudor, Elizabeth's elder sister then on the throne — all of whom opposed the Reformation. Throughout Europe, the religious reformation was linked with the rise of nationalism, and Knox was strongly influenced by John Calvin, for whom religion and politics were inseparable and the foundation of a theocratic state a fundamental objective. Eager to discredit the opposition to religious reform and hasten the establishment of a "godly nation," Knox drew upon two traditions, one that represented women as weak, foolish, mad, inconstant, cruel, willful, and disorderly, and another that interpreted a bad ruler (and a child or a female monarch) as God's punishment of a wicked people. For the Protestants, a Catholic queen opposed to the Reformation was (somewhat paradoxically) an *offense* against God's plan, and Knox drew on two traditional if contradictory arguments to undermine these female monarchs and admonish the men who misguidedly supported them.

To illustrate the monstrosity of female rule, Knox used the image of the "body politic," a commonplace that was linked with both church and state. The Christian community of believers was scripturally represented as a well-functioning body in which each member made the appropriate contribution — "the eye to see, the ear to hear, and the tongue to speak" (Romans 12:1–8, 1 Corinthians 12:4–13) — and the commonwealth, as well, was conceptualized as a body in which the ruler was the head, councillors the eyes, craftsmen the hands, and so forth. Since each part of the body was divinely created to perform its proper function and no other, the image of the body politic was customarily invoked to authorize hierarchy and discourage rebellion. Knox, however, enlists the image of the natural body of man made by God in his likeness to *incite* rebellion against the monstrous body politic misruled by idolatrous women.

However, even as the Amazon served as an emblem of monstrosity, Queen Elizabeth and her admirers enlisted qualities associated with the Amazon, such as skill, courage, and independence, to cleanse the taint of monstrosity from her reign. During her lifetime, Queen Elizabeth was identified with several Amazonian personages, including Diana and Britomart, the virtuous British warrior maiden who triumphed over the malevolent female ruler, Radigund, in Spenser's *Faerie Queene* (5.7.24). The comparison was apt: like an Amazon she governed, lived in a female community, and ultimately secured her own succession. Overseas and after her death, Elizabeth began to appear in iconography as an Amazonian warrior, and occasionally, even seemed to fashion herself as an Amazon, as in her reputed speech at Tilbury to the troops awaiting an invasion from the Spanish Armada.

The defeat of the Spanish Armada in 1588 has been understood as the moment when English nationalism crystallized, the glow of this victory suffusing the land, and the spirit of national pride and optimism unleashing a torrent of literary masterpieces by Spenser, Shakespeare, and others. This national transcendence was, supposedly, made possible by the policies and person of the great reconciler Elizabeth, simultaneously Prince (ruler of a modern state) and Virgin Warrior (leader of an ancient nation), who like Henry V at Agincourt inspired her countrymen to victory with a combination of powerful address and courageous example. The circumstances and sources of the speech, however, cast doubt both on the authenticity of the speech as we know it and on the image of unity that it reproduced, as Susan Frye has argued in "The Myth of Elizabeth at Tilbury."

Before the Armada engagement, relations between Spain and England had grown steadily worse with the discovery of Spanish support for plots to place Mary, Queen of Scots, on the English throne. But with Mary executed in 1587, Elizabeth had contemplated signing an accord with Spain. However, in a plundering expedition on Cadiz in 1587, Sir Francis Drake not only sank a number of Spanish vessels, he captured several that were obviously prepared for an invasion of England. Still, the queen refused to believe that an invasion was imminent and, ever parsimonious, delayed provisioning her fleet and recruiting soldiers: two-thirds of the English fleet was provided by the merchants of London and coastal towns and were much better supplied than the queen's ships. England had no standing army; militia forces could be mustered, but even when they were finally called up and four thousand troops straggled to Tilbury, there was no food there to feed them. By the time the queen arrived, the Spanish navy was defeated, thanks neither to the queen's inspiring oration nor to her countrymen's courageous defense but to a devastating storm that dispersed the Spanish fleet and sank most of it.

The orderly and martial rhetoric of the speech that has been attributed to Elizabeth at Tilbury is not quite consistent, then, with her actual handling of the crisis. Doubt has since been cast on the legend that she dressed for the occasion like an Amazon in battle armor (Frye 96). And she may not even have made the speech at all. There are two distinct versions of the speech; the accepted version was written long after the event by the "ardent and ambitious Protestant" Leonel Sharp (99) and therefore may be less authentic than William Leigh's earlier, lesser-known version. Sharp's speech may have prevailed because the image of a unified nation embodied as an impregnable warrior maiden was an important ideological resource for later ages (114). Taken together, the two disparate and politically motivated speeches raise provocative questions about the status and uses of "documentary evidence." No document is wholly unproblematic, as Frye has demonstrated; and as we examine each more closely, we must be prepared to revise the inherited understandings that these documents were enlisted to support.

→ CHRISTINE DE PIZAN

## *From* The Book of the City of Ladies            *c. 1405, 1521*

*Translated by Brian Anslay*

A devout Christian and a committed feminist, Christine de Pizan (1364–1430) was born in Venice and grew up in Paris where her father was connected with the court of Charles V. Educated with her father's encouragement, well connected but without a fortune of her own, she began to earn her living as a writer when she was widowed at age twenty-five with young children to support. Pizan produced several works on commission for powerful and royal patrons, paying careful attention to the copying and illumination of her books, and has therefore been considered "the first professional writer" (Warner xx–xxi). In spite of the traditional restriction of women writers to religious subjects and translations, she produced a wide range of works in the vernacular in many different genres (xxii–xxvi): volumes of poems and ballads, essays denouncing the slander of women in Jean de Meung's popular romance *Le Roman de la rose,* a narrative poem on Joan of Arc (the only praise of Joan written in her lifetime), a book of moral proverbs, defenses of women (including *Livre de la cité des dames*), and invaded masculine territory with works on military ethics and the body politic.

*Livre de la cité des dames* survives in twenty-five manuscripts, some prepared under Pizan's supervision (Warner xliv); Brian Anslay's translation, *The Book of the City of Ladies,* printed in 1521, was the only English version until this century. The work participated in the controversy on the nature of women which began in antiquity and flourished in fourteenth- and fifteenth-century France. Pizan took Giovanni Boccaccio's defense of women *De Mulieribus Claris* (Of illustrious women) as her model and chief source, but made significant changes. Boccaccio assumed that since women were inferior to men, any accomplishment at all was remarkable, and his is a history of famous, even infamous, women; when women were laudable, he concluded that they were acting like men, and he effectively dismissed the "Christian woman" as an oxymoron. Pizan, however, focuses on women's virtue, not their "fame," and assumes that women who act with virtue and courage are behaving exactly as women do (Warner xxxvi). Pizan's tribute embraces the spectrum of female roles — virtuous daughters, devoted wives, faithful lovers, warrior women, poets and scholars, prophets and visionaries, saints and martyrs — and she also includes stories of her contemporaries along with the accounts of ancient women from Boccaccio. By calling her female community a "City of Ladies" rather than a "City of Women," she affirmed that spiritual nobility was attainable within traditional social hierarchies in which women were subordinate (xxx). And by associating her City of

Christine de Pizan, *Livre de la cité des dames* (c. 1405), translated by Brian Anslay as *The Book of the City of Ladies* (London, 1521), "Of the Amazons" (Gg2r–3r) and "How the strong Hercules and Theseus went upon the Amazons and how the two ladies Menalippe and Hippolyta had almost overcome them" (Gg4v–Hh3r).

Ladies with St. Augustine's City of God, Pizan suggested that her political vision supplemented, not challenged, the Christian tradition.

## From OF THE AMAZONS

A land there is toward the end of Europe after the great sea that holdeth in all the world, which land is called Scythia.[1] It happened sometime that the country by force of war was despoiled of all the young men dwelling in that country. And when the women of that place saw that they had lost their husbands, their brethren, and their kinsmen, and there was none left but old men and children, they assembled by great courage, and took counsel between them, and advised[2] the conclusion that from that time forth they would maintain their lordships[3] without any subjection of[4] men, and made such a commandment that no manner of man should enter into their juris-diction, yet for to have lineage[5] they would go into the nearest country by a certain season of the year, and then should they turn home again into their country. And if they were delivered of any sons, they should send them unto their fathers. And if they were maid[6] children, they would nourish them themselves to perform their ordinance.[7] Then they chose two of the most noble ladies among them to be crowned queens, of which one was called Lampheto, the other Marpasia. This done, they chased out of their country all mankind[8] that was left, both young and old. And after it they armed them,[9] and with a great battle[10] all of ladies and of maidens went upon their enemies and wasted all their land by fire and by arms, and there was none that might resist them, and to speak shortly, they avenged the death of their friends full notably. And by this way began the women of Scythia to bear arms, the which were called Amazons, that is as much to say, "unpapped."[11] For that they had such a manner[12] that the noble women, when they were little maidens, their left paps were cut off by a certain craft[13] for that they should not be cumbered[14] to bear the shield. And to them that were not gentlewomen, their right paps were cut away to shoot the more easily. So they went[15] so much delighting in the craft of arms that they increased by forte[16] right much their country and their realm in so much that their fame went all about. . . . Then they went in to diverse countries, each of them leading a great host, and did so much that they conquered a great part of

---

[1] Scythia: an ancient region covering much of European and Asiatic Russia.   [2] advised: reached.   [3] lordships: dominions.   [4] of: to.   [5] lineage: descendants.   [6] maid: female.   [7] ordinance: direction, decree, command.   [8] mankind: men.   [9] them: themselves.   [10] battle: battalion.   [11] unpapped: unbreasted; "Amazon" means "without a breast" in Greek.   [12] manner: custom.   [13] by a certain craft: in a special way.   [14] cumbered: encumbered, hindered.   [15] went: continued.   [16] forte: strength.

Europe and of the country of Asia, and put under subjection many divers countries and joined them to their lordships, and founded many cities and towns, and likewise in Asia in the city of Ephesus,[17] which is a long time hath been of great renown. Of these two queens, Marpasia died first in a battle, then the Amazons crowned her daughter in her place, a noble maid and a fair, which[18] was named Synoppe, which had so great courage and high [spirits] all the days of her life, she deigned not to be coupled to no man but remained still a maid[19] all her life. So she had none other love nor charge[20] but only in the exercise of arms,[21] and in it she had so great pleasance[22] that she might not be satisfied [except] to assail and conquer lands and realms, and by her, her mother was greatly avenged in so much that those of that country [where her mother was killed] were slain and put to the sword, and [she] wasted all the land and conquered.

## *From* How the Strong Hercules and Theseus Went Upon the Amazons and How the Two Ladies Menalippe and Hippolyta Had Almost Overcome Them

[A]ll Greece was afeared, doubting[23] that the lands of [the Amazons] should stretch in short time into their country. Then there was in Greece in the flower of his youth Hercules, the marvelous strong man, which in his time did more marvels of strength than ever man did that was born of woman, of whom is made mention in histories. For he fought with giants and lions, with serpents and monsters right marvelous, and had of all them the victory. . . . This Hercules said it were not good to abide[24] till these ladies of Amazonia came upon them, but it were much better to go upon[25] them first. [T]hen for it they . . . assembled a great company of young, lusty men to go thither in great haste, [and] when Theseus, the worshipful[26] and wise man which was King of Athens, knew this tidings, he said they should not go without him. And so he assembled a great host[27] with this host of Hercules, and when they were all assembled they put them into the sea toward the country of Amazonia. And when they approached the country, Hercules, notwithstanding his marvelous strength and hardiness, and his great host of people, durst[28] not take the port by day nor to come down upon the land, so much the strength of these Amazons was blown about[29] in diverse countries, that it were marvelous[30] to say and believe if there were

---

[17] **Ephesus:** Ionian city on the coast of Asia Minor (now Turkey).   [18] **which:** who.   [19] **maid:** virgin.   [20] **charge:** responsibility, vocation.   [21] **exercise of arms:** warfare.   [22] **pleasance:** pleasure.   [23] **doubting:** suspecting, fearing.   [24] **abide:** wait.   [25] **go upon:** attack.   [26] **worshipful:** honorable.   [27] **host:** force.   [28] **durst:** dared.   [29] **blown about:** talked about.   [30] **marvelous:** incredible.

not so many histories[31] bring witness of them that there hath been so many worshipful men overcome by women. So Hercules and his host abode till the dark night was come. And then when the hour was come that every mortal creature ought to take his rest and sleep, he and his host leaped [to] land and entered into the country, and began to set fire in cities and towns, and slew all the women that took no heed of their coming. In the meantime, great was the cry among the [Amazons and] they were not slow to run to their harness[32] all manner of women as[33] those that were most hardiest[34] to run among the people toward the seaside upon their enemies.

And then there reigned upon[35] the Amazons the queen Orythia . . . [who] armed herself and abode[36] to put in order her battalions and her hosts. Then were there two worshipful maidens of sovereign strength, of chivalry and hardiness, and wise above many others, of which the one was called Menalippe and the other Hippolyta, and they were right nigh kin[37] to the queen. . . . [A]s fast as they might be armed, their spears in their hands, their shields of strong elephant [hide] hanging upon their necks, mounted upon their well-running coursers,[38] went right fast running toward the port . . . Menalippe toward Hercules and Hippolyta to Theseus. . . . [N]otwithstanding the great strength, hardiness, and great courage of [the men], so strongly these maidens hurt them, and by so great encounter[39] each of them beat [down] their knight[s] that they also fell on the other side, but as soon as they might they recovered themselves and ran upon them with good swords. Oh, what worship[40] ought these ladies to have, that by such two women were beaten two of the best knights that were in all the world, and this thing should not be credible to be true but that so many ancient doctors[41] bear witness of it. . . . [T]hese two knights were ashamed to be thus beaten of[42] these two maidens. Notwithstanding these maidens fought with their swords against these two knights strongly, and the battle endured long, yet at last . . . these maidens were taken. . . . Of this prize, [the knights] thought them greatly honored. Hercules and Theseus were gladder than if they had taken a city. So they held them in their ships with them to refresh[43] them and to unarm them, and thought that they had well employed their will. And when they saw [the Amazons] unarmed, and that they were so fair and so seemly then doubled their joy, for they took never prey that was to them so agreeable, and so they kept them with great joy and pleasance. . . . Then the Queen, for the desire that she had to have

---

[31] **histories:** stories.   [32] **harness:** battle armor.   [33] **as:** and.   [34] **hardiest:** bravest.   [35] **upon:** over.   [36] **abode:** remained.   [37] **nigh kin:** near relations.   [38] **coursers:** fast horses.   [39] **encounter:** valor.   [40] **worship:** admiration.   [41] **doctors:** authorities.   [42] **of:** by.   [43] **refresh:** entertain.

these two demoiselles[44] again, whom that she loved so much, was constrained to make a peace with the Greeks . . . and there was much joy, yet not for that it annoyed[45] greatly Theseus to deliver Hippolyta, for he was smitten with great love. So Hercules prayed and required[46] the Queen so much for him that she granted Theseus to take Hippolyta unto his wife and so should lead her into his country. And then were the weddings made worshipfully, and after that the Greeks departed, and Theseus led home Hippolyta, which had a son afterward that was called Hippolytus, which was a knight of great worship[47] and a chosen man among many. And when it was known in Greece that the peace was made, they never had greater joy, for there was never no thing that they doubted more.[48]

[44] demoiselles: maidens.    [45] annoyed: troubled, grieved.    [46] required: implored.    [47] worship: honor.    [48] never no thing that they doubted more: i.e., the Greeks had feared that their soldiers would be conquered or slain by the Amazons.

→ **SIR WALTER RALEIGH**

*From* The History of the World                                                            *1614*

Courtier, poet, soldier, scholar, adventurer, Sir Walter Raleigh, or Ralegh (1554?–1618), was the paradigm of Renaissance versatility. The third son of the third marriage of his father, a country gentleman, Raleigh attended Oxford, served with the Protestant Huguenot army in France, outfitted a discovery expedition that failed, and fought in Ireland against the opponents of the English occupation. Handsome and charming, Raleigh the courtier came to court in 1581 and soon joined the long line of Queen Elizabeth's "favorites," which included Leicester and Hatton; as she had favored Leicester with land and title, the queen granted Raleigh land, trade monopolies, and a knighthood, and appointed him both captain of her guard and to the defense commission against Spain — all of which aroused much jealousy at court. Raleigh the poet associated with a circle of men, including Thomas Harriot and Christopher Marlowe, who were interested in literature and science and accused of atheism; Raleigh the scholar was passionately interested in history, and, like John Stow, was a member of the Society of Antiquaries. Inevitably replaced in the queen's affection (by Robert Devereaux, the earl of Essex), Raleigh left the court and was imprisoned in 1592 when the queen learned of his unsanctioned marriage to one of her ladies in waiting, Elizabeth Throckmorton.

Walter Raleigh, *The History of the World in Five Books*, Part I (London, 1614) 1617 STC 20638, "Of Thalestris, Queen of the Amazons, where, by way of digression, it is showed that such Amazons have been and are," Book 4, 162–64.

In the late 1580s, Raleigh the adventurer had organized a colonizing expedition to America that ended badly as the "lost colony of Virginia" (but he has been credited with introducing tobacco and the potato to England). In 1595, he launched an expedition to Guiana to find the legendary city of gold, El Dorado: he sailed three hundred miles up the Orinoco, brought back some gold trinkets and reports that confirmed the presence of Amazons in the area, and published his account, *The Discovery of the Large, Rich, and Beautiful Empire of Guiana*, in 1596. He continued to decline in court favor, and on King James' accession to the throne in 1603 was imprisoned in the Tower of London for plotting against the king.

Between 1607 and 1614 while in the Tower, Raleigh began the first of the projected three volumes of *The History of the World*, from which the following selection on the Amazons is taken. Volume I began with the creation; related the rise and fall of Babylon, Assyria, and Macedon; and recounted the pinnacles of Hebrew, Greek, and Roman history up to 139 B.C. The other two volumes were never written. The work is both a medieval warning to rulers of the disastrous consequences of violating divine and human laws and a modern work mindful of chronology, facticity, and geography. Raleigh's *History* was eminently popular except with King James, who believed that Raleigh's effeminate character Ninus resembled him; the work was temporarily suppressed, but other editions appeared in 1617, 1621, 1624, 1628, 1634, and 1652. In 1616, Raleigh was permitted to return to the Orinoco region, but not only did he not find gold, he offended the Spanish governor there and on his return to England was executed under his original sentence of treason.

## OF THALESTRIS, QUEEN OF THE AMAZONS; WHERE, BY WAY OF DIGRESSION IT IS SHOWED, THAT SUCH AMAZONS HAVE BEEN, AND ARE

Here it is said that Thalestris or Minothea, a queen of the Amazons, came to visit [Alexander],[1] and her suit was, (which she easily obtained) that she might accompany him[2] till she were made with child by him: which done (refusing to follow him into India) she returned into her own country.

Plutarch citeth many historians, reporting this meeting of Thalestris with Alexander, and some contradicting it. But indeed, the letters of Alexander himself to Antipater,[3] recounting all that befell him in those parts, and yet omitting to make mention of this Amazonian business, may justly breed suspicion of the whole matter as forged. Much more justly may

[1] **Alexander:** Alexander the Great (356–323 B.C.) conquered Syria, Egypt, India, spreading Greek culture to the east. [2] **accompany him:** i.e., have sex with him. [3] **Antipater:** general under Alexander, regent of Macedonia during his campaigns.

we suspect it as a vain[4] tale, because an historian of the same time reading one of his books to Lysimachus (then King of Thrace) who had followed Alexander in all his voyage was laughed at by the king for inserting such news of the Amazons, as Lysimachus himself had never heard of. One that accompanied Alexander took it upon himself to write his acts, which to amplify, he told how the king had fought single with an elephant and slain it. The king hearing such stuff, caught the book, and threw it into the River of Indus,[5] saying that it were well done to throw the writer after it, who by inserting such fables, disparaged the truth of his great exploits. Yet as we believe and know that there are elephants, though it were false that Alexander fought with one, so may we give credit unto writers making mention of such Amazons, whether it were true or false that they met with Alexander, as Plutarch leaves the matter undetermined. Therefore I will here take leave to make digression, as well to show the opinions of the ancient historians, cosmographers, and others, as also of some modern discoverers touching these warlike women, because not only Strabo[6] but many others of these times make doubt, whether, or no, there were any such kind of people. Julius Solinas[7] seats them in the north parts of Asia the Less.[8] Pom[ponius] Mela[9] finds two regions filled with them, the one on the river Thermodoon,[10] the other near the Caspian Sea. . . . The former of these two had the Cimmerians[11] for their neighbors. . . . It is certain that the Cimmerians were the next nations to the Amazons. Ptolemy[12] sets them farther into the land northwards . . . [a]nd that they had dominion in Asia itself toward India, Solinus and Pliny[13] tell us, where they governed a people called the Pandeans, or Padeans, so called after Pandea, the daughter of Hercules, from whom all the rest derive themselves. Claudian[14] affirms that they commanded many nations, for he speaks (largely perhaps as a poet) thus:

> Over the Medes, and light Sabeans, reigns
> This female sex: and under arms of Queen,
> Great part of the barbarian land remains.

---

[4] **vain:** worthless.  [5] **River of Indus:** river that runs through what is now Pakistan and northern India.  [6] **Strabo:** Stoic and traveller (64 B.C.–19 A.D.) who wrote about his travels in the *Geographica*.  [7] **Julius Solinas:** naturalist of the third century A.D.  [8] **Asia the Less:** Asia Minor.  [9] **Pom[ponius] Mela:** Roman geographer in Spain, wrote the *Chorographia*, or *De Situ Orbis*, c. 43 A.D.  [10] **river Thermodoon:** river running into the Black (Euxine) Sea.  [11] **Cimmerians:** according to Herodotus, a people who lived to the north of the Euxine Sea (Black Sea), around the eighth century B.C.; nomadic invasions from the north led them to invade Assyria and Asia Minor.  [12] **Ptolemy:** Greco-Egyptian astronomer, mathematician, and geographer, of the second century A.D.; his thirteen-volume *Almagest* preserved Greek mathematics and astronomy, and his *Geography* was influential through the sixteenth century.  [13] **Pliny:** the Elder (c. 24–79 A.D.) known for the *Naturalis Historia*.  [14] **Claudian:** Greek poet from Alexandria, lived in Rome c. 395–404 A.D., wrote official poems in Latin praising rulers and generals.

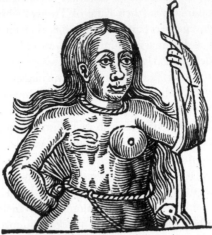

that the *Amazon*
much helping
themselves in
the wars with
Bows and Ar-
rows, and find-
ing that in this
and other exer-
cises of Armes
their Dugs or
Breasts were a
very great hin-
derance to them,
they used to
burne off the right Pap, both of themselves and
their Daughters, and thereupon they were called
*Amazons,* which signifieth in the Greeke Tongue,
No Breasts.

Purch, *Pilgr.* 3.
lib. 7.

The chiefe of
the Guard of
the King of *Con-*
*go* are left-han-
ded *Amazons,*
who seare off
their left Paps
with a hot Iron,
because it should
be no hinde-
rance to them in
their shooting.
*Pigafetta* in his
reports of the

*Pigafetta* in
*his relation of*
*Congo.*

Kingdome of *Congo,* makes the like mention of
these

FIGURE 14 *Amazons, each with a breast removed. The engravings from John Bul-wer's* Anthropometamorphosis, Or, The Artificial Changeling *emphasize the monstrosity of Amazonian self-mutilation; the accompanying text offers an explanation of the breast-burning of these African Amazons.*

Diodorus Siculus[15] hath heard of them in Libya, who were more ancient (saith he) than those which kept the banks of the Thermodoon, a river falling into the Euxine Sea[16] near Heraclium.

Herodotus[17] doth also make report of these Amazons, whom he tells us that the Scythians[18] call Aorpatas, which is as much as Viricidas, or "Men-killers." And that they made incursion into Asia the Less, sacked Ephesus,[19] and burnt the Temple of Diana, Manethon[20] and Aventinus report, which they performed forty years after Troy was taken. At the siege of Troy itself we read of Penthesilea, that she came to the succor[21] of Priam.[22]

Am[mianus] Marcellinius[23] gives the cause of their inhabiting upon the river of Thermodoon, speaking confidently of the wars they made with divers nations, and of their overthrow.

Plutarch in the "Life of Theseus," out of Philochorus, Hellanicus,[24] and other ancient historians, reports the taking of Antiopa, Queen of the Amazons, by Hercules,[25] and by him given to Theseus, though some affirm that Theseus himself got her by stealth when she came to visit him aboard his ship. But in substance, there is little difference, all confessing[26] that such Amazons there were. The same author in the "Life of Pompey" speaks of certain companies of the Amazons, that came to aid the Albanians against the Romans, by whom, after the battle, many targets[27] and buskins[28] of theirs were taken up; and he saith farther that these women entertain[29] the Gelae[30] and Lelages once a year, nations inhabiting between them and the Albanians.

But to omit the many authors making mention of Amazons that were in old times, Fran[cisco] Lopez who hath written of the navigation of Orel-

---

[15] **Diordorus Siculus:** contemporary of Julius Caesar, wrote a history of Rome from mythical times to Caesar's conquest. [16] **Euxine Sea:** "hospitable sea," now the Black Sea. [17] **Herodotus:** Greek historian (c. 480–425 B.C.), first to make the events of the past a subject of research and verification. [18] **Scythians:** peoples of the ancient region covering much of European and Asiatic Russia. [19] **Ephesus:** Ionian city on the coast of Asia Minor. [20] **Manethon:** priest of Heliopolis in Egypt, wrote Egyptian history in Greek. [21] **succor:** aid. [22] **Priam:** King of Troy at the time of the Trojan War. [23] **Am[mianus] Marcellinius:** c. 330 A.D., continued the history of Tacitus, c. 55–117 A.D., Roman historian who was perhaps best known for his writing on the Germanic tribes. [24] **Philochorus, Hellanicus:** chroniclers of early Attica, the area of Greece surrounding Athens, of, respectively, the fifth and third centuries B.C. [25] **Hercules:** (in Greek, Heracles) mythological Greek hero noted for his strength. [26] **confessing:** affirming. [27] **targets:** small, round shields. [28] **buskins:** boots. [29] **entertain:** meet to have sex with. [30] **Gelae:** people of Gela, a city on the coast of Sicily.

lana,[31] which he made down the River of Amazons from Peru, in the year 1542 (upon which river, for the divers turnings, he is said to have sailed six thousand miles) reports from the relation of the said Orellana to the Council of the Indies that he both saw these women and fought with them, where they sought to impeach his passage toward the East Sea.

It is also reported by Ulricus Schmidel[32] that in the year 1542, where he sailed up the Rivers of Parana and Parabol, that he came to a king of that country, called Scherves,[33] inhabiting under the Tropic of Capricorn, who gave his captain, Ernando Rieffere, a crown of silver, which he had gotten in fight from a queen of the Amazons in those parts.

Ed[uardo] Lopes, in his description of the kingdom of Congo, makes relation[34] of such Amazons, telling us that (agreeable to the reports of elder times) they burn off their right breast and live apart from men, save at one time of the year when they feast and accompany them for one month. These (saith he) possess a part of the kingdom of Monomotapa in Africa, nineteen degrees to the southward of the line,[35] and that these women are the strongest guards of this Emperor, all of the East Indian Portugals know.

I have produced these authorities, in part, to justify mine own relation of these Amazons, because that which was delivered me for truth by an ancient Casique of Guiana, how upon the River of Papamena[36] (since the Spanish discoveries called Amazons) that these women still live and govern, was held for a vain and unprofitable report.

[31] **Francisco Lopez . . . Orellana:** Lopez and Francisco de Orellana were sixteenth-century Spanish explorers of the Amazon. [32] **Ulricus Schmidel:** sixteenth-century explorer of what is now Argentina and Paraguay. [33] **country, called Scherves:** people called Scherves. [34] **makes relation:** tells. [35] **line:** equator. [36] **Papamena:** meaning "minus a breast."

→ JOHN KNOX

## *From* The First Blast of the Trumpet against the Monstrous Regiment of Women                1558

John Knox (1505–1572) was active throughout his life in reformist rebellions in Scotland, where he established the Presbyterian Church. As a young man, Knox studied law and divinity, was appointed to the priesthood, and worked as a notary, but his progressive principles soon led him to reject a career in the

John Knox, *The First Blast of the Trumpet against the Monstrous Regiment of Women* (London, 1558) STC 15070, "The First Blast to Awake Women Degenerate" (9r–11r).

church, and he became a tutor in vernacular studies. He found his vocation as a preacher in an uprising in 1547 over the burning for heresy of the Lutheran reformist George Wishart; rather, his vocation found him, for he was appointed by popular demand, the first time in Scotland that a congregation had chosen its spiritual guide. Knox was welcomed in England during the Protestant reign of Edward VI, where he preached and participated in the revision of *The Book of Common Prayer* of 1552, but declined a bishopric because of doctrinal differences with the Anglican Church. After the accession of the Catholic Queen Mary, he withdrew to France and Switzerland, where he associated with Henry Bullinger and John Calvin.

In 1558, Knox published *The First Blast of the Trumpet against the Monstrous Regiment of Women*, one of six of his tracts printed in the same year, the others dealing with the conflict in Scotland and urging England to remember its Protestant martyrs and embrace the true faith. Written in the fiery, exhortational style of the preacher, *The First Blast* was printed without attribution, but the identity of its author was common knowledge. Queen Mary died almost immediately after its publication, and the Protestant Elizabeth, the most powerful advocate of the reformists, assumed the throne. However, Queen Elizabeth was deeply offended by *The First Blast*. Though Knox had sought to promote religious reform and weaken the opposition by attacking influential Catholic queens, Elizabeth took personally his impassioned, if conventional, assertions of female deficiency, and of the monstrosity of female rulers whose "sight in civil regiment is but blindness; their strength, weakness; their counsel, foolishness; and judgment, frenzy" (see p. 212). For a time, she would not let Knox pass through England, and always remained lukewarm toward the Scottish Reformation.

## *From* The First Blast to Awake Women Degenerate

To promote a woman to bear rule, superiority, dominion, or empire above any realm, nation, or city, is repugnant to nature, contumely[1] to God, a thing most contrarious to his revealed will and approved ordination, and finally is the subversion of good order, of all equity and justice.

In the probation[2] of this proposition, I will not be so curious[3] as to gather whatsoever may amplify, set forth, or decore[4] the same, but I am purposed, even as I have spoken my conscience in most plain and few words, so to stand content with a simple proof of every member,[5] bringing in for my witness God's ordinance in nature, his plain will revealed in his word, and the minds of such as be most ancient amongst godly writers.

---

[1] **contumely:** insulting. [2] **probation:** trial, testing. [3] **curious:** vain, excessive. [4] **decore:** decorate, embellish. [5] **member:** component (of the argument).

And first, where that I affirm the empire of a woman to be a thing repugnant to nature, I mean not only that God by the order of his creation hath spoiled[6] woman of authority and dominion, but also that man hath seen, proved, and announced just causes why that it so should be. Man, I say, in many other cases blind, doth in this behalf see very clearly. For the causes be so manifest that they cannot be hid. For who can deny but it repugneth to[7] nature that the blind shall be appointed to lead and conduct such as do see? That the weak, the sick, and impotent[8] persons shall nourish and keep the whole and strong, and finally, that the foolish, mad, and frenetic shall govern the discreet, and give counsel to such as be sober of mind? And such be all women, compared unto man in bearing of authority. For their sight in civil regiment[9] is but blindness; their strength, weakness; their counsel, foolishness; and judgment, frenzy,[10] if it be rightly considered.

I except such as God by singular privilege, and for certain causes known only to himself, hath exempted from the common rank of women, and do speak of women as nature and experience do this day declare them. Nature, I say, doth paint[11] them forth to be weak, frail, impatient, feeble, and foolish, and experience hath declared them to be unconstant, variable, cruel, and lacking the spirit of counsel and regiment. And these notable faults have men in all ages espied in that kind, for the which not only they have removed women from rule and authority, but also some have thought that men subject to the counsel or empire of their wives were unworthy of all public office. For thus writeth Aristotle in the second of his *Politics*:[12] what difference shall we put, saith he, whether that women bear authority, or the husbands that obey the empire of their wives be appointed to be magistrates? For what ensueth the one must needs follow the other, to wit, injustice, confusion, and disorder. . . .

. . . What would this writer (I pray you) have said to that realm or nation where a woman sitteth crowned in Parliament amongst the midst of men. Oh, fearful and terrible are thy judgments (oh Lord) which thus hath abased man for his iniquity![13] I am assuredly persuaded that if any of those men, which illuminated only by the light of nature, did see and pronounce causes sufficient, why women ought not to bear rule nor authority, should this day live and see a woman sitting in judgment, or riding from Parliament in the midst of men, having the royal crown upon her head, the sword and sceptre borne before her, in sign that the administration of justice was in her power: I am assuredly persuaded, I say, that such a sight should so astonish

---

[6] spoiled: deprived. [7] repugneth to: offends, contradicts. [8] impotent: feeble. [9] regiment: order, rule. [10] frenzy: madness. [11] paint: represent. [12] the second of his *Politics: Politics,* 2.9.9. [13] iniquity: sin.

them, that they should judge the whole world to be transformed into Amazons, and that such a metamorphosis and change was made of all the men of that country as poets do say was made of the companions of Ulysses,[14] or at least, that albeit the outward form of men remained, yet should they judge that their hearts were changed from the wisdom, understanding, and courage of men to the foolish fondness and cowardice of women. Yea, they further should pronounce, that where women reign or be in authority, that there must needs vanity be preferred to virtue, ambition and pride to temperance and modesty, and finally, that avarice, the mother of all mischief, must need devour equity and justice. . . .

Augustine[15] defineth order to be that thing, by the which God hath appointed[16] and ordained[17] all things. Note well, reader, that Augustine will admit no order where God's appointment is absent and lacketh. . . . That God hath subjected womankind to man by the order of his creation, and by the curse[18] that he hath pronounced against her, is before declared. Besides these, he hath set before our eyes two other mirrors and glasses,[19] in which he will,[20] that we should behold the order, which he hath appointed and established in nature: the one is the natural body of man, the other is the politic or civil body of that commonwealth, in which God by his own word hath appointed an order. In the natural body of man, God hath appointed an order, that the head shall occupy the uppermost place. And the head hath he joined with the body, that from it doth life and motion flow to the rest of the members. In it hath he placed the eye to see, the ear to hear, and the tongue to speak, which offices[21] are appointed to none other member of the body. The rest of the members hath every one their own place and office appointed: but none may have neither the place nor the office of the head. For who would not judge that body to be a monster, where there was no head eminent above the rest, but that the eyes were in the hands, the tongue and mouth beneath the belly, and the ears in the feet. Men, I say, should not only pronounce this body to be a monster: but assuredly they might conclude that such a body could not long endure. And no less monstrous is the body of that commonwealth where a woman beareth empire.[22]

---

[14] **companions of Ulysses:** the sorceress Circe transformed Ulysses' companions into swine. Ulysses is the Latin name for Odysseus, whose many adventures with monstrous creatures and women with supernatural powers were recounted in Homer's *Odyssey.*  [15] **Augustine:** St. Augustine (354–430), influential theologian, author of the *Confessions* and *City of God.*  [16] **appointed:** ordered.  [17] **ordained:** decreed, predestined.  [18] **curse:** childbirth: "in sorrow thou shalt bring forth children; and thy desire shall be to thy husband, and he shall rule over thee," Genesis 3:16.  [19] **mirrors and glasses:** examples.  [20] **will:** wishes, commands.  [21] **offices:** functions.  [22] **empire:** rule.

... And such, I say, is every realm and nation where a woman beareth dominion. . . . [I]mpossible it is to man and angel to give unto her the properties and perfect offices of a lawful head. For the same God that hath denied power to the hand to speak, to the belly to hear, and to the feet to see, hath denied to woman power to command man, and hath taken away wisdom to consider, and providence to foresee the things that be profitable to the commonwealth: yea, finally he hath denied to her in any case to be a head to man, but plainly hath pronounced that man is head to woman, even as Christ is head to all man. . . . For that honor he hath appointed before all times to his only son, and the same will he give to no creature besides: no more will he admit, nor accept woman to be the lawful head over man. . . . For seeing he hath subjected her to one (as before is said) he will never permit her to reign over many. Seeing he hath commanded her to hear and obey one, he will not suffer that she speak, and with usurped authority command realms and nations.

→ QUEEN ELIZABETH I

# Address to the Troops at Tilbury
*1612 and c. 1624*

The following are two versions of the "Address to the Troops at Tilbury" that Queen Elizabeth supposedly gave on August 9, 1588. The first is from a sermon by William Leigh, printed in *Queen Elizabeth, Paralleled in Her Princely Virtues* in 1612. The second, the familiar version, was taken from a letter written sometime after 1624 by Leonel Sharp to the Duke of Buckingham. In both, the queen presents herself, or is represented, as warrior first and woman second, not a Diana on a summer progress ready for "recreation and disport" (Sharp, see p. 215) but a fighter among "companions at arms, and fellow soldiers, in the field" (Leigh, see p. 215) resolved to lay down honor and blood even in the dust (Sharp, see p. 215). While both speeches invoke Amazonian martiality, the queen is imagined not within a community of fighting women, but as a "fellow soldier," part of a community of men — an Amazon yet not an Amazon. In each address, the purpose of the anticipated battle with Spain is defined somewhat differently (Frye, "Myth" 100–01): for Leigh, it is the protection of

Queen Elizabeth I, two versions of the "Address to the Troops at Tilbury," August 9, 1588. Speeches modernized from Susan Frye, "The Myth of Elizabeth at Tilbury," in *Sixteenth Century Journal* 23, no. 1 (1992): 95–114. They come from a sermon by William Leigh printed in *Queen Elizabeth, Paralleled in Her Princely Virtues* (London, 1612) STC 15426; and from a letter from Leonel Sharp to the Duke of Buckingham, sometime after 1624, printed in *Cabala, Mysteries of State* (London: Bodell and Collins, 1654).

Protestantism, and for Sharp, the defense of a nation threatened by Parma, Spain, "or any prince of Europe." In the latter, nation and Queen reciprocally cross boundaries of gender, and the nation becomes the warrior maiden defended by the queen as general, judge, and feudal lord.

## TILBURY SPEECH, AS COMPOSED BY WILLIAM LEIGH (1612)

Come on now, my companions at arms, and fellow soldiers, in the field, now for the Lord, for your Queen, and for the kingdom. For what are these proud Philistines, that they should revile the host[1] of the living God? I have been your Prince in peace, so will I be in war; neither will I bid you go and fight, but come and let us fight the battle of the Lord. The enemy perhaps may challenge my sex for that I am a woman, so may I likewise charge their mould[2] for that they are but men, whose breath is in their nostrils, and if God do not charge England with the sins of England, little do I fear their force. . . . *Si deus nobiscum quis contra nos?*[3]

## TILBURY SPEECH, AS COMPOSED BY LEONEL SHARP (AFTER 1624)

My loving people, we have been persuaded by some, that are careful of our safety to take heed how we commit our self to armed multitudes for fear of treachery: but I assure you, I do not desire to live to distrust my faithful, and loving people. Let tyrants fear, I have always so behaved my self, that under God I have placed my chief strength, and safeguard in the loyal hearts and good will of my subjects. And therefore I am come amongst you as you see, at this time, not for my recreation and disport;[4] but being resolved in the midst, and heat of the battle to live, or die amongst you all, to lay down for my God, and for my kingdom, and for my people, my honor, and my blood even in the dust. I know I have the body, but of a weak and feeble woman; but I have the heart and stomach[5] of a King, and of a King of England, too, and think foul scorn that Parma[6] or Spain[7] or any prince of Europe should dare to invade the borders of my realm, to which rather than any dishonor should grow by me, I myself will take up arms, I myself will be your general, judge, and rewarder of every one of your virtues in the field. I know already for your forwardness,[8] you have deserved rewards and crowns, and we do assure you in the word of a Prince, they shall be duly paid you. In the mean-

---

[1] **host:** armed force.   [2] **mould:** form.   [3] *Si deus nobiscum quis contra nos?*: "If God is for us, who can be against us?"   [4] **disport:** enjoyment.   [5] **stomach:** disposition, courage; thought in Elizabethan times to be the inward seat of passion and emotion.   [6] **Parma:** Alessandro Farnese, Duke of Parma.   [7] **Spain:** Medina Sidonia led the Spanish forces.   [8] **forwardness:** readiness, eagerness, zeal.

FIGURE 15  *Queen Elizabeth I as an Amazon. In this Dutch engraving of 1598, Queen Elizabeth is represented as a bare-breasted Amazon warrior dominating the continent with her sword. When the engraving is turned on its side, the figure of the Queen becomes a map of Europe, with her lowered arm as Italy, and her sword-wielding arm the Isle of England.*

time, my lieutenant-general[9] shall be in my stead, than whom never prince commanded a more noble or worthy subject, not doubting but by your obedience to my general, by your concord in the camp, and your valor in the field, we shall shortly have a famous victory over those enemies of my God, of my kingdoms, and of my people.

[9] **lieutenant-general:** Charles Howard, later earl of Nottingham, commanded the English fleet; the earl of Leicester was captain-general of the armies.

## Gossips

With masculine supremacy challenged by the presence of a queen and her powerful female court, women were kept in their place not only by stories of Amazons tamed and poems about harmless little shepherdesses and sprites, but also by satirical attacks on female communities that were closer to home. In an age when the good woman was expected to be chaste, silent, and obedient,

FIGURE 16  *Gossips. The frontispiece of Samuel Rowland's* 'Tis Merry When Gossips Meet *represents the three categories — maid, wife, and widow — by which women were identified in relation to men, enjoying an evening without them — a custom reprehended by writers from Becon to Stubbes.*

one of the signs of a bad one was talking, particularly with other women. Household manuals were replete with stipulations of feminine silence and confinement: "a modest and chaste woman who loveth her husband must also love her house. . . . For the woman who gaddeth from house to house to prate confoundeth herself, her husband, and her family" (Dod and Cleaver 217). The female fondness for "gossip," which threatened hierarchy by reinforcing horizontal alliances, and occupied women with each other at the expense of home and husband, was a standard target in pamphlets, ballads, and plays.

Edward Gosynhyll's *The Schoolhouse of Women* enumerates the ways in which gossip threatened household stability and masculine supremacy. "Gossip" turned household order upside down, encouraging feminine conspiracy, idleness, and disobedience. Gosynhyll's gossip does not bear her share of the marital burden but glowers while her husband works; she does not cater to his moods and afflictions but subjugates him to hers; she does not enrich him by her domestic labor, but wastes his earnings on servants; she does not nourish him with food and drink, but presents him with an empty cup. Worst of all, in a kind of Amazonian act of autogeneration, the community of gossips perpetuates itself and even multiplies.

In early modern usage, however, "gossip" had several meanings. Etymologically derived from the linking of "God" and "syb" (kin), "gossip" referred to godparent or baptismal sponsor, or to the spiritual bond of that relationship. It also signified a same-sex friendship, at first among both men and women and later primarily between women. "Gossip" also referred to the female intimates who attended childbirth (and the "gossips' cup" to the drinking that celebrated such an event). And finally, it was used in the familiar sense of malicious or idle chatter, or the person, usually female, who indulged in it. Many of these meanings reverberate in *A Midsummer Night's Dream,* and the speech in which Titania refuses to relinquish the Indian boy to Oberon and recalls her friendship with the Indian Votaress is particularly rich.

> The fairy land buys not the child of me.
> His mother was a vot'ress of my order,
> And in the spicèd Indian air by night
> Full often hath she gossiped by my side
> And sat with me on Neptune's yellow sands,
> Marking th'embarkèd traders on the flood,
> When we have laughed to see the sails conceive
> And grow big-bellied with the wanton wind;
> Which she, with pretty and with swimming gait,
> Following — her womb then rich with my young squire —
> Would imitate, and sail upon the land

To fetch me trifles, and return again
As from a voyage, rich with merchandise.
But she, being mortal, of that boy did die;
And for her sake do I rear up her boy,
And for her sake I will not part with him.    (2.1.122–37)

Not only did Titania and the Votaress share quiet evening chats, Titania presumably attended her childbed, and fostered her son.

*A Midsummer Night's Dream* witnesses the end of Titania's loyalty to the Votaress, and of the intimacy between Hermia and Helena that was forged in shared sweet counsel (1.1.214–16 and 3.2.198–208) and evening "gossip"; in accordance with the prescriptions in household books, women's talk is silenced and their tenderness redirected towards their husbands. In the play, the dissolution of these female bonds is represented as laudable, a confirmation that these women have honorably come of age. However, while "gossip" as idle female chatter is silenced over the course of the play, and even the "god-syb" relation is undone, female bonds are not entirely severed. The female community of midwives and "gossips" who attended the childbed, in fact, will soon have much to do in assisting the imminent arrival of the flawless progeny without mole, harelip, or scar (5.1.387) promised to the wedding couples. "Gossips," then, are a female community that cannot be eradicated — indeed, since the childbearing on which masculine society depended was the province of an exclusively female domain, it had to be preserved.

→ **EDWARD GOSYNHYLL**

# *From* The Schoolhouse of Women    *1541*

The poem by Edward Gosynhyll (no dates) commonly known as *The Schoolhouse of Women* was printed anonymously in 1541. A first strike in the "pamphlet wars" on the nature of women, it provoked several responses in women's defense, among them Robert Vaughan's *A Dialogue Defensative* (1542) and Edward More's *The Defense of Women* (1560). However, Gosynhyll himself had almost immediately reconsidered his position (and reputation) and had published a poem, *Praise of All Women Called Mulierium Paen* (1542) in the same meter as *Schoolhouse*, in which he confirmed his authorship of the earlier poem and attempted to redress his incivility. Two more editions of *Schoolhouse* appeared in 1560 and 1572, and a second edition of the *Praise of All Women* in 1560: evidently there was more of a market for slander of women than for tributes to them.

---

Edward Gosynhyll, *Here Beginneth a Little Book Named the Schoolhouse of Women* (London, 1541) STC 12104.5.

Wed them once, and then adieu,
Farewell all trust[1] and housewifery.[2]
Keep their chambers and themselves mew[3]
For staining[4] of their schism[5]
And in their bed all day do lie,
Must once or twice every week
Feign themselves for[6] to be sick.
 Send for this, and send for that,
Little or nothing may them please.
Come in, good gossip,[7] and keep me chat,[8]
I trust it shall do me great ease,
Complain of many a sundry disease,
A gossip's cup,[9] between, or twain,[10]
Till she be gotten up again.
 Then must she have maidens[11] two or three
That may then gossips together bring,
Set them to labor, to blear the eye,[12]
Themselves will neither wash nor wring,
Bake nor brew, nor other thing.
Sit by the fire, let the maidens trot,
Brew[13] of the best in a halfpenny[14] pot.
 Play who will, the man must labor,
And bring to house all that he may.
The wife again doth nought but glower,
And hold him up with yea and nay.
But of her cup, he shall not assay
Other[15] she sayeth it is to thine,
Other[16] else, ywis,[17] there is nothing in.
 And when these gossips are once met,
Of every tale and new tiding
They babble fast, and nothing forget.
They put (I warrant) between riding[18]

---

[1] **trust:** duty.   [2] **housewifery:** thrift; housekeeping.   [3] **mew:** coop up.   [4] **staining:** disdaining (disregarding).   [5] **schism:** discord, division (that they create in the household).   [6] **feign themselves for:** pretend.   [7] **gossip:** familiar acquaintance; woman who delights in idle chatter; close women friends invited to a birth.   [8] **keep me chat:** keep me company, entertain me with gossip. [9] **gossip's cup:** warm ale or spiced wine given to the sick, childbearing, or their visitors. [10] **between, or twain:** a drink or two between complaints.   [11] **maidens:** young girls (to do her housework).   [12] **to blear the eye:** to deceive.   [13] **brew:** make ale.   [14] **halfpenny:** worth a halfpenny, i.e., cheap.   [15] **Other:** the rest.   [16] **Other:** or.   [17] **ywis:** surely, truly.   [18] **riding:** a mock procession holding timid husband, scolding wife, or quarreling couple up to ridicule.

This learn the younger of the elders' guiding.
Day by day, keeping such schools,
The simple men they make as fools.

## Nuns

The two alternatives to obedient marriage that Theseus presents the rebellious Hermia in *A Midsummer Night's Dream* are death or the perpetual virginity of the cloister. The latter, however, had not been an option in England since the Reformation, when the profession of nun had been abolished with the dissolution of the monasteries between 1536 and 1539 (although some women continued to take holy orders in English convents in France). By the time it was officially dissolved, the monastic system had long been in decline and under attack; indeed, the dissolution of the lesser monasteries and convents had begun as early as the fifteenth century. Monastic life had, however, been briefly revived under Mary Tudor when she restored the nation to Catholicism, and were a Catholic to succeed after Queen Elizabeth's reign, female religious communities might again have been reinstated.

In the late Middle Ages, convent life had offered women an honorable profession and an opportunity to survive and flourish independent of marriage. Within the religious community, women could be landowners, managers, and scholars, performing the same social and cultural functions as men. However, with the new importance of secular, classical studies in the Renaissance, the center of learning moved from the monasteries and convents to the universities, and with the growth of the universities, the intellectual status of the convents, formerly competitive with the monasteries, declined. Some female institutions were dissolved to found educational institutions for men (Eckenstein 435); the nunnery of St. Radigund, for instance, dissolved in 1496, was subsequently transformed into Jesus College, Cambridge. Since pre-Reformation ecclesiastic reformers emphasized worship over learning, the duties of nuns had gradually dwindled to chants, prayer, and silence. With the Reformation, the convents' devotional purpose ceased to exist (434), and their closure was lamented only by those who, like Thomas Fuller, believed that the education they provided to women was socially beneficial (3: 336). Perhaps the dissolution did not cause the end of the convents as much as symbolize with a transfer of church lands to the Crown (432–33) the cultural shifts in the woman's role that were long in progress.

When Theseus threatens Hermia with the fate of a barren sister in a thorny convent, his image might well have amused Shakespeare's audiences,

FIGURE 17 *Female Community. The woodcut from Brian Anslay's translation of Pizan's* City of Ladies *shows an ideal female society: orderly, equitable, spiritual, and learned.*

for the licentiousness of monks and nuns had long been rumored, and it was the carnal activities "discovered" during official inspections or "visitations" that provided a pretext for the termination of the cloistered life. In his report on the convent of Syon, Richard Layton reveals the sexual corruption under the convent's chaste facade: in one example, a young nun "meddles" with her confessor, who offers her absolution "whensoever and as oft" as she might require it. However, the supposed incontinency of nuns that Layton certifies in order to justify the dissolution of the convent seems rather to certify the incontinency of old monks who take advantage of lonely young nuns.

Ultimately, the vocation of nun was a casualty of the Reformation dogma that marriage was the most dependable antidote to sin and the only "godly" condition for women since they were prone to weakness (Eckenstein 433). Though Desiderius Erasmus never broke with the Roman Church, he was an early and persuasive advocate of this doctrine, whose circulation was an important part of the "pre-history of the destruction of religious life and the denial of its ideals" (Knowles 3:141) that began long before Martin Luther's (1483–1546) critique of the church that would spark the Reformation. For Erasmus, as for the Protestant reformers, marriage was the practical way for Christians, even priests, to avoid sin and enhance spirituality. In "A Maid Hating Marriage," Erasmus shows the young Catherine captivated by the idea of convent life, particularly by its aesthetic and sentimental attractions. Refusing to be persuaded by her suitor's arguments about the relative virtue and freedom of domestic over monastic life, she determines to enter a convent. (In the debate following the one presented below, however, she sees the error of her ways.)

In "A Maid Hating Marriage," the patriarchal household is praised as having all of the qualities that the convent ideally possessed. The father's house is both a sanctuary from sin and a way to spiritual perfection, offering countless appealing and virtuous activities: reading or singing, praying or listening to sermons at church, conversing with virtuous women, learning from virtuous men, selecting the most sincere of preachers. The convent, on the other hand, offers "strange mothers" and "counterfeit fathers" rather than natural ones, servitude to "masters and mistresses" rather than freedom, and vulnerability to predatory monks rather than the power to make the household "more holy."

→ RICHARD LAYTON

# A Letter, Certifying the Incontinency of the Nuns of Syon
*1535*

Syon, the Brigettine abbey that Layton's letter describes, was a wealthy community of sixty nuns, many from distinguished families, in existence for more than a hundred years. The nuns were supervised by religious men who were unusually well educated, some at Oxford and Cambridge, and Syon was an institution long known for its library, learning, and strict observance. However, the residents refused to endorse King Henry VIII's divorce, the Act of Succession that would legitimize the children of his succeeding marriages, and the Oath of Supremacy that declared him the supreme head of the Church of England (Knowles 3: 213–15). In 1535, with several leaders of this opposition executed, further inspections by deputies of Thomas Cromwell were made to ensure compliance. Cromwell had managed the suppression of the minor monasteries under Cardinal Wolsey, who was later disgraced for his failure to obtain Henry VIII a speedy divorce from Katherine of Aragon. Thereafter, Cromwell became Henry's chief minister, responsible for the Reformation statutes, the inspection and suppression of the monasteries between 1536 and 1539, and the confiscation of church land and wealth.

The visitation of Syon in 1535 was performed by Richard Layton, a former colleague of Cromwell under Cardinal Wolsey, and Master Bedyll, a council for the king in the divorce from Katherine; both men had assisted in the interrogation of Sir Thomas More, who opposed the divorce, and Layton also took part in the trial of Anne Boleyn. At Syon, Layton found the necessary evidence of moral corruption, detailed in this letter reprinted by Thomas Fuller in *The Church History of Britain*. The government hesitated to apply too much pressure since the residents of Syon were well connected, but finally in November of 1539, Syon was seized. Although many monks were content to be pensioned off with the Reformation, the nuns of Syon were not: they never formally surrendered their house, but took their books and vestments to France, returning to Syon and reestablishing their order when Mary Tudor restored Catholicism in 1553. After the accession of the Protestant Elizabeth I in 1558, the remaining nuns fled to the continent, settled in Lisbon for two centuries, and finally returned to England where they remain to this day (Knowles 3: 441–42). In spite of government insistence that monastics were weary of the religious life (Layton, see p. 226), these women clung tenaciously to their community.

---

Richard Layton, "A Letter, certifying the incontinency of the Nuns of Syon with the Friars, and after the act done, the Friars reconcile them to God" (1535), in *The Church History of Britain, from the Birth of Jesus Christ until the Year M.DC.XLVIII*, by Thomas Fuller (Oxford: Oxford UP, 1845) 391–92.

To the Right Honorable Master Thomas Cromwell,[1] chief secretary to the king's Highness.

It may please your goodness to understand that Bishop[2] this day preached, and declared the King's title[3] very well, and had a great audience, the church full of people. One of the [men] in his said declaration openly called him false knave, with other foolish words; it was the foolish fellow with the curled head that kneeled in your way when you came forth of the confessor's chamber. I can no less do but set him in prison, *ut pena ejus sit metus aliorum.*[4] Yesterday I learned many enormous[5] things against Bishop in the examination of the lay brethren,[6] first that Bishop persuaded two of the brethren[7] to have gone their ways by night, and he himself with them, and to the accomplishment of that they lacked but money to buy them secular apparel; further, that Bishop would have persuaded one of his lay brethren, a smith, to have made a key for the door, to have in the nighttime received in wenches for him and his fellows, and especially a wife of Uxbridge, now dwelling not far from the old lady Derby, nigh Uxbridge, which wife his old customer hath been many times here at the grates communing with the said Bishop, and much he was desirous to have had her conveyed in to him.

The said Bishop also persuaded a nun to whom he was confessor, *ad libidinem corporis perimplendam;*[8] and thus he persuaded her in confession, making her to believe that whensoever and as oft as they should meddle together, if she were immediately after confessed by him, and took of him absolution, she should be clear forgiven of God, and it should be none offense unto her before God. And she wrote divers and sundry letters unto him of such their foolishness and unthriftiness,[9] and would have his brother the smith to have pulled out a bar of iron out of that window [whereat] ye examined the lady abbess, that he might have gone into her by night; and that same window was their commoning place[10] by night. He persuaded the sexton that he would be in his contemplation in the church by night, and by that means was many nights in the church talking with her at the said grate

---

[1] **Thomas Cromwell:** (1485?–1540), the earl of Essex who managed the suppression of the minor monasteries under Cardinal Wolsey.    [2] **Bishop:** one of the religious men who officiated at Syon, long considered a troublemaker (Knowles 3: 219).    [3] **King's title:** the Supreme Head of the Church of England.    [4] *ut pena ejus sit metus aliorum:* so that his punishment may make others fear.    [5] **enormous:** monstrous.    [6] **lay brethren:** unordained members of the parish.    [7] **brethren:** friars.    [8] *ad libidinem corporis perimplendam:* to fulfill the pleasure of the body.    [9] **unthriftiness:** excess.    [10] **commoning place:** meeting place; dancing place, with dancing as a euphemism for sexual intercourse.

of the nuns' choir, and there was their meeting place by night, besides their day communications, as in confession.

It were too long to declare all things of him that I have heard, which I suppose is true. This afternoon I intend to make further search, both of some of the brethren and some also of the sisters of such like matters; if I find anything apparent to be true, I shall (God willing) thereof certify your mastership tomorrow by seven in the morning. And after this day I suppose there will be no other things to be known as yet here, for I have already examined all the brethren and many of them would gladly depart hence, and be right weary of their habit.[11] Such religion and feigned sanctity God save me from. If Master Bedyll[12] had been here a friar, and of Bishop's counsel, he would right well have helped him to have brought his matter to pass, without breaking up of any grate or counterfeiting of keys, such capacity God hath sent him.

From Syon, this Sunday, 12th December. By the speedy hand of your assured poor priest, Richard Layton.

[11] **be right weary of their habit:** are tired of monastic life.   [12] **Master Bedyll:** one of Cromwell's agents during the visitation, a council for the king in the divorce suit, and assistant in the interrogation of Sir Thomas More. Layton is complimenting Bedyll's efficiency.

→ DESIDERIUS ERASMUS

## *From* A Maid Hating Marriage                    *1523*

Humanist scholar and writer, Catholic priest, and sometime tutor of young English gentlemen, Desiderius Erasmus (1465?–1536) was born in Rotterdam and served as a boy chorister in the Cathedral Church at Utrecht. At the death of his parents he entered a monastery. Though he did not enjoy monastic life, his intellect brought him to the attention of a bishop who sent him to study at the Sorbonne in Paris. To support himself, he took on English gentlemen as pupils, and returned with them to England, later tutoring Alexander, son of James V of Scotland. He had many friends in England, including Henry VIII and Sir Thomas More, in whose honor he wrote the *Morae encomium* (1509), translated as *The Praise of Folly* (More increasingly differed with the king and was finally beheaded for treason in 1534 for his refusal to take the oath of the Act of Supremacy).

Desiderius Erasmus, "A Maid Hating Marriage" (1523), in *The Colloquies, or Familiar Discourses of Desiderius Erasmus of Rotterdam, Rendered into English,* translated by H. M., Gent. (London, 1671) STC 12316, 140–48.

The influence of Erasmus was widely felt in England and on the continent through his writings on religion, learning, and education and his translations of Latin and Greek texts. He wrote in Latin, still regarded as the "permanent instrument of communication and literary expression in civilized life" (Thompson xv); his works, printed in Basel by Johannes Froben, include the *Enchiridion militis christiani* (1503, 1518) (Manual of a Christian knight), *Ecclesiastes* (1535), on Christian faith and the church, and the *Institutio principis christiani* (1516) (Education of a Christian prince), on education. Although he was well known for his criticism of the clergy and church institutions, Erasmus never left the Catholic Church. Though he agreed with Martin Luther's criticism of ecclesiastical abuses and was widely condemned for Lutheran sympathies, Erasmus disapproved of the extremes of Luther and his followers, maintaining that reform should come from within the church.

The colloquy was a form of the dialogue, the genre of Platonic argumentation, in which an issue was explored dialectically in the imagined conversation of two characters. This genre was particularly suited to the ongoing controversy over monasticism since it replicated the process of debate but unfairly weighted one side of the argument. The *Colloquies (Familiarium colloquiorum formulae, et alia quedam, per Des. Erasmum Roterodamum)* were published in Latin in 1518 without authorization. Initially, the essays were exercises for teaching Latin, probably written around 1497 and 1498; Erasmus was annoyed at their publication, but became involved with later editions, which included "A Maid Hating Marriage," first printed in 1523. The *Colloquies* enjoyed great success on the continent and in England, appearing in at least eighty-seven printings of sixteen subsequent editions before Erasmus's death in 1536 (Thompson xxii–xxv). Popular as well as controversial (the theological faculty of the Sorbonne denounced them), the *Colloquies* were well known in Latin and in translation to educated Englishmen such as Lyly, Nashe, Jonson, Webster, and, perhaps, Shakespeare (Thompson xxxi).

If Erasmian antimonasticism was part of the prehistory of the Reformation, Erasmus's colloquy had a prehistory of its own. An English poem entitled "Why I Can't Be a Nun" (Furnivall, *Poems* 139–48) from the time of Henry VI (iii), tells much the same story, but without the suitor: a young girl named Katherine wishes to enter a convent but is opposed by her parents; however, when she is shown the corruption of convent life, she exhorts other young ladies to follow the example of saintly women who were not professed nuns.

EUBULUS:    I'm glad that supper is done at last, that we may enjoy this walking abroad,[1] than which there is nothing more pleasant.

CATHERINE:    And I was already wearied with sitting.

EUB:    How fresh and green, how pleasant is the world all abroad! Surely this is its youth.

---

[1] **abroad:** outdoors.

CATH:   It is so.

EUB:   But why is not thy springtime as pleasant?

CATH:   Why so?

EUB:   Because thou art somewhat sad.

CATH:   Do I look otherwise than I use to do?

EUB:   Wilt thou have me show thee to thyself?

CATH:   Yes, do.

EUB:   Dost thou see this rose, its leaves being drawn up together, night being at hand?

CATH:   I see it. What then follows?

EUB:   Thou lookest like it.

CATH:   A fine comparison!

EUB:   If thou dost not believe me, view thyself in this little spring. I pray thee what meant those thy so often sighs even while we were at supper.

CATH:   Forbear to inquire of that which belongs, not to thee to know.

EUB:   Yea, it concerns me very much, who cannot be merry unless I see thee merry, too. But lo, another sigh! Oh, how deep it was!

CATH:   There is something that troubles my mind, but it's not safe to speak it.

EUB:   Wilt not tell me, who love thee more than mine own sister? My Catherine! Fear not, whatever thing it is thou shalt safely reveal it to me.

CATH:   Though I may speak it safely, I am afraid lest I shall tell it to one that will not help me. . . .

EUB:   I do not at all perceive what thou wantest[2] to make thee fully happy. . . . To be short,[3] I would not choose myself any other wife among all the maids which are in this country,[4] besides thee, if any lucky star would shine upon me.

CATH:   Nor would I choose any other husband, if I had any mind to marry at all.

EUB:   And yet it must needs be some great matter which so troubles thy mind. . . .

CATH:   Seeing that thou so press me, I'll tell thee. I have had a certain wonderful affection[5] even from my childhood.

EUB:   What, pray thee?

CATH:   To be put into the College of the Nuns.[6]

EUB:   To be made a nun?

CATH:   It's even so. . . . My parents always stiffly withstood this my inclination.

[2] wantest: lack.   [3] short: brief.   [4] country: neighborhood.   [5] affection: desire.   [6] College of the Nuns: convent.

EUB:  I understand thee.

CATH:  On the other side,[7] I strove against the natural affection of my parents with entreaties, fair words, and tears.

EUB:  A wonderful thing.[8]

CATH:  At length, when I would not give over entreating and weeping, they gave me a promise that when I had attained to seventeen years of age, they would submit to my desire, if so be that then I were of the same mind. The year is come, I am still of the same mind, but on the contrary, my parents stiffly deny their promise. This is it that troubles my mind. I have told thee my disease, now do thou play the physician, if thou canst do any thing.

EUB:  First of all, most sweet maid, I will give thee this counsel, to govern[9] thy affections, and if that will not fall out[10] which thou desirest, desire that which thou mayest do.

CATH:  I shall die if I have not my will.

EUB:  How camest thou by this fatal affection?

CATH:  Heretofore when I was a very little girl I was carried[11] into a certain College of Virgins.[12] We were carried about it, they showed us all things; I liked the Virgins[13] for their beautiful faces: methought they looked like angels. All things were neat in the church, the gardens were very neat and well looked to,[14] and also cast a very fragrant smell; to be short, everything gave content wherever I looked. There were over and above these things the most pleasant discourses of the Virgins. I found one or two there with whom I used often to play once, when I was a little one. From that time my mind hath been exceedingly affected with that kind of life.

EUB:  I will not find fault with the Nuns' manner of life, although all things are not expedient for all persons. But considering thy inclination,[15] which methinks I have gathered by thy countenance and manners, I would counsel thee to be married to a husband like thy self, and to set up a new College at thine own house, whereof thy husband may be the father, and thou the mother.

CATH:  I'll die first, before I will forsake my purpose to be a Virgin.

EUB:  Virginity is an excellent thing if it be undefiled, but there's no necessity for this cause to put thyself into a College from whence thou canst not be freed afterwards. Thou mayest preserve thy Virginity while thou art with thy parents.

[7] side: hand.   [8] wonderful thing: a fine approach.   [9] govern: control.   [10] that will not fall out: it will not work out.   [11] carried: taken.   [12] College of Virgins: convent.   [13] Virgins: nuns.   [14] to: after.   [15] inclination: temperament.

CATH:   I may, but not so safely.

EUB:   Yea, as I think, somewhat more safely, than with those blockish and bursting-bellied monks. For they are not gelded,[16] I would have thee know. They are called "fathers," and they oftentimes take an order that this name may very well agree with them. In former times, Virgins lived nowhere more honestly[17] than with their parents, nor had any other "father" than the bishop. . . .

CATH:   I am troubled at the frequent feasts at my father's house, and they are not always chaste words which are spoken there among married folk. And oftentimes it falls out that I cannot deny a kiss.

EUB:   He that endeavors to shun whatever is offensive must depart out of the world. Thou must so accustom thy ears that they can hear all things, and yet set nothing into thy heart but good things. Thy parents, I suppose, suffer thee to have a bedchamber of thine own.

CATH:   Yes, they do.

EUB:   Thou mayest withdraw thyself thither if there shall fall out to be any troublesome feast; and while they drink and dally, do thou discourse with thy Husband, Christ: pray, sing psalms, give thanks. Thy father's house will not pollute thee, but thou mayest make it more holy.

CATH:   But it's safer to be in the company of Virgins.

EUB:   I do not disallow a chaste society, but I would not have thee be fooled with a vain show. When thou shalt have been there a little while and hast more narrowly[18] looked into things, all things will not be so gay as once thou thought they were. Neither, believe me, are they all virgins who wear a veil. . . .

CATH:   But my mind is bent that way, and hence I gather that the spirit comes from God, because it hath continued constantly so many years already, and it is every day more eager.[19]

EUB:   Yea, in this respect I have a jealousy[20] of that spirit of thine, because thy very honest parents do so withstand thee; God would have inspired their minds too, if it had been a godly thing which thou assayest.[21] But thou hast gotten that spirit from those gallantries which thou sawest when thou wast a very little girl, from the kind words of the Virgins to thee, from the affection towards thy old companions, from the holy attire, from the ceremonies being indeed very godly to see to, from the wicked exhortations of the foolish monks, and who for this purpose hunt after thee, that they may drink more freely. . . . Therefore, I would advise

[16] gelded: castrated.   [17] honestly: chastely.   [18] narrowly: closely.   [19] eager: strong.   [20] jealousy: suspicion.   [21] assayest: attempt.

thee to adventure upon no new thing against thy parents' minds, at whose disposing God will have us to be.

CATH: In this thing it's a pious thing to neglect[22] father and mother.

EUB: To neglect father and mother upon some occasion for Christ's sake is a pious thing . . . if now thy parents should force thee to ungodliness or dishonesty, their authority were not to be regarded. But what is this to a College? Thou hast Christ even at home. Nature dictates, God proves,[23] Paul exhorts, and human laws confirm that children should be obedient to their parents. Wilt thou withdraw thyself from the authority of thy most honest parents that thou mayest put thyself in the power of a counterfeit father instead of a true one, and instead of a true mother, take to thyself a strange one, or rather choose to thyself masters and mistresses instead of thy parents? . . . [C]onsider me but this, how many conveniences thou losest together with thy liberty. Thou hast now liberty to read in thy bed-chamber, to sing, as much and at what time thou pleasest. And if thou be weary of thy bed-chamber, thou mayest hear singing at the church, be at prayers, hear sermons. And if thou shalt see any matron or virgin who is very virtuous, thou mayest get good by discoursing with her; if thou shalt see any noted, honest man, thou mayest learn of him that which may benefit thee; and thou shalt have liberty to choose a preacher who teacheth Christ most sincerely. When thou art once tied to a College, thou losest all things by which true piety is most increased.

CATH: But in the meantime, I shall not be a nun. . . . Thou dost press me with many and weighty reasons indeed, and yet I cannot be rid of this desire.

EUB: If I cannot persuade thee (which yet I have wished) at least see thou remember this, that Eubulus hath given thee warning. In the meantime, I intreat thee for the love I bear thee, that this affection of thine may be better[24] for thee than my advice.

[22] **neglect:** disregard.  [23] **proves:** ordains.  [24] **better:** more successful; i.e., "I hope this works out better for you than giving advice did for me."

## The Virgin Queen

Although the convent no longer provided an active threat to the institution of marriage, in *A Midsummer Night's Dream* the "livery of the nun" is presented in bleak Erasmian terms, as imprisonment in a "shady cloister" of barren sisters "withering on the virgin thorn" (1.1.70–78). However, since

Elizabeth I, like Hermia, had also refused to yield her virgin patent up to an unwished yoke (80), Theseus's disparagement of the unmarried woman is double-edged. In relation to men and marriage, Queen Elizabeth played many roles: unattainable virgin, ardent beloved, and consenting or censuring parent with the patriarchal privilege of arranging or approving the marriages of her ladies and courtiers. But she never deliberately played the virgin withering on the thorn, even as the role became more and more appropriate. The ambivalence engendered in her subjects by Queen Elizabeth, who never flowered as wife and mother, whose virginity powerfully challenged the ideology of marriage and created a national crisis of succession, emerged ill-disguised in Theseus's warning.

Queen Elizabeth resisted marriage from the beginning of her reign and frequently made it clear that given a choice, she would never marry. In her first speech to Parliament she stated that her epitaph of choice would read "that such a queen, having reigned such a time, lived and died a virgin" (Hartley 45). As a ruler, however, her duty was to present the nation with an heir to the throne in order to ensure a smooth succession and avoid civil war. And as a Protestant, she was responsible for producing a successor to prevent the country from once again falling under Catholic rule.

Constantly pestered by the Commons, threatened by the proximity of other claimants such as Mary, Queen of Scots, goaded by her own sense of obligation, and aware that the prospect of marriage with the queen of England was a strong card in the game of foreign policy, Elizabeth entertained marriage embassies from Archduke Charles of the Holy Roman Empire and the Duke of Anjou (future King Henry III of France). But she was always ambivalent toward marriage; the year after her visit to Kenilworth she expressed her dilemma in the pastoral mode:

> if I were a milkmaid with a pail upon my arm, whereby my private person were little set by, I would not forsake the poor and single state to match with the greatest monarch. . . . Yet, for [the nation's] behalf, there is no way so difficult, that may touch my private person, which I will not well content myself to take; and this case as willingly to spoil myself of myself . . . if the present state might not thereby be encumbered. (Neale 366)

Archduke Charles lost patience and the Duke of Anjou finally demurred, but his indefatigable mother Catherine de' Medici offered Elizabeth Anjou's younger brother Alençon. For once, the queen seemed favorably disposed to the candidate, though he was twenty years younger and conspicuously unattractive. The prospect of this marriage, however, evoked strong opposition among both aristocracy and Puritans; in 1597, John Stubbes published a pamphlet against the marriage, *The Discovery of a*

*Gaping Gulf Whereinto England is Like to be Swallowed,* an impertinence that cost Stubbes his writing hand. (As his right hand was publicly removed, Stubbes is reported to have lifted his hat with his left and shouted, "God Save the Queen!")

William Camden's account of Alençon's visit of 1581 (*Annals* 134–37) captures the atmosphere of high drama surrounding the issue of the queen's marriage among courtiers, ladies in waiting, and within the queen herself — all of whom emphasize rather curiously (since the queen was then forty-eight) the danger to the queen of giving birth. Perhaps the explanation of the queen's single state that was both the simplest truth and the greatest mystification was that which Camden reports (16) from her first speech to Parliament in 1558: "'I have already joined myself in marriage to a husband, namely the kingdom of England. And behold . . . this pledge of my wedlock and marriage with my kingdom,' and therewith, she stretched forth her finger and showed the ring of gold."

→ **QUEEN ELIZABETH I**

## *From* Speech to Parliament on Marriage and Succession                                      *1566*

In 1566, when marriage to Archduke Charles was still a possibility, the queen was urged by members of Parliament in the strongest of terms and in the form of a bill, to marry and/or settle the succession. In his argument, the speaker — to whom Elizabeth's speech was a response — invoked the metaphor of the body politic to justify the impertinence with which he might be charged in urging a course of action upon the queen.

> The word or name of king doth signify a ruler or governor, an high officer . . . and may well be termed an head. . . . The office of the head consisteth in these two points: first, carefully to devise and put into execution all things most commodious for the whole body and every member thereof; then, wisely to foresee and prevent the evils that may come to any part thereof, and to that end God hath put the brain to devise, and every member giveth place thereunto, and patiently perform their duties. He hath also (for helps) placed therein the eye to look about and the ear to hearken to all things, either beneficial or discommodious. And lastly, to his great glory he

---

Queen Elizabeth I, a speech to Parliament on marriage and succession, 1566. Modernized from *Proceedings in the Parliaments of Elizabeth I,* Vol. 1, 1558–1581, edited by T. E. Hartley (Leicester: Leicester UP, 1981) 146–48.

hath created the tongue to utter the same, where the good may be received and the evil prevented. This king, this head, with the consent of the whole body and through the providence of God, weighing that his eye and ear cannot be in every corner of the kingdom . . . hath established this honorable counsel of every part absent from the king's eye and ear, the which is termed a parliament. (Hartley 129–30)

Elizabeth responded with indignation, understandably, since negotiations were in progress to accomplish the dreaded event, and smartly inverted the Parliamentary image of the body politic, reducing the Parliament from eyes, ears, and voice to the foot (and at the same time issued a sharp rebuke to Knox for his image of a woman-ruled realm as a monstrous, headless body): "A strange thing that the foot should direct the head in so weighty a cause . . . it is monstrous that the feet should direct the head" (see pp. 235–36).

If that order had been observed in the beginning of the matter, and such consideration had in the prosecuting of the same as the gravity of the cause had required, the success thereof might have been otherwise than now it is. But those unbridled persons whose heads were never snaffled by the rider did rashly enter into it in the common house, a public place, where Mr. Bell with his accomplices[1] alleged that they were natural Englishmen and were bound to their country, which they saw must needs perish and come to confusion unless some order were taken for the limitation of the succession[2] of the crown. And further to help the matter, must needs prefer their speeches to the upper house, to have you, my Lords, consent with them, whereby you were seduced and of simplicity did consent unto it, which you would not have done if you had foreseen before considerately[3] the importance of the matter. So that there was no malice in you, and so I do ascribe it. For we[4] think and know you have just cause to love us, considering our mercifulness showed to all our subjects since our reign. But there, two bishops with their long orations sought to persuade you also with solemn matter, as though you, my lords, had not known that when my breath did fail me I had been dead unto you, and that then dying without issue,[5] what a danger it were to the whole state, which you had not known before they told it you. And so it

---

[1] **Mr. Bell with his accomplices:** the leaders of the House of Commons committee that submitted a bill for the nomination of a successor to the crown. [2] **succession:** transfer of power from one ruler to the next. [3] **foreseen before considerately:** considered. [4] **we:** i.e., Queen Elizabeth. Royalty traditionally use first person plural pronouns to refer to themselves. [5] **issue:** offspring, children.

was easily to be seen *quo oratio tendit*.[6] For those that should be stops and stays[7] of this great good, and avoiding so many dangers and perils, how evil might they seem to be, and so to aggravate the cause against me. Was I not born in this realm? Were my parents born in any foreign country? Is there any cause I should alienate myself from being careful over[8] this country? Is not my kingdom here? Whom have I oppressed? Whom have I enriched to other's harm? What turmoil have I made in this commonwealth that I should be suspected to have no regard to the same? How have I governed since my reign? I will be tried[9] by envy itself. I need not to use many words, for my deeds do try me.

Well, the matter whereof they would have made their petition (as I am informed) consisteth in two points: in my marriage, and in the limitation of the succession of the crown,[10] wherein my marriage was first placed, as for manners' sake. I did send them answer by my council I would marry (although of my own disposition I was not inclined thereunto), but that was not accepted or credited[11] although spoken by their Prince. And yet I used so many words that I could say no more and were it not now I had spoken those words, I would never speak them again. I will never break the word of a prince spoken in public place, for my honor's sake. And therefore I say again, I will marry as soon as I can conveniently, if God take not him away with whom I mind to marry, or myself, or else some other great let[12] happen. I can say no more except [Archduke Charles] were present. And I hope to have children, otherwise I would never marry. . . .

The second point was the limitation of the succession of the crown, wherein was nothing said for my safety, but only for themselves. A strange thing that the foot should direct the head in so weighty a cause. . . . You would have a limitation[13] of succession. Truly, if reason did not subdue will in me, I would cause you to deal in it, so pleasant a thing it should be unto me. But I stay it for your benefit. For if you should have liberty to treat of it there be so many competitors — some kinsfolk, some servants, and some tenants; some would speak for their master, and some for their mistress, and every man for his friend — that it would be an occasion of greater charge than a subsidy.[14] And if my will did not yield to reason it should be the thing I would gladliest desire to see you deal in it.

---

[6] *quo oratio tendit*: where the speech is heading.   [7] **stops and stays**: supporters.   [8] **careful over**: concerned for.   [9] **tried**: judged.   [10] **limitation of the succession of the crown**: statutory specification of the succession; they wanted to announce officially who would inherit the throne.   [11] **credited**: believed.   [12] **let**: hindrance.   [13] **limitation**: statutory specification.   [14] **greater charge than a subsidy**: cost more than it's worth.

Well, there hath been error; I say not errors, for there were too many in the proceeding in this matter. But we will not judge that these attempts were done of any hatred to our person but even for lack of good foresight. I do not marvel, though *Domini Doctores*[15] with you, my lords, did so use[16] themselves therein, since after my brother's death they openly preached and set forth that my sister and I were bastards.[17] Well, I wish not the death of any man, but only this I desire: that they which have been the practicers therein may before their deaths repent the same, and show some open confession of their fault, whereby the scabbed sheep may be known from the whole.[18] As for mine own part I care not for[19] death, for all men are mortal; and though I be a woman yet I have as good a courage answerable to my place as ever my father had. I am your anointed Queen. I will never be by violence constrained to do any thing. I thank God I am indeed endued with such qualities that if I were turned out of the realm in my petticoat[20] I were able to live in any place of Christendom.

Your petition is to deal in the limitation of the succession. At this present it is not convenient, nor never shall be without some peril unto you, and certain danger unto me. But were it not for your peril, at this time I would give place,[21] notwithstanding my danger. Your perils are sundry ways, for some may be touched[22] who resteth now in such terms with us as is not meet to be disclosed either in the common house or in the upper house.[23] But as soon as there may be a convenient time and place that it may be done with least peril unto you, although never without great danger unto me, I will deal therein for your safety, and offer it unto you as your prince and head, without request. For it is monstrous that the feet should direct the head.

---

[15] *Domini Doctores:* master teachers.  [16] use: misuse, deceive, misconduct.  [17] my sister and I were bastards: In an attempt to ensure that the country remained Protestant after the death of Edward VI, his protector, the Duke of Northumberland, persuaded the sickly young king to declare Mary and Elizabeth illegitimate and to name Northumberland's Protestant daughter-in-law as his heir. Lady Jane Grey, fifteen years old, reigned for nine days, but the English people rallied behind Mary, and Northumberland's army deserted him.  [18] scabbed sheep may be known from the whole: the diseased sheep may be known from the healthy; i.e. guilty parties may be determined.  [19] care not for: do not fear.  [20] petticoat: allusion to the medieval folktale, retold by Chaucer and Boccaccio, of "patient Griselda" who was subjected by her husband to numerous trials of her devotion and was finally turned out of her home wearing nothing but a petticoat.  [21] give place: yield, reconsider.  [22] touched: affected.  [23] common house . . . upper house: the Houses of Parliament: the House of Commons and the House of Lords.

→ **WILLIAM CAMDEN**

## *From* The Annals of Queen Elizabeth          *1581*

William Camden (1551–1623), London historian and antiquary, who shared John Stow's interests in documentary evidence and in chorography (mapping local regions), first published his monumental geographical history of the British Isles, *Britannia,* translated as *Britain, or a chorographical description of the most flourishing kingdoms of England, Scotland, and Ireland, and the adjoining islands from the most profoundest antiquity,* in 1586. Written in Latin, it was immensely influential, with seven editions by 1607 and an English translation printed in 1610, 1637, and many editions thereafter. The first part of the history of Queen Elizabeth's reign, *The Annals or the History of the most renowned and victorious Princess Elizabeth, Late Queen of England, all the most important and remarkable pasages of state, both at home and abroad (so far as they were linked with English affairs) during her long and prosperous reign,* was printed in Latin in 1615, the second part in 1627; the first English translation was made in 1624 from the French, and English editions of the whole work were issued in 1635, 1675, and 1688. "Annals" was dropped from the title after 1675 and was therefore omitted in Macaffrey's edition from the printing of 1688; however, the work is usually referred to as "Camden's *Annals.*"

### FROM *The Four and Twentieth Year, 1581*

. . . The French King promised with all his heart to enter into a league of defense; but as for a league offensive, he flatly refused to hear any more thereof before the marriage [of Queen Elizabeth to the Duke of Anjou] were solemnized.

Not long after, the Duke of Anjou came himself into England . . . [and on the subject of the marriage] the courtiers' minds were diversely affected; some leaped for joy, some were seized with admiration,[1] and others were dejected with sorrow. Leicester,[2] who had lately plotted and contrived to cross the marriage, Hatton,[3] Vice-Chamberlain, and Walsingham,[4] stormed

---

[1] **admiration:** approbation, pleased surprise.  [2] **Leicester:** Robert Dudley, earl of Leicester, courtier and favorite of the queen, whom he entertained at Kenilworth in 1575.  [3] **Hatton:** Sir Christopher Hatton, the queen's spokesman in the House of Commons.  [4] **Walsingham:** Sir Francis Walsingham, a militant Protestant.

---

William Camden, *The Annals or the History of the most renowned and victorious Princess Elizabeth, Late Queen of England, all the most important and remarkable passages of state, both at home and abroad (so far as they were linked with English affairs) during her long and prosperous reign.* London, 1615 (vol. 1) and 1627 (vol. 2) (Latin edition), 1635, 1675, 1688 (English translations). Edited by Wallace T. Macaffrey as *The History of the Most Reknowned and Victorious Princess Elizabeth Late Queen of England* (Chicago: U of Chicago P, 1970), from "The Four and Twentieth Year, 1581," 134–37.

at it, as if the Queen, the realm and religion were now quite undone. The Queen's gentlewomen, with whom she used to be familiar,[5] lamented and bewailed, and did so terrify and vex her mind, that she spent the night in doubts and cares without sleep amongst those weeping and wailing females. The next day she sent for the Duke of Anjou, and they two, all bystanders being removed, had a long discourse together. He at length withdrew himself to his chamber, and throwing the ring [that the Queen had given him] from him, a while after took it again, taxing[6] the lightness[7] of women and the inconstancy of islanders,[8] with two or three biting and smart scoffs. . . .

In the midst of [her] perplexed cogitations concerning marriage, into which the consideration of the times did necessarily ever and anon cast her, some were of the opinion that she was fully resolved in her mind that she might better provide both for the commonwealth and her own glory[9] by an unmarried life than by marriage; as forseeing that if she married a subject, she should disparage herself by the inequality of the match, and give occasion to domestical heart-burnings, private grudges and commotions; if a stranger, then she should subject both herself and her people to a foreign yoke, and endanger religion: having not forgotten how unhappy the marriage of her sister Queen Mary[10] with King Philip, a foreigner, had been; also how unfortunate that marriage of her great-grandfather Edward the Fourth had proved, who was the first of all the kings of England since the Norman conquest that ever took one of his subjects to wife.[11] Her glory also, which whilst she continued unmarried she retained entire to herself and uneclipsed, she feared would by marriage be transferred to her husband. And besides, the perils by conception and child-bearing, objected[12] by the physicians and her gentlewomen for private reasons, did many times run in her mind, and very much deter her from thoughts of marrying.

[5] **familiar:** intimate, close.   [6] **taxing:** censuring.   [7] **lightness:** fickleness.   [8] **islanders:** i.e., people of the British Isles.   [9] **glory:** honor, distinction, reknown.   [10] **marriage of her sister Queen Mary:** Elizabeth's older half-sister married Philip of Spain, who did not reciprocate her affection.   [11] **marriage of Edward the Fourth:** Edward IV married a commoner, Elizabeth Woodville.   [12] **objected:** brought as an objection.

## A Poet and Her Patron

Toward the end of *A Midsummer Night's Dream*, Theseus seems to reinstate Athenian rationality over woodland magic, love, and poetry, but his speech is so ravishing that instead it actually empowers the "lunatic, the lover, and the poet . . . of imagination all compact" (5.1.7–8). In the play, the poetic imagination that Theseus celebrated was the imagination of the masculine subject, but in early modern England, some women, too, had a poetic imagination, as the work of Amelia Lanyer attests. If Christine de Pizan was the "first professional writer" to write on commission and to attend to the process of publication, Amelia Lanyer (1569–1645) was the first Englishwoman to publish a volume of poems and to solicit patronage as male poets did. (Moreover, Lanyer's romanticized tribute to Margaret Clifford in "The Description of Cooke-ham" conformed to the masculine tradition of poet as impassioned lover and patron as cherished beloved.) *Salve Deus Rex Judeorum (Hail, King of the Jews)* (1611), with which "The Description of Cooke-ham" was printed, was a collection of religious poems (the acceptable genre for women writers) that were explicitly feminist and praised good women from Eve to Jacobean patronesses. "The Description of Cooke-ham," like *A Midsummer Night's Dream,* commemorates the termination of female attachments — of the poet Amelia Lanyer with her patron, Margaret Clifford, and with Margaret's daughter Anne — by marriage.

Lanyer was the daughter, wife, and mother of court musicians, and her father, Baptist Bassano, was, like many court musicians, Italian and perhaps Jewish. Lanyer was a peripheral figure in the courts of Elizabeth and James; most of what is known about her life comes from the diaries of Simon Forman, astrologer and self-described lecher who dreamed about Queen Elizabeth (Chapter 2), and advised Lanyer about her future. The young Lanyer enjoyed privileges above her birth, serving in the household of the Countess of Kent and receiving some education. She became the mistress of Henry Cary, Lord Hunsdon, forty-five years her senior, the queen's Lord Chamberlain and the patron of Shakespeare's company of players, and married the musician Alfonso Lanyer in 1592 when she was pregnant with her son Henry, probably Hunsdon's child. After her marriage, her fortunes declined; she was nostalgic for her glamorous past and hoped in vain that her husband's success with Essex on the Azores expedition in 1597 would restore her position.

Sometime before the marriage of Anne Clifford in 1609, Lanyer visited Cooke-ham, crown property held by William Russell, who was the brother of Margaret Clifford (1560–1616), Anne's mother and countess of Cumberland. Lanyer's "Description of Cooke-ham" was published, and probably written, before Ben Jonson's "To Penshurst" (1616), supposedly the first of the genre of English country-house poems. In the tradition of the Virgilian "valediction to a place" (Lewalski 235) and the pastoral poem (Michael Drayton's *Poly-Olbion*) that celebrated the English landscape, the country-house poem praised the great estates like Penshurst, Kenilworth, and Elvetham; the splendid concord of natural beauty and human achievement to which they aspired; and the social order that they represented. Where these country-house poems usually extolled masculine spaces, however, Lanyer eulogized a community of women.

Laneham's Kenilworth was a resort filled to bursting with deer, hounds, statuary, fireworks, music, mythical personages, lords and ladies, lakes, servants, country folk, all organized in holiday celebration of the queen. Jonson's Penshurst, Sir Robert Sidney's estate, was an enduring little kingdom in which every creature bustled eagerly to serve Sidney, game waiting patiently to be captured and fish jumping helpfully out of the water. Justice reigned and class hostility was nonexistent, for the stone walls were "reared with no man's ruin, no man's groan" (line 46) and none that lived about them wished them down. Women kept their place, and Lady Sidney, "noble, fruitful, chaste" (line 90), exceeded her domestic duty with superlative and cheerful huswifery.

Lanyer's "Cooke-ham," in contrast, honors a quiet, intimate, and vanishing, female community of three. "Cooke-ham" is an elegy to "lost Eden," a "female paradise, an ageless, classless society in which Amelia, Margaret, and Anne lived together in happy intimacy" (Lewalski 237). In this sanctuary, Lanyer, who experiences a religious conversion, finds her poetic vocation, discovers a spiritual union with other women, and finds an identity beyond her social role of wife. But the idyll must end for the same reason that feminine intimacy must dissolve in *A Midsummer Night's Dream*: it is incompatible with the demands of a masculine social order.

"Unconstant Fortune" has created an insurmountable barrier between the women in the form of Amelia's social decline and Anne's marriage, and like Hippolyta, Titania, Hermia, and Helena, Anne must cease to gossip and redirect her attention to home and husband. *A Midsummer Night's Dream* ends with the successful union of four couples, who are promised happiness and fruitfulness; there is no hint that the end of female attachments is lamented as it is in Lanyer's poem. However, like the country house, the stage is finally empty: the women are silent, the fairy king a little too reassuring, the reconciliation a little too complete. One wonders whether the representation of women's loss of one another was "no more yielding than a dream" for Shakespeare's audience.

→ AMELIA LANYER

## *From* The Description of Cooke-ham                     *1611*

Farewell (sweet Cooke-ham) where I first obtained
Grace[1] from that Grace where perfect Grace remained;
And where the Muses gave their full consent,
I should have power the virtuous to content:
Where princely palace willed me to indite,[2]                    5
The sacred story[3] of the soul's delight.
Farewell (sweet place) where Virtue then did rest,
And all delights did harbor in her breast:
Never shall my sad eyes again behold
Those pleasures which my thoughts did then unfold:            10
Yet you (great Lady) Mistress of that place
From whose desires did spring this work of Grace,
Vouchsafe to think upon these pleasures past,
As fleeting worldly joys that could not last,
Or as dim shadows of celestial pleasures,                        15
Which are desired above all earthly treasures.
Oh, how (me thought) against[4] you thither came,
Each part did seem some new delight to frame!
The house received all ornaments to grace it,
And would endure no foulness[5] to deface it.                    20
The walks put on their summer liveries,[6]
And all things else did hold like similes:
The trees with leaves, the fruits with flowers clad,
Embraced each other, seeming to be glad,
Turning themselves to beauteous canopies,                        25
To shade the bright sun from your brighter eyes.
The crystal streams with silver spangles graced,
While by the glorious sun they were embraced:
The little birds in chirping notes did sing,
To entertain both you and that sweet spring.                     30

[1] **Grace:** favor; member of the nobility; virtue.   [2] **indite:** write.   [3] **sacred story:** Christ's passion; perhaps a reference to her poem *Salve Deus Rex Judaeorum*.   [4] **against:** in anticipation of.   [5] **foulness:** imperfection.   [6] **liveries:** distinctive clothing worn by servants.

Amelia Lanyer, "The Description of Cooke-ham" with *Salve Deus Rex Judaeorum* (London, 1611) STC 15227, H2r–I1r.

And Philomela[7] with her sundry lays,[8]
Both you and that delightful place did praise.
Oh how me thought, each plant, each flower, each tree
Set forth their beauties then to welcome thee!
The very hills right humbly did descend,                    35
When you to tread upon them did intend.
And as you set your feet, they still did rise,
Glad they could receive so rich a prize.

. . . . . . . . . . . . .

And that sweet Lady sprung from Clifford's race,[9]
Of noble Bedford's blood, fair stream of Grace,
To honorable Dorset[10] now espoused,                      95
In whose fair breast true virtue then was housed:
Oh, what delight did my weak spirits find
In those pure parts of her well-framed[11] mind;
And yet it grieves me that I cannot be
Near unto her, whose virtues did agree                     100
With those fair ornaments of outward beauty,
Which did enforce from all both love and duty.
Unconstant Fortune, thou art most to blame,
Who casts us down into so low a frame,[12]
Where our great friends we cannot daily see,              105
So great a difference is there in degree.[13]
Many are placed in those orbs of state,[14]
Parters in honor,[15] so ordained by fate;
Nearer in show,[16] yet farther off in love,
In which the lowest always are above.[17]                  110
But whither am I carried in conceit?[18]
My wit too weak to conster[19] of the great.
Why not? although we are but born of earth,
We may behold the heavens, despising death,
And loving heaven that is so far above,                    115
May in the end vouchsafe[20] us entire love.

---

[7] Philomela: the nightingale.  [8] lays: songs.  [9] Clifford . . . Bedford: Anne, the countess of Cumberland's daughter, was a Clifford (earls of Cumberland) on her father's side, and a Russell (earls of Bedford) on her mother's.  [10] Dorset: Anne married into the Sackville family (earls of Dorset).  [11] framed: fashioned, taught.  [12] frame: order, i.e., place in the social order.  [13] degree: social rank.  [14] orbs of state: court circles.  [15] parters in honor: those whom social differences have separated.  [16] show: demonstrations of affection.  [17] the lowest always are above: the subordinate always loves the most.  [18] conceit: fanciful imagination.  [19] conster: understand.  [20] vouchsafe: grant.

Therefore sweet Memory, do thou retain
Those pleasures past, which will not turn again:
Remember beauteous Dorset's former sports,
So far from being touched by ill reports,                              120
Wherein my self did always bear a part,
While reverend love presented my true heart.
Those recreations let me bear in mind,
Which her sweet youth and noble thoughts did find:
Whereof deprived, I evermore must grieve,                             125
Hating blind Fortune, careless to relieve.[21]
And you, sweet Cooke-ham, whom these ladies leave,
I now must tell the grief you did conceive[22]
At their departure: when they went away,
How every thing retained[23] a sad dismay.                            130
Nay, long before, when once an inkling came,
Me thought each thing did unto sorrow frame:
The trees that were so glorious in our view,
Forsook both flowers and fruit, when once they knew
Of your depart, their very leaves did wither,                         135
Changing their colors as they grew together.
But when they saw this had no power to stay you,
They often wept, though speechless could not pray[24] you,
Letting their tears in your fair bosoms fall,
As if they said, "Why will ye leave us all?"                          140
This being vain, they cast their leaves away,
Hoping that pity would have made you stay:
Their frozen tops, like Age's hoary[25] hairs,
Shows their disasters,[26] languishing in fears.
A swarthy, riveled rind[27] all over spread,                          145
Their dying bodies half alive, half dead.
But your occasions[28] called you so away,
That nothing there had power to make you stay.
Yet did I see a noble, grateful mind,
Requiting each according to their kind,                               150
Forgetting not to turn and take your leave
Of these sad creatures, powerless to receive
Your favor, when with grief you did depart,

---

[21] **careless to relieve:** indifferent.    [22] **conceive:** experience.    [23] **retained:** possessed.    [24] **pray:** beg.    [25] **hoary:** frosty, white.    [26] **disasters:** devastation.    [27] **riveled rind:** wrinkled crust or bark.    [28] **occasions:** duties.

Placing their former pleasures in your heart,
Giving great charge[29] to noble Memory,                                    155
There to preserve their love continually.
But specially the love of that fair tree,
That first and last you did vouchsafe[30] to see,
In which it pleased you oft to take the air,
With noble Dorset, then a virgin fair,                                      160
Where many a learned book was read and scanned.
To this fair tree, taking me by the hand,
You did repeat the pleasures which had past,
Seeming to grieve they could no longer last.
And with a chaste yet loving kiss took leave,                               165
Of which sweet kiss I did it soon bereave,[31]
Scorning a senseless creature should possess
So rare a favor, so great happiness.
. . . . . . . . . . . .

Yet this great wrong I never could repent,
But of the happiest made it most forlorn                                    175
To show that nothing's free from Fortune's scorn,
While all the rest with this most beauteous tree,
Made their sad consort[32] sorrow's harmony.
The flowers that on the banks and walks did grow,
Crept in the ground, the grass did weep for woe.                            180
The winds and waters seemed to chide[33] together,
Because you went away they know not whither;
And those sweet brooks that ran so fair and clear,
With grief and trouble, wrinkled did appear.
Those pretty birds that wonted[34] were to sing,                            185
Now neither sing, nor chirp, nor use their wing,
But with their tender feet on some bare spray,
Warble forth sorrow, and their own dismay.
Fair Philomela leaves her mournful ditty
Drowned in dead sleep, yet can procure no pity.                             190
Each arbor, bank, each seat, each stately tree,
Looks bare and desolate now for want of thee,
Turning green tresses into frosty gray,
While in cold grief they wither all away.

---

[29] charge: commands.   [30] vouchsafe: agree, consent.   [31] bereave: deprive; Lanyer kissed the tree to take back the kiss.   [32] consort: company of musicians; music.   [33] chide: complain.   [34] wonted: accustomed.

The sun grew weak, his beams no comfort gave,                    195
While all green things did make the earth their grave:
Each briar, each bramble, when you went away,
Caught fast your clothes, thinking to make you stay.
Delightful Echo, wonted to reply
To our last words, did now for sorrow die.                       200
The house cast off each garment that might grace it,
Putting on dust and cobwebs to deface it.
All desolation then there did appear,
When you were going, whom they held so dear.
This last farewell to Cooke-ham here I give,                     205
When I am dead thy name in this may live,
Wherein I have performed her noble hest,[35]
Whose virtues lodge in my unworthy breast,
And ever shall, so long as life remains,
Tying my heart to her by those rich chains.                      210

[35] **hest:** bidding, wish.

## Family Ties

Titania's refusal to surrender the Indian boy to Oberon might strike readers today, unaware of the threat to the Elizabethan social order that female disobedience posed, as highly commendable. Since Titania has vowed to care for her friend's orphaned boy, she quite responsibly refuses to deliver him to a man who is acting like a spoiled child himself, disrupting the supernatural and natural worlds, menacing human society, and blaming Titania for the damage (2.1.81–117). Likewise, Hermia's refusal to submit to an unwished yoke seems admirable to us, and the demands made by her father and the punishments approved by Theseus seem arrogant and cruel. And when Hermia and Helena lapse into distance and silence at the end of the play, it troubles us. Yet according to sixteenth-century rules of behavior for daughters and wives, presented in the following selections, women's disobedience was always a fault, and their silence always a virtue.

The social position of women in early modern England was not analyzed as were the ranks of men (see Chapter 2), since legally a woman's rank was determined by that of her father and husband. There were, however, general categories for women based on marital status (maiden, wife, widow) or sexual behavior (virgin, wife, whore). As Richard Hyrde observed in the dedication of his translation of Vives's *Instruction of a Christian Woman* (1529), though the precepts for men be innumerable, women yet may be informed of a few words. For men must be occupied both at home and abroad, both in their own matters and for the commonweal. . . . As for a woman hath no charge to see to but her honesty and chastity. (B2v)

*A Midsummer Night's Dream* celebrates the happy transition from maid to wife accomplished by Hippolyta, Hermia, and Helena and the rehabilitation of Titania from unruly to obedient wife. Under the auspices of Theseus and Oberon, the shifting amorous entanglements that animate the play are resolved into a universal unity of future households natural and supernatural, a tidy conclusion that supported the Protestant ideology of marriage.

The English commonwealth was composed of heads of households, not individual citizens. These households were structured like miniature monarchies, with the father at the top ruling his dependents: "A family is a little commonwealth," wrote William Gouge, "a school wherein the first principles and grounds of government and subjection are learned" (17). Women were subordinated first to father then to husband: the good woman was chaste, silent, and obedient, and the bad one was licentious, talkative, and willful. Children were subordinate to their parents all their lives and were expected to kneel for their parents' blessing ("To you, your father should be as a god" [1.1.47]) and stand silently in their presence even as adults. The power and property of the father was transferred to the eldest son according to the principle of primogeniture, and property was also transferred between men by means of arranged marriages; the obedience of the daughter and the chastity of the wife were crucial to the success of these exchanges.

Under the Roman Church, celibacy was venerated, marriage regarded with ambivalence ("it is better to marry than to burn," 1 Corinthians 7:9), and monastic life afforded an honorable alternative to marriage. But religious reformers, doubting monastic chastity and disdaining the contemplative life as idle (Crawford, *Religion* 46), opposed church institutions as corrupt and man-made, and celebrated marriage as a divine mandate (Maclean 84). Marriage was a consecrated antidote to sin, "instituted of God to the intent that man and woman should live lawfully in a perpetual friendly fellowship, to bring forth fruit, and to avoid fornication" (*Homily of the State of Matrimony* 239). The convent was not the only female space to wither with the Reformation: the legal brothels were closed in 1546 (Crawford, *Religion* 42–43), and trades like brewing formerly dominated by women were taken over by men (Fletcher 243). After the Reformation, although women continued to participate in the marketplace and assist their husbands outside the household, officially, woman's place — "whom nature hath made to keep home and children, and not to meddle with matters abroad" (Thomas Smith 29) was in the home.

Religious opposition to the customs of the Roman Church coincided with political necessity, for the rise of monarchical power depended on reducing the influence of the old aristocratic factions that had disputed the succession, and encouraging absolute loyalty to the crown. In the absence of a universal church and an unquestioned belief system, the family acquired additional moral and political force, and not without reason does Elyot liken the body politic to a hierarchy of household stuff (See Chapter 2). Family and state were explicitly linked in the sermons and official homilies read in church that were an important aspect of the national religious observance. In *A Homily of Obedience* (1547, 1623), the order of heaven, state, body, and society are represented as structurally identical and divinely appointed, and the observance of that order as a devotional act.

> Almighty God hath created and appointed all things in heaven, earth, and waters, in a most excellent and perfect order. In Heaven, he hath appointed distinct and several orders and states of Archangels and Angels. In earth he hath assigned and appointed kings, princes, with other governors under them, in all good and necessary order. . . . A man himself also hath all his parts both within and without, as soul, heart, mind, memory, understanding, reason, speech, with all and singular corporal members of his body, in a profitable, necessary, and pleasant order; every degree of people in their vocation, calling and office, hath appointed to them their duty and order: some are in high degree, some in low, some kings and princes, some inferiors and subjects, priests, and lay men, masters and servants, fathers and children, husbands and wives, rich and poor, and every one have need of other, so that in all things is to be lauded and praised the goodly order of God, without the which, no house, no city, no commonwealth can continue and endure or last. (69)

The divinely appointed hierarchy that supported the power of the crown was, in turn, confirmed by household hierarchies of "masters and servants, fathers and children, husbands and wives," with fathers at the top. Wifely subordination was bolstered by a litany of biblical citations: Man was superior to woman because he alone was created in the image of God (Genesis 1:26–27); as he was the glory of God, the obedient woman was the glory of man (1 Corinthians 11:7). Woman was "the weaker vessel" (1 Peter 3:7), "not endued with like strength and constancy of mind [as a man]; therefore, they be the sooner disquieted, and they be the more prone to all weak affections and dispositions of mind, more than men be, and lighter they be, and more vain in their fantasies and opinions" (*Matrimony* 140). Since Eve misled

Adam and caused their fall from Grace, as just punishment all women were cursed with pain, sorrow, and subordination (Genesis 3:16) and sentenced to "[l]earn in silence with all subjection . . . [not] to teach nor to usurp authority over a man, but to be in silence" (1 Timothy 2:11–12). Submitting to male rule was represented as both a social and a devotional act for a woman and the way to redemption: "Wives, submit yourselves unto your own husbands as unto the Lord" (Ephesians 5:22).

As humanist manuals on the education of the young man proliferated, so did the household and conduct books, many by conservative clerics, that detailed women's domestic duties. This flourishing genre affirmed marriage as the only virtuous path and dispensed practical advice — most stringent for daughters and wives — for the maintainance of family stability. The position of the wife within the family was genuinely contradictory, since she was simultaneously ruled (by her husband) and ruler (of children and servants), but that of the daughter was entirely unambiguous: she ranked below father, mother, eldest son, and all brothers, at the bottom of the family hierarchy, the polar opposite of her father.

Thomas Becon's *A New Catechism* (1560) was the first major domestic advice book of the Reformation (Crawford, *Religion* 39). Although Becon wrote more than thirty years before *A Midsummer Night's Dream*, his assertions concerning the appropriate conduct of daughters are remarkably congruent with those that the play seems first to parody, then affirm. Daughters should be "seen and not heard," a spectacle of reticence adorned, decked, trimmed, and garnished only with silence. They should submit to the authority of their fathers, and marry, only with their fathers' consent, a husband who enhanced family property and status. All daughters were expected to be chaste, silent, and obedient, but other valued qualities were determined by social rank. For the lady of high status, beauty, grace, wit, and musical skills were prized, but in the lower classes, women had to be hardworking. Therefore, as within the household a woman's position was contradictory, the disparate accomplishments demanded of women of different ranks placed additional contradictory demands on a woman who moved (with father or husband) up or down in the social hierarchy.

In Becon's *Catechism* the injunction against filial speech is absolute, and his ideal maiden is a decorative, quasi-courtly vision of femininity adorned in men's eyes by her silence. However, in *The Christian State of Matrimony, wherein husbands and wives may learn to keep house together with love* (1541), Henry Bullinger, apparently addressing a less affluent readership, qualifies the rule of female silence and emphasizes the importance of woman's work. Constructive conversation among friends, Bullinger argues, can provide a young woman with valuable practical knowledge, and the maiden accomplished in household skills will enrich her future husband like a merchant's ship. Deeply influenced by Calvinism and its ethic of hard work, responsibility, and frugality — the "work ethic" that supported the growth of trade and industry and expedited the rise of capitalism — Bullinger recommends the "companionate" marriage of husband and wife yoked together for the long haul, as diligent and uncomplaining as oxen ploughing a field.

But keeping house was not all there was to marriage for Bullinger; as his subtitle suggests, there was also "love." If family structure was changing, so was the conception of the nature and purpose of the family. Lawrence Stone has suggested (in a model that has been hotly debated) that a shift occurred in early modern England from the feudal, extended family for which marriage was a chilly arrangement that served to consolidate property and power to the "affective," nuclear family, organized by obedience, characterized by the sexual division of labor, and sustained by affection. Neither feudal nor modern family formation was monolithic or exclusive, however: there was no precise moment of transition between them, elements of both coexisted, and both "feudal" and "affective" formations also varied over time, place, and social rank.

Fragments from Bullinger resonate in *A Midsummer Night's Dream* — the image of the merchant's ship, the fables of fond and light love, the lovesick Titania yoking herself to the hapless Bottom ("Out of this wood do not desire to go" [3.1.125]) — but Bullinger's manual was not necessarily "the source." Most household books, while differing on details of the feminine ideal, have (like the antifestive pamphlets of Chapter 1) strong similarities to one another in their rhetoric, images, and biblical citations: Dod and Cleaver also envision the marital relationship in terms of husbandry, with the man and wife yoked together in matrimony (I2r), which serves as a "strong bridle" for "brutish lust" (I4r). While each household book may have been the "work of a single author," collectively they articulated a dominant discourse of family relations, one probed and examined on the stage. Echoes of household prescriptions in *A Midsummer Night's Dream* might have reminded Shakespeare's audiences of the contradictory demands of the family structures that were evolving in a time of competing value systems of work and leisure and paradoxical norms of feminine behavior. By enlisting "household discourse" to refuse to yield her virgin patent up to an "unwishèd yoke" (1.1.80–81), Hermia focuses attention on the contradictions inherent in an ideal of marriage that demanded wifely subordination as well as equal labor, filial obedience as well as marital love.

William Gouge's treatise on wives' "Particular Duties" in *Of Domestical Duties* (1626) was generated by the great Reformation marriage text, Ephesians 5:22–23: "Wives, submit yourselves unto your husbands, as unto the

Lord. For the husband is the head of the wife, even as Christ is the head of the Church." Among Protestant reformers, the nature of the sacraments was much disputed and marriage was no longer a sacrament, but all conceived of married life as a ritual of faith. The family formation that served to consolidate state power was itself reinforced by Protestant doctrine, both Anglican and Puritan, that defined female obedience as a form of worship.

Readers may find in *Domestical Duties* a first flowering of the familiar ideology of marriage as hard work, especially for the wife. As does Bullinger, Gouge emphasizes wifely labor, but for him, huswifery goes far beyond culinary skills: the most important household chore appears to be a kind of autobrainwashing by which a wife keeps her conduct and spirit immaculate. She must, Gouge asserts, cast aside the delusion of her own good judgment, actively shape her opinions to those of her husband, and bend to his will though it contradicts her own — in fact, the more his wishes run counter to hers, the greater is her virtue when she obeys him. One aspect of the sexual division of labor in the modern family becomes clearer and clearer: the wife bears the sole responsibility for the family's moral and emotional health, which she must ensure by relinquishing her autonomy. And, as Gouge (and Oberon) assert, if the wife is responsible for the welfare of the family, it follows that she bears the ultimate responsibility for the stability of the nation.

The ideal of feminine conduct prescribed by Bullinger and Gouge is realized in the actions of Katherine Stubbes, wife of Philip Stubbes (author of *The Anatomy of Abuses*), as described in his eulogy, *A Crystal Glass for Christian Women* (1591). Katherine obediently married the man of her parents' choice; asserted her opinions only in defense of the true faith; never blabbed to her gossips but kept at home; read the Bible but not fables of light love; spoke only of theology, and only with her husband. If Katherine was ravished, it was with the Holy Spirit, ennobling rather than dishonoring her husband. She exceeded her duty, shunned flighty entertainments, stayed home in her husband's absence, devoted herself to his every mood, and even encouraged him to spend money on his friends. She delivered a son, and having achieved her earthly purpose, bequeathed the child to her husband as she died to raise in all true religion.

Katherine embodies the paradigm of Protestant womanhood in every respect; her good example underscores the bad behavior of Hermia, Helena, Titania, and the Indian Votaress and distinguishes them from the pacified Hippolyta, who even before she marries behaves with a Katherinesque submission to Theseus. But while the women of *A Midsummer Night's Dream*, in all of their rebellion and imperfections, seem sympathetic and comprehensible to the modern reader for most of the play, Katherine remains distant and enigmatic, and *The Crystal Glass* is one of those texts that forces us to engage the enormous differences between the values of Shakespeare's time and those of our own.

→ **THOMAS BECON**

## *From* A New Catechism                                      *1564*

*Set Forth Dialogue Wise between the Father and the Son*

Thomas Becon (1512–1567) was a Protestant minister, a contemporary of Henry Machyn whom Machyn mentions in his diary. Associated with Canterbury Cathedral during the reign of Edward VI, Becon was imprisoned in the Tower for treasonous preaching at the beginning of Mary Tudor's reign; on his release, Becon lived in Strasbourg until the accession of Queen Elizabeth, when he was appointed to several London parishes. He gained a wide following for his preaching, and his *Works,* entered in the Stationer's Register May 14, 1560, were published in 1563–64. His arguments in favor of maidenly silence and filial obedience locate him in the early stages of the cultural transition from Catholicism to Protestantism, for while he supports his argument for obedience by referring to the Scriptures, which reformists privileged over church tradition, he affirms the virtue of feminine silence with the example of the Virgin Mary, who would soon be replaced by the Virgin Queen as an object of veneration in England.

### *From* OF THE DUTY OF MAIDS AND YOUNG UNMARRIED WOMEN

From *Silence in a maid is greatly commendable.*

[T]his also must honest maids provide, that they be not full of tongue[1] and of much babbling, nor use many words, but as few as they may, yea, and those wisely and discreetly, soberly and modestly spoken, ever remembering this common proverb: "a maid should be seen and not heard." Except that the gravity of some matter do require that she should speak, or else an

---

[1] **full of tongue:** talkative.

---

Thomas Becon, *A New Catechism set forth dialogue wise between the father and the son, lately made and now first of all published by Thomas Becon. The Works of T. Becon, which he hath hitherto made and published,* 3 vols. (London: J. Day, 1564) STC 1710. "Of the Duty of Maids and Young Unmarried Women": "Silence in a maid is greatly commendable," BBb2r, and "Children ought not to contract matrimony without consent of their parents," Bbb3v–4r.

answer is to be made to such things as are demanded of her, let her keep silence. For there is nothing that doth so much commend, advance, set forth, adorn, deck, trim, and garnish a maid as silence. And this noble virtue may the virgins learn of that most holy, pure, and glorious virgin Mary, which when she either heard or saw any worthy and notable thing, blabbed it not out straightaways[2] to her gossips, as the manner of women is at this present day, but being silent, she kept all those sayings secret and pondered them in her heart, saith blessed Luke.[3]

*From Children ought not to contract matrimony without consent of their parents*

[W]hen the time cometh when they feel themselves apt unto marriage, and are desirous to contract matrimony to them, that they may avoid all uncleanness[4] and bring forth fruit according to God's ordinance, as their parents have done before them, they must diligently take heed that they presume not to take in hand so grave, weighty, and earnest matter, nor entangle themselves with the love of any person before they have made their parents, tutors, friends, or such as have the governance of[5] them, privy of[6] their intent, yea, and also require their both counsel and consent in the matter, and by no means to establish or appoint[7] any thing in this behalf without the determination of their rulers. For this is part of the honor that the children owe to their parents and tutors by the commandment of God, even to be bestowed in marriage, as it pleaseth the godly, prudent, and honest parents or tutors to appoint, with this persuasion;[8] that they for their age, wisdom, and experience, and yea, for the tender love, singular benevolence, and hearty good will that they bear toward [the children], both know and will better provide for them than they will be able to provide for themselves. The histories of the Holy Bible teach evidently that the godly fathers in times past appointed the marriages of their children, and that the children attempted nothing in this behalf without the counsel, consent, determination,[9] and appointment of their parents. And that authority, which parents at that time had over their children, have fathers and mothers also at this present. And as the children then did not take upon them to marry without the consent of their parents, no more ought they to do so in this our age. The children which presume to marry without the counsel of their parents do greatly offend God, and are fallen away from the obedience which they owe their parents or tutors in this behalf, by the commandment of God. Let

[2] **straightaways:** immediately.  [3] **Luke:** Luke 2:19; "But Mary kept all these things, and pondered them in her heart."  [4] **uncleanness:** inchastity, sin.  [5] **governance of:** authority over.  [6] **privy of:** acquainted with.  [7] **appoint:** arrange, decide.  [8] **persuasion:** assurance.  [9] **determination:** decision.

all godly maids take heed therefore, that they snarl[10] not themselves with the love of any other, nor marry with any person before they have the good will of their parents.

[10] snarl: entangle.

→ HENRY BULLINGER

## From The Christian State of Matrimony 1541

### Wherein Husbands and Wives May Learn to Keep House Together with Love

*Translated by Miles Coverdale*

Henrich (Henry) Bullinger (1504–1575) was a Swiss Protestant cleric and activist, pastor of the major Protestant church in Zurich who inherited the leadership of the reform movement in Switzerland after the death of Ulrich Zwingli (1484–1531), Bullinger's father-in-law. Early in his career, he sided with Martin Luther (1483–1546) in condemning the abuses of the Roman Church, declaring the Scripture as ultimate authority and affirming the justification by faith. Later, however, he redirected the Swiss church towards the beliefs of John Calvin in a nationalist church, a "godly nation," and the "work ethic" that supported the development of a capitalist economy. In the hard-working godly nation, a girl trained for productive womanhood by avoiding idleness and "unhonest games and pastimes," and the paradigm of Protestant womanhood labored gladly with her hands to enrich her husband's household like a merchant ship and cheerfully pulled her share of the burden in the marital yoke. *The Christian State of Matrimony* was influential both on the continent and in England, and in the century following the publication of Miles Coverdale's translation in 1541, it was reprinted in eight English editions. Miles Coverdale (1488–1569) was an English reformer and translator of the Bible. A bishop during the reign of Edward VI, he fled to the continent during the reign of Queen Mary, but returned after Elizabeth I assumed the throne and became the rector of a London parish well known for his sermons. Coverdale's name is on the title page of this edition, and he is sometimes referred to as the author, as by David Cressy in *Birth, Marriage, and Death*.

Henry (Heinrich) Bullinger, *The Christian State of Matrimony, wherein husbands and wives may learn to keep house together with love,* translated by Miles Coverdale (London, 1541, 1575), Chapter 24, "How daughters and maidens must be kept," 91r–92v; and Chapter 2, "What Wedlock Is," 5–6.

### *From* How Daughters and Maidens Must Be Kept

Now to return to young daughters how they should be instructed in prayer and knowledge of their Christian religion . . . yet shall they not be too busy in teaching or reasoning openly, but there to use[1] silence and to learn at home, openly[2] to hear, and at home let them reason and teach each other. Neither would I have them ever shut up as it were in a cage, never to speak nor to come forth, but some times to see the good fashions[3] and honest behavior of others. . . . As for this thing every discreet parent shall know by the foresaid rules how to order them to avoid all wantonness and niceness[4] in words, gestures, and deeds, to eschew all unhonest[5] games and pastimes, to avoid all unhonest loves and occasions of the same, [such] as unhonest dancing, wanton communications, company with ribalds,[6] and filthy speakers. Teach them to avert their sight and senses from all such inconveniences,[7] let them avoid idleness, be occupied either doing some profitable thing for your family or else reading some goodly book. Let them not read books of fables of fond[8] and light love, but call upon God to have pure hearts and chaste, that they might cleave only to their spouse Christ, unto him married by faith, which is the most purest wedlock of us all, pure virgins being both married and unmarried. . . . *Books of Robin Hood, Bevis of Hampton,*[9] *Troilus* and such like[10] fables do but kindle in liars like lies and wanton love. . . . If ye delight to sing songs ye have the psalms and many godly songs and books in English, right fruitful and sweet. Take the New Testament in your hands, and study it diligently, and learn your profession[11] in baptism, to mortify[12] your flesh, and to be received in the spirit; learn the use of the Lord's Supper[13] to remember his death, and to give him perpetual thanks for thy redemption. Mothers must also teach their daughters to work, to love their husbands and children, and let them lay their hands to spin, sew, weave, etc., for the noblest women both among the heathen Romans and Greeks, and Hebrews, had great commendations for their huswifely[14] working with their hands, as ye may read of Solomon saying, He that findeth an honest faithful woman, she is more worth than precious pearls. The heart of her husband may surely trust to her. All the days of her life will she seek his profit. She occupieth wool and flax,[15] and laboreth gladly with her hands. She is like a merchant's ship,[16] etc. It is

---

[1] **use:** practice.   [2] **openly:** unreservedly.   [3] **fashions:** manners.   [4] **niceness:** foolishness.   [5] **unhonest:** immoral, improper.   [6] **ribalds:** immoral persons.   [7] **inconveniences:** unseemly behavior.   [8] **fond:** foolish.   [9] *Bevis of Hampton:* popular romance of the late fourteenth century.   [10] **like:** similar.   [11] **profession:** declaration, promise, vow.   [12] **mortify:** discipline, chastise.   [13] **the Lord's Supper:** the sacrament of Holy Communion.   [14] **huswifely:** housewifely.   [15] **occupieth wool and flax:** busies herself with spinning and weaving.   [16] **merchant's ship:** see the description of the good wife in Proverbs 31:10–31.

expedient that a man handfast[17] not his daughter before he hath good experience of her huswifery and governing of a house, for it becometh her better to have a pair of rough and hard hands than to be fair and soft and glittering with rings, or covered continually with smooth gloves. And let the parents beware that they bring them not up tenderly, wantonly, and delicately, or too nicely.[18] And at due time let them be provided for so that they may govern their own houses with their own husbands.

## From WHAT WEDLOCK IS

[F]irst will I show what wedlock is. Then when I have described the same, I shall open and declare the articles thereof particularly.

That we call wedlock is in the German tongue called Ge, which as it is a very old word, so is it sometime taken for a law or statute, sometime for a bond or covenant . . . because that term consisteth[19] not only the law that God gave to the old and new people,[20] but also the covenant which he made with them both. The Latinists call [wedlock] *Conjugium*, a joining or yoking together, like as when two oxen are coupled together under one yoke, they bear or draw together like burden and weight. . . . Now if wedlock be the coupling or yoking together of one thing, then must it be excepted from other knittings,[21] and we must give unto it the own nature and property pertaining to itself. Namely, that it is a right knot unto God acceptable, a yoking together of one man and one woman with the good consent of them both. Hereunto also must we add why and wherefore they should and must be yoked together: even to the intent that they may live honestly and friendly[22] the one with the other, that they may avoid uncleanness,[23] that they may bring up children in the fear of God, that the one may help and comfort the other.

Out of this may we comprehend[24] a short description of wedlock, and say: wedlock is a lawful knot and unto God an acceptable yoking together of one man and one woman with the good consent of them both, to the intent that they two may dwell together in friendship and honesty, one helping and comforting the other, eschewing uncleanness, and bringing up children in the fear of God. Or else set it after this manner following: Wedlock is the yoking together of one man and one woman, whom God hath coupled according to his word, with the consent of them both, from thence forth to

---

[17] handfast: betroth, engage to marry.   [18] tenderly, wantonly, and delicately, or too nicely: indulgently, immorally, pretentiously, and foolishly.   [19] consisteth: includes.   [20] old and new people: people of the Old and New Testaments.   [21] knittings: connections.   [22] honestly and friendly: chastely, as companions.   [23] uncleanness: sin.   [24] comprehend: understand, construct.

dwell together, and to spend their life in the equal partaking of all such things as God sendeth, to the intent that they may bring forth children in the fear of Him, that they may avoid whoredom,[25] and that according to God's good pleasure the one may help and comfort the other.

[25] **whoredom:** fornication, i.e., sexual relations outside of marriage.

→ WILLIAM GOUGE

## *From* Of Domestical Duties                                    *1626*

Abstemious in his life and devoted to his religious practice, William Gouge (1578–1653) was a Puritan's Puritan. Born into a family of merchants and preachers, he was educated at Eton and at Cambridge, where he later lectured on logic and philosophy. The revival of Greek and Hebrew studies facilitated biblical scholarship in the Reformation, and Gouge was among the first to learn Hebrew and teach it. A dutiful son, Gouge married according to his father's wishes and left Cambridge in 1604. As an Anglican minister, he preached at St. Anne's Church in London for thirty-five years and developed a large following. Like Becon and many other ministers with Puritan sympathies, Gouge was briefly imprisoned for sedition, or subversive teachings. Throughout his life, Gouge played an energetic part in ecclesiastical governance and fundraising, but unlike the activists Bullinger and Knox, took no role in politics, disapproving of the trial of Charles I in 1647 as a breach both of the divine covenant and of the state constitution. He published *Of Domestical Duties* in 1622 (reprinted in 1626 and 1634) and many volumes of sermons throughout his career, including over a thousand on Paul's "Letter to the Hebrews."

Gouge's tedious mode of argument, with its obsessive enumeration of propositions and relentless biblical citations, contrasts strongly with the comparatively anecdotal presentations of Becon and Bullinger. This stylistic trait may reflect a "defensive attempt to maintain an outdated order" (Fletcher 206); Gouge may have been addressing on the familial level increasing social instability or battling an increasing individual resistance (like that of Titania and Hermia) to patriarchal family formations. Whether the moral breakdown was societal or individual, it required a forceful response invoking masculine logic as well as divine authority.

William Gouge, *Of Domestical Duties: Eight Treatises* (London, 1626), STC 12120. "The Third Treatise: Of wives' particular duties": §3 "Of an husband's superiority over a wife, to be acknowledged by the wife," 158–59; §43 "Of a wife's active obedience," 183; §63 "Of the extent of a wife's obedience," 195; §64 "Of a wife's laboring to bring her judgment to the bent of her husband's," 195–96; §65 "Of wives' overweening conceit of their own wisdom," 196; §66 "Of a wife's yielding to her husband in such things as she thinketh not to be the meetest," 196.

## *From* THE THIRD TREATISE: OF WIVES' PARTICULAR DUTIES

Ephesians 5:22–24. "Wives, submit yourselves unto your husbands, as unto the Lord. For the husband is the head of the wife, even as Christ is the head of the Church, and he is the Savior of the body. Therefore, as the Church is subject to Christ, so let wives be subject to their husbands in every thing."

*Of an husband's superiority over a wife, to be acknowledged by a wife*

. . . I will lay down some evident and undeniable proofs, to show that an husband is his wife's superior. The proofs are the following:

1. God, of whom the powers that be ordained are, hath power to place His image in whom he will; and to whom God giveth superiority and authority, the same ought to be acknowledged to be due unto them. But God hath said of the man to the woman, "He shall rule over thee" (Genesis 3:16).

2. Nature hath placed an eminency in the male over the female, so where they are linked together in one yoke, it is given by nature that he should govern, she obey. . . .

3. The titles and names whereby an husband is set forth do imply a superiority and authority in him, as "Lord" (1 Peter 3:6), "Master," "Guide" (Proverbs 2:17), "Head" (1 Corinthians 11:3), "Image and glory of God" (1 Corinthians 11:7).

4. The persons whom the husband by virtue of his place, and the wife by virtue of her place, represent, most evidently prove as much, for the husband representeth Christ, the wife, the Church (Ephesians 5:23).

5. The circumstances noted by the Holy Ghost at the woman's creation imply no less, as that she was created "after man, for man's good and out of man's side" (Genesis 2:18).

6. The very attire which nature and custom of all times and places have taught woman to put on confirmeth the same, as long hair, veils, and other coverings over the head. This and the former argument doth the Apostle himself use to this very purpose (1 Corinthians 11:7).

The point then being so clear, wives ought in conscience to acknowledge as much, namely that an husband hath superiority and authority over a wife. The acknowledgment hereof is a main and principal duty, and a ground of all other duties. Till a wife be fully instructed therein, and truly persuaded thereof, no duty can be performed by her as it ought, for subjection hath relation to superiority and authority. The very notation of the word implieth as much. How then can subjection be yielded if husbands be not acknowledged superiors? It may be forced, as one king conquered in battle by another may be compelled to yield homage to the conqueror, but yet because he still thinketh with himself that he is no whit inferior, he will hardly be brought willingly to yield a subject's duty to him, but rather expect a time when he may free himself and take revenge of the conqueror.

### Of a wife's active obedience

It is a good proof and trial of a wife's obedience, to abstain from doing such things as otherwise she should do, if her husband's contrary will did not restrain her: but yet that is not sufficient, there must be an active, as well as a passive obedience yielded. That old Law before mentioned ("thy desire shall be subject to thy husband, and he shall rule over thee")[1] implieth so much also. If she refuse to do what he would have her to do, her desire is not subject to him but to herself, neither doth he rule over her. This active part of her obedience hath respect:

1. To his commandments, readily to do what he lawfully commands.
2. To his reproofs, carefully to redress what he justly blameth.

For the first, so far ought a wife to be from thinking scorn to be commanded by her husband that the very knowledge which by any means she hath of her husband's mind and will ought to have the force of a straight[2] commandment with her. . . .

### Of the extent of a wife's obedience

The extent of a wife's subjection (which remaineth now to be handled) is set down under these general terms (in everything) which are not so generally to be taken, as if they admitted no restraint or limitation, for then would they contradict such cautions as these, "in the fear of the Lord," "as to the Lord," "in the Lord." For man is so corrupt by nature, and of so perverse a disposition, that oft he willeth and commandeth that which is contrary to God's will and commandment, which when he doth, that Christian principle laid down as a ruled case[3] by [Scripture] must take place, "we ought rather to obey God than men."

Question: Why then is this extent laid down in such general terms?

Answer: 1. To teach wives that it is not sufficient for them to obey their husbands in some things, as they themselves think meet, but in all things,

---

[1] ("thy desire . . . thee"): Genesis 3:16.  [2] straight: direct; immediate.  [3] ruled case: legal precedent; scriptural authority should prevail over man-made laws.

whatsoever they be, wherein the husband, by virtue of his superiority and authority hath power to command his wife. Thus this general extent excludeth not God's will, but the wife's will. She may do nothing against God's will, but many things must she do against her own will, if her husband require her. 2. To show that the husband's authority and power is very large. It hath no restraint but God's contrary command, whereof if a wife be not assured, she must yield to her husband's will. . . .

*Of a wife's laboring to bring her judgment to the bent* [4] *of her husband's*

From that extent I gather these two conclusions:

1. A wife must labor to bring her judgment and will to that of her husband's.

2. Though in her judgment she cannot think that most meet[5] which her husband requireth, yet she must yield to it in practice.

In the former of these I say not simply that a wife is bound to bring her judgment to the bent of her husband's, for he may be deceived in his judgment and she may see his error, and then unless her understanding should be blinded, she cannot conceive that to be true which he judgeth so; but I speak of endeavor[6] when she hath not sure and undeniable grounds to the contrary to suspect her judgment when it is contrary to her husband's, and to think she may be in an error and thereupon not be too peremptory and resolute in contradicting her husband's opinion. This submission even of her judgment respecteth not only things necessary, for which the husband hath an express determinate warrant[7] out of the Scripture, but also things doubtful and indifferent,[8] for even so far doth this clause ("in every thing") extend, and the subjection of a wife respecteth not her practice only but her judgment and opinion also, which if she can bring to the lawfulness and meetness of that which her husband requireth, she will much more cheerfully perform it. To this purpose (as I take it) may be applied that exhortation of the Apostle unto women, that they "learn in silence with all subjection,"[9] which though it be principally meant of learning in the Church, yet it excludeth not her learning at home of her husband, for in the next word he addeth, "I suffer not a woman to usurp authority over the man, but to be in silence."

---

[4] **bent:** inclination.   [5] **meet:** suitable, proper.   [6] **endeavor:** effort.   [7] **warrant:** authorization, guarantee.   [8] **indifferent:** insignificant.   [9] **"learn . . . subjection":** 1 Timothy 2:11.

*Of wives' overweening* [10] *conceit of their own wisdom*

Contrary is the presumption of such wives as think themselves wiser than their husbands, and able better to judge matters than they can. I deny not but that a wife may have more understanding than her husband, for some men are very ignorant and blockish,[11] and on the other side, some women well instructed, who thereby have attained to a great measure of knowledge and discretion.[12] But many, though they have husbands of sufficient and good understanding, wise and discreet men, yet think that that which they have once conceived to be a truth must needs be so, and such is their peremptoriness that they will not be brought to think that they may err, but say they will never be brought to think otherwise than they do, though all the husbands in the world should be of another opinion, not much unlike to the wise man's fool, "who thinketh himself wiser than seven men that can render a reason."

*Of a wife's yielding to her husband in such things as she thinketh not to be the meetest*

The latter conclusion concerning a wife's yielding in practice to that which her husband requireth, though she cannot bring her judgment to think as he doth about the meetness of it, hath respect to indifferent things, namely, to such as are neither in their particulars commanded, nor forbidden by God, as the outward affairs of the house, ordering it, disposing goods, entertaining guests, etc.

Question: May she not reason with her husband about such matters as she thinketh unmeet, and labor to persuade her husband not to persist in the pressing[13] thereof, yea, endeavor to bring her husband to see the unmeetness (as she thinketh) of that which she seeth?

Answer: With modesty, humility, and reverence she may so do, and he ought to hearken unto her, as the husband of the Shunamite did (2 Kings 4:23–24), but yet, if notwithstanding all that she can say, he persist in his resolution and will have it done, she must yield.

First, her subjection is most manifested in such cases wherein she apparently[14] showeth that what she doth, she doth in respect of her husband's place and power; were it not for that she would not do it. Other things are not so evident proofs of her subjection to her husband, for if he command her to do that which God hath expressly commanded, and so she ought to do it whether her husband command it or no, it may be thought she doth it

---

[10] **overweening:** arrogant.   [11] **blockish:** stupid.   [12] **discretion:** judgment.   [13] **pressing:** urging, demanding.   [14] **apparently:** openly.

on God's command, and not on her husband's. If her husband command her to do that which God hath expressly forbidden, then ought she by no means to yield unto it; if she do, it may rather be termed a joint conspiracy of husband and wife together against God's will . . . than subjection to the image of God in her husband.

Secondly, her yielding in indifferent things tendeth much to the peace of the family, as subjects yield to their magistrates in such cases maketh much to the peace of the commonwealth. For in differences and dissensions one side must yield, or else great mischief is like to follow. Now of the two, who should yield but the inferior?

→ PHILIP STUBBES

## *From* A Crystal Glass[1] for Christian Women      *1591*

*Wherein They May See Most Wonderful and Rare Examples of a*
*Right Virtuous Life and Christian Death, as in the Discourse Following*
*May Appear*

If Stubbes's satirical diatribe *Anatomy of Abuses* (see Chapter 1) was a popular success, he enjoyed an even greater one with his biographical eulogy for his wife Katherine, *A Crystal Glass for Christian Women*, printed in 1591 with seven subsequent editions. Stubbes praises Katherine as an exemplary Puritan wife and believer, in the form of the medieval *speculum,* a textual "mirror" (or "glass") that, traditionally, reflected either actions to avoid or conduct to emulate. A model of womanly conduct while she lived — modest, courteous, gentle, affable, zealous, industrious, homebound, solitary, indulgent — Katherine was a perfect pattern of true Christianity in her death, seeking only to be delivered from "this body subject to sin," and bequeathing her son to his father to bring up "in good letters, in learning and discipline, and above all . . . in the exercise of true religion."

Calling to remembrance (most Christian reader) the final end[2] of man's creation, which is to glorify God, and to edify one another in the way of godliness, I thought it my duty, as well in respect of the one as in regard of the other, to publish this rare and wonderful example of the virtuous life and

---

[1] **crystal glass:** a fine mirror; example to follow.    [2] **final end:** ultimate purpose.

---

Phillip Stubbes, *A Crystal Glass for Christian Women. Wherein They May See Most Wonderful and Rare Examples of a Right Virtuous Life and Christian Death, as in the Discourse Following May Appear* (London, 1591) A2r–A3r.

Christian death of Mistress Katherine Stubbes, who whilst she lived was a mirror[3] of womanhood, and now being dead, is a perfect pattern of true Christianity. . . .

At fifteen years of age, her father being dead, her mother bestowed her in marriage to one Master Philip Stubbes with whom she lived four years and almost a half very honestly[4] and godly, with rare commendation of all that knew her, as well for her singular wisdom as also for her modesty, courtesy, gentleness, affability, and good government;[5] and above all, for the fervent zeal which she did bear to the truth, wherein she seemed to surpass many, in so much that if she chanced at any time to be in place where either Papists or Atheists were and heard them talk of religion, whatsoever countenance or credit[6] [what]ever they seemed to be of, she would not yield to them a jot,[7] or give place to them at all, but would most mightily justify the truth of God against their blasphemous untruths, and convince them, yea, and confound them by the testimonies of the word of God. Which thing, how could it be otherwise? For her whole heart was bent to seek the Lord, her whole delight was to be conversant in the Scriptures, and to meditate upon them day and night. Insomuch as you could seldom or never have come into her house and have found her without a Bible or some other good book in her hand. And when she was not reading, she would spend her time conferring, talking, and reasoning with her husband of the word of God, and of religion: asking him, what is the sense of this place, and what is the sense of that? . . . so as she seemed to be ravished with the same spirit David was, when he said, "the zeal of thy house hath eaten me up."[8]

She followed the commandment of our Savior Christ who biddeth us search the scriptures, for in them you hope to have eternal life. She obeyed the commandment of the Apostle who biddeth women to be silent, and to learn of their husbands at home.[9] She would never suffer any disorder or abuse in her house to be unreproved or unreformed. And so gentle was she, and courteous of nature, that she was never heard to give to any the lie[10] in all her life, not so much as "thou"[11] to any in anger. She was never known to fall out with any of her neighbors, nor with the least[12] child that lived, much less to scold or brawl,[13] as many will nowadays, for every trifle, or rather for no cause at all; and so [selthanly][14] was she given that she would very seldom or never, and not then neither, except her husband were in company, go abroad[15] with any, either to banquet or feast, to gossip or make merry, as

---

[3] **mirror:** paragon, example.   [4] **honestly:** respectably.   [5] **government:** behavior.   [6] **countenance or credit:** respect or authority.   [7] **a jot:** in the least.   [8] **"the zeal of thy house . . .":** Psalm 69:9.   [9] **biddeth women be silent . . . :** 1 Timothy 2:11–12.   [10] **to give to any the lie:** to call anyone a liar.   [11] **thou:** familiar form of "you," sometimes used in contempt as an insult.   [12] **least:** smallest.   [13] **brawl:** argue.   [14] **[selthanly]:** conscientiously.   [15] **abroad:** outdoors.

they term it, insomuch that she was noted by some (though most untruly) to do it in contempt and disdain of others. When her husband was abroad in London or elsewhere, there was not the dearest friend she had in the world that could get her abroad to dinner or supper, or to plays or interludes,[16] nor to any other pastimes or disports whatsoever. . . . [S]he was so far from dissuading her husband to be beneficial[17] to his friends, that she would rather persuade him to be more beneficial unto them. If she saw her husband was merry, then she was merry; if he were heavy[18] or passionate,[19] she would endeavor to make him glad; if he were angry, she would quickly please him, so wisely she demeaned[20] herself toward him. She would never contrary[21] him in anything, but by wise counsel and sage advice, with all humility and submission, seek to persuade him. And also, so little was she given to this world that some of her neighbors marvelling why she was no more careful of it,[22] would ask her sometimes, saying, "Mistress Stubbes, why are you no more careful for the things of this life, but sit always poring upon a book, and reading?" To whom she would answer, "If I should be a friend unto this world, I should be an enemy unto God, for God and the world are two contraries. . . . I have enough in this life, God make me thankful, and know I have but a short time to live here, and it standeth upon me to have a regard to my salvation in the life to come."

Thus this godly young gentlewoman held on her course three or four years after she was married, at which time it pleased God, that she conceived with a man-child; after which conception she would say to her husband, and many other her good neighbors and friends yet living, not once nor twice, but many times, that she should never bear more children, and that child should be her death, and that she should live but[23] to bring that child into the world, which thing no doubt was revealed unto her by the spirit of God, for according to her prophecy so it came to pass.

The time of her account[24] being come, she was delivered of a goodly man-child, with as much speed and as safely in all women's judgment as any could be. And after her delivery she grew so strong that she was able within four or five days to sit up in her bed, and to walk up and down her chamber, and within a fortnight after to go abroad, being thoroughly well and past all danger, as everyone thought.

But presently upon this sudden recovery, it pleased God to visit her again with an exceeding hot and burning quotidian ague,[25] in which she lan-

---

[16] **interludes:** short secular plays; comic scenes played between the scenes of a religious cycle, or later, musical intervals in a play. [17] **beneficial:** generous, liberal. [18] **heavy:** gloomy. [19] **passionate:** excitable. [20] **demeaned:** humbled; conducted. [21] **contrary:** contradict. [22] **no more careful of it:** unconcerned about it. [23] **but:** only. [24] **time of her account:** time of her delivery, end of her pregnancy. [25] **quotidian ague:** daily fever.

guished for the space of six weeks or thereabout, during all which time . . .
she never showed any sign of discontentment or impatience,[26] neither was
there ever heard one word to come forth of her mouth sounding either of
indiscretion[27] or infidelity,[28] of mistrust or distrust, or of any doubting or
wavering, but always remained faithful and resolute in her God. And so
desirous she was to be with the Lord, that these golden sentences were never
out of her mouth: "I desire to be dissolved and to be with Christ," and "Oh,
miserable wretch that I am, who shall deliver me from this body subject to
sin? Come quickly, Lord Jesus, come quickly." . . .

. . . And so calling for her child, which the nurse brought unto her, she
took it up in her arms and kissed it, and said, "God bless thee, my sweet
babe, and make thee an heir of the kingdom of heaven," and kissing it again,
delivered it to the nurse with these words to her husband standing by:
"Beloved husband, I bequeath this my child unto you. He is no longer mine,
he is the Lord's and yours, I forsake him, you, and all the world, yea, and
mine own self, and esteem all things but dung, that I may win Jesus Christ.
And I pray you, sweet husband, bring up this child in good letters, in learning and discipline, and above all, see that he be brought up and instructed in
the exercise of true religion."

[26] **impatience:** restlessness; failure to bear suffering patiently as a Christian should.    [27] **indiscretion:** imprudence, lack of judgment.    [28] **infidelity:** lack of faith in God.

# CHAPTER 4

# *Natural and Supernatural*

>‹

In contemplating *A Midsummer Night's Dream*'s representation of the supernatural, we should begin by noting two things. One is that modern understanding of the supernatural differs substantially from that of the Elizabethans. Two is that, because Elizabethan playgoers were drawn from different ranks of society and had different levels of education, sophistication, and religious training, beliefs about the supernatural differed even *within* the first audiences — as they differ in today's audience. Furthermore, since the play's supernatural action and effects revolve around the fairies, the question of how seriously to take the play's myth-making inevitably arises. As Keith Thomas has argued, "the more sophisticated Elizabethans tended to speak as if fairy-beliefs were a thing of the past." But, he goes on, "commentators have always attributed them to the past," which suggests the difficulty of thinking and writing historically about beliefs typically associated with children or other "simple" people (Thomas 725–26). Pondering how much of the play's magical action was *literally* incredible to an Elizabethan audience, or whether indeed everyone in the audience would have found the same events equally impossible, brings us to key questions about what different parts of Elizabethan society did and did not, could and could not believe about the nature of the world, about how and why things happen as they do. It brings us to the question of magical belief considered historically.

As with any term locked in a binary opposition, the "supernatural" is defined in relation to its opposite. Natural and supernatural are interdependent categories, so much so that each logically produces the other: the natural is what the supernatural is not, and vice versa. Both terms change over time in response to changes in the nature of agreed-upon reality — that which most people in a society accept as true and verifiable in nature or that which most people accept as true about the divine. Certainly beliefs about reality have changed in many essential details as the theological and geocentric cosmology dominant in early modern Europe was gradually replaced over the course of the seventeenth century by the secular-scientific world view most Westerners can agree upon today.

In *A Midsummer Night's Dream*, natural and supernatural are brought together through plot and characters deeply influenced by mythopoesis, the literary creation of myth. We might define myth for our purposes here as any fictitious narrative that involves supernatural characters or actions and also, says the *Oxford English Dictionary*, "embodies some popular idea concerning natural or historical phenomena." Myth thus explains (or like Shakespeare's play pretends to explain) occurrences and things, especially mysterious ones, of general if not universal importance. Myth tends to concern things like creation, the gods, the founding of a people or nation, the unusual manifestation of natural forces, or any event that resists easy explanation. Myth seeks to create in its audience a community of belief, especially supernatural belief. Sometimes, as in the case of *A Midsummer Night's Dream*, belief is offered as mock-belief and only temporary. As Robin says at the play's end:

If we shadows have offended,
Think but this, and all is mended,
That you have but slumbered here
While these visions did appear.
And this weak and idle theme,
No more yielding but a dream.  (5.1.399–404)

From this point of view, *A Midsummer Night's Dream* qualifies as myth proper only in part. Certainly it qualifies by way of its inclusion of supernatural characters and events. Along with *The Tempest*, it stands out from other Shakespeare comedies in relying upon magic to move the plot. Its magic includes Oberon's love juice (which transforms the eyesight of Lysander, Demetrius, and Titania), Puck's substitution of an ass's head for Bottom's own human one, and the ability of all the fairy folk to be invisible. But does *A Midsummer Night's Dream* also embody popular ideas about natural or historical phenomena? What does the action of *A Midsummer Night's*

*Dream,* if it is mythopoetic, seek to explain to its audience? And, in a comedy as joyously and eclectically make-believe as this one, what is the social status and function of such an explanation? Psychoanalytic critic Joel Fineman has argued that public theater functions something like a collective dream, representing anxieties and at the same time providing narrative defenses against those anxieties (Fineman 73). Perhaps this collective psychological function is especially true for a play, like this one, that emphasizes its resemblance to a dream. If so, then we should ask what anxieties are aroused and dispelled by the mythic action of *A Midsummer Night's Dream.*

The texts selected below, rather than addressing these questions directly, are intended to open up the mythic implications of *A Midsummer Night's Dream.* They focus on phenomena that, for Shakespeare's contemporaries, required but also resisted explanation. Some of these texts concern natural and historical events — unusual weather, local unrest, monstrous births, aberrant sexual desire. Some texts are themselves the product of poetic mythmaking (Ovid's *Metamorphoses*) and some texts involve contested beliefs — the possibility of miracles, the existence of fairies. They are alike, however, in representing invisible agency and unusual occurrences in terms that may reveal the dynamics of collective mentalities at a time of important transition in early modern England.

## Bad Weather and Dearth

As we suggested in the introduction, the 1590s were a difficult decade all across Europe. The single biggest disaster was a spate of spectacularly bad weather causing harvest failures. Wet springs and cold summers were part of the general worsening of the European climate in the sixteenth century known as the "Little Ice Age" (Clark, "Introduction" 8). Shakespeare alludes to the suffering this bad weather caused when Titania and Oberon meet onstage for the first time. As Titania rehearses the grounds of their quarrel, she speaks poignantly of widespread suffering: "The plowman lost his sweat, and the green corn / Hath rotted ere his youth attained a beard" (2.1.94–95).

Today, the causes of long-term global climate change baffle scientists, despite the obvious diagnostic advantages we enjoy of superior record-keeping and computer-modeling. Given the "intensely insecure environment" of early modern Europe (Thomas 5), it is not surprising that the succession of terrible winters and cold, wet summers should have perplexed and distressed people. Earth scientists today discuss the relative importance of factors such as deforestation, automobile and industrial exhausts, and bovine flatulence in determining the nature, pace, and effects of global warming.

They believe that, for the first time in the history of the world, human behavior has the capacity to produce massive and potentially disastrous climatic changes. The early moderns, too, believed that human behavior was able to affect the climate. In their theological world view, however, the causes were not industrial or developmental in nature, but rather moral and religious: human beings sinned and God punished them, collectively with bad weather or individually with personal misfortune. Certainly this doctrine of judgments, as we call it, did not eclipse all other forms of explanation available to early modern people. Any unusual occurrence, including a succession of harvest failures, produced specific natural explanations as well as references to divine causation. But it is true to say that a general acceptance of providential history — a belief that all events in the world, even local ones, fit a divine plan — would make the human suffering caused by weather in some sense *deserved* and *justified*. The debate could then arise as to who were the sinners and what were their sins, and such a debate would, almost by definition, be partisan, endless, and irresolvable.

In the agricultural economy of late sixteenth-century England, bad weather, however it was understood, had widespread social consequences. These consequences are taken up into the mythic action of *A Midsummer Night's Dream* and translated into private conflicts in the search for personal happiness on the part of aristocratic lovers, fairy king and queen, and amateur actors. Even as his magical plot alludes to the real experiences of food scarcity, plague epidemics, and social disorders occurring in Elizabethan society at large, Shakespeare plays openly with popular forms of supernatural explanation. Let us pretend, suggests the play, that bad weather is created by a fierce domestic quarrel among fairy rulers about the custody and rearing of a foster child. And let us also pretend for a moment that when the fairy couple settle their differences — as, in comedy, we can expect that they will — the terrors that trouble our nights and the real social problems that vex our days will magically disappear.

Understanding themselves as woodland deities, the fairy king and queen claim responsibility for the climate and accept blame for its unintended consequences. Titania speaks powerfully of bad weather, poor harvests, disease, loss of pastime and festivity: "And this same progeny of evils comes / From our debate, from our dissension" (2.1.115–16). Hearing these words, Shakespeare's audience would have been reminded that England had suffered four successive harvest failures in the mid-1590s. John Stow notes in his *Annals* for those years that great spring storms threw down trees and buildings. The cold, wet summers that followed not only swamped the grassy turf of the "nine-men's morris" dance (2.1.98), but more disastrously produced food shortages and general dearth, or scarcity. Dearth in turn caused price inflation. In 1594, the price of wheat was 30 percent above normal, in 1595, 36 percent above normal, in 1596, a record 83 percent above normal, and finally in 1597, 65 percent above normal. With the good harvest of 1598, prices fell back again to pre-1594 levels (Outhwaite 28). The great suffering of poor people — the laborers and poor householders whom historians describe as "harvest-sensitive" — led to local uprisings and food riots in several locations, London among them. Dearth exposed the disparity not only between rich and poor but also between those who prospered from high food prices and those who did not. Even in a time of general crisis, some could still feast while others hungered. As a 1595 leaflet distributed in the city of Norwich exclaimed, "for seven years space they [the rich] have fed on our flesh, on our wives and children . . . ; oh, who is the better for all the dearth? The rich" (quoted in Clark, "A Crisis" 44). At first the poor looked for relief from their suffering from local authorities: "I hope the Justices of peace will take order that we that are poor men shall have corn without such violence," said one laborer. Yet when in despair of redress, the poor contemplated direct action: "if they could not have remedy, they would seek remedy themselves, and cast down hedges and ditches, and knock down gentlemen" (quoted in Walter, "A Rising" 98). In London, recurrent disturbances began in 1590 and peaked in 1595 with two riots led by apprentices (Williams 62). Though the riots' leaders were executed, ballads and leaflets appeared that suggest massive discontent in the capital survived (Walter, "A Rising" 92).

Such civil unrest may seem predictable to us, given the obvious inequalities of Elizabethan society and the extreme stress brought on by repeated harvest failures. But Stow's *Annals* for those years evoke a general sense of crisis for the nation as a whole. Bad weather and poor harvests are not themselves the problem, he suggests, but merely symptomatic of it. He seems to discern the invisible hand of judgment when he intones, upon noting the rise in prices for staple foods, "such was our sins deserving it." The conclusion is conventional piety as well as Stow's dismayed reaction, as an aged and conservative Londoner, to the worst civil disturbances in memory. The crisis began on June 13, 1595, when apprentices in Southwark seized butter that was being sold at high prices and offered what they considered fair market value. In spurning violence and offering money, they behaved according to ordinary communal norms for protesting what they believed to be extortionate pricing. The government responded to this first disorder by flogging and pillorying the ringleaders; perhaps this response seemed excessively harsh. But the government imposed an even severer punishment on the large group of young men who, led by a veteran soldier, stormed up Tower Hill on June 29. In July, five of those men were executed, horribly, as traitors (Clark, "A Crisis" 53–54). Stow's final invocation of divine judgment for what may have seemed like a breakdown in social order is complicated: on one hand, he accepts the justice of the government's actions against the young rioters; on the other, he accepts a collective responsibility — "our sins" — for the actions of the few.

The government's response during dearth years was to authorize local justices to ensure the delivery of grain supplies from the countryside to local market towns, to keep markets open and prices reasonable, and to compel an informal sort of rationing. To prevent wholesalers from buying too much grain, the government required agents for large householders to bring "testimony" from their employers that they were buying grain for household use only. To prevent withholding grain from the market, producers were required to sell whatever grain they brought to market at prevailing prices, to display all the grain they had to sell, and to leave in the market town unsold grain for the next market day. Such measures were only partly successful because the government, fearful of riots in the capital, continued to allow the transportation of grain to London. The poor were finally relieved, says Peter Clark, when local officials "organized corn stocks which sold grain, flour, and bread at below market prices" ("A Crisis" 57–58).

This is a picture of crisis in which misfortunes brought about by nature aggravate and are aggravated by long-term social stresses of poverty and inequality. The question for literary interpretation is whether and to what degree invoking this model can help to explain characters' behaviors and events in *A Midsummer Night's Dream*. Evidence in the play is mixed and subtle. Unlike the London apprentices who protested food prices, the Athenian artisans who assemble at night in the woods in *A Midsummer Night's Dream* have no grievances. Titania has spoken eloquently of suffering among the people, but Peter Quince's troop has preoccupations other than hunger or disease (who will write the prologue of their play, whether or not the moon will shine on performance night, how to avoid frightening the ladies and how to "present Wall" and moonshine [3.1.52]). Although a war against a foreign enemy, the Amazons, has just been fought and won, the mechanicals seem not to have participated. Whatever memory the artisans might have had of the conflict seems eclipsed by the imminence of Theseus's wedding, a celebration in which they are determined to be included. And, while they are anxious to profit from their venture into court theatricals, to be "made men" (4.2.14), their ambitions are designed not to disturb the Athenian hierarchy. But some traces of Elizabethan social tensions may nevertheless still be found. In the hilarious discussions about their production of "Pyramus and Thisbe," the mechanicals express fears of being misunderstood by their audience when Bottom, playing Pyramus, is to draw a sword or when Snout, playing the lion, is to roar: "An you should do it too terribly, you would fright the Duchess and the ladies, that they would shriek; and that were enough to hang us all" (1.2.59–61). As Theodore Leinwand has concluded, "performance, especially strife- and sword-filled performance, is potentially life-threatening in the world of *A Midsummer Night's Dream*" (Leinwand, "'I believe,'" 14). The play's depiction of work ingmen meeting after dark in the woods outside town to rehearse their parts in a theatrical rather than a political venture could conceivably have been double-sided, both stirring and obscuring an audience's knowledge of local uprisings.

Social legislation enacted during the years of crisis held out the prospect of relief for the suffering poor, but the Elizabethan state lacked policing mechanisms and perhaps the political will to bring it about. Its aim was not social reform but maintenance of order. Similarly, perhaps, the play's action works to dispel the anxieties it notices. When Bottom's transformation leaves him alone in the woods, his experience there is one of pleasure and magical abundance (even if his food is mostly fruit and hay). When the ambitious mechanicals perform "Pyramus and Thisbe" before Theseus and his wedding guests, they are punished only with ridicule, and they are rewarded as well. In this sense, *A Midsummer Night's Dream* might be understood as a mythic transformation of actuality, a fantasy of escape from urgent social tensions and the uncertainties of nature.

→ JOHN STOW

# *From* The Annals of England

1601

John Stow (1525?–1605) began publishing his *Annals of England* in 1580, updating and reissuing the text at intervals until his death in 1605. Two subsequent editions by Edmund Howes appeared in 1615 and 1631. According to Howes, Stow "always protested never to have written anything either for malice, fear, or favour, nor to seek his own particular gain or vainglory, and that his only pains and care was to write truth" (quoted in *Dictionary of National Biography* 19: 5).

The format of annals, the historical record of a given year, is more like that of a diary than that of a historical narrative proper. Annals lack the shaping and foreshortening techniques characteristic of narration and are organized merely by the order of events rather than by theme. Here Stow follows the practice of beginning each year's annals on March 25, the start of the legal and administrative year.

John Stow, *The Annals of England* (London, 1601) 1274–81.

[1594]

In this month of March was many great storms of wind, which overturned trees, steeples, barns, houses, etc.; namely, in Worcestershire in Bewdley Forest, many oaks were overturned. In Norton Wood of the said shire, more than 1,500 oaks were overthrown in one day; namely, on the Thursday next before Palm Sunday. In Staffordshire, the steeple in Stafford town was rent[1] in pieces along through the midst and thrown upon the church, wherewith the said roof is broken. One thousand pound will not make it good. Houses and barns were overthrown in most places of those shires. In Canke Wood more than 3,000 trees were overthrown. Many steeples, more or less above 50, in Staffordshire were perished or blown down.

The 11. of April, a rain continued very sore more than 24 hours long and, withal, such a wind from the north as pierced the walls of houses, were they never so strong.

The 14. of April, a woman was burned in Smithfield[2] for murdering of her husband.

[On April 16 Ferdinando Stanley, the young earl of Derby,[3] dies after a brief, violent illness. Though rumors circulated that Stanley had been poisoned, Stow's narrative insinuates that Stanley had been the victim of witchcraft.]

In the month of May, namely on the second day, came down great water floods by reason of sudden showers of hail and rain that had fallen, which bore down houses, iron mills, the provision of coals prepared for the said mills. It bore away cattle, etc., in Sussex and Surrey to the great loss of many . . .

This year in the month of May fell many great showers of rain, but in the months of June and July, much more. For it commonly rained every day or night till St. James Day[4] and two days after together most extremely. All which notwithstanding, in the month of August there followed a fair harvest. But, in the month of September fell great rains which raised high waters such as stayed the carriages[5] and bore down bridges at Cambridge, Ware, and elsewhere, in many places. Also the price of grain grew to be such as a strike[6] or bushel of rye was sold for five shillings, a bushel of wheat for six, seven, or eight shillings, etc. For still it rose in price, which dearth hap-

---

[1] rent: torn.   [2] Smithfield: open area north of London, site of fairs, livestock markets, and executions.   [3] Ferdinando . . . earl of Derby: Ferdinando Stanley (1559–1594), fifth earl of Derby, sometime patron of the company of actors to which Shakespeare belonged.   [4] St. James Day: July 25.   [5] stayed the carriages: stopped traffic.   [6] strike: dry measure (now obsolete), usually identical to a bushel.

pens (after the common opinions) more by means of overmuch transporting by our own merchants for their private gain than through the unseasonableness of the weather passed.

## [1595]

The 20. of April, being Easter day, in the afternoon about five of the clock, it thundered and lightened sore, with some rain. Notwithstanding, the weather very cold and so continued the rest of that month, and also the month of May.

This year, by means of the late transporting of grain into foreign countries, the same was here grown to an excessive price, as in some places from fourteen shillings to four marks[7] the quarter[8] and more. As the poor did feel, for all things else, whatsoever was sustenance for man was likewise raised without all conscience and reason. For remedy whereof, our merchants brought back from Dansk[9] much rye and some wheat (not of the best) but passing dear,[10] yet served the turn in such extremity. Some prentices[11] and other young people about the city of London, being pinched of their victuals more than they had been accustomed, took from the market people in Southwark[12] butter for their money, paying for the same but 3 d.[13] the pound, whereas the owners would have had 5 d. For the which disorder, the said young men, on the 27. of June were punished by whipping, setting on the pillory, and long imprisonment.

The 29. of June, being Sunday in the afternoon, a number of unruly youths on the Tower Hill, being blamed by the warders[14] of Tower Street ward, threw at them stones and drove them back into Tower Street, being heartened[15] thereunto by sounding of a trumpet. But the trumpeter, having been a soldier, and many other of that company were taken by the sheriffs of London and sent to prison. About 7 of the clock the same night, Sir John Spencer, Lord Mayor, rode to the Tower Hill, attended by his officers and others, to see the hill cleared of all tumultuous persons. Where about the middle of the hill, some warders of the Tower and lieutenants' men being there told the mayor that the sword ought not in that place to be borne up. And therefore, two or three of them catching hold of the sword, some bickering there was and the sword-bearer with other hurt and wounded. But the

---

[7] **marks:** silver coins worth 13 shillings, 4 pence.   [8] **quarter:** eight bushels.   [9] **Dansk:** Denmark.   [10] **passing dear:** very expensive.   [11] **prentices:** apprentices.   [12] **Southwark:** borough on south bank of the Thames.   [13] **3 d.:** three pence; d. is the common abbreviation for Latin *denarius*, penny.   [14] **warders:** guardsmen.   [15] **heartened:** emboldened.

Lord Mayor, by his wise and discreet pacification, as also by proclamation of Her Majesty's name, in short time cleared the hill of all trouble and rode back, the sword-bearer bearing up the sword before him.

The Queen's Majesty, being informed of these and sundry other disorders committed in and about her city of London, by unlawful assemblies; and some, attempting to rescue out of the hands of public officers such as had been lawfully arrested, whereby the peace had been violated and broken. Her Majesty, for reformation thereof by proclamation dated the 4. of July, straightly[16] charged all her officers, both in the city and places near adjoining in the counties of Middlesex, Kent, Surrey, and Essex that had authority to preserve the peace and to punish offenders, more diligently, to the best of their powers, see to the suppression of all offenders against the peace, upon pain to be not only removed from their offices, but to be also punished as persons maintaining or comforting such offenders. And, because the late unlawful assemblies and routs were compounded of sundry sorts of base people, some prentices, and some others wandering, idle persons (of condition rogues and vagabonds), and some coloring their wandering by the name of soldiers, Her Majesty, for better direction to her officers of justice and inquisition to be made, notified her pleasure to her council to prescribe orders to be published and straightly observed. And for that purpose, a provost marshal with sufficient authority to apprehend all such as should not be readily reformed and corrected by the ordinary officers of justice and that, without delay, to execute upon the gallows by order of martial law. The orders prescribed were the same day also by proclamation published. Sir Thomas Wilford, knight, was appointed provost marshal for the time. He rode about and through the City of London daily with a number of men on horseback, armed, with their cases of pistols, etc. This marshal apprehended many vagrant and idle people, brought them before the justices who committed them to divers prisons. On the 22. of July were arraigned in the Guildhall[17] of London 5 of those unruly youths that were apprehended on the Tower Hill. They were condemned of high treason, had judgment to be drawn,[18] hanged, and quartered. And, on the 24. of the same month, they were drawn from Newgate to the Tower Hill and there executed accordingly.

In this time of dearth and scarcity of victuals, at London, an hen's egg was sold for a penny or three eggs for two pence at the most, a pound of sweet butter for 7 d. and so the like of fish or flesh, exceeding measure in price, such was our sins deserving it.

[16] **straightly:** directly, immediately.   [17] **Guildhall:** London's city hall.   [18] **drawn:** disembowelled.

## Metamorphosis and Monstrosity

The idea of metamorphosis is so common in European literature that it is tempting to see its fascination as universal. As Leonard Barkan has argued, "what, amid all the transformations of transformations, makes its bewitching power and meaning abide so intensely and so uniformly for two millenia?" His answer is that "in the image of magical transformation there is always the mystery of the divine embedded in the real" (Barkan 1, 18). But, just as the terms "natural" and "supernatural" change in meaning over time, so do the meanings accorded to the divine and the real. There might be, as Barkan claims, universal interest in physical transformation, but that does not mean that literary uses of metamorphosis are immune to social conflict or historical variation. Indeed, with the following documents from early modern England, we want to argue just the reverse.

Shakespeare's play and Ovid's great poem of changes, *Metamorphoses*, are both myths. But Ovid's stories embody his culture's myths of creation and the gods, while Shakespeare's play is frankly and explicitly invented from a combination of materials, including an eclectic mix of classical and local mythologies. For Ovid, who certainly does not demand his audience's literal belief, the morality of truth is less crucial than aesthetic delight. His stories are fictions that are serious in the sense that they focus upon great cosmic questions and often represent extreme physical and emotional pain. Their eroticism is often intense. Because of their sheer narrative power and beauty, the *Metamorphoses* were widely read in early modern England, by schoolboys in the original Latin and by other readers in translations like Arthur Golding's, which we use here. Educated members of Shakespeare's first audiences would have recognized the literary allusions embedded in Bottom's transformation. Like many characters in Ovid's *Metamorphoses*, Bottom loses the comfort and dignity of human form without knowing how or why. Perhaps like King Midas, punished by Apollo with ass's ears for failing to keep a secret, Bottom is being punished for his presumption in wanting to play all the parts in the mechanicals' "Pyramus and Thisbe." (The latter was itself a tale of illicit lovers that the audience would have found in *Metamorphoses*, Book 4.) Like the narrator-turned-ass in Apuleius's second-century Latin novel, *The Golden Ass*, Bottom becomes for a time the sexual object, we might even say the sexual obsession, of a woman socially his superior. And, like the young Englishman turned into an ass in Reginald Scot's *The Discovery of Witchcraft* (see p. 287), Bottom wants to eat hay rather than bread.

But many members of Shakespeare's audience — most of its women, many of its lower-class men — were virtually untouched by classical education. For them, Bottom's animal-head costume might have evoked memories of holiday celebrations like those described in Chapter 1, communal feasts where celebrants, some of them wearing animal masks or garbed as hobby-horses, entertained their fellow townsfolk. In the details of his transformation, Bottom takes on other meanings as well, becoming the protagonist of a popular sort of tale told at home by the fireside. He undergoes something like the legendary fate of travelers and other folk who, lost in the woods, are taken up mysteriously by the English fairies and sprites and treated with uncommon benevolence.

Bottom's is a hybrid metamorphosis. The astonished weaver is the center of a complex of traditions — learned and popular, classical and local, magical and theatrical. He is an ordinary mortal transported into a frightening and delightful mythological encounter. He is an amateur player cast in a starring part not of his own making. Without knowing it, he appears in public in an animal role unanticipated by the preparations for "Pyramus and Thisbe." Having been transformed by an English sprite who is chief henchman to a fairy king of Celtic extraction, Bottom is multiply, if comically, victimized. However besotted Titania may be by his voice and appearance, she commands her fairies to "tie up my lover's tongue" (3.1.172) and forbids him from even desiring to escape: "Out of this wood do not desire to go" (125). His transformation offers sensual pleasure but also passivity and complete subjection. The helpless beneficiary of magical abundance, Bottom has only the humblest of requests, for a good scratch and a "bottle of hay" (4.1.28).

There are, then, good historical reasons for drawing attention to the mixture of traditions involved in Bottom's transformation. These traditions seem to mingle and interact effortlessly in the play, seem to make up the play's heterogeneity of time, atmosphere, and population. Yet the differences among the traditions play off against the structure of social differences of Shakespeare's audience — differences in education, social privilege, literacy, and gender. In the play's central image of an ass-headed artisan embraced by the queen of fairies, specific social and theatrical meanings converge.

## OVID AND REGINALD SCOT

Sudden magical transformation is so central to *A Midsummer Night's Dream* that almost any part of Ovid's great poem might be invoked as a context. Ovid's story of Pyramus and Thisbe (*Metamorphoses* 4) is the play's only direct literary source, but Titania's dotage upon Bottom does echo the mythical Cretan Queen Pasiphaë's passion for her husband King Minos's beautiful bull (*Metamorphoses* 8 and 9). That passion's offspring — the half-man, half-bull known as the Minotaur — is the monster lurking at the center of the labyrinth whom Theseus must kill. Forced to choose among Ovid's many stories, we have selected his representation of the island of the witch-enchantress Circe in Book 14. Here, direct links to Shakespeare's play are minute but telling: Ovid calls Circe "Titania," or "the Titaness," three times. But, in this play, even an oblique allusion to the powerful Circe may send out danger signals about the seductiveness and aggressiveness of women. Theseus may have conquered Hippolyta, queen of the Amazons, and he may attract Titania's devotion (on the occasion of their onstage quarrel, Oberon exclaims to his wife: "How canst thou thus for shame, Titania, / Glance at my credit with Hippolyta, / Knowing I know thy love to Theseus?" [(2.1.74–76)], but the play insists upon the conquerability of unruly women even as it thereby acknowledges that there will always be more of them. While the audience recognizes that Robin Goodfellow has brought about Bottom's metamorphosis, Bottom himself does not. He has reason to imagine himself in thrall to a female sorceress, a Circe. As the image of Titania's physical dominance over Bottom suggests, male anxiety about female seductiveness persists. What is important to look for in Ovid's Circe, then, are resemblances within the play to Titania and outside it to Queen Elizabeth.

For many medieval and Renaissance readers, Ovid's stories of transformation became an opportunity for moral allegorization, that is, for seeing actions and characters as having hidden moral symbolism. This was especially true, perhaps, for the story of Circe, who seduced the sailors of Ulysses with a magical drink which transformed them into swine. To moral interpreters like the medieval philosopher Boethius, the sailors' physical transformation symbolized the inner corruption by temptation and sin: "the vicious, though they keep the outward shape of men, are in their inward state of mind changed into brute beasts" (*The Consolation of Philosophy* bk. 4, ch. 4). A reader with Elizabethan court culture rather than moral allegory in mind might see Circe less as a demonic agent of the soul's deterioration than as an unflattering mirror image of a jealous and powerful queen — whether Titania, queen of fairies, or Elizabeth I, queen of subject male courtiers. If Ovid's Circe is witch-like in her power to transform unsuspecting men who accept her offers of food and hospitality, she is queen-like in her desire to keep crowds of subject males in captivity. Ovid calls Circe's bower a "beautiful retreat." Golding's translation turns it into a version of a Renaissance royal presence chamber: "She sat underneath a traverse in a chair / Aloft right rich and stately, in a chamber large and fair" (14: 300–01).

It is important to remember, as we saw in Chapter 1, that godlike powers of transformation were routinely credited to European kings and queens as part of the protocols of flattery. The entertainments that greeted Elizabeth I while on summer progresses featured characters in classical or Arthurian costumes — a Savage Man, the woodland god Sylvanus, the Lady of the Lake — who asked her advice, required her taming, or sought her help and intercession. These characters, performed by professional actors hired for the occasion or occasionally by aspiring courtier-poets like George Gascoigne, were themselves stand-ins for the peers who commissioned their verses and desired the queen's good will (Smith 57–115). Such requests, although political in nature, tended to employ the eroticized address the queen often demanded of her courtiers and to portray the queen as herself a benevolent enchantress. But the queen's great power, anomalous in this patriarchal society, must have left powerful peers and councillors feeling somewhat degraded by subjection to a woman (Montrose, *Purpose* 167–69). They must have felt vulnerable to the kind of woeful transformation, even social death, visited upon courtiers in disgrace. The queen, like a jealous goddess, was capable of rage and revenge when the attentions of her male courtiers were directed elsewhere. Metamorphosis from royal favorite to political exile is precisely what Sir Walter Ralegh experienced in 1584 when he embarked on an indiscreet liaison and eventual marriage with Elizabeth Throckmorton, one of the queen's ladies-in-waiting. Elizabeth sent them both first into imprisonment in the Tower of London and then into exile in the country, transforming them socially.

Ovid's Circe transforms both women and men, though apparently out of jealousy and vengefulness in the first case and desire for power and adoration in the second. At the beginning of *Metamorphoses* 14, the fisherman Glaucus, naïve and hopeful, swims to Circe's island hoping that the goddess will help him in his love affair with Scylla. But Circe, like Elizabeth I, becomes enraged when her subject (in this case, Glaucus) spurns her advances and vows fidelity to another (in this case, Scylla). Unable to punish Glaucus directly, Circe wreaks vengeance on Scylla instead, turning her into a hideous monster, half-woman, half-dog, a rock of shipwreck and disaster. In the ugliness of its lower parts — "misshapen loins and womb remaining sound" (bk. 14, line 76) — the body of Scylla can be seen to represent a nightmarish version of the female reproductivity that Titania wishes to honor in the memory of her dead votaress. Titania remembers the pregnant body of her votaress as beautiful and weightless, moving along the seashore "with pretty and with swimming gait" (2.1.130), imitating the fluid movement of ships offshore, their sails impregnated by wind. In such imagery, reproductivity becomes for a moment incorporeal, the pregnant body as buoyant as a billowing sail and magically pain-free.

Compared to her punishment of Scylla, Circe's transformations of Ulysses' sailors seem comic, in part because their swinish bodies, though clumsy and inflexible, are less painful and frightening than Scylla's canine lower limbs. But their metamorphoses are also, unlike Scylla's, merely temporary. Ulysses has not only resisted Circe's seductions but entered into a form of joint government with her. In returning to their human shape, Ulysses' men are rescued from their subjection to a female enchantress and restored to their male leader.

If we transport Ovid's pagan story of mythological magic into the polarized realm of European religious conflict, we move from a world of aesthetically delightful, if frightening, fictions into a social landscape of witch-hunts and executions where lives did depend on questions of belief. Magic, which is treated comically in Shakespeare's play, became a topic of intense debate for Protestant reformers, who regarded the rituals of the Catholic church as spurious magic and belief in them as superstition. In 1547, an Englishman was forbidden to engage in such religious acts as "casting holy water upon his bed, . . . bearing about him holy bread, . . . ringing of holy bells; or blessing with the holy candle, to the intent thereby to be discharged of the burden of sin, or to drive away devils" (quoted in Thomas 60). Reginald Scot, an Elizabethan country squire unusually well read in Continental demonology, took up Protestant cudgels against Roman Catholicism in his powerful treatise, *The Discovery of Witchcraft* (1584). Scot's strategy, according to Keith Thomas, was to demonstrate "the magical elements in medieval Catholicism and their affiliation with other contemporary kinds of magical activity" (Thomas 61). For Scot, Christ had given the apostles the miraculous gift of exorcism, but it did not pass from them into the later church fathers. Hence he did not see any difference between Catholic priests and conjuring charlatans who preyed on the gullible in late sixteenth-century London.

What sets Scot apart from most of his European contemporaries, both ordinary people and theologians, is his disbelief in the literal existence of the Devil. He rejects the idea that Satan could take on corporeal existence; Satan is real only in the sense that credulous, weak-minded people use Satan symbolically to rationalize or personify their own temptations (Thomas 560–61). Witchcraft, rather than being an organized cult of malevolent women who have made a diabolical compact, is the self-delusion of weak, old women frightened by their own imaginations or what others have led them to believe possible. A logical extension of Scot's general skepticism about demonology and magical practice was to deny the possibility of metamorphosis. Metamorphosis compromises the omnipotence of God:

"whosoever believeth that any creature can be made or changed into better or worse, or transformed into any other shape . . . is an infidel and worse than a pagan" (see p. 291).

Scot's *Discovery of Witchcraft* works to refute metamorphosis by calling up the biblical, classical, and early Christian stories of metamorphosis and the doctrinal controversies surrounding the lore of demonism and witchcraft in Europe. For Scot, these stories, no matter how old or how remote in provenance, seem remarkably urgent, timely, and meaningful; they bear responsibility for the outbreak of witchcraft trials and executions that so horrified and dismayed him. He must attack and refute them with the most powerful of rhetorical arsenals, lawyer-like arguments, and withering sarcasm that he can muster. But, ironically, the stories tend to be more vivid and memorable than Scot's refutation of them, especially when they are given a dense social reality, as in his story of the witch in Cyprus and the young English sailor, which we reproduce below, and which is often cited as an analogue to Titania and Bottom. Scot's Circe figure is a poor egg-woman whose motive for transforming the young sailor seems to be her need for a beast of burden. Her capricious victimization of the young man does not prevent Scot from pointing out the bad faith of her inquisitors, who extract a confession from her under torture and execute her after promising not to. Scot demolishes the story by attacking its climax. The witch's transformation of the young sailor is revealed by the miracle of an ass kneeling down for the Elevation of the Host at Mass. But if that miracle suggests the miraculous power of the Mass, why, he asks mockingly, is the ass's return to human shape still dependent on the witch? Scot also criticizes the story, which he himself has preserved by retelling, by pointing out its improbability, suggesting ironically that English sailors do not speak Greek nor old Cypriot women English (we might also point out the story's flagrant anachronism in imagining the sailor as an Englishman long before such identification would have been possible).

But the big questions that Scot asks of his material are also crucial for the multiple transformations of *A Midsummer Night's Dream*: is the idea of transformation more than a literary fiction and, if it occurs at all, does it take place through change in the body or change in the mind? The young sailor, the story seems to suggest, endures his transformation until he hears the church bells. The unexpected memory of his human experience of divine worship causes him to react against his animal body and reenact the human posture of kneeling in adoration that his new life as a beast of burden had caused him to forget. Bottom is less aware than the sailor of his transformation, perhaps because it is only partial and much more temporary. What amuses us is how much he takes for granted the adoration of the fairy queen and the complete obedience of her servants, how unconcerned he is by his strange new appetite for hay. That so little in Bottom's *personality* has been changed by metamorphosis may imply Shakespeare's wry recognition of the impossibility of deep or lasting transformation.

→ OVID

## *From* Metamorphoses, *Book 14*                                    *c. 1–8 A.D.*
Translated by Arthur Golding

The Roman poet Publius Ovidius Naso (43 B.C.-17 A.D.) began writing his greatest work, the *Metamorphoses*, in c. 1 A.D. He was still revising it when, in 8 A.D., having deeply offended the emperor Augustus, he was sent into an exile from which he never returned.

An epic poem in hexameter of fifteen books, the *Metamorphoses* was studied intensively in the sixteenth-century English grammar school curriculum (Bate 21). English schoolboys read Ovid in Latin and could reread Ovid in English with Arthur Golding's translation of the poem in 1567. In the *Metamorphoses* students found a group of interlinked stories of transformation that encompassed all of classical mythology (including the story of Pyramus and Thisbe that provides a source for *A Midsummer Night's Dream*). More than a source, however, the *Metamorphoses* is "primary in the genesis of this play, [which is] Shakespeare's best attempt to respond to the inspiration of Ovidian materials" (Barkan 252).

Although the witch Circe first enters the *Metamorphoses* in Book 4, the fullest glimpse of her powers and her court comes in the passages from Book 14 excerpted here. Especially relevant to the reader of *A Midsummer Night's Dream* is the first-person account by Macareus, a companion of Ulysses, of how it feels to be transformed into a swine.

Now had th'Euboean fisherman[1] (who lately was become
A god of sea to dwell in sea for ay[2]) already swum
Past Etna which upon the face of giant Typho[3] lies,
Together with the pasture of the Cyclops[4] which defies

---

[1] **Euboean fisherman:** Glaucus of Anthedon in the ancient Greek province of Boeotia who, in an earlier book of the *Metamorphoses* eats a magic herb and becomes a god thereby.   [2] **ay:** always.   [3] **Typho:** monstrous giant who, having stolen the thunderbolts of Zeus, was buried under Sicily's volcano as punishment.   [4] **Cyclops:** one-eyed giants, sons of Neptune the god of the sea dwelling on the Sicilian coast; a Cyclops named Polyphemus (line 287) eats two of Ulysses' companions and loses his eye as punishment.

---

*Shakespeare's Ovid, Being Arthur Golding's Translation of the "Metamorphoses,"* edited by W. H. D. Rouse (London: Centaur, 1961), Book 14, lines 1–84, 281–356.

Both plough and harrow and by teams of oxen sets no store,5
And Zancle and racked Rhegium⁵ which stands o' tother shore.
And eke⁶ the rough and shipwreck sea which, being hemmed in
With two mainlands on either side, is as a bound between
The fruitful realms of Italy and Sicil. From that place
He, cutting through the Tyrrhene sea with both his arms, apace10
Arrivèd at the grassy hills and at the palace high
Of Circe,⁷ Phoebus' imp,⁸ which full of sundry beasts did lie.
When Glaucus in her presence came, and had her greeted, and
Receivèd friendly welcoming and greeting at her hand,
He said: "O goddess, pity me, a god, I thee desire.15
Thou only (if at least thou think me worthy so great hire⁹)
Canst ease this love of mine. No wight¹⁰ doth better know than I
The power of herbs who late ago transformèd was thereby.
And now to open unto thee of this my grief the ground:¹¹
Upon th'Italian shore against Messine walls I found20
Fair Scylla. Shame it is to tell how scornful she did take
The gentle words and promises and suit that I did make.
But if that any power at all consist in charms, then let
That sacred mouth of thine cast charms. Or if more force be set
In herbs to compass¹² things withal, then use the herbs that have25
Most strength in working. Neither think I hither come to crave
A med'cine for to heal myself and cure my wounded heart.
I force no end;¹³ I would have her be partner of my smart."
　　But Circe (for no natures are more lightly set on fire
　　Than such as she is, whether that the cause of this desire30
Were only in herself, or that dame Venus bearing ay
In mind her father's deed in once disclosing of her play¹⁴
Did stir her hereunto) said thus: "It were a better way
For thee to fancy such a one whose will and whole desire
Is bent to thine, and who is singèd with self-same kind of fire.35
Thou worthy art of suit to thee and (credit¹⁵ me) thou shouldst
Be wooed indeed if any hope of speeding¹⁶ give thou wouldst.

---

⁵ **Zancle and racked Rhegium:** the Sicilian city of Zancle, otherwise called Messina (line 20), faces the Calabrian city of Rhegion across the Sicilian Strait.　⁶ **eke:** also.　⁷ **Circe:** legendary enchantress of Greek mythology, dwelling on an island called Aeaea off the Italian coast. ⁸ **imp:** child, but also witch or demon.　⁹ **hire:** reward.　¹⁰ **wight:** creature.　¹¹ **ground:** occasion.　¹² **compass:** obtain.　¹³ **I force no end:** i.e., I seek not to end my love.　¹⁴ **disclosing of her play:** gossiping about her love affairs.　¹⁵ **credit:** believe.　¹⁶ **speeding:** succeeding.

And therefore doubt not, only of thy beauty liking have.[17]
Lo, I who am a goddess and the imp of Phoebus brave,
Who can so much by charms, who can so much by herbs, do vow          40
Myself to thee. If I disdain, disdain me also thou.
And if I yield, yield thou likewise, and in one only deed
Avenge thyself of twain." To her entreating, thus too speed:[18]
"First trees shall grow," quoth Glaucus, "in the sea, and reek[19] shall thrive
On tops of hills, ere I (as long as Scylla is alive)                   45
Do change my love." The goddess waxed right wroth,[20] and sith[21] she could
Not hurt his person (being fallen in love with him), ne[22] would,
She spited her that was preferred before her. And upon
Displeasure ta'en of this repulse, she went her way anon.
And wicked weeds of grisly juice[23] together she did bray,[24]          50
And in the braying, witching charms she over them did say.
And, putting on a russet cloak, she passèd through the rout
Of savage beasts that in her court came fawning round about,
And going unto Rhegium cliff which stands against the shore
Of Zancle, entered by and by the waters that do roar                   55
With violent tides, upon the which she stood as on firm land,
And ran and never wet her feet a whit. There was at hand
A little plash[25] that bowèd like a bow that standeth bent,
Where Scylla wonted was to rest herself and thither went
From rage of sea and air what time the sun amid the sky               60
Is hottest, making shadows short by mounting up on high.
This plash did Circe then infect against that[26] Scylla came,
And with her poisons which had power most monstrous shapes to frame,
Defiled it. She sprinkled there the juice of venomed weeds,
And thrice nine times with witching mouth she, softly mumbling, reads  65
A charm right dark of uncouth[27] words. No sooner Scylla came
Within this plash and to the waist had waded in the same,
But that she saw her hinder loins with barking bugs[28] attent.[29]
And at the first, not thinking with her body they were meant
As parts thereof,[30] she started back and rated[31] them. And sore     70
She was afraid the eager curs should bite her. But the more

---

[17] **only . . . have:** i.e., believe in the power of your own beauty.  [18] **speed:** speedily, rashly.
[19] **reek:** seaweed.  [20] **wroth:** angry.  [21] **sith:** since.  [22] **ne:** nor.  [23] **grisly juice:** thick liquid.
[24] **bray:** compound.  [25] **plash:** pool.  [26] **against that:** in preparation for when.  [27] **uncouth:**
strange, powerful.  [28] **bugs:** monsters (here dog-shaped).  [29] **attent:** stung.  [30] **with . . . parts
thereof:** that they had become parts of her body.  [31] **rated:** drove away.

She shunned them, the surer still she was to have them there.
In seeking where her loins and thighs and feet and ankles were,
Chaps,[32] like the chaps of Cerberus,[33] instead of them she found.
Nought else was there than cruel curs'[34] from belly down to ground.          75
So underneath, misshapen loins and womb remaining sound,
Her mannish masties'[35] backs were ay within the water drowned.
    Her lover Glaucus wept thereat and Circe's bed refused,
    That had so passing[36] cruelly her herbs on Scylla used.
But Scylla in that place abode; and, for hate she bore          80
To Circe-ward[37] (as soon as meet occasion served therefore),
She spoiled[38] Ulysses of his mates. And shortly after, she
Had also drowned the Trojan fleet but[39] that (as yet we see)
She was transformed to rock of stone which shipmen warily shun.

[Scylla, having become a rock, does not succeed in wrecking the ships of
Aeneas, whose sojourn in Dido's Carthage occupies this next portion of
Ovid's narrative. After leaving Dido and surviving a journey to the under-
world, Aeneas sails to Caieta where he encounters Macareus, one of Ulysses'
companions, who recounts his own transformation on Circe's island.]

. . . . . . . . . . . . . . . . . . . . . . . . . . . . . "And thou,
Aeneas, goddess Venus' son, the justest knight of all
The Trojan race (for since the war is done, I cannot call
Thee foe), I warn thee get thee far from Circe's dwelling place.
For when our ships arrivèd there, rememb'ring oft the case          285
Of cruel king Antiphates[40] and of that hellish wight
The round-eyed giant Polyphemus, we had so small delight
To visit uncouth places that we said we would not go.
Then cast we lots. The lot fell out upon myself as tho,[41]
And Polites, and Eurylochus, and on Elpenor[42] (who          290
Delighted too too much in wine), and eighteen other mo.[43]
All we did go to Circe's house. As soon as we came thither,
And in the portal of the hall had set our feet together,
A thousand lions, wolves, and bears did put us in a fear
By meeting us. But none of them was to be fearèd there.          295
For none of them could do us harm, but with a gentle look

---

[32] **Chaps:** jaws.   [33] **Cerberus:** three-headed watchdog of Hades, the hell of Greek myth.
[34] **curs':** (jaws) belonging to dogs.   [35] **mannish masties':** i.e., human flesh in the shape of mas-
tiffs.   [36] **passing:** very.   [37] **To Circe-ward:** toward Circe.   [38] **spoiled:** deprived.   [39] **but:**
except.   [40] **Antiphates:** king of the Laestrygonians, mythological Greek cannibals.   [41] **as tho:**
then.   [42] **Polites . . . Eurylochus . . . Elpenor:** names of Ulysses' companions.   [43] **mo:** more.

FIGURE 18 *Circe transforming Ulysses' sailors into animals. "Homines voluptatibus transformantur" from Geoffrey Whitney,* A Choice of Emblems.

And following us with fawning feet their wanton[44] tails they shook.
Anon did damsels welcome us and led us through the hall
(The which was made of marble — stone, floors, arches, roof, and wall)
To Circe. She sat underneath a traverse[45] in a chair                         300
Aloft right rich and stately, in a chamber large and fair.
She wore a goodly, long, trained gown and all her rest attire
Was every whit[46] of goldsmith's work. There sat me also by her
The sea-nymphs and her ladies whose fine fingers never knew
What tozing[47] wool did mean, nor thread from whorlèd[48] spindle drew.        305

---

[44] **wanton:** frisky.   [45] **traverse:** curtain, canopy.   [46] **whit:** piece.   [47] **tozing:** combing.
[48] **whorlèd:** twirled.

They sorted herbs and, picking out the flowers that were mixed,
Did put them into mounds and, with indifferent[49] space betwixt,
Did lay the leaves and stalks on heaps according to their hue.
And she herself the work of them did oversee and view.
The virtue[50] and the use of them right perfectly she knew,          310
And in what leaf it lay and which in mixture would agree.
And so, perusing every herb by good advisement, she
Did weigh them out. As soon as she us ent'ring in did see,
And greeting had both giv'n and ta'en, she lookèd cheerfully,
And granting all that we desired, commanded by and by          315
A certain potion to be made of barley parchèd dry,
And wine and honey mixed with cheese; and with the same she sly
Had meynt[51] the juice of certain herbs which, unespied, did lie[52]
By reason of the sweetness of the drink. We took the cup
Delivered by her wicked hand and quaffed it clearly up          320
With thirsty throats. Which done, and that the cursed witch had smit[53]
Our highest hair-tips with her wand (it is a shame but yet
I will declare the truth), I waxed[54] all rough with bristled hair,
And could not make complaint with words. Instead of speech I there
Did make a roughtish[55] grunting and, with groveling[56] face, gan[57] bear    325
My visage downward to the ground. I felt a hookèd groin[58]
To waxen hard upon my mouth, and brawnèd[59] neck to join
My head and shoulders. And the hands with which I late ago[60]
Had taken up the charmèd cup were turned to feet as tho.
Such force there is in sorcery. In fine, with other mo          330
That tasted of the selfsame sauce,[61] they shut me in a sty.
From this mishap Eurylochus only scaped. For why
He only would not taste the cup; which, had he not fled fro,[62]
He should have been a bristled beast as well as we. And so
Should none have borne Ulysses word of our mischance, nor he    335
Have come to Circe to revenge our harms and set us free.
The peace-procurer Mercury had given to him a white
Fair flower whose root is black and of the gods it moly[63] hight.[64]
Assured by this and heavenly hests,[65] he entered Circe's bower
And, being bidden for to drink the cup of baleful[66] power,          340

---

[49] **indifferent:** equal.  [50] **virtue:** power.  [51] **meynt:** mixed.  [52] **unespied, did lie:** went undetected.  [53] **smit:** struck.  [54] **waxed:** grew.  [55] **roughtish:** harsh.  [56] **groveling:** lowered.
[57] **gan:** began.  [58] **groin:** snout.  [59] **brawnèd:** thickened.  [60] **late ago:** recently.  [61] **sauce:** liquid.  [62] **fro:** from.  [63] **moly:** mythological plant given to Ulysses by Mercury as a charm against Circe; sometimes identified with the mandrake, sometimes with wild garlic.  [64] **hight:** was called.  [65] **hests:** directions.  [66] **baleful:** deadly.

As Circe was about to stroke her wand upon his hair,
He thrust her back and put her with his naked sword in fear.
Then fell they to agreement straight and faith in hand was plight.[67]
And, being made her bedfellow, he claimed as in right
Of dowry for to have his men again in perfect plight.[68]          345
She sprinkled us with better juice of uncouth herbs and strake[69]
The awk[70] end of her charmèd rod upon our heads, and spake
Words to the former contrary. The more she charmed, the more
Arose we upward from the ground on which we dared[71] before.
Our bristles fell away, the cleft our cloven clees[72] forsook.          350
Our shoulders did return again and next our elbows took
Our arms and hands their former place. Then weeping, we embrace
Our lord and hung about his neck who also wept apace.
And not a word we rather spake than such as might appear
From hearts most thankful to proceed. We tarried there a year.          355
  I in that while saw many things and many things did hear.

[67] **faith in hand was plight:** contracted marriage by clasping hands.   [68] **plight:** condition.
[69] **strake:** struck.   [70] **awk:** opposite.   [71] **dared:** crept fearfully.   [72] **clees:** hooves.


→   **REGINALD SCOT**

# *From* The Discovery of Witchcraft          *1584*

Reginald Scot (1538?–1599) is best known to students of sixteenth-century England as a vigorous defender of the Protestant Reformation and a source of witchcraft lore, thanks to the virulent anti-Catholic rhetoric in *The Discovery of Witchcraft* (1584). This historical legacy might have surprised Scot, given that he spent most of his adult life in his native county of Kent as a married landowner with a practical interest in the cultivation of hops. But *The Discovery*'s publication was widely noted by contemporaries, especially the clergy. Writer Gabriel Harvey praised the book: it "dismasketh sundry egregious impostures and in certain principal chapters, and special passages, hitteth the nail on the head with a witness" (quoted in *Dictionary* 17: 1002).

But James VI of Scotland did not want to be argued out of his belief in witchcraft, and his own *Daemonology* of 1597 sought to confute Scot. In 1603, having ascended the English throne as James I, he ordered copies of Scot's book

Reginald Scot, *The Discovery of Witchcraft* (London, 1584), Book 5, 94–101.

to be burned. Like the persecutions against witches themselves, persecutions of Scot's book continued until the last quarter of the seventeenth century. Details from *The Discovery* make their way into Shakespeare's treatment of the witches in *Macbeth* and in Thomas Middleton's play, *The Witch*.

## CHAPTER III

*Of a man turned into an ass, and returned again into a man by one of Bodin's witches; St. Augustine's opinion thereof.*

It happened in the city of Salamis[1] in the kingdom of Cyprus (wherein is a good haven) that a ship laden with merchandise stayed there for a short space. In the meantime, many of the soldiers and mariners went to shore to provide fresh victuals. Among which number, a certain Englishman, being a sturdy young fellow, went to a woman's house a little way out of the city and not far from the seaside to see whether she had any eggs to sell. Who, perceiving him to be a lusty young fellow, a stranger,[2] and far from his country (so as upon the loss of him there would be the less miss or inquiry), she considered with herself how to destroy him and willed him to stay there awhile, while she went to fetch a few eggs for him. But she tarried long, so as the young man called unto her, desiring her to make haste, for he told her that the tide would be spent[3] and, by that means, his ship would be gone and leave him behind. Howbeit, after some detracting of time,[4] she brought him a few eggs, willing him to return to her if his ship were gone when he came. The young fellow returned towards his ship, but, before he went aboard, he would needs eat an egg or twain[5] to satisfy his hunger and, within short space, he became dumb and out of his wits (as he afterwards said). When he would have entered into the ship, the mariners beat him back with a cudgel saying, "What a murrain[6] lacks the ass? Whither the devil with this ass?" The ass or young man (I cannot tell by which name I should term him), being many times repelled[7] and understanding their words that called him ass, considering that he could speak never a word and yet could understand everybody, he thought that he was bewitched by the woman at whose house he was. And, therefore, when by no means he could get into the boat but was driven to tarry and see her[8] departure, being also beaten from place to place as an ass, he remembered the witch's words and the words of his own

---

[1] **Salamis:** city of ancient Cyprus; its haven, or harbor, silted up c. 200 B.C. [2] **stranger:** foreigner. [3] **spent:** ebbed. [4] **detracting of time:** delay. [5] **twain:** two. [6] **murrain:** plague or pestilence, often used (as here) as a curse. [7] **repelled:** beaten back. [8] **her:** i.e., the boat's.

fellows that called him ass, and returned to the witch's house. In whose service he remained by the space of three years, doing nothing with his hands all that while but carried such burdens as she laid on his back; having only this comfort, that, although he were reputed an ass among strangers and beasts, yet that both this witch and all other witches knew him to be a man.

After three years were passed over, in a morning betimes,[9] he went to town before his dame,[10] who, upon some occasion (of like to make water), stayed a little behind. In the meantime, being near to a church, he heard a little sacring-bell[11] ring to the elevation of a morrow-mass.[12] And, not daring to go into the church lest he should have been beaten and driven out with cudgels, in great devotion he fell down in the churchyard upon the knees of his hinder legs and did lift his forefeet over his head as the priest doth hold the sacrament[13] at the elevation. Which prodigious sight, when certain merchants of Genoa espied and with wonder beheld, anon cometh the witch with a cudgel in her hand, beating forth the ass. And, because (as it hath been said) such kinds of witchcrafts are very usual in those parts, the merchants aforesaid made such means as both the ass and the witch were attached by the judge. And she, being examined and set upon the rack,[14] confessed the whole matter and promised that, if she might have liberty to go home, she would restore him to his old shape. And, being dismissed, she did accordingly. So as notwithstanding, they apprehended her again and burned her. And the young man returned into his country with a joyful and merry heart.

Upon the advantage of this story, M. Mal.,[15] Bodin,[16] and the residue of the witchmongers triumph and specially because St. Augustine[17] subscribeth[18] thereunto or, at the least, to the very like. Which, I must confess, I find too common in his books insomuch as I judge them rather to be foisted in[19] by some fond papist[20] or witchmonger than so learned a man's doings. The best is that he himself is no eyewitness to any of those his tales, but

---

[9] **morning betimes:** early morning.  [10] **dame:** mistress.  [11] **sacring-bell:** bell rung at mass to signal the elevation of the Host.  [12] **morrow-mass:** morning service.  [13] **sacrament:** the Host.  [14] **rack:** instrument of torture.  [15] **M. Mal.:** Scot's abbreviation for *Malleus Maleficarum* (The hammer of witches), a book of demonology, published in 1486, by Dominican monks Heinrich Kramer and Jacob Sprenger.  [16] **Bodin:** Jean Bodin (1530–1596), French jurist and author of another influential demonology, *On the Demon-Mania of Witches* (1580), written to help judges recognize what Bodin regarded as an organized witchcraft cult. Bodin, who had presided over witch trials, advocated brutal measures.  [17] **St. Augustine:** (354–430), Bishop of Hippo in north Africa. In *The City of God*, Book 18, chs. 17–18, Augustine argues that real metamorphosis is impossible but that, under the influence of evil spirits, a man's "phantom" may appear to others in the form of a beast.  [18] **subscribeth:** supports, concurs.  [19] **foisted in:** inserted surreptitiously.  [20] **fond papist:** credulous Catholic.

speaketh only by report, wherein he uttereth these words, to wit, that it were a point of great incivility,[21] etc., to discredit so many and so certain reports. And, in that respect, he justifieth the corporeal transfigurations of Ulysses' mates through the witchcraft of Circe[22] and that foolish fable of Praestantius's father,[23] who (he saith) did eat provender and hay among other horses, being himself turned into a horse. Yea, he verifieth the starkest lie that ever was invented of the two alewives that used to transform all their guests into horses and to sell them away at markets and fairs. And, therefore, I say with Cardanus[24] that, how much Augustine saith he hath seen with his eyes, so much I am content to believe. Howbeit St. Augustine concludeth against Bodin. For he affirmeth these transubstantiations[25] to be but fantastical and that they are not according to the verity[26] but according to the appearance.[27] And yet, I cannot allow of such appearances made by witches or yet by devils, for I find no such power given by God to any creature. And I would wit[28] of St. Augustine where they became[29] whom Bodin's transformed wolves[30] devoured. But

> _____ô quàm
> *Credula mens hominis, & erectoe fabulis aures!*[31]
> Good Lord! how light of credit is
>   the wavering mind of man!
> How unto tales and lies his ears
>   attentive all they can?

General councils[32] and the pope's Canons,[33] which Bodin so regardeth, do condemn and pronounce his opinions in this behalf to be absurd and the residue of the witchmongers, with himself in the number, to be worse than infidels. And these are the very words[34] of the Canons, which elsewhere I

---

[21] **incivility:** disrespect, here against ancient authorities. [22] **Ulysses'** . . . **Circe:** allusion to the sojourn of Ulysses and his men with the witch Circe in Book 10 of the *Odyssey;* Ulysses alone escaped transformation into a beast. For Bodin's reference to Ulysses, see *On the Demon-Mania of Witches,* trans. Randy A. Scott, ed. Randy A. Scott and Jonathan L. Pearl (Toronto: Centre for Reformation and Renaissance Studies, 1995) 143. [23] **foolish fable of Praestantius's father:** cited by Augustine. [24] **Cardanus:** Girolamo Cardano or Jerome Cardan (1501–1576), Milanese physician and philosopher. [25] **transubstantiations:** here, metamorphoses in general. [26] **according to the verity:** corresponding to truth. [27] **appearance:** apparition, illusion. [28] **wit:** learn. [29] **where they became:** what became of those. [30] **transformed wolves:** allusion to myths of classical Arcadia, cited by Augustine and Bodin, in which certain men became wolves and were allowed to reassume human form only if they refused to eat human flesh. [31] *ô quàm* . . . *aures!*: lines translated by Abraham Fleming. [32] **General councils:** synods called to establish church doctrine; many councils sought to penalize belief in witchcraft. [33] **Canons:** ecclesiastical laws or decrees, here canon laws known as the Canon or Capitulum Episcopi of c. 906, which held that belief in witchcraft was pagan, hence heretical. [34] **very words:** Scot translates the Latin text.

have more largely repeated: "whosoever believeth that any creature can be made or changed into better or worse, or transformed into any other shape or into any other similitude by any other than by God himself the creator of all things, without all doubt is an infidel and worse than a pagan. And therewithal this reason is rendered; to wit, because they attribute that to a creature which only belongeth to God, the creator of all things."

## CHAPTER IV

*A summary of the former fable, with a refutation thereof, after due examination of the same.*

Concerning the verity or probability of this interlude betwixt Bodin, *M. Mal.*, the witch, the ass, the mass, the merchants, the inquisitors, the tormentors, etc. First, I wonder at the miracle of transubstantiation.[35] Secondly, at the impudency of Bodin and James Sprenger for affirming so gross a lie, devised belike by the knight of the Rhodes,[36] to make a fool of Sprenger and an ass of Bodin. Thirdly, that the ass had no more wit than to kneel down and hold up his forefeet to a piece of starch or flour which neither would, nor could, nor did help him. Fourthly, that the mass could not reform that which the witch transformed. Fifthly, that the merchants, the inquisitors, and the tormentors could not either severally[37] or jointly do it, but refer the matter to the witch's courtesy and good pleasure.

But where was the young man's own shape all these three years wherein he was made an ass? It is a certain and a general rule that two substantial forms cannot be in one subject[38] *simul et semel,*[39] both at once; which is confessed by themselves. The form of the beast occupied some place in the air and so, I think, should the form of a man do also. For, to bring[40] the body of a man, without feeling, into such a thin, airy nature[41] as that it can neither be seen nor felt, it may well be unlikely but it is very impossible. For the air is inconstant[42] and continueth not in one place, so as[43] this airy creature would soon be carried into another region, as elsewhere I have largely proved. But indeed our bodies are visible, sensitive,[44] and passive,[45] and are

---

[35] **transubstantiation:** here, doctrine that the communion bread is literally transformed into Christ's body at the Mass.  [36] **knight of the Rhodes:** Grand Master of the Knights of Rhodes, also known as the Knights Hospitallers, a military and religious order headquartered on the islands of Rhodes and Cyprus. In the sixteenth century, they fought against the Turks.  [37] **severally:** separately.  [38] **subject:** material body, substance from which a thing is made.  [39] *simul et semel:* Latin, "at the same time."  [40] **bring:** transform.  [41] **nature:** state, condition.  [42] **inconstant:** changeable.  [43] **so as:** for this reason.  [44] **sensitive:** endowed with sensation.  [45] **passive:** capable of suffering.

indued with many other excellent properties which all the devils in hell are not able to alter. Neither can one hair[46] of our head perish, or fall away, or be transformed without the special providence of God Almighty.

But to proceed unto the probability of this story. What luck it was that this young fellow of England landing so lately in those parts and that old woman of Cyprus, being both of so base a condition,[47] should both understand one another's communication, England and Cyprus being so many hundred miles distant and their languages so far differing? I am sure in these days wherein traffic[48] is more used and learning in more price, few young or old mariners in this realm can either speak or understand the language spoken at Salamis in Cyprus, which is a kind of Greek. And, as few old women there can speak our language. But Bodin will say, you hear that, at the inquisitor's commandment and through the tormentor's correction,[49] she promised to restore him to his own shape. And so she did, as being thereunto compelled. I answer that, as the whole story is an impious fable, so this assertion is false and disagreeable[50] to their own doctrine, which maintaineth that the witch doth nothing but by the permission and leave of God. For if she could do or undo such a thing at her own pleasure, or at the commandment of the inquisitors, or for fear of the tormentors, or for love of the party,[51] or for remorse of conscience, then is it not either by the extraordinary leave nor yet by the like direction of God, except[52] you will make Him a confederate with old witches. I for my part wonder most how they can turn and toss a man's body so and make it smaller and greater, to wit, like a mouse or like an ass, etc., and the man all this while to feel no pain. And I am not alone in this maze, for Danaeus[53] a special maintainer[54] of their follies saith that, although Augustine and Apuleius[55] do write very credibly of these matters, yet will he never believe that witches can change men into other forms, as asses, apes, wolves, bears, mice, etc.

---

[46] **one hair:** allusion to Acts 28:34, where St. Paul tells frightened mariners, "there shall not an haire fall from the head of any of you."  [47] **base a condition:** low in rank.  [48] **traffic:** trade, travel.  [49] **tormentor's correction:** Bodin based his belief in witchcraft cults in part on similarities in witches' confessions under torture. See *On the Demon-Mania of Witches*, 42.  [50] **disagreeable:** contradictory.  [51] **love of the party:** love for the affected person (the English sailor).  [52] **except:** unless.  [53] **Danaeus:** Lambert Daneau (1530–1595), French Calvinist whose *A Dialogue of Witches* (1574) was the first Protestant demonology translated into English. Scot alludes to the third chapter here.  [54] **maintainer:** defender.  [55] **Apuleius:** Latin writer (c. 123–?), best known for his novel *The Golden Ass*, whose protagonist is punished for necromancy by being turned into an ass until rescued by the goddess Isis.

## Chapter V

*That the body of a man cannot be turned into the body of a
beast by a witch is proved by strong reasons, scriptures, and authorities.*

But was this man an ass all this while? Or was this ass a man? Bodin saith
(his reason only reserved)[56] he was truly transubstantiated into an ass, so as
there must be no part of a man but reason remaining in this ass. And yet
Hermes Trismegistus[57] thinketh he hath good authority and reason to say:
*Aliud corpus quàm humanum non capere animam humanam; nec fas esse in cor-
pus animae ratione carentis animam rationalem corruere.* That is, an human
soul cannot receive any other than an human body, nor yet can light into a
body that wanteth reason of mind. But St. James[58] saith, the body without
the spirit is dead. And surely, when the soul is departed from the body, the
life of man is dissolved. And, therefore, Paul wished to be dissolved[59] when
he would have been with Christ. The body of man is subject to divers kinds
of agues, sicknesses, and infirmities whereunto an ass's body is not inclined.
And man's body must be fed with bread, etc., and not with hay. Bodin's ass-
headed man must either eat hay or nothing, as appeareth in the story. Man's
body also is subject unto death and hath his days numbered. If this fellow
had died in the meantime (as his hour might have been come for anything
the devils, the witch, or Bodin knew), I marvel then what would have
become of this ass, or how the witch could have restored him to shape, or
whether he should have risen at the day of judgment in an ass's body or
shape. For Paul saith that that very body[60] which is sown and buried a natural body is raised a spiritual body. The life of Jesus is made manifest in our
mortal flesh and not in the flesh of an ass.

God hath endowed every man and every thing with his proper nature,
substance, form, qualities, and gifts, and directeth their ways. As for the
ways of an ass, he taketh no such care, howbeit[61] they also have their properties and substance several to themselves. For there is one flesh[62] (saith Paul)
of men, another flesh of beasts, another of fishes, another of birds. And,
therefore, it is absolutely against the ordinance of God (who hath made me

[56] **(his reason only reserved):** except for the transformed man's reason.   [57] **Hermes Trismegistus:** mythical Egyptian, thought to be a contemporary of Moses and author of the *Hermetica,*
philosophical and magical works actually written in Alexandria in the second century A.D. Scot
quotes from *Book on the Power and Wisdom of God, Whose Title is Pimander* (Book 4, par. 67), a
Latin translation of the *Hermetica* by the Florentine scholar Marsilio Ficino.   [58] **St. James:**
James 2:26.   [59] **Paul . . . dissolved:** Philippians 1:23, "For I am greatly in doubt on both sides,
desiring to be loosed and to be with Christ, which is best of all" (Geneva Bible).   [60] **very body:**
I Corinthians 15:44, "It is sown a natural body, and is raised a spiritual body. There is a natural
body and there is a spiritual body."   [61] **howbeit:** although.   [62] **one flesh:** I Corinthians 15:39.

a man) that I should fly like a bird, or swim like a fish, or creep like a worm, or become an ass in shape. Insomuch as if God would give me leave, I cannot do it, for it were contrary to his own order and decree and to the constitution of any body which he hath made. Yea, the spirits themselves[63] have their laws and limits prescribed, beyond the which they cannot pass one hair's breadth. Otherwise, God should be contrary to himself, which is far from him. Neither is God's omnipotency hereby qualified but the devil's impotency manifested, who hath none other power but that which God from the beginning hath appointed unto him, consonant to his nature and substance. He may well be restrained from his power and will, but beyond the same he cannot pass, as being God's minister, no further but in that in which he hath from the beginning enabled him to do. Which is, that he, being a spirit, may with God's leave and ordinance vitiate and corrupt the spirit and will of man, wherein he is very diligent.

What a beastly assertion is it that a man, whom God hath made according to his own similitude and likeness, should be by a witch turned into a beast? What an impiety is it to affirm that an ass's body is the temple of the Holy Ghost?[64] Or an ass to be the child of God and God to be his Father, as it is said of man? Which Paul to the Corinthians so divinely confuteth, who saith that our bodies are the members of Christ,[65] in the which we are to glorify God, for the body is for the Lord and the Lord is for the body.[66] Surely he meaneth not for an ass's body as, by this time, I hope appeareth. In such wise as Bodin may go hide him for shame, especially when he shall understand that even into these our bodies, which God hath framed after his own likeness, he hath also breathed that spirit which Bodin saith is now remaining within an ass's body, which God hath so subjected in such servility under the foot of man. Of whom God is so mindful[67] that he hath made him little lower than angels, yea than himself, and crowned him with glory and worship, and made him to have dominion over the works of his hands, as having put all things under his feet, all sheep and oxen, yea wolves, asses, and all other beasts of the field, the fowls of the air, the fishes of the sea, etc. Bodin's poet, Ovid, whose *Metamorphoses* make so much for him, saith to the overthrow of this fantastical imagination:

*Os homini sublime dedit, coelúmque videre*
*Jussit, & erectos ad sydera tollere vultus.*

The effect of which verses is this:

[63] spirits themselves: Psalm 119 (Scot's note; the reference is obscure).    [64] temple of the Holy Ghost: I Corinthians 6:19.    [65] our bodies . . . Christ: I Corinthians 6:15.    [66] body . . . body: I Corinthians 6:13.    [67] God is so mindful: Psalm 8:5–8.

The Lord did set man's face so high,
That he the heavens might behold,
And look up to the starry sky,
To see his wonders manifold.

Now, if a witch or a devil can so alter the shape of a man as contrarily to make him look down to hell like a beast, God's work should not only be defaced and disgraced, but his ordinance should be wonderfully[68] altered and thereby confounded.

[68] **wonderfully:** magically.

## Bestiality and Monstrosity

In *A Midsummer Night's Dream,* Bottom and Titania may have a sexual union offstage. This is one predictable result of the monstrous desire that Oberon through Puck has inflicted on his wife as punishment for her rebellion over the care of the Indian boy. "My mistress with a monster is in love," reports Puck triumphantly to his master (3.2.6). In an audience's imagining, this possible union of immortal queen and metamorphosed weaver could be scandalous for several reasons. The image, with its fairy gloss removed, is that of a ruling-class woman aggressively wooing a passive, bewildered lower-class man and finding him surpassingly beautiful. It is a love that manipulates not only customary hierarchies of gender and class but customary notions of bodily grace and beauty, the dignity of human form. Titania's ear is "much enamored" of Bottom's voice, her eye is "enthrallèd" to Bottom's shape (3.1.114–15). Such mistaking is what amorous dotage means.

But the really scandalous nature of their imaginary liaison, if scrutinized carefully by an Elizabethan playgoer, would lie elsewhere. To recognize the scandal is to understand what Shakespeare dares to evoke onstage here — the powerful sexual and religious taboos manipulated for the sake of comic delight. Insofar as Titania was played by a boy actor and Bottom was played by an adult male (probably the famous comedian Will Kempe), envisioning them together sexually is to imagine an act of same-sex, male-male intercourse. This is always the case, of course, for lovers played by an all-male acting company. Sodomy, though almost never prosecuted in early modern England, was nonetheless a capital crime. But even beyond flirting with an allusion to criminal sexuality, the play subverts the customary sexual dynamics of dominance and attraction. Instead of an older man loving a beautiful young man, the play gives us a "boy" Titania making love to the man Bottom. Insofar as the union would have to take place while Bottom is, technically speaking, only part human, their liaison could be also be seen as bestiality,

the act of sexual intercourse between human and animal. But Bottom, captured and dominated by the fairy queen, is not only Titania's beloved, he is
also symbolically her changeling child, a substitute in her bower for the
Indian boy whose care has provoked the fairy dispute in the first place. In
the popular religious imagination of early modern Europe, any forbidden
act of sexual intercourse would be — or should be — punished with a monstrous offspring. Thus doubly monstrous in his overlapping roles as lover
and baby, Bottom is the object of a forbidden love like that of Queen
Pasiphaë for the bull, and he is the monstrous offspring too. His complicated, even perhaps unique experience is, as Bottom himself understands,
the sensational stuff of the popular press, material ripe for a ballad writer.

Here we wish to suggest something of the possible range of attitudes
towards those sexual experiences which, like Bottom and Titania's, stretched
the imaginations and provoked the moral judgments of early modern
people. We want to suggest that taboos do not always work prescriptively or
effectively to circumscribe behaviors or determine attitudes. The documents
reproduced below — selections from Elizabethan court records and from
the French surgeon Ambroise Paré's *Of Monsters and Prodigies* — deal with
bestiality and monstrosity from two non-religious points of view, one legal
and juridical, the other scientific and medical.

### PROSECUTING BUGGERY

In the Bible, bestiality is treated with particular horror and severity: "the
man that lieth with a beast shall die the death and ye shall slay the beast.
And if a woman come to any beast and lie therewith, then thou shalt kill the
woman and the beast. They shall die the death, their blood shall be upon
them" (Leviticus 20:15–16). In early modern England, an act of sexual intercourse with an animal became a felony crime, punishable by death, in 1533
(Baker 430–31). Before that time, the offence was part of the jurisdiction of
the ecclesiastical courts, known colloquially as "bawdy courts." Court
records invariably describe this act as "buggery" — thereby conflating it
with other transgressive sexual acts, especially sodomy. The offender judged
guilty in bawdy court faced a number of possible penalties, the worst of
which was excommunication, the equivalent of social and spiritual death.
The guilty one was required to undergo the humiliation of a public penance,
confessing his fault openly at a church service and perhaps also in the marketplace, and appearing in public for a specified amount of time wearing a
penitent's white gown and carrying a white wand.

After the act was criminalized and its jurisdiction changed to the civil
courts, the accused appeared before officers of the crown at the local county

assizes (circuit courts sitting twice a year). Statistically, bestiality cannot be considered a major crime in England, compared to such crimes as theft, larceny, assault, or murder; surviving legal records show that indictments were rare and convictions even rarer. Nor did English courts carry out the biblical injunction that the animals involved should be destroyed (Sharpe 66). The court records included here reproduce legal findings for a few cases of bestiality in the mid-1590s. We can assume that more such offences were committed than reported. All the offenders are men; some of them are judged guilty, some not. The spare language of names, dates, acts, and judgments may look clear, even conclusive, but the data may conceal as much or more than it reveals. Perhaps the men brought before the authorities were accused by the animals' owners, who interpreted the act (or even fabricated it) as a crime against property rights; perhaps this is why the animals were not destroyed. Perhaps the authorities were sympathetic to the owners when they judged a man guilty; perhaps they found the perpetrator mentally unfit and let him go. The fate of some offenders, such as those merely reported to be dead or at large, is left unclear. The official records do not allow us to know the full social life in the community of the persons accused. Without knowledge about the local contexts of such cases or the motives and social positions of the people involved, the historian must be extremely careful in making inferences about actual sexual behavior in the period and attitudes towards sexual misconduct on the part of local people or the officials. By allowing us to see evidence of both tolerance and punitive disapproval, the records become almost as rich for interpretation as Shakespeare's text.

→ *From* Calendar of Assize Records                                    *1583–98*

### SUSSEX INDICTMENTS

*E*ast Grinstead Assizes,[1] before Robert Clarke, B[aron of the Exchequer],[2] and Sergeant[3] John Puckering.

Charlett, *William,* of West Dean, husbandman,[4] indicted for buggery. On 16 March 1589 at West Dean he buggered a horse belonging to Richard Lewkenor.
    Guilty; to hang.
*Craddock, William,* of Heathfield, laborer, indicted for buggery. At Lewes sessions, 22 April 1596, before Walter Covert, Thomas Pelham, *et al.,* J.P.s, a grand jury — [the names of twelve men are listed] — presented[5] that, on 1 March 1596 at Heathfield, Craddock buggered a white horse in the stable of George Cruttenden.
    At the same sessions Joseph Barnes of Heathfield, husbandman, entered a recognizance[6] to give evidence against Craddock.
    Dead.

### HERTFORDSHIRE INDICTMENTS

*St. Albans Assizes, 31 July 1590.*

Gerson, *William,* of Thorley, laborer, indicted for buggery. On 27 May 1590 at Thorley he buggered a horse.
    Guilty; to hang.

*Hertford Assizes, 4 March 1597.*

Rice, *Thomas,* of Bushey, yeoman,[7] indicted for buggery. On 11 June 1596 in a close[8] called "Shepperds" at Bushey he committed buggery with a steer, and

---

[1] *Assizes:* court sessions held periodically in each county presided over by specially commissioned justices.   [2] *B[aron of the Exchequer]:* presiding judge of the Court of Exchequer, name for one of the law courts.   [3] *Sergeant:* officer of the court, usually the arresting officer.   [4] **husbandman:** married householder.   [5] **presented:** offered evidence.   [6] **recognizance:** formal pledge.   [7] **yeoman:** landowner below rank of gentry, hence a respectable countryman.   [8] **close:** enclosed field.

---

*Calendar of Assize Records: Elizabeth I,* edited by J. S. Cockburn, 5 vols. (London: Her Majesty's Stationery Office, 1975–80). Sussex Indictments I: 230, 324; Hertfordshire Indictments II: 76, 130; Essex Indictments III: 240, 433; Surrey Indictments: V: 377, 379.

on 19 July 1596 in a close there called "Hartescrofte" he committed buggery with another steer.

Not guilty.

## Essex Indictments

*Witham Assizes, 29 July 1583, before Thomas Gawdy, Judge, and Sergeant Francis Gawdy.*

*Wodward, John,* of Great Leighs, laborer, indicted for buggery. On 17 June 1583 at Gubbion's Green in Great Leighs he committed buggery with a heifer.

Not guilty.

*Chelmsford Assizes, 3 March 1595, before Robert Clarke, Baron and Sergeant Edward Drewe.*

*Dawson, George,* of Dedham, glazier, indicted for buggery. At Chelmsford sessions, 9 January 1595, a grand jury presented that on 30 August 1594 he committed buggery with a bitch in the house of William Bryan at Dedham.

Guilty; to hang.

## Surrey Indictments

*Southwark Assizes, 17 February 1592, before Robert Clarke, Baron of the Exchequer, and Sergeant John Puckering.*

*Twyner, Thomas,* of Burstow, husbandman, indicted for buggery. On 25 July 1591 at Horne he committed buggery with a sheep belonging to Walter Tickner.

Guilty; to hang.

*Coote, Richard,* of Kingston upon Thames, yeoman, indicted for buggery. At Croydon sessions, 10 January 1592, before Sir Francis Carew [and nine other justices of the peace] a grand jury — [of twelve men, whose names appear here] — presented that on 15 March 1591 he entered the close of William Style at Kingston upon Thames and buggered a gray mare.

At large.

## Monsters and Prodigies

The formal study of monstrosity, known as teratology, has from ancient classical and early Christian times taken several characteristic forms. Some of it was scientific writing, represented first by Aristotle's massively influential *Generation of Animals*. In another form, represented both by Cicero and St. Augustine, monstrous births were portents or divine signs. Finally, there is what we would now call an anthropological discourse, focusing upon the monstrous human races thought to inhabit remote regions of Asia and Africa. During the sixteenth century, monsters were identified less as extraordinary phenomena like earthquakes than as ordinary symptoms of natural plenitude — "signs of nature's fertility rather than God's wrath" (Park and Daston 23). Eventually, the study of monsters was absorbed into anatomy and embryology, and monsters themselves became pathological — signs of conceptions gone wrong. Among the learned, interest in monsters almost disappeared by the end of the seventeenth century, but it continued to flourish in the ballads and broadsheets of popular culture. There monsters remained signs of divine disapproval.

*Of Monsters and Prodigies,* by the French royal surgeon Ambroise Paré, was written during a crucial transition in the history of teratology. The publication history of the text suggests where it belongs in this complex transition. It was first published in 1573 as the second part of a medical text on human reproduction; the volume outraged the Parisian medical faculty, in part because Paré wrote about matters such as genitalia in French rather than in Latin, the more exclusive language of science and learning. (The second edition of 1575 was revised slightly in response to their charges.) Within this scientific context, Paré alludes to divine wrath and the machinations of the devil and confuses the rare — ostriches, for example — with the monstrous. Of the eleven causes he introduces as possible explanations for monsters, however, only the first and last are truly supernatural. All the others seek to trace monstrosity to flaws in the act of conception or to deficiencies in the parents.

Of particular interest for readers of *A Midsummer Night's Dream* is belief in the force of maternal imagination and the power of images in determining outcome at birth. At the beginning of the play, Theseus seeks to enforce Hermia's obedience to her father by reminding her in Aristotelian terms of a father's role as the formative and shaping influence in generation. He is "One that compos'd your beauties, yea, and one / To whom you are but as a form in wax / By him imprinted" (1.1.48–50). Paré would agree, attributing to the mother's womb the power of nourishment only. But, after conception has taken place and the father's role in shaping the child has been completed, the mother could still mark the child in disastrous ways. The pregnant woman, impressionable and fearful, was prey to imaginings or bizarre cravings. Just as the father's seed had given the child its form, so the mother's mental *impressions*, transferred to the infant in the brief course of its uterine life, now malformed it. This destructive potential of the maternal imagination was one explanation for birth defects in early modern science, just as fairies were the explanation in popular culture. Oberon, when he alters Titania's imagination and causes her quasi-amorous, quasi-maternal dotage upon the monstrous baby Bottom, may be said to participate in both traditions — that of science and that of fairy lore. His magic lies in having Puck use the mind-altering power of a particular plant, love-in-idleness. What he makes happen in Titania's imagination is an excess of maternal love and devotion, the comic counterpart to early modern fears that mothers in the terror and vulnerability of their imaginations caused the malformation of their babies. It is this terror that, at the end of the play, Oberon seeks to dispel by pronouncing a fairy blessing upon the bridebeds:

> And the blots of Nature's hand
> Shall not in their issue stand;
> Never mole, harelip, nor scar,
> Nor mark prodigious, such as are
> Despisèd in nativity,
> Shall upon their children be. (5.1.385–90)

→ AMBROISE PARÉ

# *From* Of Monsters and Prodigies
*Translated by Thomas Johnson*

*1582*

Ambroise Paré's book was translated into English in 1634 by Thomas Johnson from the 1582 Latin version of Paré's works. Janis Palliser, Paré's modern translator, has described this Latin version as "extremely faulty" and Johnson's translation of it has been described as "very crude" (Palliser xxvii–xxviii). But since Johnson's version is what most English readers would have read, we have included it rather than a modern English translation here.

Ambroise Paré, *Of Monsters and Prodigies*, in *The Works of Ambroise Paré*, translated by Thomas Johnson (London, 1634) 961–82.

*The effigies of a monster halfe man and halfe swine.*

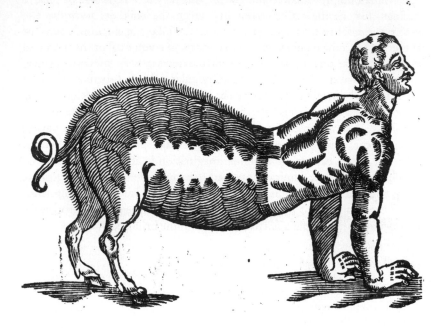

FIGURE 19 *Monster, half-man, half-pig. From Ambroise Paré,* Works; *Paré's "Of Monsters and Prodigies" contains pictures of many such hybrid creatures.*

## THE PREFACE

We call "monsters" what things soever are brought forth contrary to the common decree[1] and order of nature. So we term that infant monstrous which is born with one arm alone or with two heads. But we define "prodigies" those things which happen contrary to the whole course of nature, that is, altogether differing and dissenting from nature, as if a woman should be delivered of a snake or a dog. Of the first sort are thought all those in which any of those things which ought and are accustomed to be, according to nature, is wanting,[2] or doth abound; is changed, worn, covered or defended, hurt, or not put in his right place. For sometimes some are born with more fingers than they should, other some but with one finger, some with those

---

[1] **decree:** purpose.   [2] **wanting:** lacking.

parts divided which should be joined, others with those parts joined which should be divided. Some are born with the privities[3] of both sexes, male and female. And Aristotle saw a goat with a horn upon her knee. No living creature was ever born which wanted the heart, but some have been seen wanting the spleen, others with two spleens, and some wanting one of the reins.[4] And none have been known to have wanted the whole liver, although some have been found that had it not perfect and whole. And there have been those which wanted the gall,[5] when by nature they should have had it. And besides, it hath been seen that the liver, contrary to his[6] natural site, hath lain on the left side and the spleen on the right. Some women also have had their privities closed and not perforated, the membraneous obstacle, which they call the hymen, hindering.[7] And men are sometimes born with their fundaments,[8] ears, noses, and the rest of the passages shut and are accounted monstrous, nature erring from its intended scope.[9] But, to conclude, those monsters are thought to portend some ill which are much differing from their nature.

## CHAPTER I

*Of the causes of monsters; and first of those monsters which appear for the glory of God, and the punishment of men's wickedness.*

There are reckoned up many causes of monsters, the first whereof is the glory of God that His immense power may be manifested to those which are ignorant of it by the sending of those things which happen contrary to nature. For thus our Savior Christ answered the disciples[10] asking whether he or his parents had offended, who, being born blind, received his sight from him: That neither he nor his parents had committed any fault so great but this to have happened only that the glory and majesty of God should be divulged by that miracle and such great works.

Another cause[11] is that God may either punish men's wickedness or show signs of punishment at hand because parents sometimes lie and join themselves together without law or measure, or luxuriously and beastly.[12] Or at such times as they ought to forbear, by the command of God and the Church, such monstrous, horrid, and unnatural births do happen.

---

[3] **privities:** private parts, genitalia.   [4] **reins:** kidneys.   [5] **gall:** gall bladder.   [6] **his:** its.   [7] **hindering:** obstructing (the vaginal opening).   [8] **fundaments:** anuses.   [9] **scope:** purpose.   [10] **answered the disciples:** allusion to John 9:1–3.   [11] **Another cause:** allusion to scriptural prohibitions about times for intercourse, such as Leviticus 15:19–33.   [12] **luxuriously and beastly:** lecherously and in the manner of beasts.

At Verona, *Anno Domini* 1254, a mare foaled a colt with the perfect face of a man but all the rest of the body like a horse. A little after that, the war between the Florentines and Pisans[13] began by which all Italy was in a combustion.

About the time that Pope Julius the Second[14] raised up all Italy and the great part of Christendom against Lewis the Twelfth,[15] the king of France, in the year of our Lord 1512 (in which year, upon Easter Day, near Ravenna was fought that mortal battle in which the Pope's forces were overthrown), a monster was born in Ravenna having a horn upon the crown of his head and besides two wings and one foot alone, most like to the feet of birds of prey; and, in the knee thereof, an eye, the privities of male and female, the rest of the body like a man. . . .

The third cause is an abundance of seed[16] and overflowing matter.[17] The fourth, the same in too little quantity[18] and deficient. The fifth, the force and efficacy of imagination.[19] The sixth, the straitness of the womb.[20] The seventh, the disorderly sight of the party with child and the position of the parts of the body.[21] The eighth, a fall, strain, or stroke,[22] especially upon the belly of a woman with child. The ninth, hereditary diseases or effects by any other accident.[23] The tenth, the confusion and mingling together of the seed.[24] The eleventh, the craft and wickedness of the Devil. There are some others which are accounted for[25] monsters because they have their original, or essence, full of admiration[26] or do assume a certain prodigious form by the craft of some begging companions. Therefore we will speak briefly of them in their place in this our treatise of monsters.

---

[13] **war between the Florentines and Pisans:** Florence and Pisa were on opposite sides of the factional struggles between the papal Guelph party and their rivals, the Ghibellines.    [14] **Julius the Second:** Giulano della Rovere (1443–1513), Pope Julius II (1503–1513). In 1510, he founded the Holy League to fight against French occupation of Italian city-states.    [15] **Lewis the Twelfth:** Louis XII (1462–1515), King of France (1498–1515), occupied Milan and Genoa but failed to conquer Naples.    [16] **abundance of seed:** excess of semen, thought to cause hermaphroditism (two sets of sexual organs), extra limbs or organs, and multiple births.    [17] **overflowing matter:** bodily fluids.    [18] **too little quantity:** deficiency of semen, thought to cause missing limbs or organs.    [19] **imagination:** i.e., mother's imagination affecting the fetus.    [20] **straitness of the womb:** narrowness of the birth canal, causing difficult labor and malformed babies.    [21] **position of the parts of the body:** Paré writes elsewhere that women who cross their legs during pregnancy — as seamstresses and tapestry weavers do — risk bearing misshapen children.    [22] **stroke:** blow.    [23] **accident:** non-congenital illness.    [24] **confusion and mingling together of the seed:** copulation between members of different species.    [25] **accounted for:** taken as. Paré, in another chapter, details the tricks of beggars who pretend to have missing or extra limbs.    [26] **have their original, or essence, full of admiration:** because of where they come from or because of specific features, seem to be marvels.

## CHAPTER VII

*Of monsters which take their cause and shape by imagination.*

The ancients, having diligently sought into all the secrets of nature, have marked and observed other causes of the generation of monsters. For, understanding the force of imagination to be so powerful in us as, for the most part, it may alter the body of them that imagine, they soon persuaded themselves that the faculty which formeth the infant may be led and governed by the firm and strong cogitation of the parents[27] begetting them (often deluded by nocturnal and deceitful apparitions) or by the mother conceiving them. And so, that which is strongly conceived in the mind imprints the force into the infant conceived in the womb. Which thing, many think to be confirmed by Moses[28] because he tells that Jacob increased and bettered the part of the sheep granted to him by Laban, his wife's father, by putting rods[29] having the bark in part pulled off finely stroked with white and green in the places where they used to drink, especially at the time they engendered, that the representation apprehended in the conception[30] should be presently impressed[31] in the young. For the force of imagination hath so much power over the infant that it sets upon it the notes[32] or characters of the thing conceived.

We have read in Heliodorus[33] that Persina, Queen of Ethiopia, by her husband Hidustes, being also an Ethiope, had a daughter of a white complexion because, in the embraces of her husband, by which she proved with child, she earnestly fixed her eye and mind upon the picture of the fair Andromeda[34] standing opposite to her. Damascene[35] reports that he saw a maid, hairy like a bear, which had that deformity by no other cause or occasion than that her mother earnestly beheld, in the very instant of receiving and conceiving the seed, the image of St. John covered with camel's skin hanging upon the posts of the bed.

---

[27] **parents:** fathers.　[28] **Moses:** allusion to Jacob's experiment in selective breeding of spotted goats and sheep in Genesis 30:31–42.　[29] **rods:** twigs.　[30] **representation apprehended in the conception:** image taken into the mind at the moment of conception.　[31] **impressed:** stamped upon.　[32] **notes:** marks.　[33] **Heliodorus:** (c. 220–250 A.D.) writer of Greek romances best known for his novel *Aethiopica*, first translated into English in 1569. Its albino heroine, Charicleia, though exposed at birth by her fearful mother Persina, is finally reunited with her parents after many adventures.　[34] **Andromeda:** in Greek mythology, daughter of Cepheus, king of Ethiopia, and his wife Cassiopoeia. In punishment for Cassiopoeia's boast that she was more beautiful than the sea nymphs, the daughter was chained to a sea-rock and exposed to a monster; she was rescued by Perseus.　[35] **Damascene:** St. John of Damascus (c. 675–750), theologian and polemicist.

They say Hippocrates,[36] by this explication of the causes, freed a certain noble woman from suspicion of adultery who, being white herself and her husband also white, brought forth a child as black as an Ethiopian, because in copulation she strongly and continually had in her mind the picture of an Ethiop.

There are some who think the infant, once formed in the womb, which is done at the utmost within two and forty days after the same conception, is in no danger of the mother's imagination, neither of the seed of the father which is cast into the womb because, when it hath got a perfect figure, it cannot be altered with any external form of things. Which, whether it be true or no, is not here to be inquired of. Truly, I think it best to keep the woman all the time she goeth with child, from the sight of such shapes and figures.

## CHAPTER XII

### Of monsters by the confusion of seed of divers kinds.

That which followeth is a horrid thing to be spoken. But the chaste mind of the reader will give me pardon and conceive that which not only the Stoics but all philosophers who are busied about the search of the causes of things must hold: That there is nothing obscene or filthy to be spoken. Those things that are accounted obscene may be spoken without blame but they cannot be acted or perpetrated without great wickedness, fury, and madness. Therefore, that ill which is in obscenity consists not in word but wholly in the act. Therefore, in times past there have been some who, nothing fearing the Deity, neither law, nor themselves — that is, their soul — have so abjected and prostrated themselves that they have thought themselves nothing different from beasts. Wherefore atheists, sodomites, outlaws, forgetful of their own excellency and divinity and transformed by filthy lust, have not doubted[37] to have filthy and abominable copulation with beasts. This so great, so horrid a crime, for whose expiation all the fires in the world are not sufficient, though they, too maliciously crafty, have concealed and the conscious beasts[38] could not utter. Yet the generated misshapen issue hath abundantly spoken and declared, by the unspeakable power of God, the revenger and punisher of such impious and horrible actions. For of this various and promiscuous confusion of seeds of a different kind, monsters have been generated and born, who have been partly men and partly beasts.

---

[36] **Hippocrates:** Greek physician (469–399 B.C.) considered the founder of scientific medicine. The reference, according to the authoritative edition of Paré's works, is probably apocryphal.
[37] **doubted:** been afraid.   [38] **conscious beasts:** beasts aware of their guilt.

The like deformity of issue is produced if beasts of a different species do copulate together, nature always affecting[39] to generate something which may be like itself. For wheat grows not but by sowing of wheat, nor an apricot but by the setting or grafting of an apricot. For nature is a most diligent preserver of the species of things.

[39] affecting: intending, desiring.

## Fairy Belief

It is hard today to understand why fairies should have ever have been controversial, even if we know that in medieval times fairies were believed to be large, menacing creatures rather than the small mischief-makers they became by the late sixteenth century. But just as Reginald Scot could not tolerate belief in metamorphosis because he believed it compromised the sovereignty of God, so too the status of fairies became caught up in the ideological controversies of late Elizabethan England. Shakespeare seems careful to distance the fairies of *A Midsummer Night's Dream* in time, space, and action from the great ideological warfare between European Protestantism and Catholicism. His fictive Athenians are pagans, serenely unaware of disputatious points of Christian faith. The relationship between make-believe Athenian lovers, artisans, and equally fictional supernatural beings bears no direct, obvious relation to current controversies about the practices of belief. Yet Shakespeare also takes pains to make many-layered connections between the play's fairies and his audience: interplay between familiarity and distance, between the play's Englishness and its quaintly anachronistic classicism, is central both to historical interpretation and to the play's particular charm.

What seem to be Shakespeare's playful allusions to popular beliefs about mischievous spirits of the household or of the forest belong, then, to a vigorous contemporary debate about the nature of the spirit world and the realm of the invisible. In fact, the late sixteenth century in England, as in much of Europe, is a particularly interesting period for questions of this sort because the decades before and after the turn of that century witnessed a general decline in magical belief and magical thinking. This was a consequence partly of the Protestant Reformation and partly of the related emergence of what we now recognize as scientific thought. The English Reformation had taken hold within the living memory of older members of Shakespeare's audience. The matter of supernatural belief could not have seemed trivial to Shakespeare's audience, caught up as they were in the ideological warfare between Protestant reformers and the Catholic Church. Bottom's interaction with fairy creatures named Mustardseed and Peaseblossom might have seemed like a comic displacement of more urgent matters of faith or it might have seemed somewhat subversive.

The role of the fairies in the disputes of faith between Protestantism and Catholicism is a deeply ironic one. Fairy belief had been prohibited by medieval Catholicism. Such practices as leaving out food and drink in order to propitiate the fairies had seemed like pagan worship, the practice of a rival faith. For Protestant reformers, however, the rival faith was Catholicism itself. Clerical hostility to fairies thus continued but Protestant reformers, perhaps unfairly, charged the Catholic church rather than paganism with promoting popular belief in fairies along with belief in saints. In fact, Protestant reformers accused Catholic priests of inventing fairies and fairy practices in order to conceal their own misdeeds. Fairies, wrote Thomas Cooper in *The Mystery of Witchcraft* in 1617, were "conceits . . . whereby the Papists kept the ignorant in awe" (quoted in Thomas 729). The abandoned baby on the doorstep, rumored in earlier days to be left by the fairies, was now said to be a priest's illegitimate offspring.

Even within English Protestantism, however, there was ample room for disagreement about belief in spirits in general, fairies in particular. Thus the rationalist Reginald Scot, whose writings on metamorphosis we included earlier in this chapter, believes in fairies no more than he believes in the possibility of metamorphosis. In *The Discovery of Witchcraft* he protests the idea of a world inhabited by good and evil spirits, such as Robin Goodfellow, who are to be feared, cajoled, and placated by means of superstitious practices and beliefs. Insofar as he wishes to lay blame for fairy belief anywhere, he does so by castigating cowardly household authorities who seek to arouse fear in weak or simple-minded people, especially women, children, servants. "Our mothers' maids have so terrified us," writes Scot indignantly, "with spirits, witches, urchins, elves, hags, fairies, satyrs" and so forth, "that we are afraid of our own shadows" (86). Such fearfulness reproduces itself and spreads, as when nursemaids, for their own amusement or in order to compel obedience, terrify children.

Bishop Richard Corbett and John Aubrey, whose writings about fairies we reproduce below, take positions different from Scot's and from each other. For Corbett, the fairies symbolize a lost world of religious uniformity and social integration. "The Fairies' Farewell," Corbett's best-known poem, probably dates from around 1620, a period when royal and clerical opposition to Puritan efforts at religious reform involved, among other things, official promotion of traditional holiday customs and, as a corollary, forms of popular belief like that in fairy magic. "The Fairies' Farewell" expresses benevolence towards belief in fairies as harmless creatures of the popular imagination and, more important, as nostalgic remnants of a time when English church observances and civic life were full of rituals, holidays, and festive celebrations, all of which promoted social harmony.

For a conservative, high church cleric like Corbett, nostalgic celebration of the fairies — if not actual belief in their supernatural agency — symbolized acceptance of the political and religious status quo. By the same token, attacks against fairy beliefs could be represented as hostility to the monarch or even evidence of subversion. That fairies represented vestiges of paganism mattered less to a churchman like Corbett than that they could be understood as part of a sacramental old order when "divine beneficence had been communicated through the agency of popular custom" (Marcus 18).

John Aubrey's interest in English fairy lore is not religious at all, except insofar as fairy belief is part of the history of religion and thus an appropriate object of study. Aubrey writes from the point of view of a local historian and early theorist of culture. The first Aubrey excerpt reproduced below comes from the antiquarian's notebook compilation of passages from a variety of authors and his comments upon them, a book he calls *The Remains of Gentilism and Judaism*. By "gentilism," we should note, Aubrey means classical paganism; by "Judaism" he means the practice of the ancient Hebrews. The second passage was reprinted in 1845 by the Shakespeare scholar and antiquarian James Orchard Halliwell-Phillipps; Aubrey's original manuscript, however, has been lost (see Briggs, *Encyclopedia* 34, n. 1, for a discussion of the missing pages). In *Remains*, Aubrey examines the possibility that certain beliefs and ritual practices of his own day represent survivals from ancient times, classical or biblical. By tracing the pathways of such practices over time and space, Aubrey created the beginning of what a cultural anthropologist today would call a theory of the transmission of cultural practices from epoch to epoch, from culture to culture. Hence those practices that a Protestant polemicist like Reginald Scot condemns as idolatrous and superstitious were, for a more neutral, scientifically minded observer like Aubrey, a source of knowledge. For the modern reader, though, Aubrey may seem too naïve and credulous even for an early scientist, for in him we find an idiosyncratic combination of scientific rationalism (or even skepticism) and a "credulous belief in black magic and many other supernatural phenomena" (Hunter 209). The combination makes reading Aubrey on fairies a curious and charming experience.

The third selection in this section, the ballad entitled "The Mad Merry Pranks of Robin Good-fellow," suggests how quickly Oberon's chief fairy henchman took on a popular existence outside of Shakespeare's play. The ballad, which has been attributed to Ben Jonson, is a literary offshoot of *A Midsummer Night's Dream* rather than independent evidence of the popular traditions on which Shakespeare drew for his construction of the hybrid character, Puck/Robin Goodfellow. Before the quarto publication of *A Midsummer Night's Dream* in 1600, Robin Goodfellow and Puck were distinct figures. Robin was larger, more sexual, and usually less demonic than Puck. Writers in the Stuart period follow Shakespeare in conflating them and interpreting Robin/Puck as a tiny, mischievous, but essentially harmless and asexual trickster of rural dairymaids.

→ JOHN AUBREY

# Collecting Fairy Lore                                                        *1686, 1688*

John Aubrey (1626–1697), scientist and antiquarian, has often been regarded as an unsystematic or even eccentric compiler of data — historical, geographical, archeological. Aubrey's writings partly support such an impression: almost all remained unpublished or were left incomplete in his lifetime, and the observations that fill them seem loosely interconnected. But for recent historians of scientific thought, Aubrey was part of the "intellectual *avant-garde* of his age," being thoroughly imbued with the new mechanistic, materialist, empirical science associated with Francis Bacon (Buchanan-Brown xvii). He was an early Fellow of the Royal Society, founded in 1660 by Charles II to promote scientific inquiry and experimentation.

## *From* THE REMAINS OF GENTILISM AND JUDAISM (1688)

*Fairies and Robin Goodfellow*

Theocritus,[1] Idyllium XIII:

> "Within, the nymphs, the ladies of the plain,
> The watchful nymphs that dance, and fright the swains."[2]

When I was a boy, our country people would talk much of them. They were wont to please the fairies that they might do them no shrewd turns[3] by

---

[1] **Theocritus:** Greek poet of the third century B.C., whose *Idylls* are often regarded as the origin of pastoral poetry.   [2] **swains:** shepherds, country fellows.   [3] **shrewd turns:** nasty tricks.

John Aubrey, *The Remains of Gentilism and Judaism,* in *Three Prose Works,* edited by John Buchanan-Brown (Fontwell, Sussex: Centaur Press, 1972), 203–04; "The Wiltshire Fairies," in *Illustrations of the Fairy Mythology of "A Midsummer Night's Dream,"* edited by James Orchard Halliwell [Phillipps] (London, 1845) 235–37.

sweeping clean the hearth and setting by it a dish where was set a mess[4] of milk sopped with white bread; and did set their shoes by the fire and many times on the morrow they should find a threepence in one of them. But if they did speak of it, they never had any again.

Mrs. Markey of Hereford (a daughter of Sergeant Hoskyns, the poet) told me that her mother did use that custom and had as many groats or 3ds[5] this way as made her (or bought her) a little silver cup of thirty shillings value, which her daughter preserves still.

Not far from Sir Bennet Hoskyns, there was a laboring man that rose up early every day to go to work, who for many days together found a nine pence in the way that he went. His wife, wondering how he came by so much money, was afraid he got it not honestly. At last he told her and afterwards he never found any more.

They would churn the cream, etc.

That the fairies steal away young children and put others in their places: verily believed by old women in those days and by some yet living.

And in Germany old women tell the like stories received from their ancestors that a water-monster, called the Nickard,[6] does enter by night the chamber where a woman is brought to bed[7] and stealeth, when they are all sleeping, the newborn child and supposeth[8] another in his place. Which child growing up is like a monster and commonly dumb.[9] The remedy whereof that the mother may get her own child again: the mother taketh the Supposititium and whips it so long with the rod till the said monster, the Nickard, brings the mother's own child again and takes to himself the Supposititium[10] which they call the *Wexel balg*.[11]

Some were led away by fairies, as was a hind[12] riding upon Hackpen[13] with corn,[14] led a dance to the Devises. So was a shepherd of Mr. Brown of Winterbourne-Bassett; but never any afterwards enjoy themselves. He said the ground opened and he was brought into strange places under ground where they used musical instruments, viols and lutes, such (he said) as Mr. Thomas did play on.

Elias Ashmole,[15] Esq., says there was in his time a piper in Lichfield that was entertained by the fairies and had oftentimes seen them; who said he

---

[4] **mess:** serving.   [5] **groats or 3ds:** coins of low value; d. is a common abbreviation for Latin *denarius*, or penny.   [6] **Nickard:** Aubrey's term, related to modern German *Neck* or *Nix*, merman or water sprite.   [7] **bed:** here, childbed.   [8] **supposeth:** substitutes.   [9] **dumb:** mute.   [10] **Supposititium:** substitute child.   [11] *Wexel balg:* naughty elf, Aubrey's rendering of German *Wichtel*, elf, and *Balg*, urchin, brat.   [12] **hind:** farmhand.   [13] **Hackpen:** hill in Wiltshire, one of several Wiltshire placenames here.   [14] **corn:** grain.   [15] **Elias Ashmole:** (1617–1692), antiquarian and scientist whose collections were the basis of the Ashmolean Museum at the University of Oxford.

knew which houses of the town were fairy ground. Mr. Ashmole also spoke of a cavous place,[16] e.g. that at Frensham in Surrey, where people against[17] weddings or &c. bespoke[18] spits, pewter, &c. and they had it but were to return it or else they should never be supplied anymore.

## THE WILTSHIRE FAIRIES (1686)

In the year 1633–4, soon after I had entered into my grammar school at the Latin school at Yatton-Keynall, our curate Mr. Hart was annoyed one night by these elves or fairies. Coming over the downs, it being near dark, and approaching one of these fairy dances, as the common people call them in these parts, viz.[19] the green circles made by these sprites on the grass, he all at once saw an innumerable quantity of pigmies or very small people dancing round and round, and singing, and making all manner of small odd noises. He, being very greatly amazed, and yet not being able, as he says, to run away from them, being, as he supposes, kept there in a kind of enchantment, they no sooner perceive him but they surround him on all sides and, what betwixt fear and amazement, he fell down scarcely knowing what he did. And thereupon these little creatures pinched him all over, and made a sort of quick humming noise all the time. But at length they left him and, when the sun rose, he found himself exactly in the midst of one of these fairy dances. This relation I had from him myself, a few days after he was so tormented. But when I and my bedfellow[20] Stump went soon afterwards at nighttime to the dances on the downs, we saw none of the elves or fairies. But indeed it is said they seldom appear to any persons who go to seek for them.

As to these circles, I presume they are generated from the breathing out of a fertile subterraneous vapor, which comes from a kind of conical concave and endeavors to get out at a narrow passage at the top, which forces it to make another cone inversely situated to the other, the top of which is the green circle. Every tobacco-taker knows that 'tis no strange thing for a circle of smoke to be whiffed out of the bowl of the pipe, but 'tis done by chance. If you dig under the turf of this circle, you will find at the roots of the grass a

---

[16] **cavous place:** hollow hill, here the Fairy Mound of Frensham. In his natural history of Surrey, Aubrey mentions the Frensham vicarage's large Fairy Kettle, which local women believed to have come from the fairies: "These stories are verily believed by most of the old women of this parish, and by many of their daughters who can hardly be of any other opinion. So powerful a thing is custom joined with ignorance" (*The Perambulation of Surrey*, quoted in *Three Prose Works* 429). [17] **against:** in preparation for. [18] **bespoke:** ordered. [19] **viz.:** short for Latin *videlicet*, namely. [20] **bedfellow:** i.e., boarding school roommate; beds were often shared at the time.

hoar[21] or moldiness. But as there are fertile streams, so contrary-wise there are noxious ones which proceed from some minerals, iron, etc., which also, as the others, *caeteris paribus*,[22] appear in a circular form. *Mem[orandum]*. that pigeon's dung and nitre, steeped in water, will make the fairy circles; it draws to it the nitre of the air and will never wear out.

Let me not omit a tradition which I had many years since, when I was a boy, from my great uncles and my father's baily,[23] who were then old men: that in the harvest time, in one of the great fields at Warminster, at the very time of the fight at Bosworth Field[24] in Leicestershire between King Richard III and Henry VII, there was one of the parish (I have forgot whether he was not a natural fool[25]) who took two wheat-sheaves, one in one hand, and the other in the other hand, and said that the two armies were engaged. He played with the sheaves, crying with some intervals, "Now for Richard!" "Now for Henry!" At last lets fall Richard, and cried, "Now for King Henry, Richard is slain!" And this action of his did agree with the very time, day, and hour. Query: might not this boy have been one changed by the fairies. The vulgar[26] call them changelings.

---

[21] **hoar:** whitish mold.   [22] *caeteris paribus:* Latin, "other things being equal."   [23] **baily:** bailiff, estate manager.   [24] **Bosworth Field:** battle fought in 1485 between Richard III and Henry Tudor, earl of Richmond, who became Henry VII, the first Tudor monarch.   [25] **natural fool:** congenital idiot.   [26] **vulgar:** common people.

→ RICHARD CORBETT

# The Fairies' Farewell                                              *1620*

Richard Corbett (1582–1635) was a clergyman and minor poet in the reign of Charles I. The poet and playwright Ben Jonson, his contemporary, held him in great affection. Anthony Wood, the biographer of Oxford alumni, writes that, even as a student, Corbett was "one of the most celebrated wits of the university, as his poems, jests, romantic fancies and exploits, which he made and performed extempore showed" (Wood 2: 584). Corbett's rapid rise through the ranks of the Church of England from the deanship of Christ Church, Oxford, to the bishoprics of Oxford and Norwich exemplifies both the influence of court politics over clerical appointments and the importance of ingratiating personal gifts.

For singing his lyrics, Corbett jocularly specifies two tune names, both presumably familiar to his audience. "The Meadow Brow" was originally a Leicestershire ballad, but no tune with that name has survived. According to

---

Richard Corbett, *The Poems of Richard Corbett*, edited by J. A. W. Bennett and H. R. Trevor-Roper (Oxford: Clarendon P, 1955) 49–52.

Claude Simpson, singing Corbett's lyric to the second tune, "Fortune," which has survived, would produce "a completely undignified jiggy effect — doubtless part of Corbet's humorous intention" (Simpson 740).

## A Proper New Ballad Entitled
## The Fairies' Farewell: or God-a-Mercy Will

*To be sung or whistled to the Tune of "The Meadow Brow" by the learned; by the unlearned to the tune of "Fortune."*

Farewell, rewards and fairies,
    Good housewives now may say;
For now foul sluts[1] in dairies
    Do fare as well as they.
And though they sweep their hearths no less        5
    Than maids were wont to do,
Who, of late, for cleanliness
    Finds six-pence in her shoe?

Lament, lament old abbeys,
    The fairies lost command.        10
They did but change[2] priests' babies,
    But some have changed your land,[3]
And all your children sprung from thence
    Are now grown Puritans,
Who live as changelings[4] ever since        15
    For love of your desmesnes.[5]

At morning and at evening both
    You merry were and glad,
So little care of sleep or sloth
    These pretty ladies had.        20
When Tom came home from labor,
    Or Ciss to milking rose,
Then merrily, merrily went their tabor,[6]
    And nimbly went their toes.

---

[1] **foul sluts:** ugly and untidy wenches, here dairymaids.   [2] **change:** exchange.   [3] **changed your land:** i.e., received your lands in 1536 when Henry VIII, breaking away from the Roman church, disbanded England's monasteries and sold or gave away monastic lands.   [4] **changelings:** babies put in place of another by the fairies; here with the sense of converts, those who have changed religious beliefs for material gain.   [5] **demesnes:** lands, here those attached to abbeys.   [6] **tabor:** small drum.

Witness those rings and roundelays[7]                                        25
   Of theirs, which yet remain,
Were footed in Queen Mary's days[8]
   On many a grassy plain.
But, since of late Elizabeth
   And later James came in,                                                  30
They never danced on any heath
   As when the time hath been.

By which we note the fairies
   Were of the old Profession.[9]
Their songs were *Ave Maries,*[10]                                           35
   Their dances were procession.[11]
But now, alas, they all are dead,
   Or gone beyond the seas,
Or farther for religion fled,
   Or else they take their ease.                                             40

A tell-tale in their company
   They never could endure,
And who so kept not secretly
   Their mirth was punished sure.

[7] **rings and roundelays:** fairy circles.   [8] **Queen Mary's days:** reign of the Catholic Mary Tudor (1553–1558).   [9] **old Profession:** former faith, i.e., Roman Catholicism.   [10] **Ave Maries:** "Hail Marys."   [11] **procession:** religious parade on saints' or holy days. Protestant reformers banned processions and stripped the church calendar of many religious holidays.

It was a just and Christian deed                                    45
    To pinch such black and blue.
O, how the commonwealth doth need
    Such justices as you!

Now they have left our quarters,
    A register[12] they have,                                      50
Who looketh to their charters,[13]
    A man both wise and grave.
An hundred of their merry pranks
    By one that I could name
Are kept in store;[14] con[15] twenty thanks                       55
    To William[16] for the same.

I marvel who his cloak would turn[17]
    When Puck had led him round,
Or where those walking-fires[18] would burn
    Where Cureton would be found.                                  60
How Broker[19] would appear to be,
    For whom this age doth mourn,
But that their spirits live in thee,
    In thee, old William Chourne.

To William Chourne of Staffordshire,                               65
    Give laud[20] and praises due,
Who every meal can mend your cheer
    With tales both old and true.
To William, all give audience,
    And pray ye for his noddle,[21]                               70
For all the fairies' evidence,
    Were lost if that were addle.[22]

---

[12] **register:** registrar, official record-keeper.   [13] **charters:** traditional rights and privileges.
[14] **kept in store:** remembered.   [15] **con:** offer.   [16] **William:** William Chourne, a servingman,
accompanied Corbett and others on a journey through woods he believed to be fairy ground.
Chourne counseled the travellers to "turn their cloaks" inside out as protection from Puck,
whereupon a forester mysteriously appeared to guide them out.   [17] **cloak would turn:** with pun
on turncoat.   [18] **walking-fires:** *ignes fatui* (Latin, "foolish fires") or will-o'-wisps; phosphores-
cent lights, possibly caused by burning gases emitted by rotting organic matter, which flit over
low swampy ground at night. Such lights lured travellers who thought they had found human
dwellings.   [19] **Cureton . . . Broker:** perhaps Staffordshire worthies symbolizing adherence to
traditional beliefs.   [20] **laud:** praise.   [21] **noddle:** head, colloquially, as seat of thought.
[22] **addle:** empty.

→ # The Mad Merry Pranks of Robin Good-fellow   *c. 1600*

This broadsheet ballad was printed by Francis Coles, Thomas Vere, and John
Wright, printers working in partnership in London between 1663 and 1674
(Blagden 162), though it originally dates from earlier in the century.

    "Dulcina," the tune name specified here, dates from before 1615 and serves as
the basis for numerous ballads throughout the seventeenth century (Simpson
204).

*To the Tune of Dulcina.*

From Oberon in Fairy Land,
    the king of ghosts and shadows[1] there,
Mad[2] Robin I at his command,
    am sent to view the night-sports here.
        What revel-rout[3]
        Is kept about                          5
In every corner where I go,
        I will o'ersee,
        And merry be,
And make good sport with, ho ho ho.           10

More swift than lightning can I fly
    and round about this air welkin[4] soon;
And in a minute's space descry
    each thing that's done beneath the moon.
        There's not a hag,[5]
        nor ghost shall wag,[6]               15
Nor cry goblin where I do go;
        but Robin I,
        their feats will spy,
And fear them home with, ho ho ho.         20

If any wanderers I meet
    that from their night-sports do trudge home,

---

[1] **shadows:** phantoms.   [2] **Mad:** crazy.   [3] **revel-rout:** boisterous merriment.   [4] **air welkin:**
heaven.   [5] **hag:** nighttime spirit, usually female.   [6] **wag:** move about.

---

*The Euing Collection of English Broadside Ballads,* edited and with an introduction by John Holloway (Glasgow: University of Glasgow Publications, 1971) 325–26.

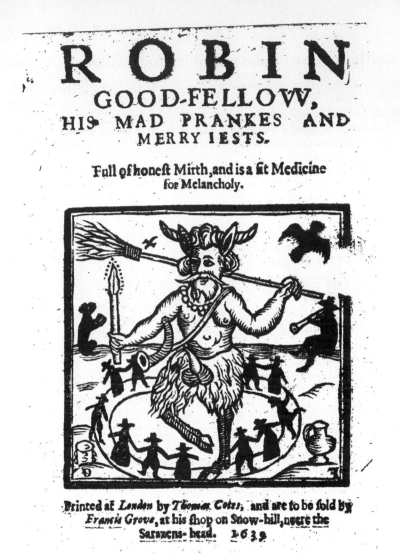

# ROBIN
## GOOD-FELLOW,
### HIS MAD PRANKES AND
### MERRY IESTS.

Full of honest Mirth, and is a fit Medicine
for Melancholy.

Printed at *London* by *Thomas Cotes*, and are to be sold by
*Francis Grove*, at his shop on Snow-hill, neere the
Sarazens- head. 1639.

FIGURE 20 *Title page from* Robin Good-fellow, His Mad Pranks. *The woodcut
shows a satyr-like, sexually erect Robin surrounded by a circle of dancers.*

With counterfeiting voice I greet
    and cause them on with me to roam;
        through woods, through lakes,
        through bogs, through brakes,[7]                    25
O'er bush and briar with them I go,
    I call upon
    them to come on,
And wend me[8] laughing, ho ho ho.                         30

Sometimes I meet them like a[9] man,
    sometimes an ox, sometimes a hound.
And to a horse I turn me can,
    to trip and trot about them round;
        but if to ride                                     35
        my back they stride,
More swift than wind away I go,
    o'er hedge and lands,
    through pools and ponds,
I whirry[10] laughing, ho ho ho.                           40

When lads and lasses merry be,
    with possets[11] and with junkets[12] fine,

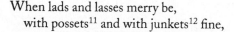

[7] **brakes:** clumps of bushes.    [8] **wend me:** go my way.    [9] **like a:** in the shape of.    [10] **whirry:**
hurry.    [11] **possets:** hot drinks of milk flavored with spices and wine.    [12] **junkets:** feasts of deli-
cacies.

Unseen of all the company,
  I eat their cakes and sip the wine;
    and to make sport,              45
    I fart and snort,
And out the candles I do blow.
    The maids I kiss,
    they shriek, "who's this?"
I answer nought, but ho ho ho.        50

Yet now and then the maids to please,
  I card at midnight up[13] their wool;
And while they sleep, snort, fart, and sneeze,
  with wheel[14] to thread their flax I pull.
    I grind at mill           55
    their malt up still,
I dress their hemp, I spin their tow;[15]
    if any awake
    and would me take,
I wend me laughing, ho ho ho.    60

*The second part, to the same Tune.*

When house or hearth doth sluttish[16] lie,
  I pinch the maids there black and blue,
And from the bed the bedclothes I
  pull off and lay them naked to view;
    'twixt sleep and wake    65
    I do them take,
And on the key-cold[17] floor them throw.
    If "Out," they cry,
    then forth fly I,
And loudly laugh, ho ho ho.    70

When any need to borrow aught,[18]
  we lend them what they do require;
And for the use demand we nought,
  our own is all we do desire.
    If to repay    75
    they do delay,

[13] **card ... up:** comb out.  [14] **wheel:** spinning wheel.  [15] **tow:** short flax or hemp fibers.
[16] **sluttish:** slovenly.  [17] **key-cold:** cold as a key.  [18] **aught:** anything.

Abroad amongst them then I go,
    and night by night,
    I them affright,
With pinching, dreams, and ho ho ho.            80

When lazy queans[19] have nought to do,
    but study how to cog[20] and lie,
To make debate and mischief too,
    'twixt one another secretly;
        I mark their gloze[21]            85
        and do disclose
To them that I had wrongèd so.
        When I have done,
        I get me gone,
And leave them scolding, ho ho ho.         90

When men do traps and engines[22] set
    in loopholes[23] where the vermin creep,
That from their folds[24] and houses fet[25]
    their ducks and geese, their lambs and sheep,
        I spy the gin[26]            95
        and enter in
And seem a vermin taken so.
        But when they there
        approach me near,
I leap out laughing, ho ho ho.         100

By wells and gills[27] in meadow green,
    we nightly dance our hey-day guise;[28]
And to our Fairy King and Queen
    we chant our moonlight harmonies.
        When larks 'gin sing,
        away we fling,           105
And babes newborn steal as we go.
        An elf in bed
        we leave instead,
And wend us laughing, ho ho ho.         110

---

[19] **queans:** harlots.   [20] **cog:** cheat.   [21] **gloze:** flattery, deceit.   [22] **engines:** snares.   [23] **loopholes:** holes in walls.   [24] **folds:** pens for animals.   [25] **fet:** snatch.   [26] **gin:** trap.   [27] **gills:** river banks.   [28] **guise:** dance.

From hag-bred Merlin's[29] time have I,
  thus mighty, revelled to and fro;
And, for my pranks, men call me by
  the name of Robin Good-fellow.
    Fiends, ghosts, and sprites           115
      that haunt the nights,
The hags and goblins do me know,
  and beldams[30] old,
    my feats have told,
So *vale, vale,*[31] ho ho ho.           120

*London,* Printed for F. Coles, T. Vere, and J. Wright.

[29] **Merlin's:** magician and prophet in Arthurian legend.   [30] **beldams:** women.
[31] *vale:* Latin, "farewell."

## → 1 Corinthians 2:1–16

The subversion of the status quo that so perturbed Bishop Corbett is faintly detectable in the last document reproduced below, the passage from 1 Corinthians that Bottom garbles after waking up from his magical encounter with Titania. The echo of 1 Corinthians 2:9 is a good example of common cultural memory at work, for the joke depends on the Elizabethan audience's recognition of the garbled scriptural text. If, as some scholars have maintained, the allusion echoes a specific translation of the Bible, it would allow us to glimpse with unusual clarity the dynamics of cultural transmission. But the case to be made is neither simple nor unambiguous.

    Two versions of the Bible in English existed in late sixteenth-century England, the Geneva Bible of 1560 and the Bishops' Bible of 1568. The Geneva Bible was by far the more popular as well as the more scholarly text: it was published in small volumes in a legible type and contained helpful marginal commentary. For most readers and owners of books, this was the Bible of choice. The Bishops' Bible was the more splendid, appearing in a large volume with nearly 150 woodcut illustrations. Once its faulty New Testament translations were revised in 1572, it served as the official Bible of the English church until the 1611 publication of the authorized version sponsored by James I. Of the ninety-two editions of the Bible published in England between 1576 (when the Geneva Bible was published in England) and 1611, only eleven were Bishops' Bibles (Shaheen 15–27).

1 Corinthians 2:1–16, in *The Bishops' Bible* (London, 1573) 82r.

Since Elizabethans were compelled to attend Sunday church services, they would regularly have heard those passages from the Bishops' Bible that were included in *The Book of Common Prayer*. In other settings, such as at home, they would probably have read from or listened to the Geneva version. The wording of Bottom's speech seems to derive not from the Geneva Bible (which reads "The things which eye hath not seen, neither ear hath heard, neither came into man's heart") but rather from the Bishops' (Shaheen 99). That would argue for audience recognition of the joke based upon their experience as listeners at church. Yet the text of I Corinthians 2 is not part of *The Book of Common Prayer;* Elizabethans would not have heard it regularly at church. (For an index to the biblical passages the *Book of Common Prayer* does include, see Booty 423–27.) Thus the source of its familiarity cannot easily be traced. To recognize the textual source of a joke, in this case, does not allow us to understand fully the route or the social means of its transmission.

Furthermore, even if we could identify how Shakespeare's audience would have recognized this misquotation, we could not claim to understand the joke's perhaps complex social function. Is Shakespeare making fun of Bottom here for misquoting the Bible or is he glorifying him at the expense of his social superiors? Certainly the biblical context is, as Annabel Patterson has argued, "one of profound spiritual leveling" (Patterson 68). Paul contrasts the unworldly, spiritual wisdom revealed to the Christian faithful with the useless, worldly knowledge of their rulers. For Patterson this scriptural levelling is transported into the play in order to evoke a "utopian vision" of social integration and interclass harmony (Patterson 69). But because the biblical text proposes an inverse relation between political power and spiritual insight, Bottom's misquotation may work more subversively than her argument suggests. By giving credit for spiritual wisdom to a workingman who will perform a play before the Duke of Athens, Shakespeare gives Bottom and his fellow actors the imaginative authority he may be claiming for himself and his theater at the expense of the imaginative authority of the state (Montrose, *Purpose* 192–94).

1 And I, brethren, when I came to you, came not in gloriousness of words, or of wisdom, showing unto you the testimony of God.

2 For I esteemed not to know any thing among you, save Jesus Christ, and him crucified.

3 And I was among you in weakness, and in fear, and in much trembling.

4 And my words and my preaching was not with enticing words of man's wisdom, but in showing of the spirit and of power.

5 That your faith should not stand in the wisdom of men, but in the power of God.

6 And we speak wisdom among them that are perfect: not the wisdom of this world, neither of the princes of this world, which come to nought.

7 But we speak the wisdom of God in a mystery, even the hid wisdom, which God ordained before the world, unto our glory.

8 Which none of the princes of this world know: for had they known it, they would not have crucified the Lord of glory.

9 But as it is written, The eye hath not seen, and the ear hath not heard, neither have entered into the heart of man, the things which God hath prepared for them that love him.

10 But God hath revealed them unto us by his spirit: for the spirit searcheth all things, yea, the deep things of God.

11 For what man knoweth the things of a man, save the spirit of man, which is in him? Even so the things of God knoweth no man, but the spirit of God.

12 And we have not received the spirit of the world, but the spirit, which is of God, that we might know the things that are given to us of God.

13 Which things also we speak, not in the words which man's wisdom teacheth, but which the holy ghost teacheth, comparing spiritual things with spiritual things.

14 But the natural man perceiveth not the things of the spirit of God: for they are foolishness unto him: neither can he know them, because they are spiritually discerned.

15 But he that is spiritual discerneth all things, yet he himself is judged of no man.

16 For who hath known the mind of the Lord that he might instruct him? But we have the mind of Christ.

# Bibliography

>‹

## Primary Sources

Ascham, Roger. *The Schoolmaster, or plain and perfect way of teaching the Latin tongue.* London, 1570. Ed. Lawrence V. Ryan. Folger Documents of Tudor and Stuart Civilization. Ithaca: Cornell UP, 1967.

Aubrey, John. *The Remains of Gentilism and Judaism. Three Prose Works.* Ed. John Buchanan-Brown. Fontwell, Sussex: Centaur, 1972.

Becon, Thomas. *A New Catechism. The Works of T. Becon, which he hath hitherto made and published.* 3 vols. London: Day, 1564.

*The Bishops' Bible.* London, 1573.

Bodin, Jean. *On the Demon-Mania of Witches.* Trans. Randy A. Scott, ed. Randy A. Scott and Jonathan A. Pearl. Toronto: Centre for Reformation and Renaissance Studies, 1995.

Bullinger, Henry (Heinrich). *The Christian State of Matrimony, wherein husbands and wives may learn to keep house together with love.* Trans. Miles Coverdale. London, 1541, 1575.

*Calendar of Assize Records: Elizabeth I.* 5 vols. Ed. J. S. Cockburn. London: Her Majesty's Stationery Office, 1975–1980.

Camden, William. *[The Annals of Queen Elizabeth] The History of the Most Reknowned and Victorious Princess Elizabeth Late Queen of England.* London, 1688. Ed. Wallace T. MacCaffrey. Chicago: U of Chicago P, 1970.

Castiglione, Baldesar. *The Book of the Courtier.* Trans. Thomas Hoby. London, 1561. London: Nutt, 1900.

Cooper, Thomas. *Thesaurus Linguae Romanae et Britannicae.* London, 1565. Menston, England: Scolar, 1969.

Corbett, Richard. "The Fairies' Farewell." *The Poems of Richard Corbett.* Ed. J. A. W. Bennett and H. R. Trevor-Roper. Oxford: Clarendon, 1955.

Coventry Records. *Records of Early English Drama: Coventry.* Ed. W. Ingram. Toronto: U of Toronto P, 1981.

Dod, John, and Robert Cleaver. *A Godly Form of Household Government.* London, 1598.

Elizabeth I. Speech to Parliament, 1566. *Proceedings in the Parliaments of Elizabeth I.* Vol. 1 (1558–1581). Ed. T. E. Hartley. Leicester: Leicester UP, 1981.

——. Tilbury Speech, 1588. Susan Frye, "The Myth of Elizabeth at Tilbury." *Sixteenth Century Journal* 23, no. 1 (1992): 95–114.

Elyot, Thomas. *The Book Named the Governor.* London, 1531.

"Entertainment at Elvetham," 1591. *Entertainments for Elizabeth I.* Ed. Jean Wilson. Woodbridge: Brewer, 1980.

Erasmus, Desiderius. "A Maid Hating Marriage." 1523. *The Colloquies.* Trans. H. M., Gent. London, 1671.

"Fetching Home of May." *The Roxburghe Ballads.* Vol. 3, Part I. Ed. William Chappell. Hertford: Austin 1875.

Forman, Simon. *The Casebooks of Simon Forman.* Ed. A. L. Rowse. London, 1974.

Gascoigne, George. "In the Commendation of the Noble Art of Venery." *The Noble Art of Venery or Hunting.* By George Turberville. London, 1575.

*Geneva Bible.* London, 1560. Facsim. ed. Intro. Lloyd E. Berry. Madison: U of Wisconsin P, 1969.

Gosynhyll, Edward. *Here Beginneth a Little Book Named the School House of Women.* London, 1541.

Gouge, William. *Of Domestical Duties, Eight Treatises.* London, 1626.

Halliwell-Phillipps, James Orchard, ed. *Illustrations of the Fairy Mythology of "A Midsummer Night's Dream."* London, 1845.

Harrison, William. *The Description of England.* In Raphael Holinshed, *Chronicles of England, Scotland, and Ireland.* London, 1587.

Heywood, Thomas. *The Exemplary Lives and Memorable Acts of the Nine Most Worthy Women in the World.* London, 1640.

"An Homily of the State of Matrimony." *The Second Tome of Homilies.* Archbishop Matthew Parker, et al. London, 1563.

"An Homily of Obedience." *Certain Sermons, or Homilies.* Bishop Edmund Bonner, et al. London, 1547; reprinted, 1623.

Jonson, Ben. *The Alchemist. The Complete Plays of Ben Jonson.* Ed. G. A. Wilkes. 4 vols. Oxford: Clarendon, 1982.

——. "To Penshurst." *Ben Jonson: The Complete Poems.* Ed. George Parfitt. New Haven: Yale UP, 1982.

Knox, John. *The First Blast of the Trumpet against the Monstrous Regiment of Women.* London, 1558.

Laneham, Robert. *A Letter.* London, c. 1575.

Lanyer, Amelia. "The Description of Cooke-ham." *Salve Deus Rex Judaeorum.* London, 1611.

Machyn, Henry. *Diary of a Resident in London (1550–1563).* Camden Society vol. 42. London, 1848.

"Mad Merry Pranks of Robin Good-fellow." *The Euing Collection of English Broadside Ballads.* Ed. John Holloway. Glasgow: U of Glasgow P, 1971.

Nashe, Thomas. *Summer's Last Will and Testament.* London, 1600.

——. *The Terrors of the Night.* London, 1594.

Ovid. *Metamorphoses.* Trans. Arthur Golding. London, 1567.

Painter, William. *The Palace of Pleasure.* London, 1567.

Paré, Ambrose. *Works.* Trans. T. Johnson. London, 1634.

Pizan, Christine de. *Livre de la cité des dames.* c. 1405. Trans. Brian Anslay: *The Book of the City of Ladies.* London, 1521.

Plutarch. *The Lives of the Noble Grecians and Romans.* Trans. Thomas North. London, 1579.

Puttenham, George. *The Art of English Poesie.* London, 1589.

Raleigh, Sir Walter. *The Discovery of the Large, Rich, and Beautiful Empire of Guiana.* London, 1596.

——. *The History of the World.* Part I. London, 1614.

"Regulating Chester Wages." *Tudor Royal Proclamations. Vol. III: The Later Tudors (1588–1603).* Ed. Paul L. Hughes and James F. Larkin. New Haven: Yale UP, 1969.

Roper, William. *The Life of Sir Thomas More.* Ed. Richard S. Sylvester and Harding Davis. New Haven: Yale UP, 1962.

Scot, Reginald. *The Discovery of Witchcraft.* London, 1584.

Smith, Thomas. *De Republica Anglorum.* London, 1583. Ed. L. Alston. Cambridge: Cambridge UP, 1906.

Spenser, Edmund. *The Faerie Queene.* London, 1596.

——. *The Shepheardes Calendar.* London, 1579.

"Statute of Artificers." *Tudor Economic Documents.* Ed. R. H. Tawney and Eileen Power. 3 vols. London: Longmans, 1951.

Stow, John. *The Annals of England.* London, 1601.

——. *A Survey of London.* London, John Windet, 1603.

Stubbes, Philip. *The Anatomy of Abuses.* London, 1583.

——. *A Crystal Glass for Christian Women.* London, 1591.

Traister, Barbara H. *A Window on Elizabethan London: The Manuscripts of Simon Forman.* Ms.

Turberville, George. *The Noble Art of Venery or Hunting.* London, 1575.

Wingfield, Sir Anthony. Letter. c. 1567. *The Losely Manuscripts.* Ed. Alfred John Kempe. London: Murray, 1836.

## Secondary Sources

Agnew, Jean-Christophe. *Worlds Apart: The Market and the Theatre in Anglo-American Thought, 1550–1750.* Cambridge: Cambridge UP, 1986.

Amussen, Susan Dwyer. "Gender, Family, and the Social Order, 1560–1725." *Order and Disorder in Early Modern England.* Ed. Anthony Fletcher and John Stevenson. Cambridge: Cambridge UP, 1985. 196–217.

——— . *An Ordered Society: Gender and Class in Early Modern England.* London: Blackwell, 1988.

Archer, Ian W. "John Stow's Survey of London: The Nostalgia of John Stow." *The Theatrical City.* Ed. David L. Smith, Richard Strier, and David Bevington. Cambridge: Cambridge UP, 1995. 17–34.

——— . *The Pursuit of Stability: Social Relations in Elizabethan London.* Cambridge: Cambridge UP, 1991.

Aubrey, John. *Aubrey's Brief Lives.* Ed. Oliver Lawson Dick. London: Secker, 1949.

Bagley, J. J. *The Earls of Derby 1485–1985.* London: Sedgwick, 1985.

Baker, J. H. *An Introduction to English Legal History.* 2nd ed. London: Butterworths, 1979.

Barber, C. L. *Shakespeare's Festive Comedy: A Study of Dramatic Form and its Relation to Social Custom.* Princeton: Princeton UP, 1959.

Barkan, Leonard. *The Gods Made Flesh: Metamorphosis and the Pursuit of Paganism.* New Haven: Yale UP, 1986.

Baskervill, Charles Read. *The Elizabethan Jig.* Chicago: U of Chicago P, 1929.

Bate, Jonathan. *Shakespeare and Ovid.* Oxford: Clarendon, 1993.

Belsey, Catherine. "Disrupting Sexual Difference: Meaning and Gender in the Comedies." *Alternative Shakespeares.* Ed. John Drakakis. London: Methuen, 1985. 166–90.

Ben-Amos, Ilana Krausman. *Adolescence and Youth in Early Modern England.* New Haven: Yale UP, 1994.

Bennett, Judith M. "Misogyny, Popular Culture, and Woman's Work." *History Workshop* 31 (Spring 1991): 166–88.

Berry, Phillipa. *Of Chastity and Power: Elizabethan Literature and the Unmarried Queen.* London: Routledge, 1993.

Blagden, Cyprian. "Notes on the Ballad Market in the Second Half of the Seventeenth Century." *Studies in Bibliography* 6 (1954): 161–80.

Boehrer, Bruce Thomas. "Bestial Buggery in *A Midsummer Night's Dream.*" *The Production of English Renaissance Culture.* Ed. David Lee Miller, Sharon O'Dair, and Harold Weber. Ithaca: Cornell UP, 1994. 123–50.

Boethius. *The Consolation of Philosophy.* Trans. H. F. Stewart. Cambridge: Harvard UP, 1946.

Booty, John E., ed. *The Book of Common Prayer, 1559: The Elizabethan Prayer Book.* Charlottesville: UP of Virginia, 1976.

Brand, John. *Popular Antiquities*. Vol. 2. Ed. W. Carew Hazlitt. London: Blom, 1879.

Briggs, Katherine. *The Anatomy of Puck: An Examination of Fairy Beliefs Among Shakespeare's Contemporaries and Successors*. London: Routledge, 1959.

———. *An Encyclopedia of Fairies: Hobgoblins, Brownies, Bogies, and Other Supernatural Creatures*. New York: Pantheon, 1976.

Brooks, Harold F., Introduction. *A Midsummer Night's Dream*. Ed. Brooks. Arden Edition. London: Methuen, 1979.

Buchanan-Brown, John. Introduction. *Three Prose Works*. By John Aubrey. Ed. Buchanan-Brown. Fontwell, Sussex: Centaur, 1972.

Bullough, Geoffrey. *Narrative and Dramatic Sources of Shakespeare*. Vol. 1. London: Routledge; New York: Columbia UP, 1966.

Burke, Peter. *Popular Culture in Early Modern Europe*. New York: Harper, 1978.

———. "Popular Culture in Seventeenth Century London." *Popular Culture in Seventeenth-Century England*. Ed. Barry Reay. London: Croom, 1985. 31–57.

Cahn, Susan. *Industry of Devotion: The Transformation of Woman's Work in England, 1500–1660*. New York: Columbia UP, 1987.

Chambers, E. K. *The Elizabethan Stage*. 4 vols. Oxford: Oxford UP, 1928.

———. *The Medieval Stage*. 2 vols. Oxford: Oxford UP, 1903.

Chappell, William, ed. *The Roxburghe Ballads*. Vols. 2 and 3. Hertford: Austin, 1875.

Clark, Alice. *The Working Life of Women in the Seventeenth Century*. Intro. Amy Louise Erickson. London: Routledge: 1919, 1992. 44–66.

Clark, Peter. Introduction. *The European Crisis of the 1590s: Essays in Comparative History*. Ed. Clark. London: Allen, 1985.

———. "A Crisis Contained? The Condition of English Towns in the 1590s." *The European Crisis of the 1590s*.

Coletti, Theresa. "Reading REED: History and Records of Early English Drama." *Literary Practice and Social Change in Britain, 1380–1539*. Ed. Lee Patterson. Berkeley: U of California P, 1990. 248–84.

Collinson, Patrick. "Protestant Culture and the Cultural Revolution." *Reformation to Revolution: Politics and Religion in Early Modern England*, ed. Margot Todd. London: Routledge, 1995. 33–52.

Crawford, Patricia. "The Sucking Child: Adult Attitudes to Child Care in the First Year of Life in Seventeenth-Century England." *Continuity and Change* 1, no. 1 (1986): 23–57.

———. *Women and Religion in England 1500–1720*. London: Routledge, 1993.

Cressy, David. *Birth, Marriage, and Death: Ritual, Religion, and the Life-Cycle in Tudor and Stuart England*. Oxford: Oxford UP, 1997.

———. *Bonfires and Bells: National Memory and the Protestant Calendar in Elizabethan and Stuart England*. Berkeley: U of California P, 1989.

———. "Describing the Social Order in Elizabethan and Stuart England." *Literature and History* 3 no. 3 (March 1976): 29–44

Culler, Jonathan. "Convention and Meaning: Derrida and Austin." *New Literary History* 13 (1981–82): 15–30.

Davidson, Clifford. "'What hempen home-spuns have we swaggering here?' Amateur Actors in *A Midsummer Night's Dream* and the Coventry City Plays and Pageants." *Shakespeare Studies* 29. Ed. Leeds Barroll and Barry Gaines. New York: Franklin, 1987. 87–99.

*Dictionary of National Biography.* 21 vols. Ed. Leslie Stephen and Sidney Lee. Oxford: Oxford UP, 1917.

Eckenstein, Lina. *Women under Monasticism: Chapters on Saint-Lore and Convent Life between A.D. 500 and A.D 1500.* Cambridge: Cambridge UP, 1896.

Erickson, Amy. *Women and Property in Early Modern England.* London: Routledge, 1995.

Ferguson, Margaret W., Maureen Quilligan, and Nancy J. Vickers, eds. *Rewriting the Renaissance: The Discourses of Sexual Difference in Early Modern Europe.* Chicago: U of Chicago P, 1986.

Fineman, Joel. "Fratricide and Cuckoldry: Shakespeare's Doubles." *Representing Shakespeare: New Psychoanalytic Essays.* Ed. Murray M. Schwartz and Coppélia Kahn. Baltimore: Johns Hopkins UP, 1980. 70–109.

Fletcher, Anthony. *Gender, Sex, and Subordination in England 1500–1800.* New Haven: Yale UP, 1995.

Foakes, R. A. Introduction. *A Midsummer Night's Dream.* Cambridge: Cambridge UP, 1984.

Frye, Susan. *Elizabeth I: The Competition for Representation.* Oxford: Oxford UP, 1993.

———. "The Myth of Elizabeth at Tilbury." *Sixteenth Century Journal* 23, no. 1 (1992): 95–114.

Fuller, Thomas. *The Church History of Britain From the Birth of Jesus Christ Until the Year MDCXLVIII.* 6 vols. Oxford: Oxford UP, 1845.

Fumerton, Patricia. *Cultural Aesthetics: Renaissance Literature and the Practice of Social Ornament.* Chicago: U of Chicago P, 1991.

Furnivall, Frederick J. *Early English Poems and Lives of Saints. Transactions of the Philological Society, 1858.* Berlin: Asher, 1862.

———, ed. *Phillip Stubbes's Anatomy of the Abuses in England in Shakespeare's Youth.* London: Trubner, 1877–79.

Goldberg, Jonathan. *Sodometries: Renaissance Texts, Modern Sexualities.* Stanford: Stanford UP, 1992.

Greenblatt, Stephen. *Renaissance Self-Fashioning: From More to Shakespeare.* Chicago: U of Chicago P, 1980.

———. *Shakespearean Negotiations: The Circulation of Social Energy in Renaissance England.* Berkeley: U of California P, 1988.

Hair, Paul, ed. *Before the Bawdy Courts.* London: Elek, 1972.

Harris, Jonathan Gil. "Puck / Robin Goodfellow." *Fools and Jesters in Art, Literature, and History.* Ed. Vicki K. Janik. Westport: Greenwood, 1996.

Hartley, T. E., ed. *Proceedings in the Parliaments of Elizabeth I.* Vol. 1 (1558–1581). Leicester: Leicester UP, 1981.

Helgerson, Richard. *Forms of Nationhood: Elizabethan Writing of England.* Chicago: U of Chicago P, 1992.

Hendricks, Margo. "'Obscured by Dreams': Race, Empire, and Shakespeare's *A Midsummer Night's Dream.*" *Shakespeare Quarterly* 47 (1996): 37–60.

Hill, Bridget. "A Refuge from Men: The Idea of a Protestant Nunnery." *Past and Present* 117 (1987): 107–30.

Holloway, John, ed. *The Euing Collection of English Broadside Ballads.* Glasgow: Glasgow UP, 1971.

Houlbrooke, Ralph. *English Family Life 1576–1717: An Anthology from Diaries.* London: Blackwell, 1988.

Howard, Jean E. *The Stage and Social Struggle in Early Modern England.* London: Routledge, 1994.

Howard, Skiles. "Hands. Feet, and Bottoms: Decentering the Cosmic Dance in *A Midsummer Night's Dream.*" *Shakespeare Quarterly* 44 (1993): 325–42.

Hunter, Michael. *John Aubrey and the Realm of Learning.* New York: Science History, 1975.

Hutton, Ronald. *The Rise and Fall of Merry England: The Ritual Year.* Oxford: Oxford UP, 1994.

——. *The Stations of the Sun: A History of the Ritual Year in Britain.* Oxford: Oxford UP, 1996.

Ingram, R. W., ed. *Records of Early English Drama: Coventry.* Toronto: U of Toronto P, 1981.

King, John N. "Queen Elizabeth I: Representations of the Virgin Queen." *Renaissance Quarterly* 43, no. 1 (Spring 1990): 30–74.

Kingsford, Charles Lethbridge, ed. *John Stow. A Survey of London, Reprinted from the Text of 1603.* 2 vols. Oxford: Clarendon, 1908, 1971.

Kipling, Gordon. *The Triumph of Honor: Burgundian Origins of the Elizabethan Renaissance.* The Hague: Leyden UP, 1977.

Knowles, David. *Religious Orders in England.* 3 vols. Cambridge: Cambridge UP, 1955, 1959.

Kuin, R. J. P., ed. *Robert Langham, A Letter.* Leiden: Brill, 1983.

Leinwand, Theodore. "'I believe we must leave the killing out': Deference and Accommodation in *A Midsummer Night's Dream.*" *Renaissance Papers*, 1986. 11–30.

——. "Shakespeare and the Middling Sort." *Shakespeare Quarterly* 44 (1993): 284–303.

Levin, Carole. *The Heart and Stomach of a King: Elizabeth I and the Politics of Sex and Power.* Philadelphia: U of Pennsylvania P, 1994.

Levin, Carole, and Jeanie Watson, eds. *Ambiguous Realities: Women in the Middle Ages and Renaissance.* Detroit: Wayne State UP, 1987.

Lewalski, Barbara Kiefer. *Writing Women in Jacobean England.* Cambridge: Harvard UP, 1993.

Livingston, Carole Rose. *British Broadsides of the Sixteenth Century, A Catalogue of Extant Sheets and an Essay.* New York: Garland, 1991.

Luborsky, Ruth Samson. "Connections and Disconnections Between Images and Text: The Case of Secular Book Illustration." *Word and Image* 3, no. 1 (Jan.–March 1987): 74–85.

MacCaffrey, Wallace. "Place and Patronage in Elizabethan Politics." *Elizabethan Government and Society.* Ed. S. T. Bindoff, Joel Hurstfield, and C. H.Williams. London: Athalone, 1961. 95–126.

Maclean, Ian. *The Renaissance Notion of Woman: A Study in the Fortunes of Scholasticism and Medical Science in European Intellectual Life.* Cambridge: Cambridge UP, 1980.

Marcus, Leah S. *The Politics of Mirth: Jonson, Herrick, Milton, Marvell, and the Defense of Old Holiday Pastimes.* Chicago: U of Chicago P, 1978.

Montrose, Louis Adrian. "'Eliza, Queene of Shepherdes,' and the Pastoral of Power." *Renaissance Historicism.* Ed. Arthur F. Kinney and Dan S. Collins. Amherst: U of Mass P, 1987. 34–63.

——. "A Kingdom of Shadows." *The Theatrical City.* Ed. David L. Smith, Richard Strier, and David Bevington. Cambridge: Cambridge UP, 1995. 31–64.

——. *The Purpose of Playing: Shakespeare and the Cultural Politics of the Elizabethan Theatre.* Chicago: U of Chicago P, 1996.

——. "'Shaping Fantasies': Figurations of Gender and Power in Elizabethan Culture." *Representing the English Renaissance.* Ed. Stephen Greenblatt. Berkeley: U of California P, 1988. 68–86.

Mowat, Barbara. "'A local habitation and a name': Shakespeare's Text as Construct." *Style* 13 (1989): 335–51.

Neale, J. E. *Elizabeth and Her Parliaments, 1559–1581.* New York: St. Martin's, 1958.

Orgel, Stephen. "Jonson and the Amazons." *Soliciting Interpretation: Literary Theory and Seventeenth-Century Poetry.* Ed. Elizabeth D. Harvey and Katharine Eisaman Maus. Chicago: U of Chicago P, 1991.

Outhwaite, R. B. "Dearth, the English Crown, and the Crisis of the 1590's." *The European Crisis of the 1590's: Essays in Comparative History.* Ed. Peter Clark. London: Allen, 1985. 23–43.

*Oxford English Dictionary.* Ed. J. A. Simpson and E. S. C. Weiner. Oxford: Clarendon, 1989.

Palliser, D. M. *The Age of Elizabeth: England Under the Late Tudors, 1547–1603.* London: Longman, 1983.

Park, Katherine, and Lorraine J. Daston. "Unnatural Conceptions: A Study of Monsters in Sixteenth and Seventeenth-Century France and England." *Past and Present* 92 (1981): 21–54.

Parker, Patricia. *Shakespeare from the Margins: Language, Culture, Context.* Chicago: U of Chicago P, 1995.

Paster, Gail Kern. *The Body Embarrassed: Drama and the Disciplines of Shame in Early Modern England.* Ithaca: Cornell UP, 1993.

Patterson, Annabel. *Shakespeare and the Popular Voice.* Cambridge: Blackwell, 1989.

Pearl, Valerie. Introduction. *The Survey of London.* By John Stow. London: Dent, 1987.

Pennino-Baskerville, Mary. "Terpsichore Reviled: Antidance Tracts in Elizabethan England." *The Sixteenth Century Journal* 22 (1991): 475–93.

Phythian-Adams, Charles. "Ceremony and the Citizen: The Communal Year at Coventry, 1450-1550." *Crisis and Order in English Towns, 1500–1700: Essays in Urban History.* Ed. Peter Clark and Paul Slack. London: Routledge, 1972. 57–85.

Pollard, A. W., ed. *The Queen's Majesty Entertainment at Woodstock, 1575.* Oxford: Dorrel, 1903, 1910.

Power, Eileen. *Medieval English Nunneries c. 1275–1535.* Cambridge: Cambridge UP, 1922.

Prior, Mary, ed. *Women in English Society, 1500–1800.* London: Methuen, 1985.

Prior, Roger. "Jewish Musicians at the Tudor Court." *The Musical Quarterly* 69, (1983). 253–65.

Rackin, Phyllis. "Historical Difference / Sexual Difference." *Privileging Gender.* Ed. Jean R. Brink. Kirksville, Mo.: 16th Century Journal, 1993. 37–64.

Rappaport, Steve. *Worlds within Worlds: Structures of Life in Sixteenth-Century London.* Cambridge: Cambridge UP, 1989.

Reay, Barry. *Popular Culture in Seventeenth-Century England.* London: Croom, 1985.

Roper, Lyndal. *Oedipus and the Devil: Witchcraft, Sexuality, and Religion in Early Modern Europe.* London: Routledge, 1994.

Schleiner, Winfried. "*Divina Virago*: Queen Elizabeth as an Amazon." *Studies in Philology* 75 (1978): 163–80.

Shaheen, Nasheeb. *Biblical References in Shakespeare's Comedies.* Newark: U of Delaware P, 1993.

Sharpe, J. A. *Crime in Seventeenth-Century England: A County Study.* Cambridge: Cambridge UP, 1983.

Shepherd, Simon. *Amazons and Warrior Women: Varieties of Feminism in Seventeenth-Century Drama.* New York: St. Martin's, 1981.

Simpson, Claude M. *The British Broadside Ballad and Its Music.* New Brunswick: Rutgers UP, 1966.

Smith, Bruce R. "Landscape with Figures: The Three Realms of Queen Elizabeth's Country-House Revels." *Renaissance Drama,* New Series VIII. Ed. Leonard Barkan. Evanston: Northwestern UP, 1977. 57–115.

——— . "Reading Lists of Plays, Early Modern, Modernist, Postmodern." *Shakespeare Quarterly* 42 (1991): 127–44.

Smith, David L., Richard Strier, and David Bevington, eds. *The Theatrical City: Culture, Theatre, and Politics in London, 1576–1649.* Cambridge: Cambridge UP, 1995.

Stallybrass, Peter. "Patriarchal Territories: The Body Enclosed." *Rewriting the Renaissance.* Ed. Margaret W. Ferguson, Maureen Quilligan, and Nancy J. Vickers. Chicago: U of Chicago P, 1986. 123–42.

Stone, Lawrence. *The Family, Sex and Marriage in England, 1500–1800.* London: Weidenfeld, 1977.

———. "Social Mobility in England, 1500–1700." *Past and Present* 33 (1966): 7–23.

Strong, Roy. *The Cult of Elizabeth.* Berkeley: U of California P, 1977.

Strutt, Joseph. *Sports and Pastimes of the People of England.* Ed. William Hone. London: Chatto, 1876.

Thomas, Keith. *Religion and the Decline of Magic: Studies in Popular Beliefs in Sixteenth- and Seventeenth-Century England.* London: Penguin, 1971.

Thompson, Craig R., ed. *The Colloquies of Erasmus.* Chicago and London: U of Chicago P, 1965.

Walter, John. "A 'Rising of the People'?: The Oxfordshire Rising of 1596." *Past and Present* 107 (1985): 90–143.

———. "The Social Economy of Dearth in Early Modern England." *Famine, Disease, and the Social Order in Early Modern Society.* Ed. John Walter and Roger Schofield. Cambridge: Cambridge UP, 1989. 75–128.

Walter, John, and Roger Schofield. *Famine, Disease, and the Social Order in Early Modern Society.* Cambridge: Cambridge UP, 1989.

———, and Keith Wrightson. "Dearth and the Social Order in Early Modern England." *Past and Present* 71 (1976): 22–42.

Warner, Marina. Foreward. *The Book of the City of Ladies.* By Christine de Pizan. Trans. Earl Jeffrey Richards. New York: Persea, 1982, 1988.

Warnicke, Retha M. *Women of the English Renaissance and Reformation.* Westport: Greenwood, 1983.

Wickham, Glynne. *The Medieval Theatre.* Cambridge: Cambridge UP, 1974.

Wiles, David. *Shakespeare's Almanac: A Midsummer Night's Dream, Marriage, and the Elizabethan Calendar.* Cambridge: Brewer, 1993.

Williams, Penry. "Shakespeare's *A Midsummer Night's Dream:* Social Tensions Contained." *The Theatrical City.* Ed. David L. Smith, Richard Strier, and David Bevington. Cambridge: Cambridge UP, 1995. 55–66.

Williamson, G. C. *George, Third Earl of Cumberland: His Life and Voyages (1558–1605).* Cambridge: Cambridge UP, 1920.

Wilson, Jean. *Entertainments for Elizabeth I.* Woodbridge: Brewer, 1980.

Wood, Anthony. *Athenae Oxonienses.* 1692. Ed. Philip Bliss. Rpt. Hildesheim: Olms, 1969.

Woods, Suzanne, ed. *The Poems of Aemilia Lanyer.* Oxford: Oxford UP, 1993.

Wright, Celeste Turner. "The Amazons in Elizabethan Literature." *Studies in Philology* 37 (1940): 433–56.

Wright, Pam. "A Change in Direction: The Ramifications of a Female Household, 1558–1603." *The English Court: From the Wars of the Roses to the Civil
War.* Ed. David Starkey, et al. London: Longman, 1987. 147–72.

Wrightson, Keith. *English Society, 1580–1680.* New Brunswick: Rutgers UP, 1982.

Yates, Frances. *Astraea: The Imperial Theme in the Sixteenth Century.* London,
1977.

Youings, Joyce. *The Dissolution of the Monasteries.* London: Allen, 1971.

*Acknowledgments*

*A Midsummer Night's Dream* from *The Complete Works of Shakespeare*. 4th ed. Ed. David Bevington. Copyright © 1992 by HarperCollins, Inc. Reprinted by permission of Addison-Wesley Educational Publishers, Inc.

Figure 1. Title page of the quarto *A Midsummer Night's Dream* (London, 1600; STC 22302). By permission of the Folger Shakespeare Library.

CHAPTER 1

Figure 2. City and Woods. Woodcuts accompanying "The Coaches Overthrow," second part, Roxburghe Ballad Collection (1: 547), and "Your Humble Servant, Madam," Roxburghe Ballad Collection (3: 248, 249). By permission of the British Library.

Figure 3. Morris Dancers. "From an Ancient Window in the House of George Tollet, Esq. at Henley in Staffordshire." Art File M875 #1. By permission of the Folger Shakespeare Library.

Figure 4. Maypole dance. Michael Drayton, *Poly-Olbion* (London, 1613; STC 7226). By permission of the Folger Shakespeare Library.

Figure 5. Lovers. Woodcut accompanying the ballad "The Crost Couple, Or a Good Misfortune." The Euing Ballad Collection (no. 56). By permission of the Glasgow University Library, Department of Special Collections.

"The Fetching Home of May." The Roxburghe Ballad Collection (1: 538, 539). By permission of the British Library.

Figure 6. Queen Elizabeth on a Hunt. George Turberville, *The Book of Falconry* (London, 1575; STC 24234). By permission of the Folger Shakespeare Library.

Coventry Records. From *Records of Early English Drama*, ed. W. Ingram. By permission of the University of Toronto Press.

"The Fourth Day's Entertainment." From *The Honorable Entertainment given to the Queen's Majesty in a Progress, at Elvetham in Hampshire by the Right Honorable Earl of Hereford, 1591. Entertainments for Elizabeth I*, ed. Jean Wilson (Woodbridge, U.K.: D. S. Brewer; and Totowa, N.J.: Rowman and Littlefield, 1980). By permission of Boydell and Brewer, Ltd.

Figure 7. *Naumachia*, Elvetham. *The Honorable Entertainment Given to the Queen's Majesty in Progress at Elvetham in Hampshire* (London, 1591). In John Nichols, *The Progresses of Queen Elizabeth* (London, 1823), 3: 100. By permission of the Folger Shakespeare Library.

Figure 8. "Aprill." Edmund Spenser, *The Shepheardes Calendar* (London, 1579; PML 78109, fol. 11v). By permission of the Pierpont Morgan Library, New York. PML 127066.

Edmund Spenser, portion of "Aprill" from *The Shepheardes Calendar* from *The Yale Edition of the Shorter Poems of Edmund Spenser*, edited by William A. Oram, et al., pp. 72–76. Copyright © 1989 Yale University Press. Reprinted by permission of the publisher.

CHAPTER 2

Figure 9. Page from Plutarch, *The Lives of the Noble Grecians and Romans* (London, 1570; STC 20065). By permission of the Folger Shakespeare Library.

Figure 10. *Catechism*, 1573, STC 18711. By permission of the Folger Shakespeare Library.

Figure 11. title page of George Turberville, *The Noble Art of Venery, or Hunting* (London, 1575; STC 24328). By permission of the Folger Shakespeare Library.

"The Statute of Artificers" (1563), *Tudor Economic Documents,* ed. R. H. Tawney and Eileen Power (London and New York: Longmans, Green and Co., 1951). By permission of Addison Wesley Longman.

Figure 12. Manuscript page from *The Autobiography of Simon Forman.* Ms. Ashmole 226, fol. 44r. By permission of the Bodleian Library.

CHAPTER 3

Figure 13. Amazons, lascivious and brutal. Hulsius, engravings from *Kurtze Wunderbar Beschreibung Desz Goldreichen Konigreiches Guianae* (Nuremburg, 1599; shelfmark C. 114 c. 15). By permission of the British Library.

Figure 14. Amazons, with right and left breast removed. John Bulwer, *Anthropometamorphosis, Man Transformed: or, The Artificial Changeling* (London, 1654, B5461). By permission of the Folger Shakespeare Library.

Figure 15. Queen Elizabeth as an Amazon ("Elizabeth as Europa"). Dutch engraving, 1598. By permission of the Department of Western Art, Ashmolean Museum, Oxford.

Elizabeth I, Two Versions of the Address to the Troops at Tilbury. From Susan Frye, "The Myth of Elizabeth at Tilbury" in *Sixteenth Century Journal* 23, no. 1 (1992): 95–114. By permission of the *Sixteenth Century Journal.*

Figure 16. Frontispiece. Samuel Rowland. "'Tis Merry When Gossips Meet" (London, 1602; STC 21410.2). By permission of the Folger Shakespeare Library.

Figure 17. Woodcut from Christine de Pizan, *The Book of the City of Ladies,* trans. Brian Anslay (London, 1521; STC 7271). By permission of the Folger Shakespeare Library.

Queen Elizabeth, From a speech to Parliament, 1566. From *Proceedings in the Parliaments of Elizabeth I, Vol. I 1558–1581,* ed. T. E. Hartley (Leicester: Leicester UP, 1981). By permission of the Leicester University Press, an imprint of Cassell, Wellington House, 125 Strand, London, WC2R OBB, England.

William Camden, From *The History of the Most Reknowned and Victorious Princess Elizabeth Late Queen of England,* ed. Wallace T. Macaffrey. (Chicago: U of Chicago P, 1970). By permission of the University of Chicago Press.

CHAPTER 4

Figure 18. Circe touching a pig with her wand. Geoffrey Whitney, *A Choice of Emblems* (London, 1586; STC 25438). By permission of the Folger Shakespeare Library.

Figure 19. Monster, half-man, half-pig. From Ambroise Paré, *Works* (London, 1634; STC 19189). By permission of the Folger Shakespeare Library.

John Aubrey, *The Remains of Gentilism and Judaism* in *Three Prose Works,* ed. John Buchanan-Brown (Fontwell, Sussex: Centaur, 1972). By permission of Centaur Press.

Ovid, From *Shakespeare's Ovid, Being Arthur Golding's Translation of the "Metamorphoses"* (London: Centaur P, 1961). By permission of Centaur Press.

Figure 20. Title page from *Robin Good-Fellow, His Mad Pranks* (London, 1628). Reprinted by permission of the Folger Shakespeare Library.

"The Mad Merry Pranks of Robin Good-fellow." The Euing Ballad Collection (no. 203). By permission of Department of Special Collections, Glasgow University Library.

# Index

338